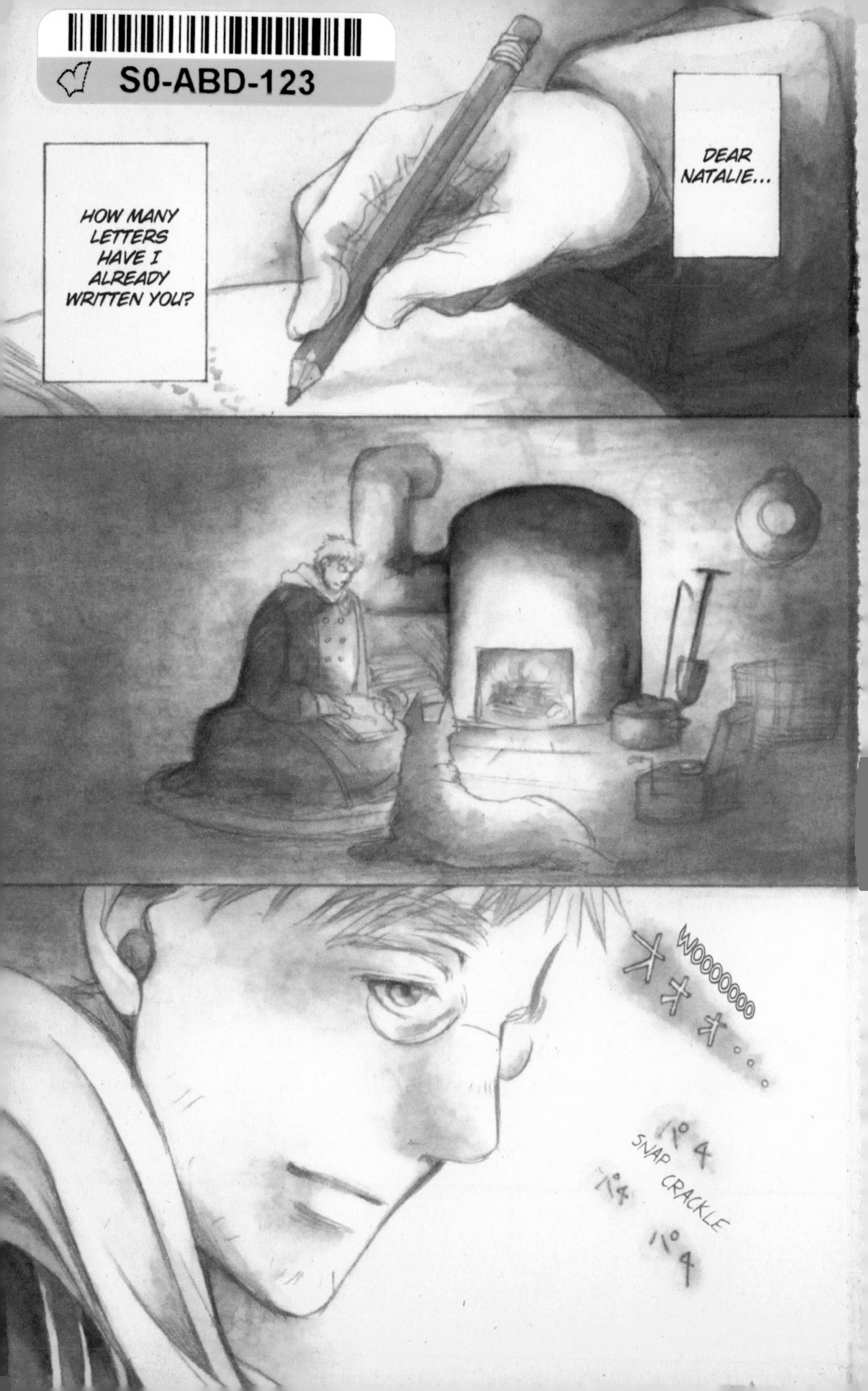
DEAR NATALIE...
HOW MANY LETTERS HAVE I ALREADY WRITTEN YOU?
オオオ・・・
WOOOOOOO
パチ パチ パチ
SNAP CRACKLE

Translation – Christine Schilling
Adaptation – Brynne Chandler
Production Assistant – Suzy Wells
Lettering & Retouch – Eva Han
Editorial Assistant – Mallory Reaves
Production Manager – James Dashiell
Editor – Brynne Chandler

A Go! Comi manga

Published by Go! Media Entertainment, LLC

Visit us online at www.gocomi.com
e-mail: info@gocomi.com

ISBN 978-1-933617-87-9

First printed in August 2008

1 2 3 4 5 6 7 8 9

Manufactured in the United States of America.

Song of the Hanging Sky

AUTHOR
TORIKO GIN

VOLUME 1

go!comi

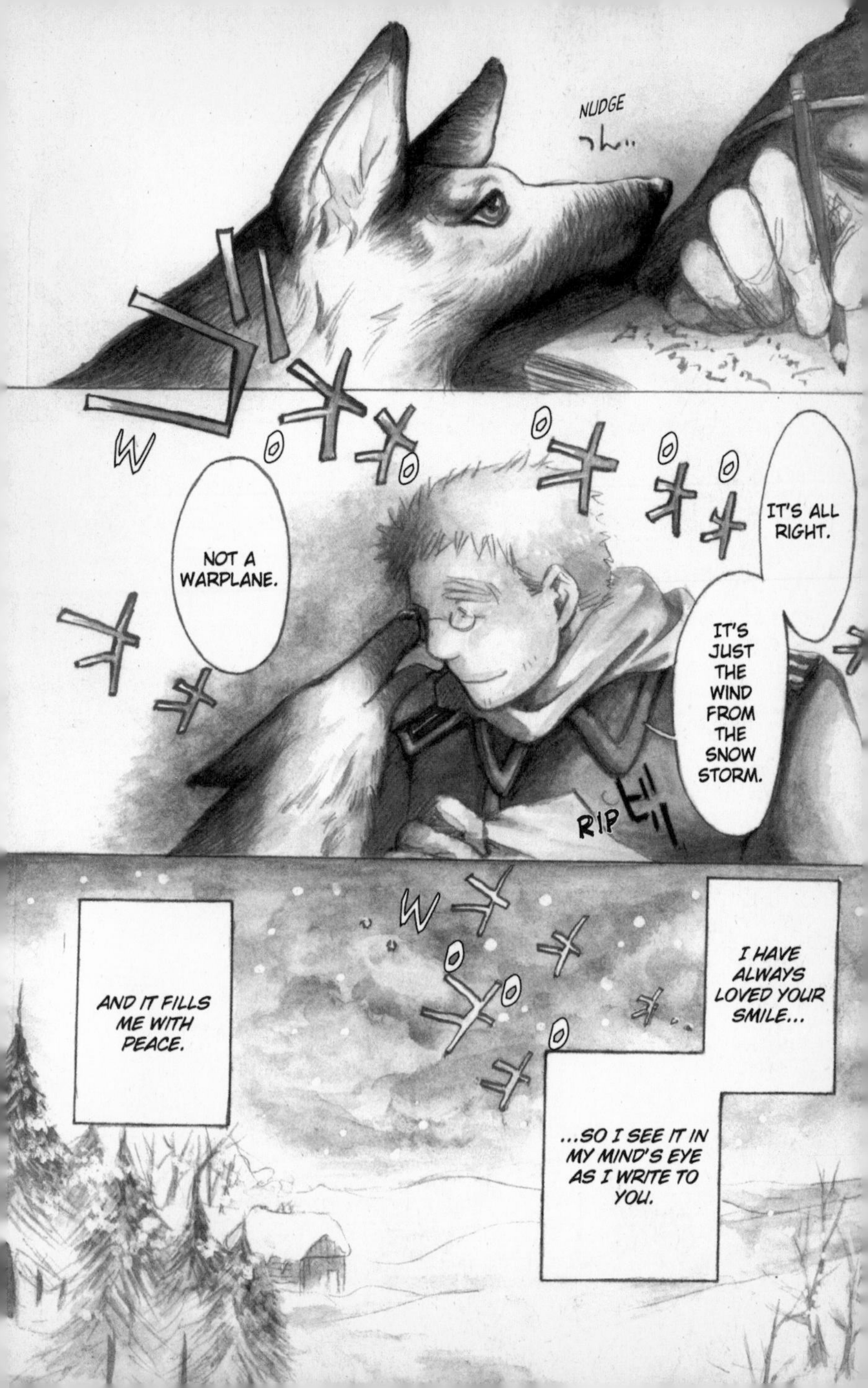
NUDGE
IT'S ALL RIGHT.
IT'S JUST THE WIND FROM THE SNOW STORM.
NOT A WARPLANE.
RIP
I HAVE ALWAYS LOVED YOUR SMILE...
...SO I SEE IT IN MY MIND'S EYE AS I WRITE TO YOU.
AND IT FILLS ME WITH PEACE.

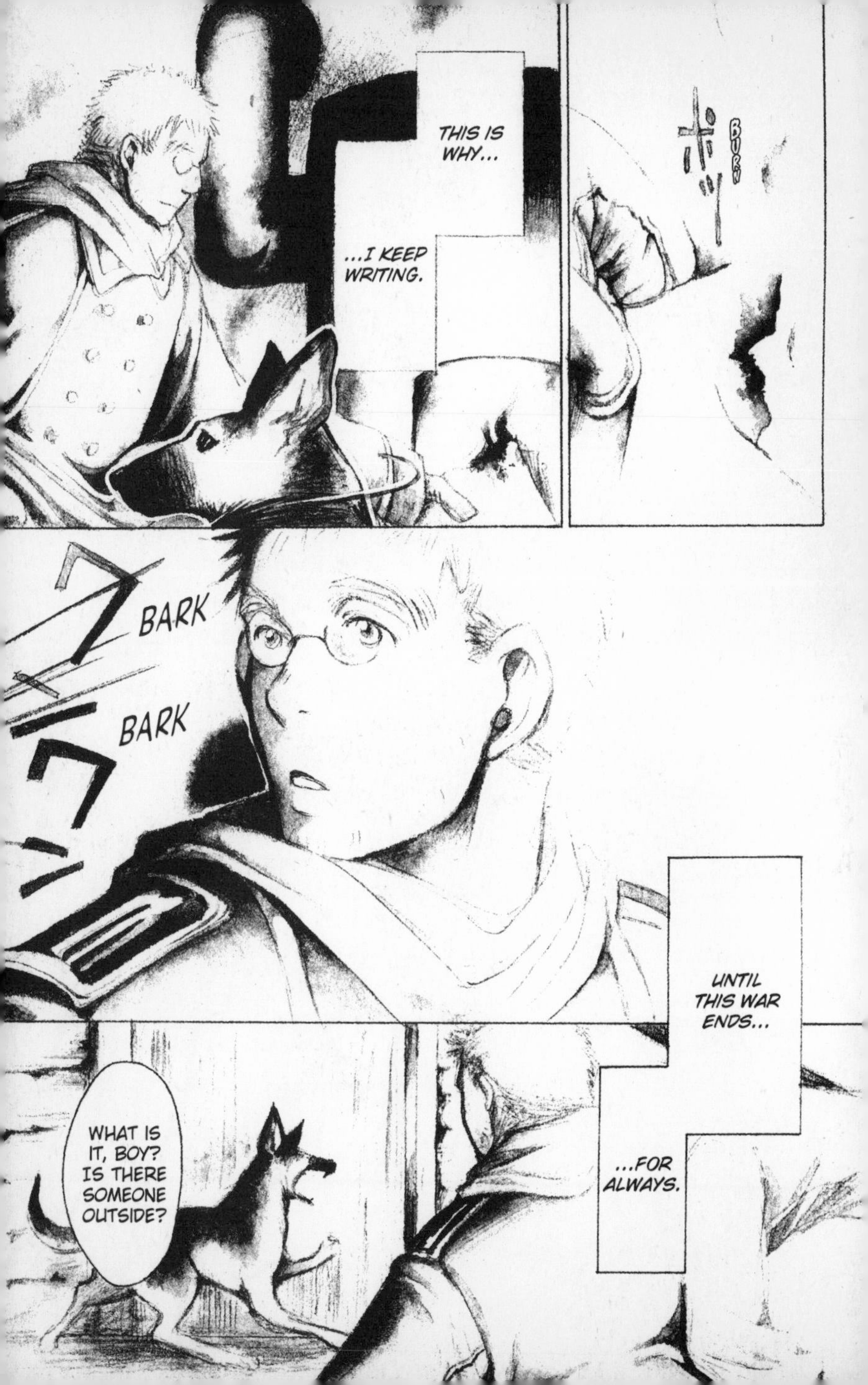
BURN
THIS IS WHY...
...I KEEP WRITING.
BARK
BARK
UNTIL THIS WAR ENDS...
...FOR ALWAYS.
WHAT IS IT, BOY? IS THERE SOMEONE OUTSIDE?

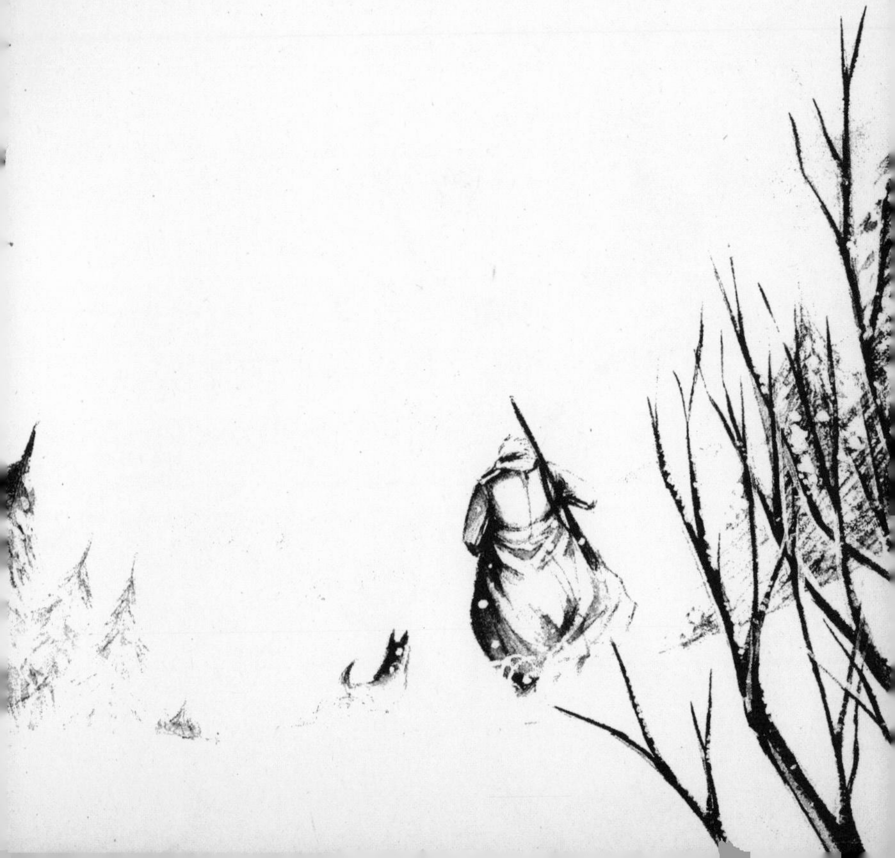

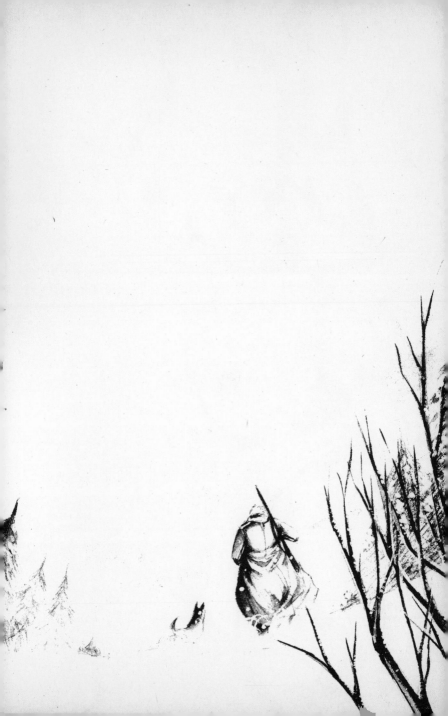

I

SONG OF THE HANGIING SKY
GIN TORIKO

CONTENTS

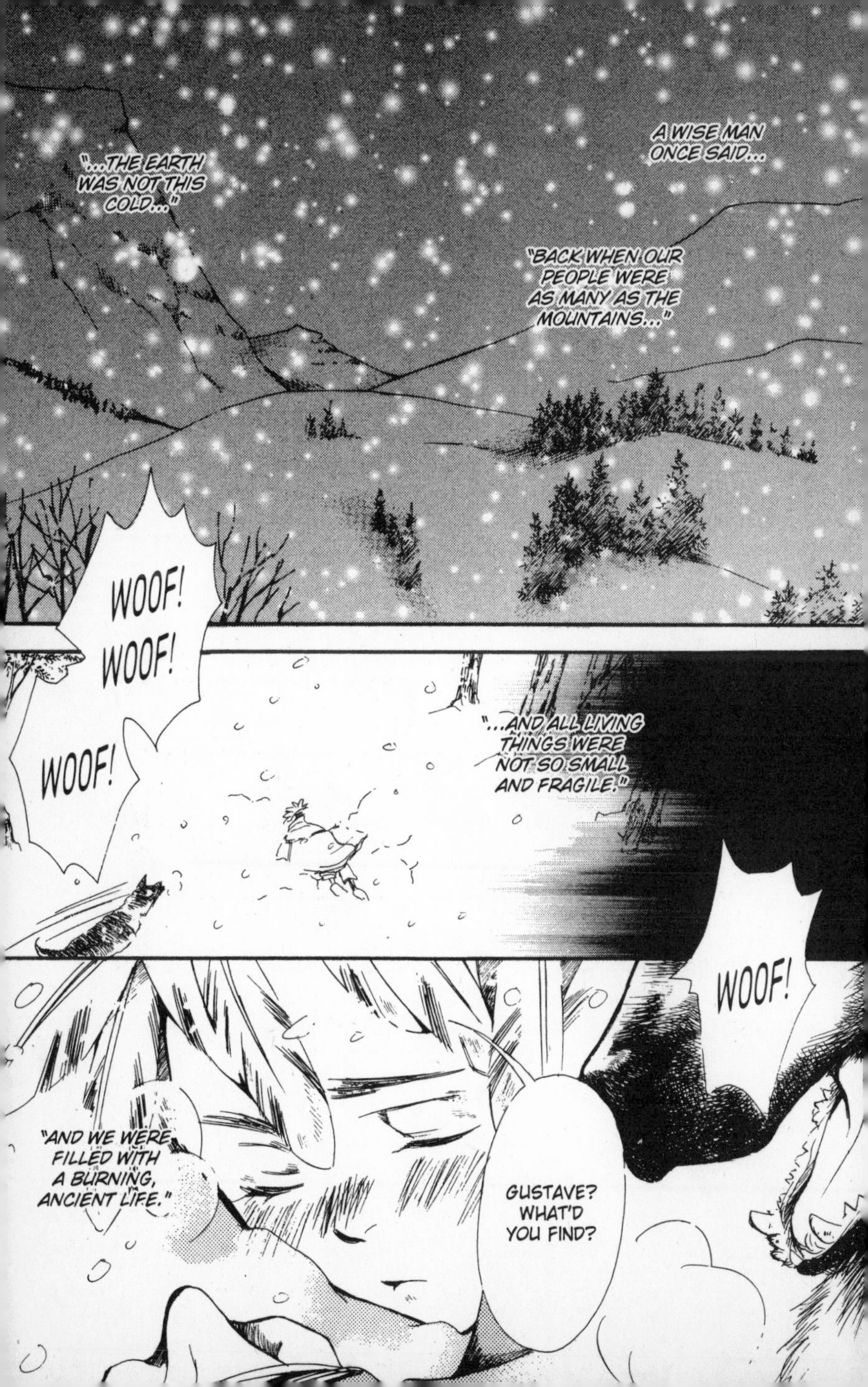
A WISE MAN ONCE SAID...
"BACK WHEN OUR PEOPLE WERE AS MANY AS THE MOUNTAINS..."
"...THE EARTH WAS NOT THIS COLD..."
WOOF! WOOF!
"...AND ALL LIVING THINGS WERE NOT SO SMALL AND FRAGILE."
WOOF!
WOOF!
GUSTAVE? WHAT'D YOU FIND?
"AND WE WERE FILLED WITH A BURNING, ANCIENT LIFE."

Song of the Hanging Sky

Chapter 1

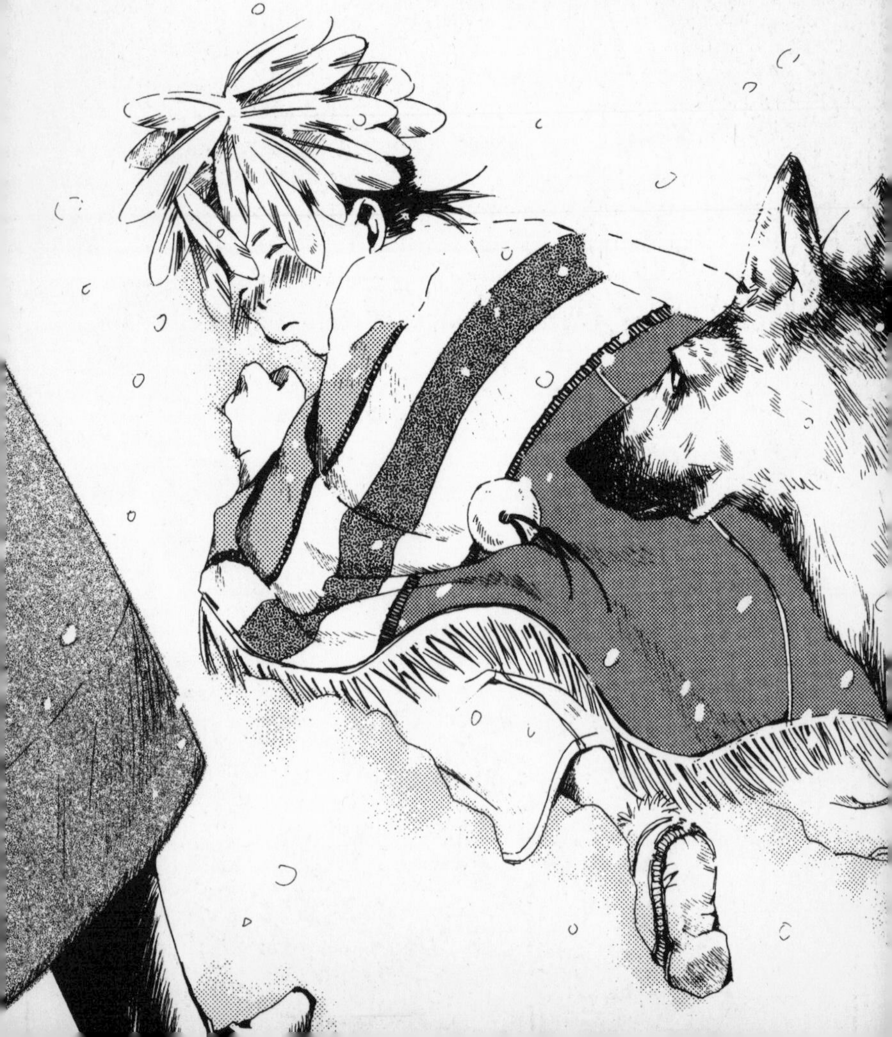

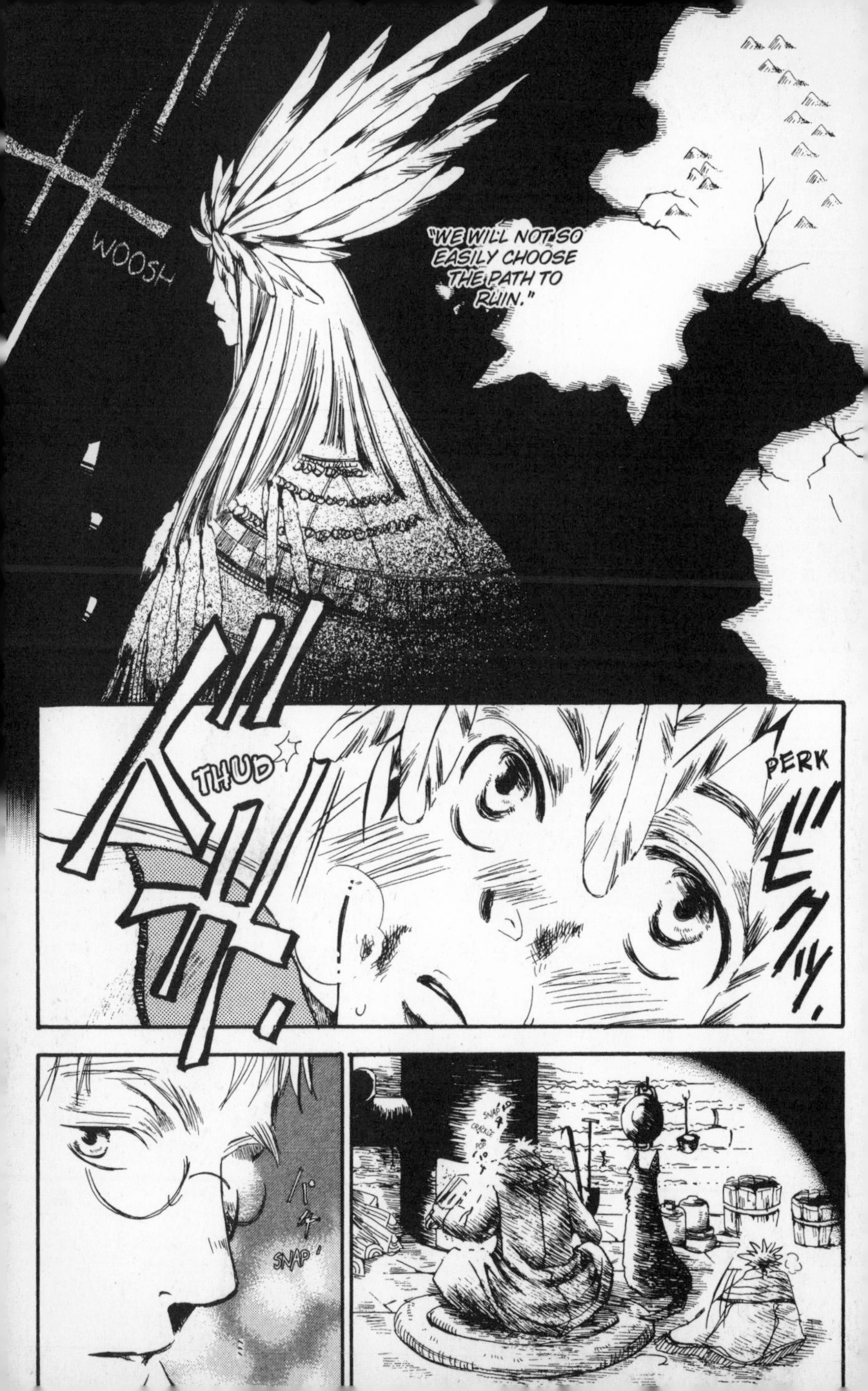
WOOSH
"WE WILL NOT SO EASILY CHOOSE THE PATH TO RUIN."
PERK
THUD
SNAP
CRACKLE
POP
SNAP

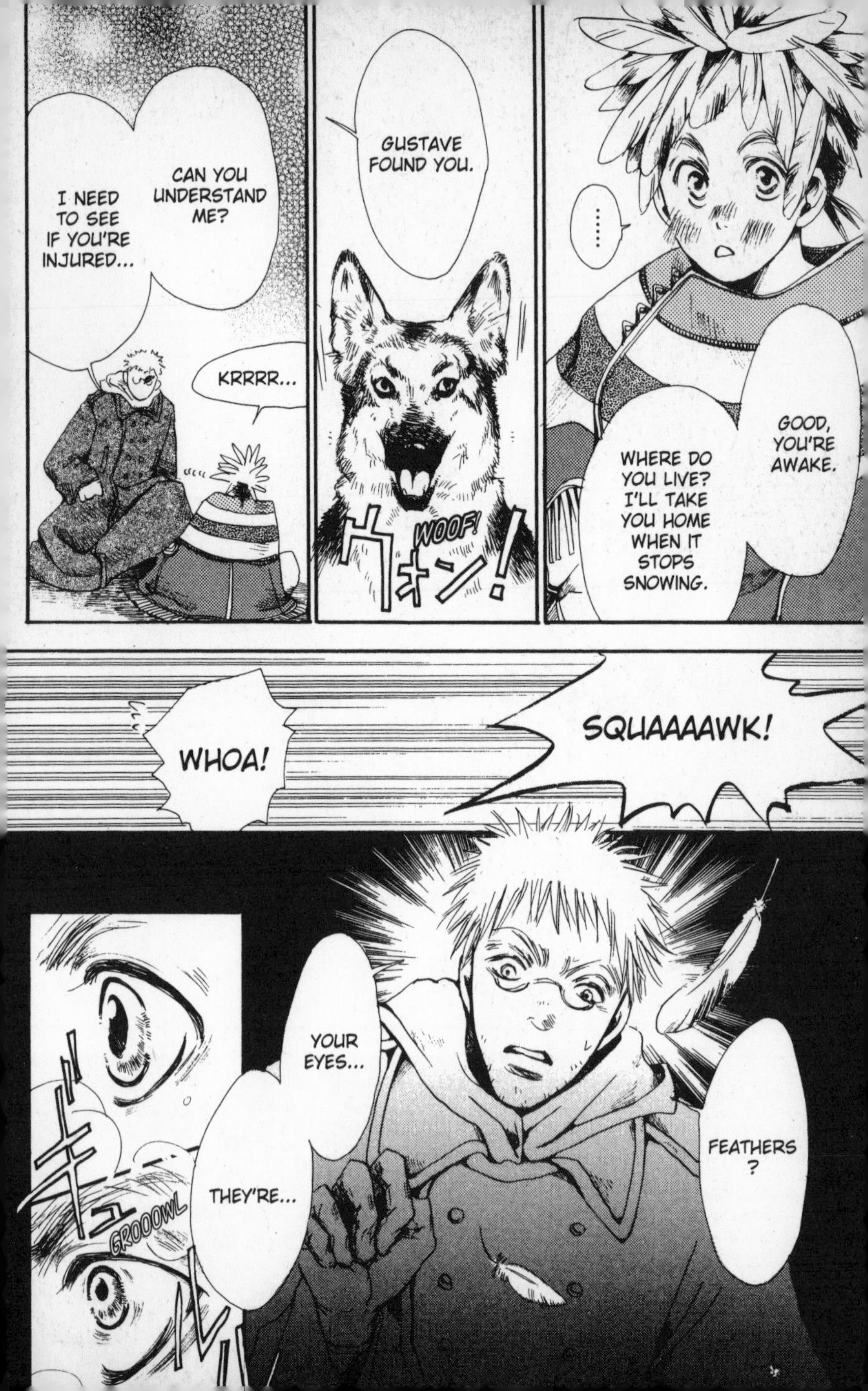
……
GOOD, YOU'RE AWAKE.
WHERE DO YOU LIVE? I'LL TAKE YOU HOME WHEN IT STOPS SNOWING.
GUSTAVE FOUND YOU.
WOOF!
ウォーン!
CAN YOU UNDERSTAND ME?
I NEED TO SEE IF YOU'RE INJURED...
KRRRR...
SQUAAAAWK!
WHOA!
FEATHERS ?
YOUR EYES...
THEY'RE...
GROOOWL

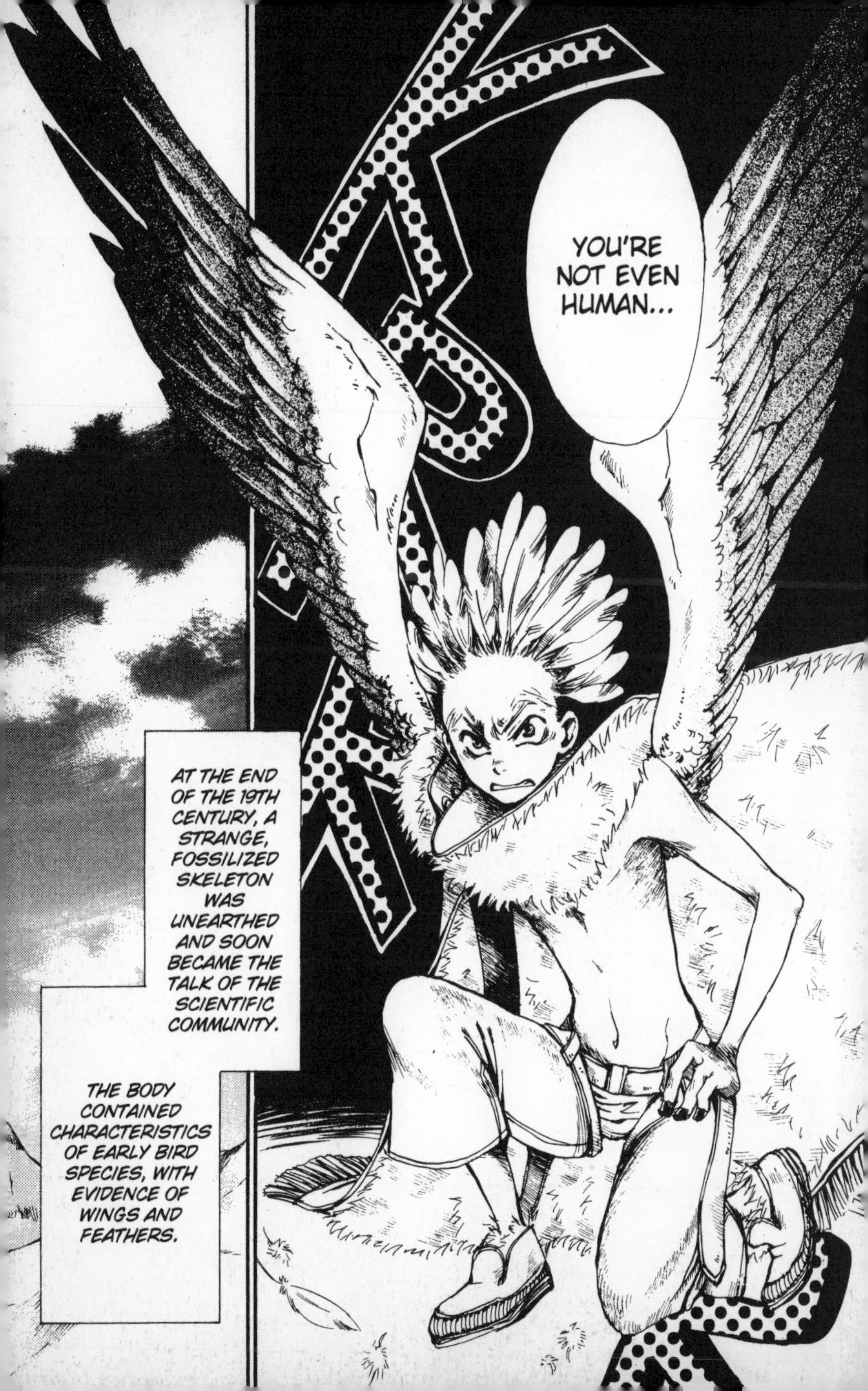
YOU'RE NOT EVEN HUMAN...
AT THE END OF THE 19TH CENTURY, A STRANGE, FOSSILIZED SKELETON WAS UNEARTHED AND SOON BECAME THE TALK OF THE SCIENTIFIC COMMUNITY.
THE BODY CONTAINED CHARACTERISTICS OF EARLY BIRD SPECIES, WITH EVIDENCE OF WINGS AND FEATHERS.

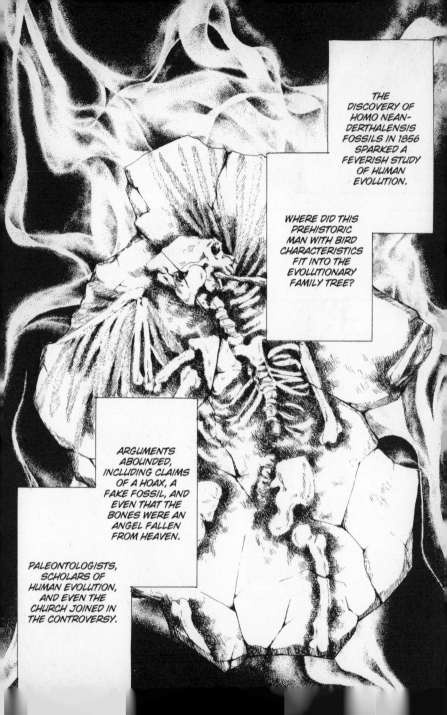

THE DISCOVERY OF HOMO NEANDERTHALENSIS FOSSILS IN 1856 SPARKED A FEVERISH STUDY OF HUMAN EVOLUTION.

WHERE DID THIS PREHISTORIC MAN WITH BIRD CHARACTERISTICS FIT INTO THE EVOLUTIONARY FAMILY TREE?

ARGUMENTS ABOUNDED, INCLUDING CLAIMS OF A HOAX, A FAKE FOSSIL, AND EVEN THAT THE BONES WERE AN ANGEL FALLEN FROM HEAVEN.

PALEONTOLOGISTS, SCHOLARS OF HUMAN EVOLUTION, AND EVEN THE CHURCH JOINED IN THE CONTROVERSY.

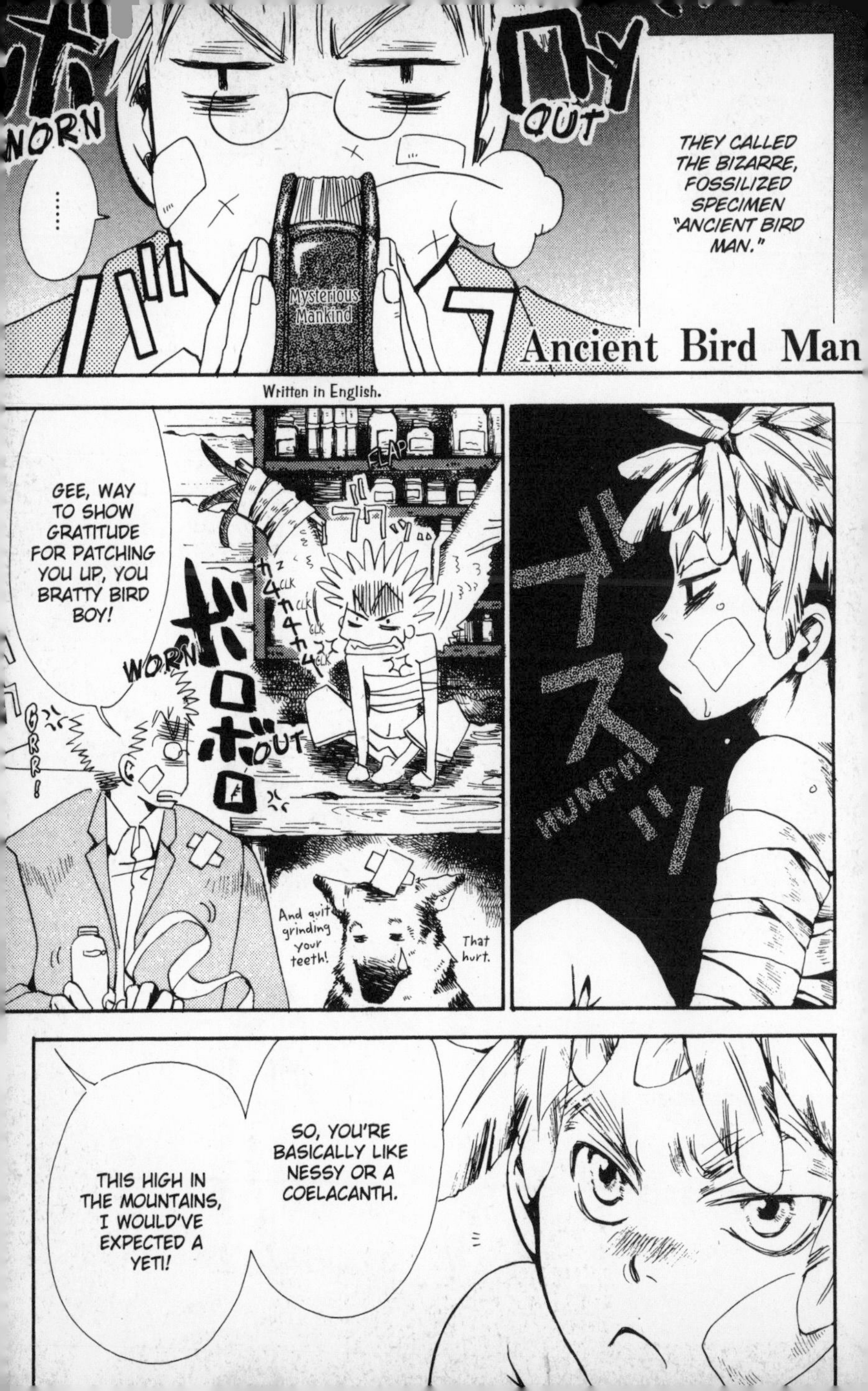
THEY CALLED THE BIZARRE, FOSSILIZED SPECIMEN "ANCIENT BIRD MAN."
OUT
WORN
......
Mysterious Mankind
Ancient Bird Man
Written in English.
HUMPH
FLAP
CLK
CLK
CLK
CLK
GEE, WAY TO SHOW GRATITUDE FOR PATCHING YOU UP, YOU BRATTY BIRD BOY!
OUT
WORN
GRRR!
That hurt.
And quit grinding your teeth!
SO, YOU'RE BASICALLY LIKE NESSY OR A COELACANTH.
THIS HIGH IN THE MOUNTAINS, I WOULD'VE EXPECTED A YETI!

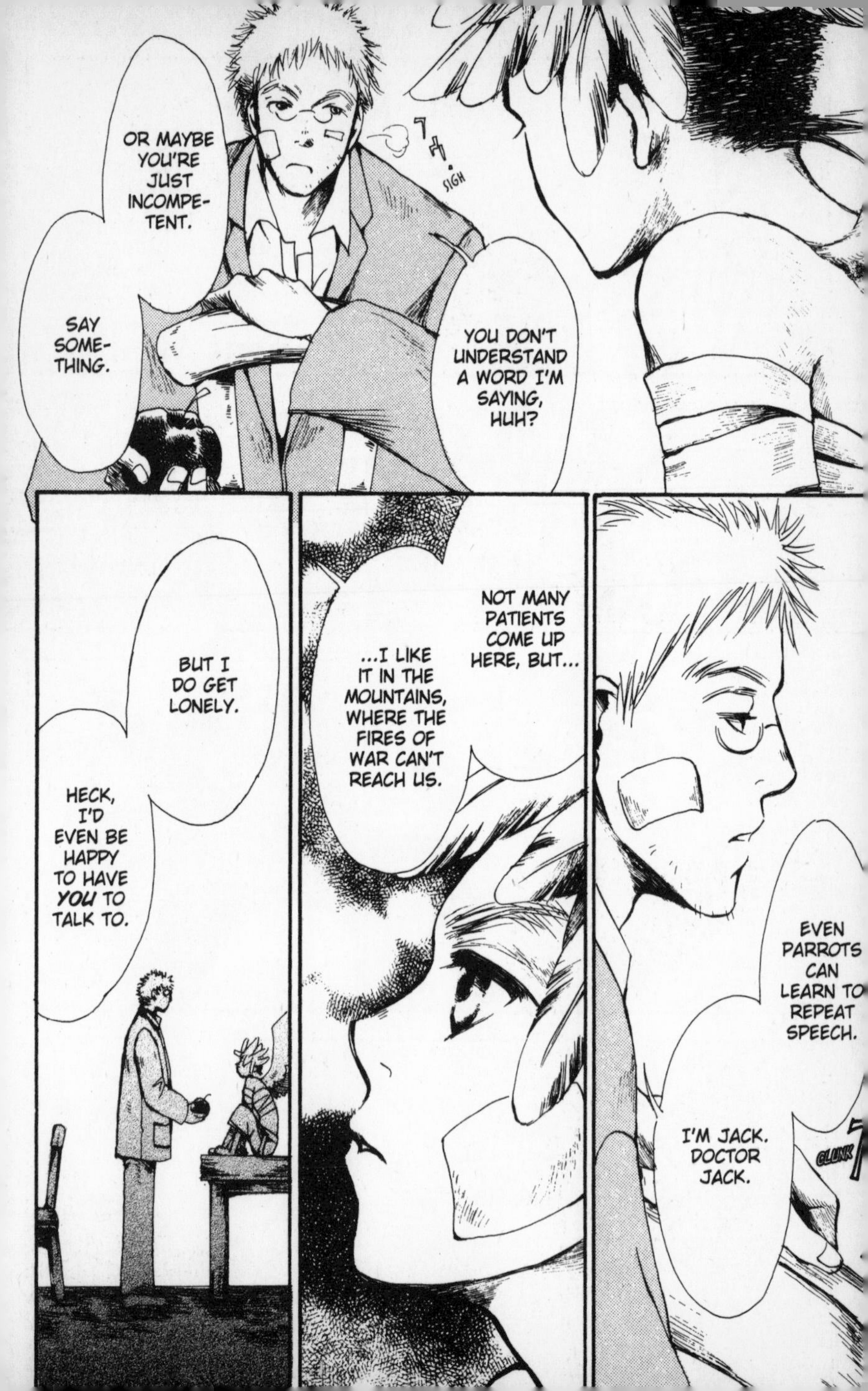
YOU DON'T UNDERSTAND A WORD I'M SAYING, HUH?
SIGH
OR MAYBE YOU'RE JUST INCOMPETENT.
SAY SOMETHING.
EVEN PARROTS CAN LEARN TO REPEAT SPEECH.
I'M JACK. DOCTOR JACK.
CLUNK
NOT MANY PATIENTS COME UP HERE, BUT...
...I LIKE IT IN THE MOUNTAINS, WHERE THE FIRES OF WAR CAN'T REACH US.
BUT I DO GET LONELY.
HECK, I'D EVEN BE HAPPY TO HAVE *YOU* TO TALK TO.

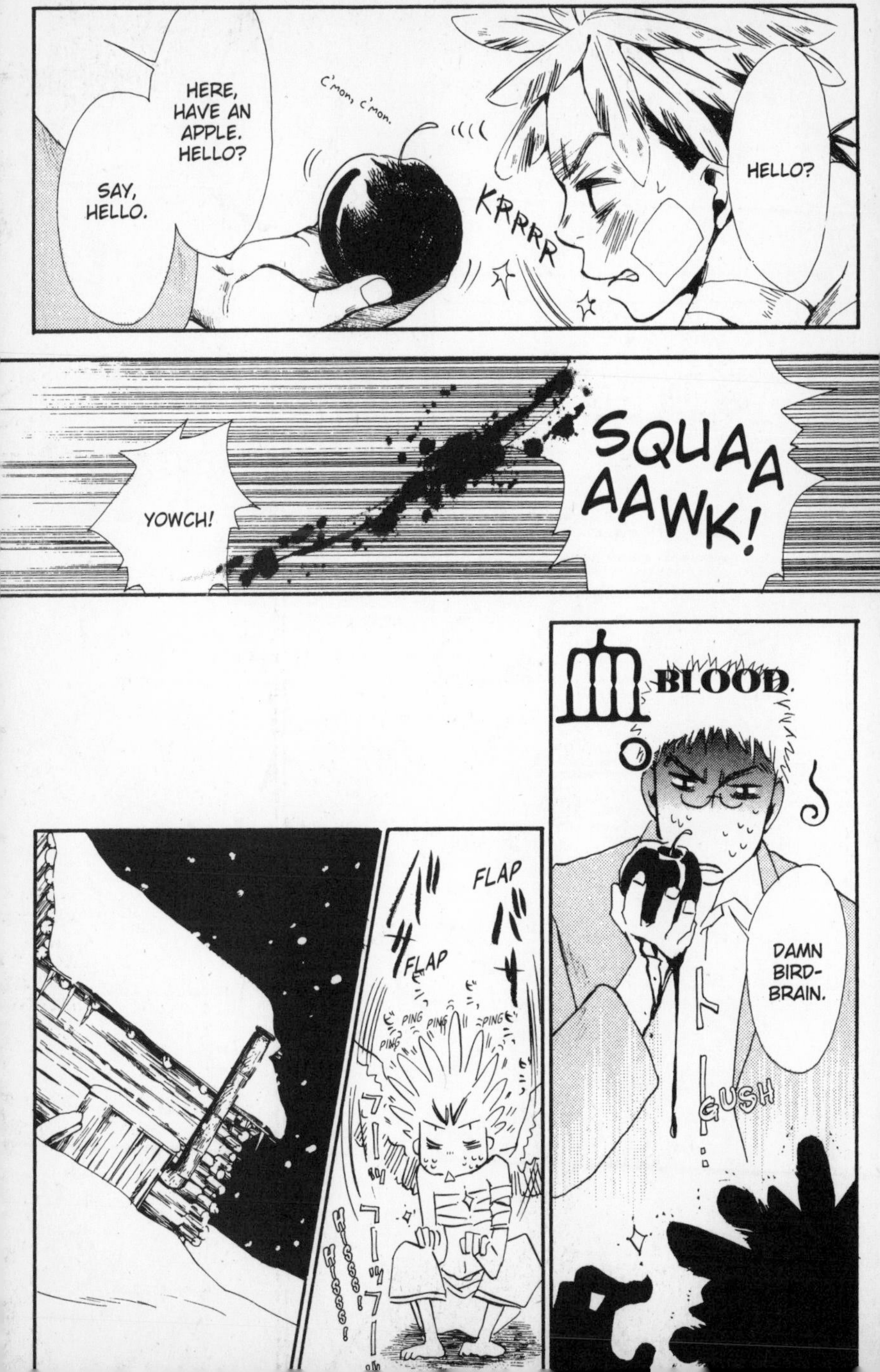
HELLO?
KRRRRR
c'mon, c'mon.
HERE, HAVE AN APPLE. HELLO?
SAY, HELLO.
SQUAAAAWK!
YOWCH!
BLOOD
DAMN BIRD-BRAIN.
GUSH
FLAP
FLAP
PING PING PING PING
HISSS! HISSS!

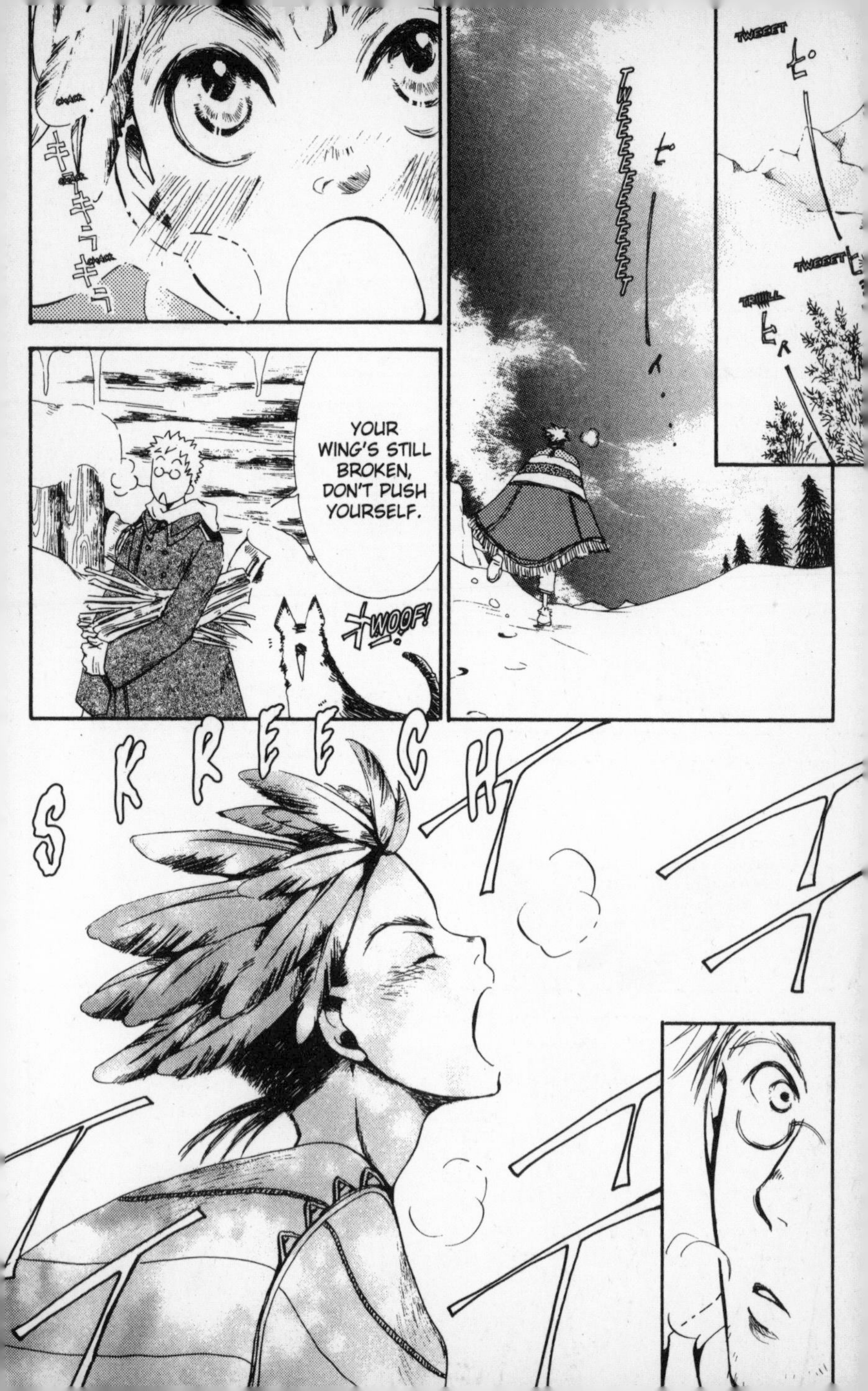
TWEEET
TWEEET
TRIIIILL
TWEEEEEEEEEEEET
YOUR WING'S STILL BROKEN, DON'T PUSH YOURSELF.
WOOF!
SKREECH

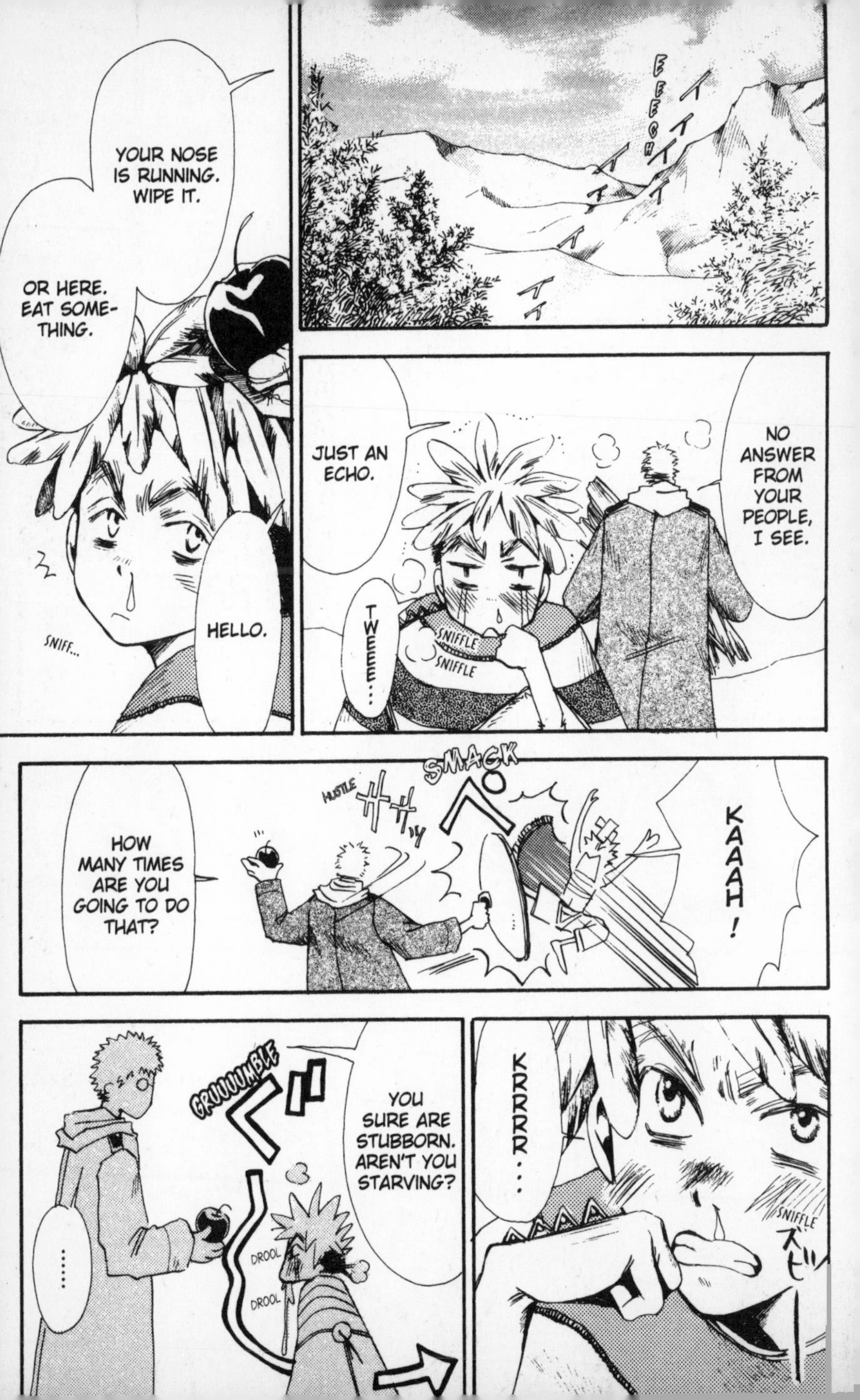
EEECH
NO ANSWER FROM YOUR PEOPLE, I SEE.
JUST AN ECHO.
TWEEE...
SNIFFLE
SNIFFLE
YOUR NOSE IS RUNNING. WIPE IT.
OR HERE. EAT SOMETHING.
HELLO.
SNIFF...
KAAAH!
SMACK
HUSTLE
HOW MANY TIMES ARE YOU GOING TO DO THAT?
KRRRR...
SNIFFLE
YOU SURE ARE STUBBORN. AREN'T YOU STARVING?
GRUUUUMBLE
DROOL
DROOL
......

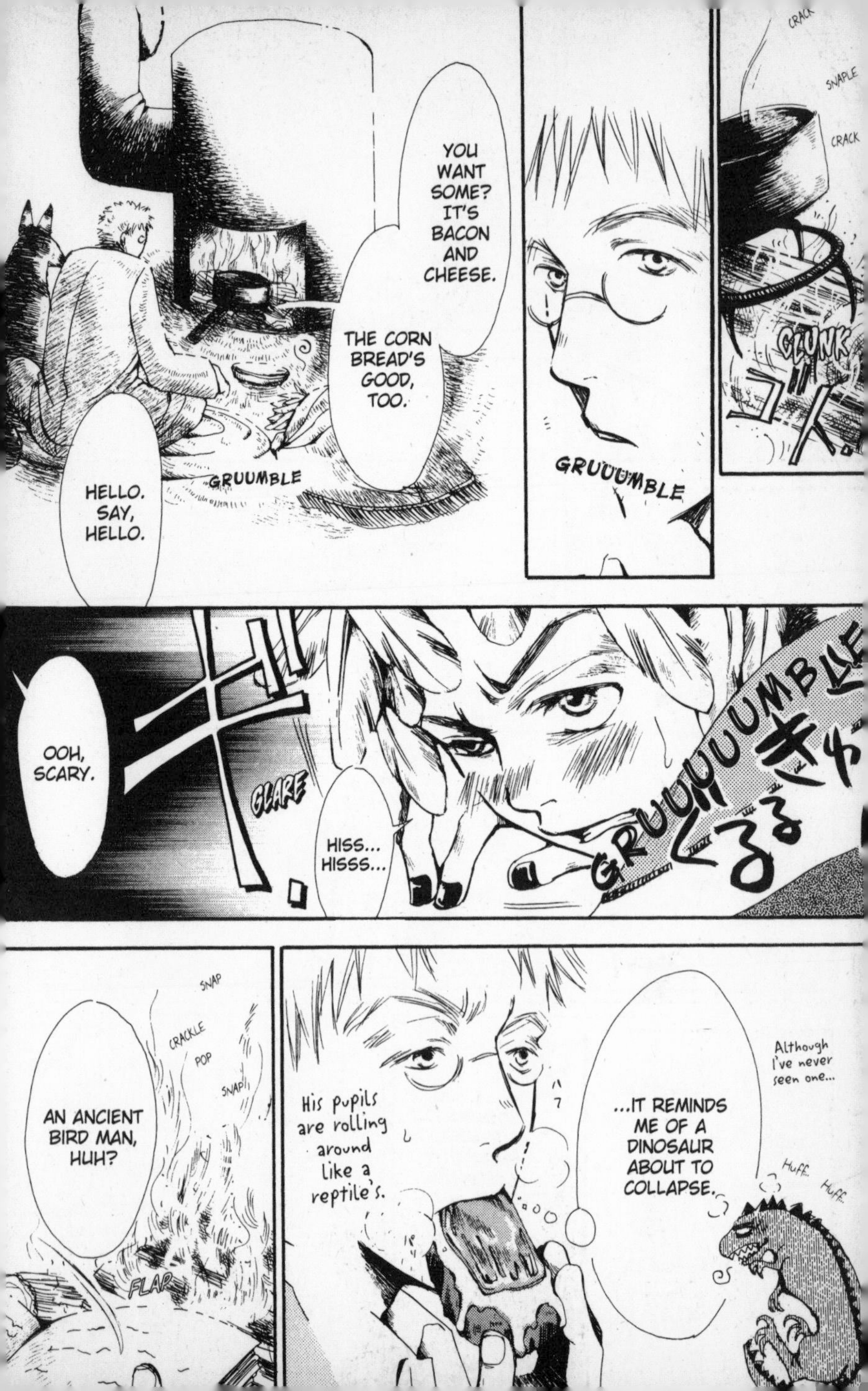
CRACK
SNAPLE
CRACK
CLUNK
GRUUUMBLE
YOU WANT SOME? IT'S BACON AND CHEESE.
THE CORN BREAD'S GOOD, TOO.
GRUUMBLE
HELLO. SAY, HELLO.
GRUUUUUMBLE
HISS... HISSS...
GLARE
OOH, SCARY.
Although I've never seen one...
...IT REMINDS ME OF A DINOSAUR ABOUT TO COLLAPSE.
Huff...
Huff...
His pupils are rolling around like a reptile's.
SNAP
CRACKLE
POP
SNAP
AN ANCIENT BIRD MAN, HUH?
FLAP

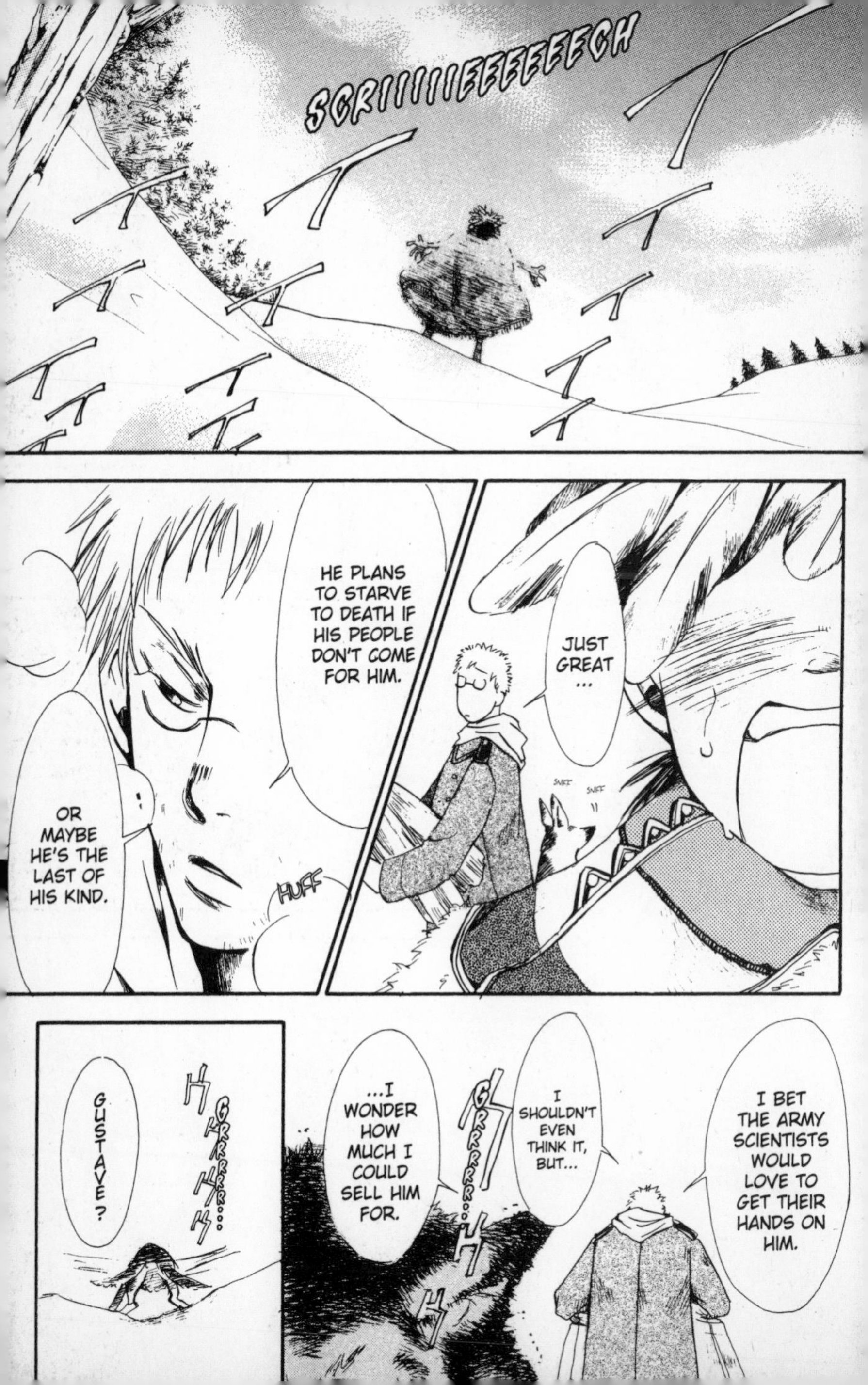
SCRIIIIIEEEEEECH
JUST GREAT ...
HE PLANS TO STARVE TO DEATH IF HIS PEOPLE DON'T COME FOR HIM.
OR MAYBE HE'S THE LAST OF HIS KIND.
HUFF
I BET THE ARMY SCIENTISTS WOULD LOVE TO GET THEIR HANDS ON HIM.
I SHOULDN'T EVEN THINK IT, BUT...
GRRRRRR...
...I WONDER HOW MUCH I COULD SELL HIM FOR.
GRRRRR...
GUSTAVE?

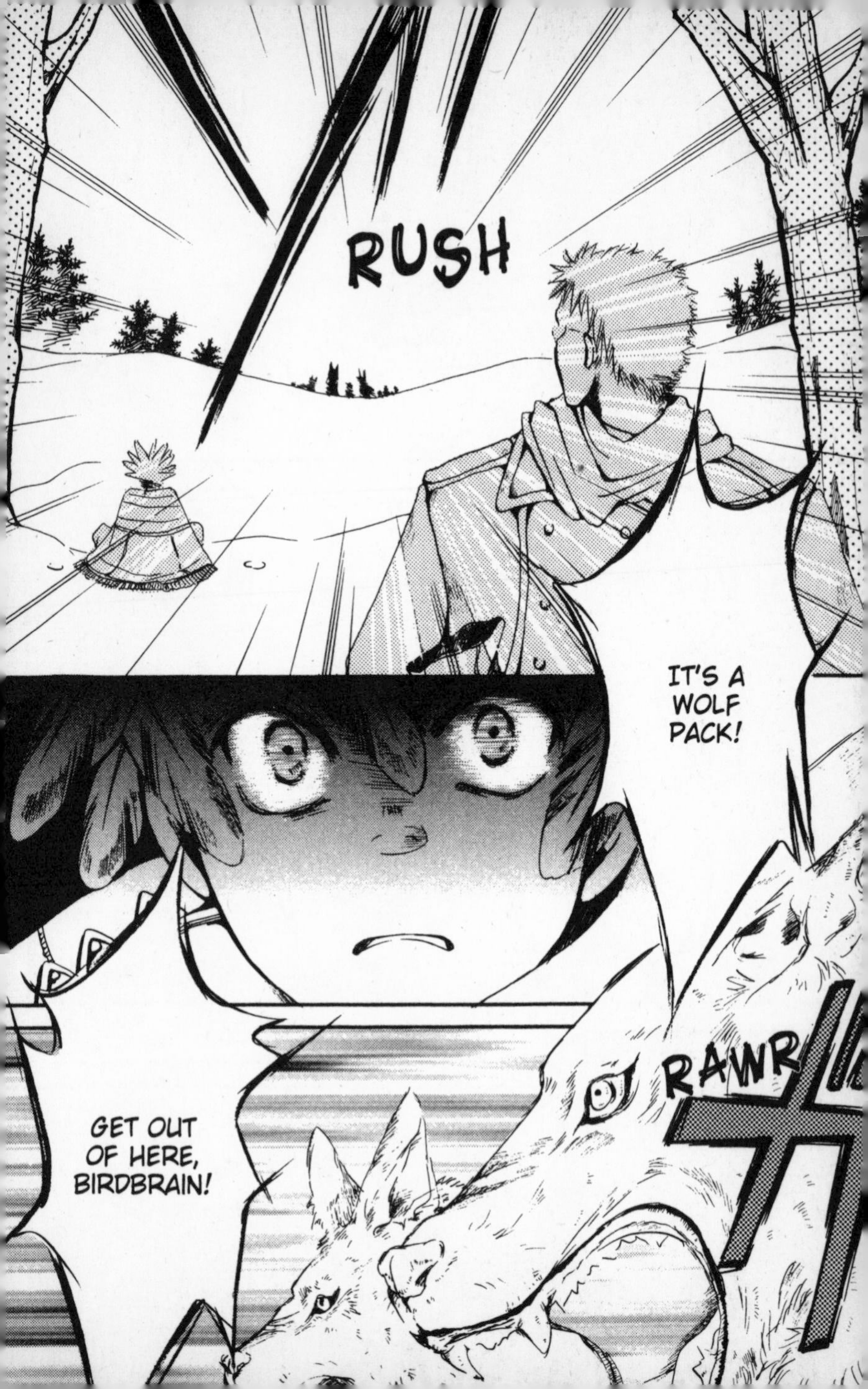
RUSH
IT'S A WOLF PACK!
RAWR
GET OUT OF HERE, BIRDBRAIN!

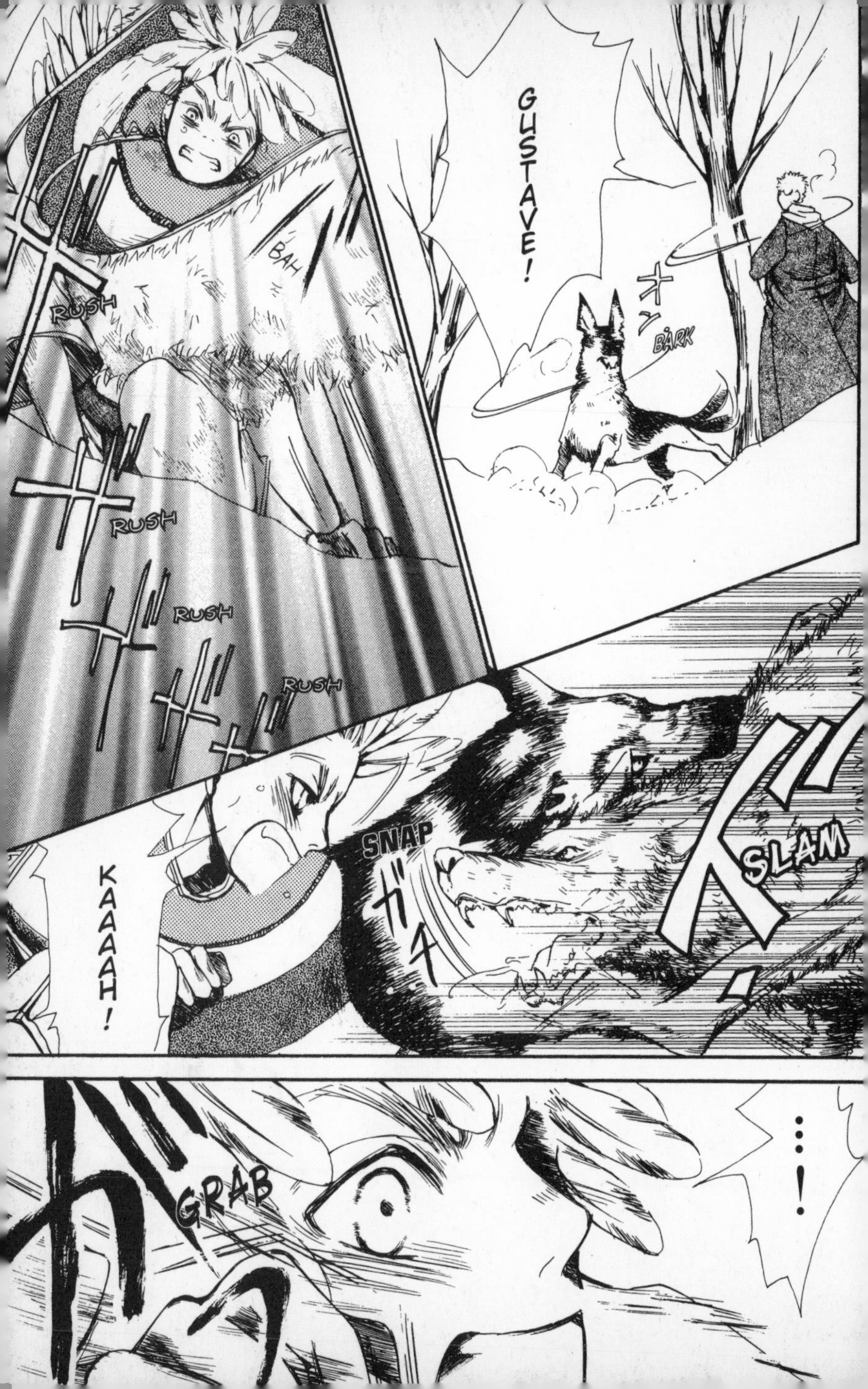
GUSTAVE!
BARK
BAH
RUSH
RUSH
RUSH
RUSH
SLAM
SNAP
KAAAAAH!
…!
GRAB

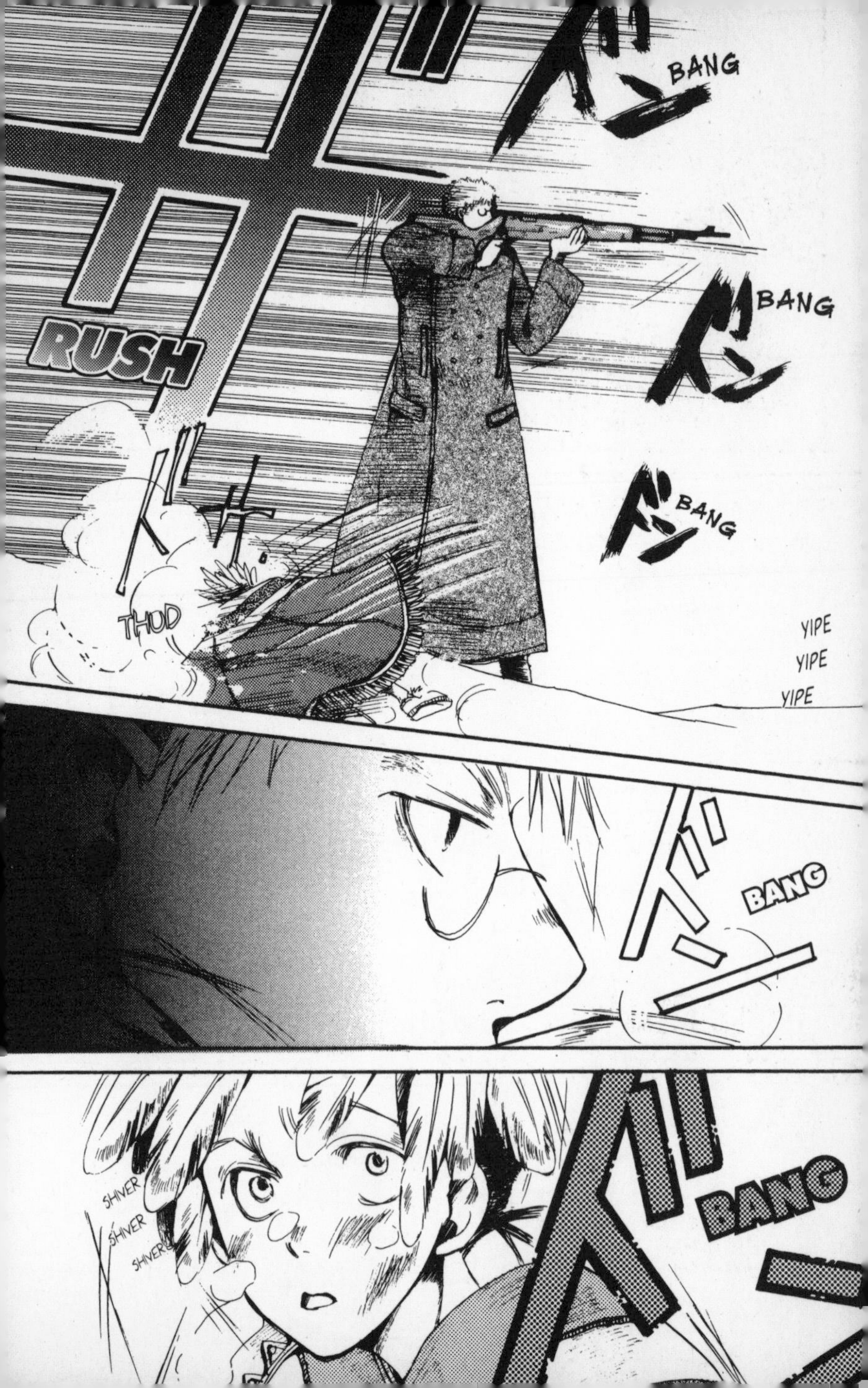
BANG
BANG
BANG
YIPE
YIPE
YIPE
RUSH
THUD
BANG
BANG
SHIVER
SHIVER
SHIVER

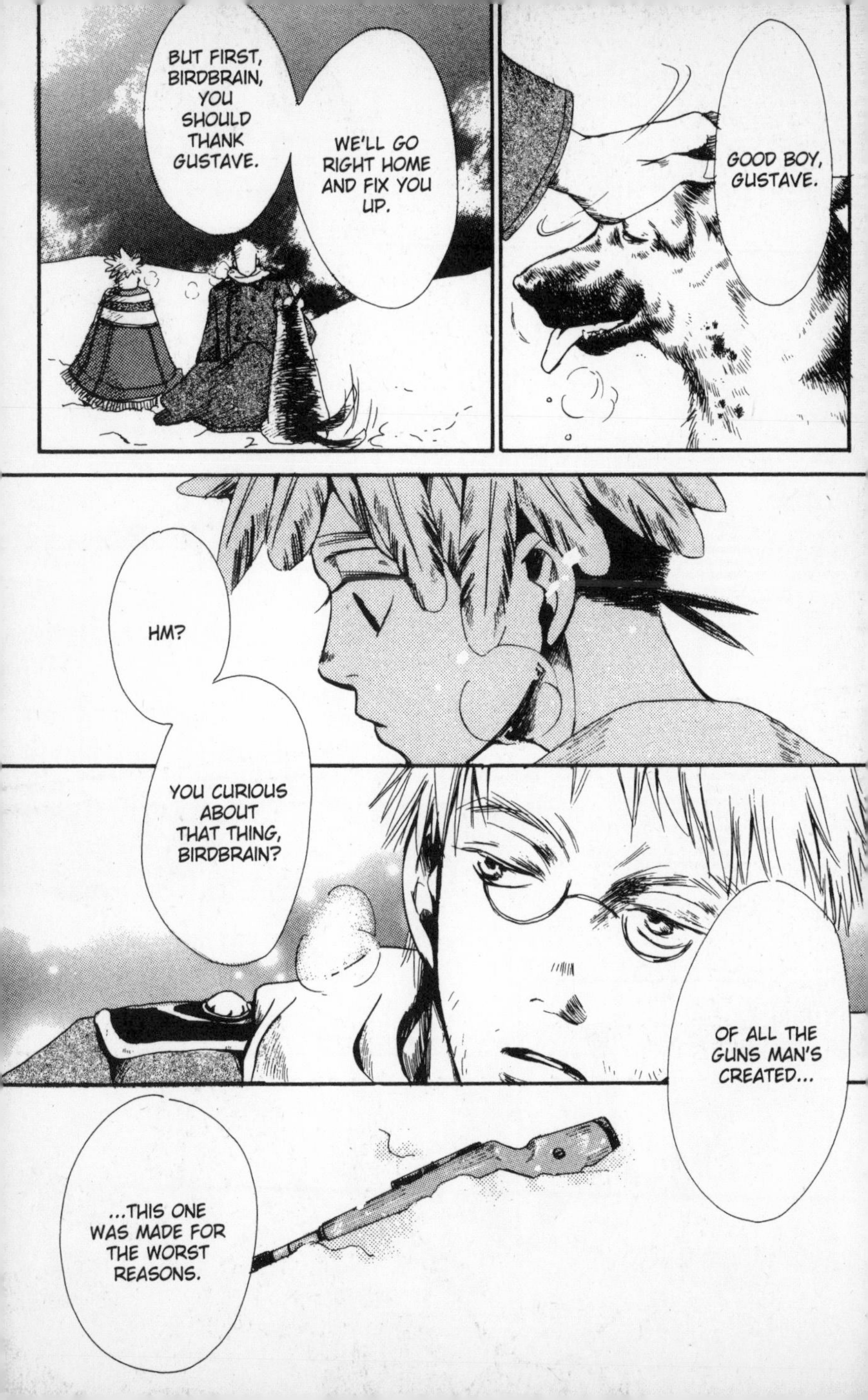
GOOD BOY, GUSTAVE.
WE'LL GO RIGHT HOME AND FIX YOU UP.
BUT FIRST, BIRDBRAIN, YOU SHOULD THANK GUSTAVE.
HM?
YOU CURIOUS ABOUT THAT THING, BIRDBRAIN?
OF ALL THE GUNS MAN'S CREATED...
...THIS ONE WAS MADE FOR THE WORST REASONS.

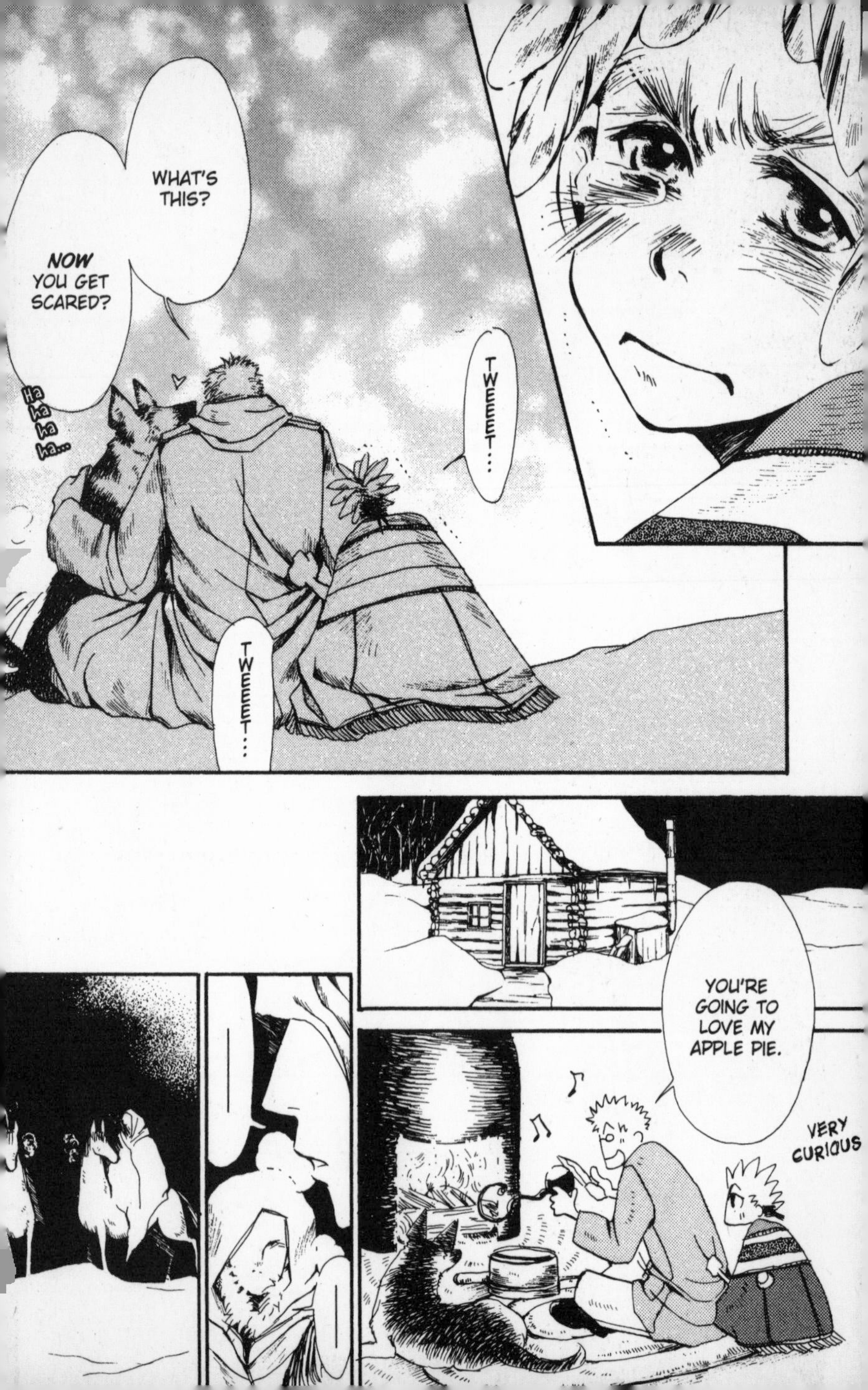
WHAT'S THIS?
NOW YOU GET SCARED?
Ha ha ha ha...
TWEEET...
TWEEET...
YOU'RE GOING TO LOVE MY APPLE PIE.
VERY CURIOUS

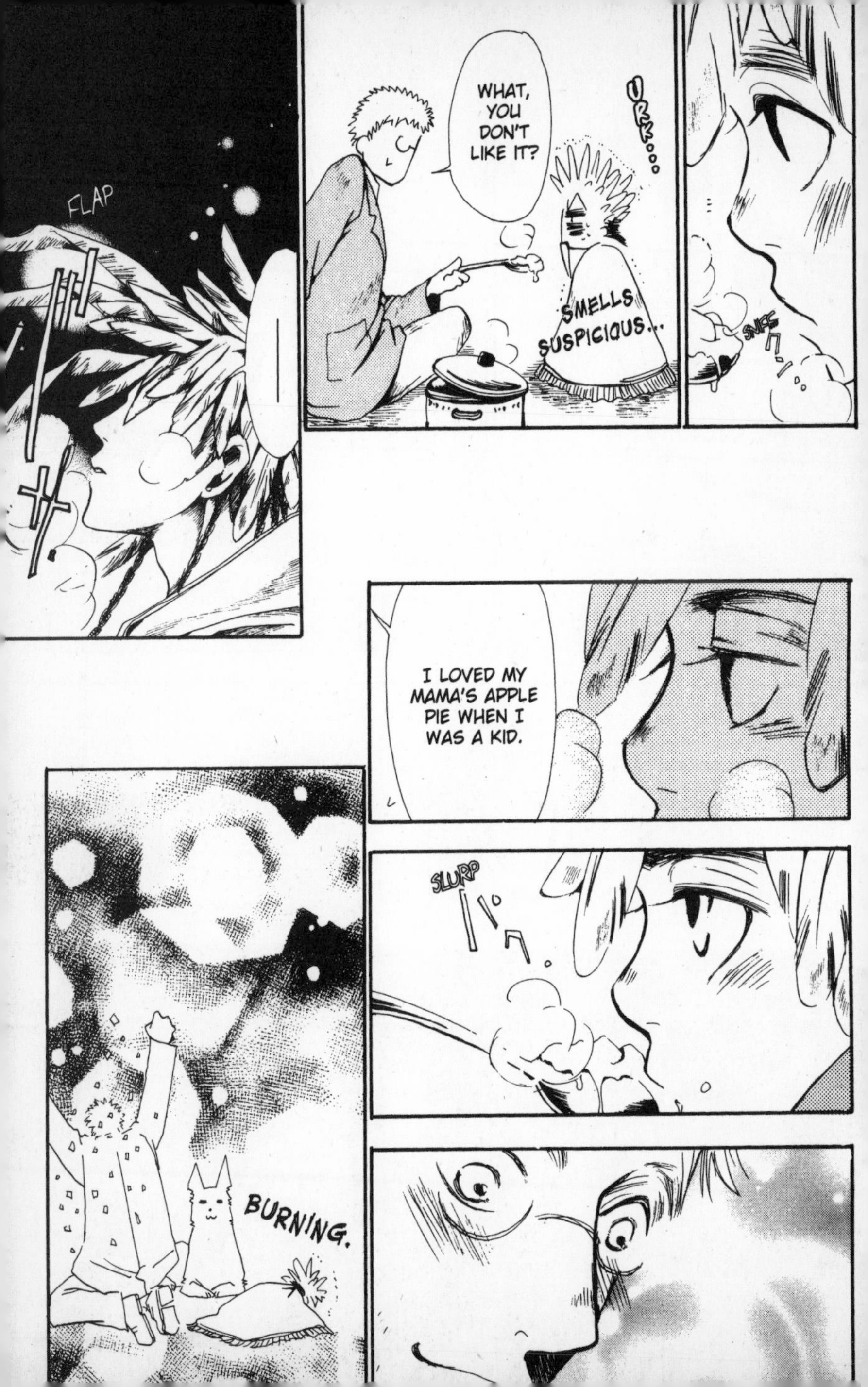
SNIFF
WHAT, YOU DON'T LIKE IT?
URRK...
SMELLS SUSPICIOUS...
FLAP
I LOVED MY MAMA'S APPLE PIE WHEN I WAS A KID.
SLURP
BURNING.

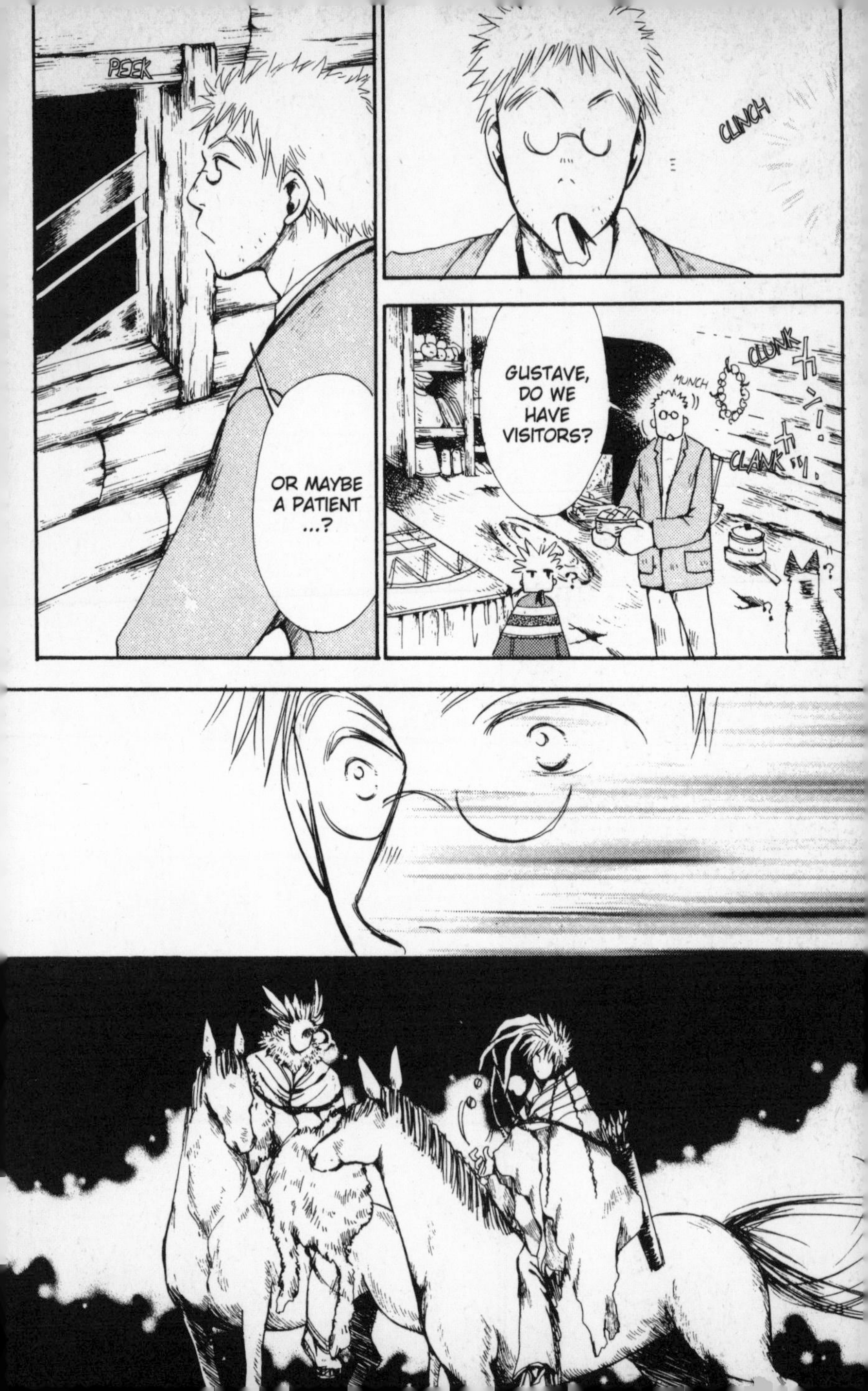
CLINCH
MUNCH
GUSTAVE, DO WE HAVE VISITORS?
CLUNK
CLANK
PEEK
OR MAYBE A PATIENT ...?

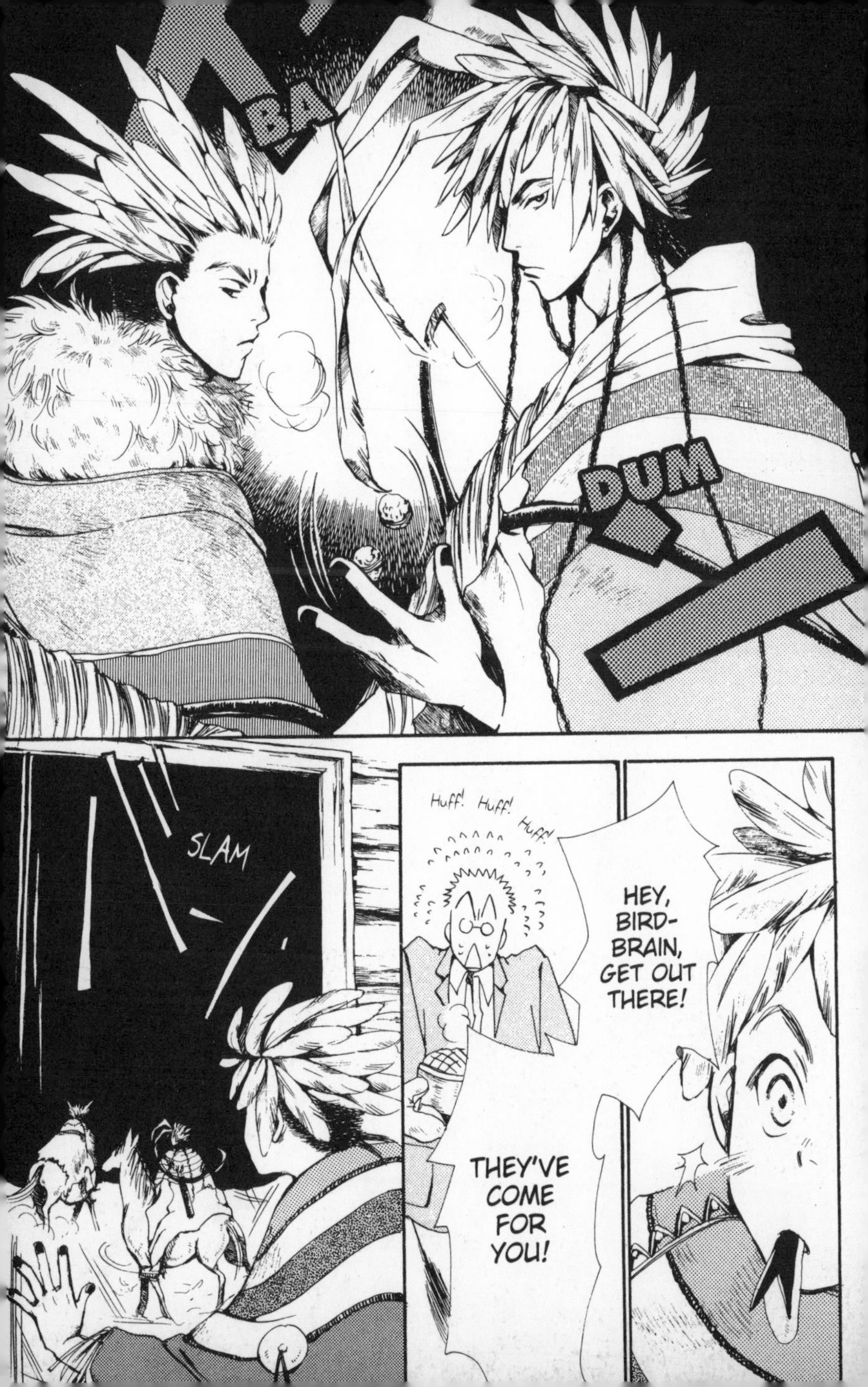
BA
DUM
HEY, BIRD-BRAIN, GET OUT THERE!
Huff! Huff! Huff!
THEY'VE COME FOR YOU!
SLAM

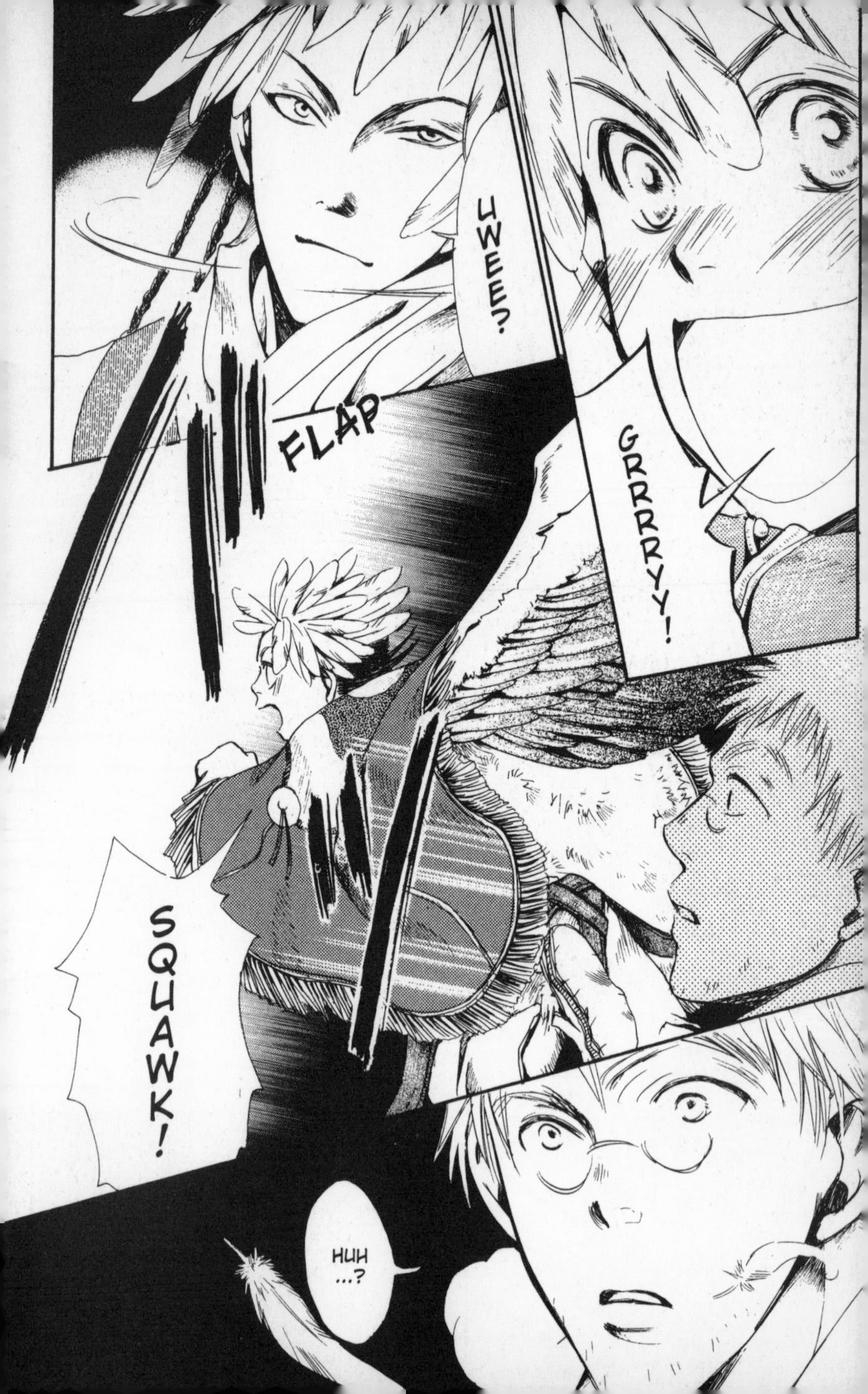
UWEE?
GRRRRYY!
FLAP
SQUAWK!
HUH ...?

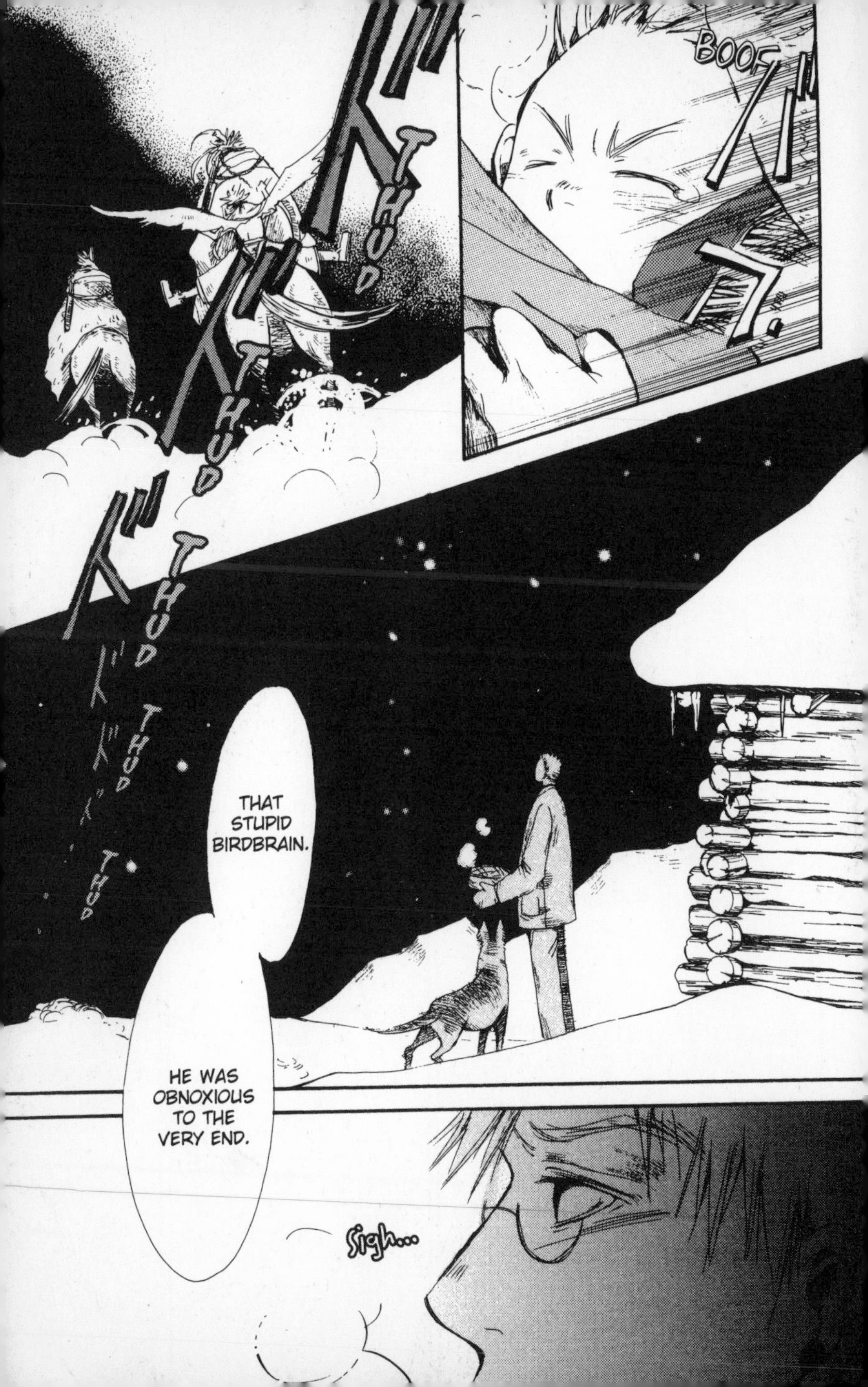
BOOF
THUD THUD THUD THUD THUD THUD
THAT STUPID BIRDBRAIN.
HE WAS OBNOXIOUS TO THE VERY END.
Sigh...

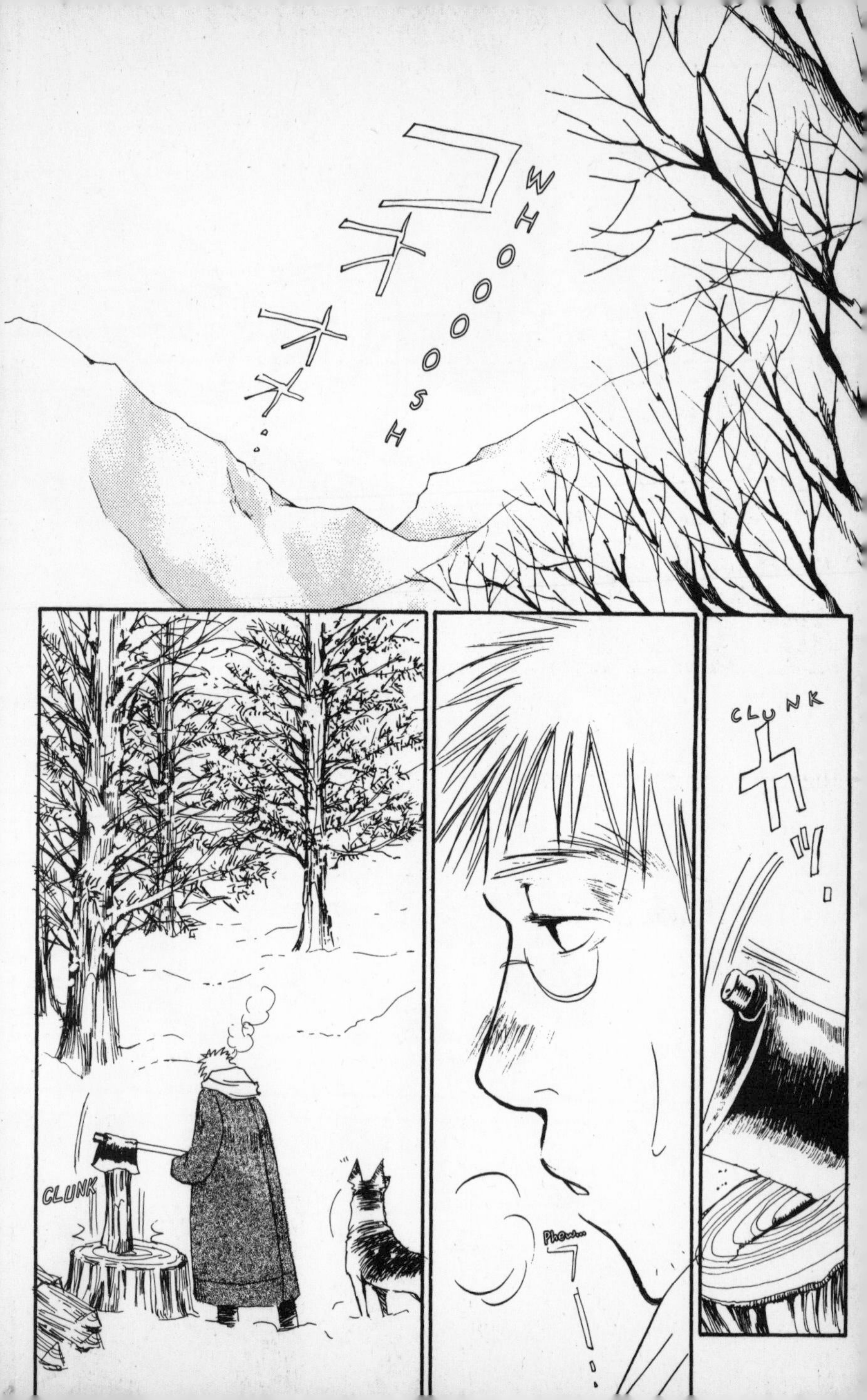

WHOOOOOSH
コオオオ…
CLUNK
カッ!
Phew...
CLUNK

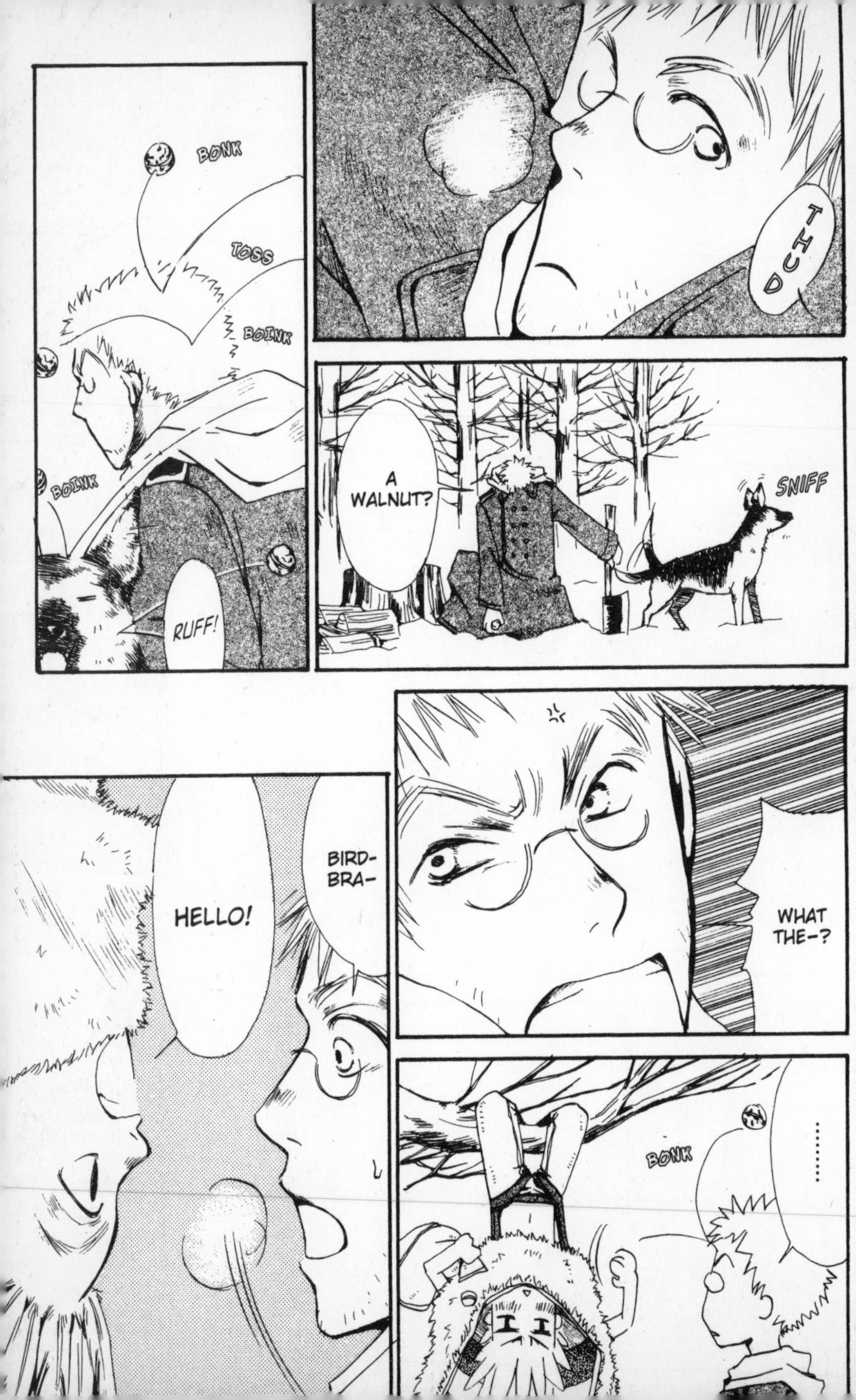
THUD
A WALNUT?
SNIFF
BONK
TOSS
BOINK
BOINK
RUFF!
WHAT THE-?
......
BONK
BIRD-BRA-
HELLO!

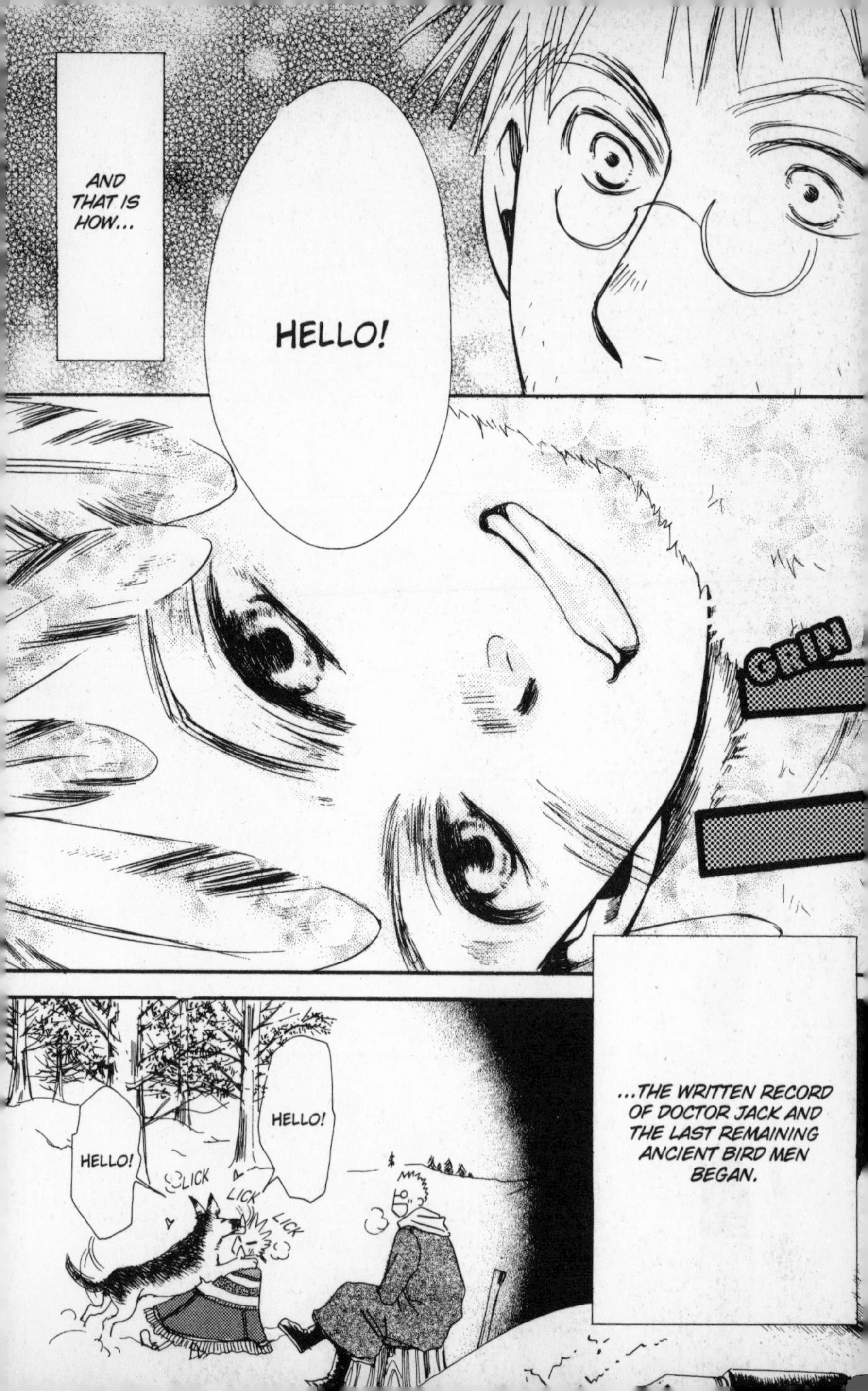
AND THAT IS HOW...
HELLO!
GRIN
...THE WRITTEN RECORD OF DOCTOR JACK AND THE LAST REMAINING ANCIENT BIRD MEN BEGAN.
HELLO!
HELLO!
LICK
LICK
LICK

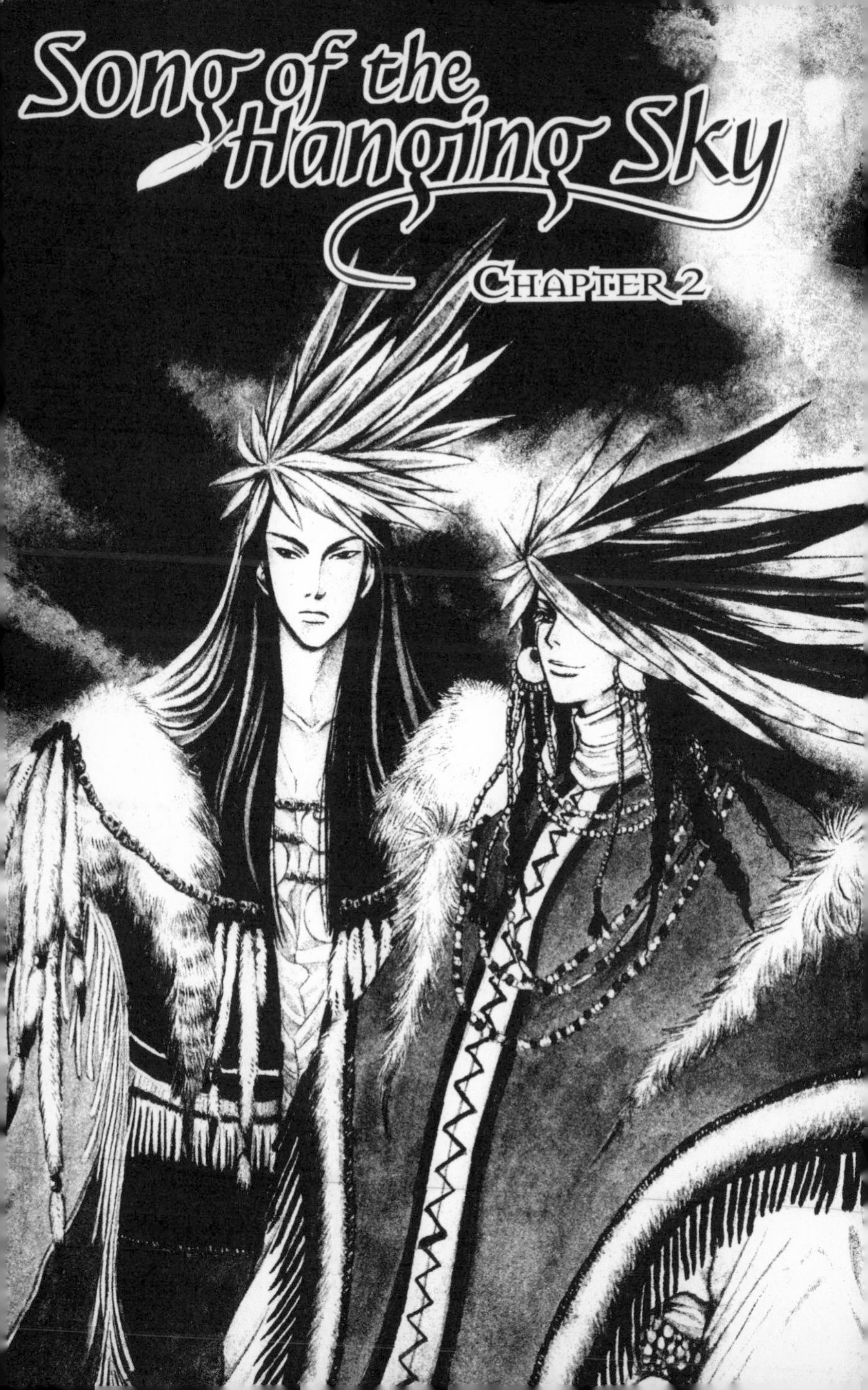
Song of the Hanging Sky
Chapter 2

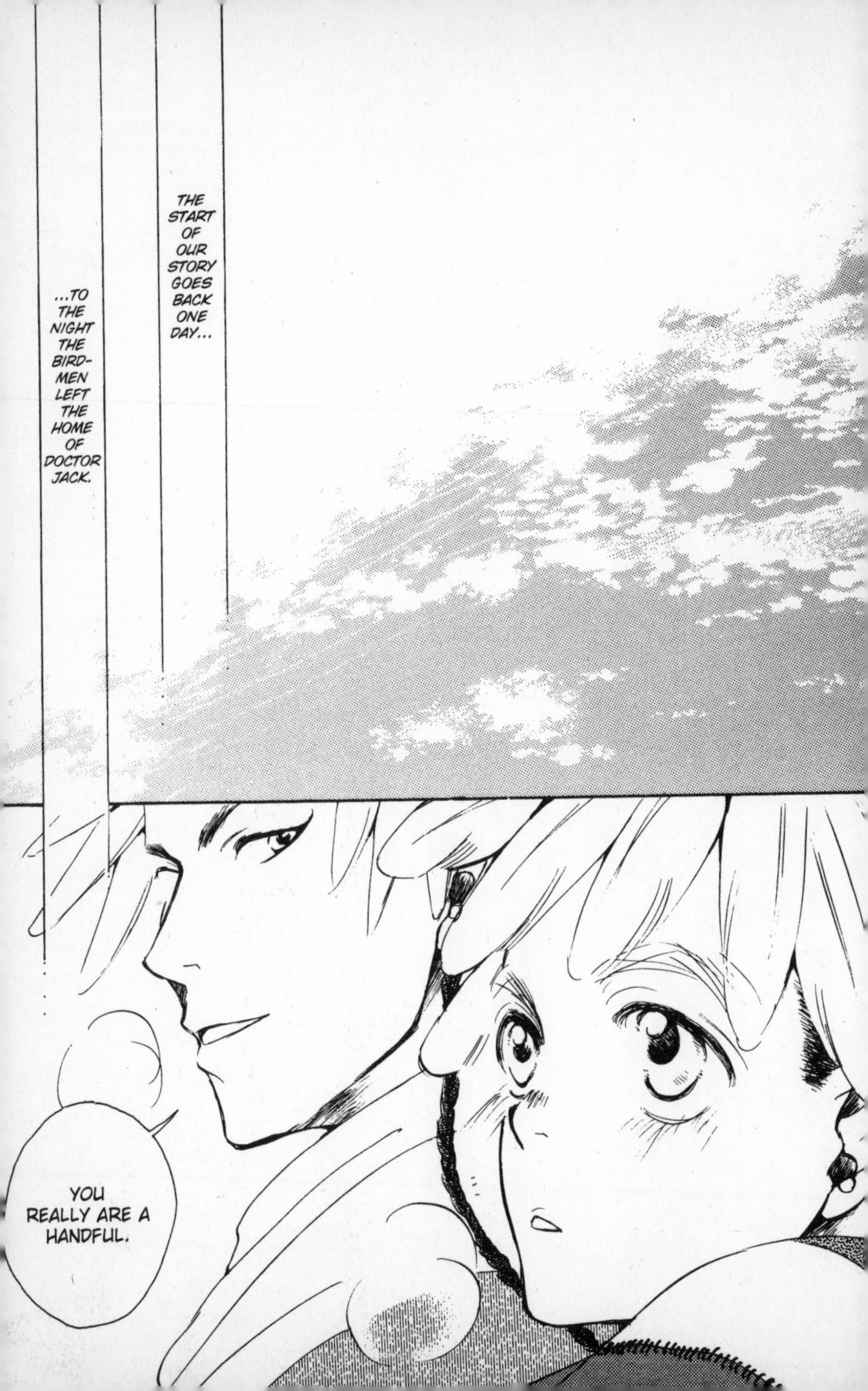
THE START OF OUR STORY GOES BACK ONE DAY...
...TO THE NIGHT THE BIRD-MEN LEFT THE HOME OF DOCTOR JACK.
YOU REALLY ARE A HANDFUL.

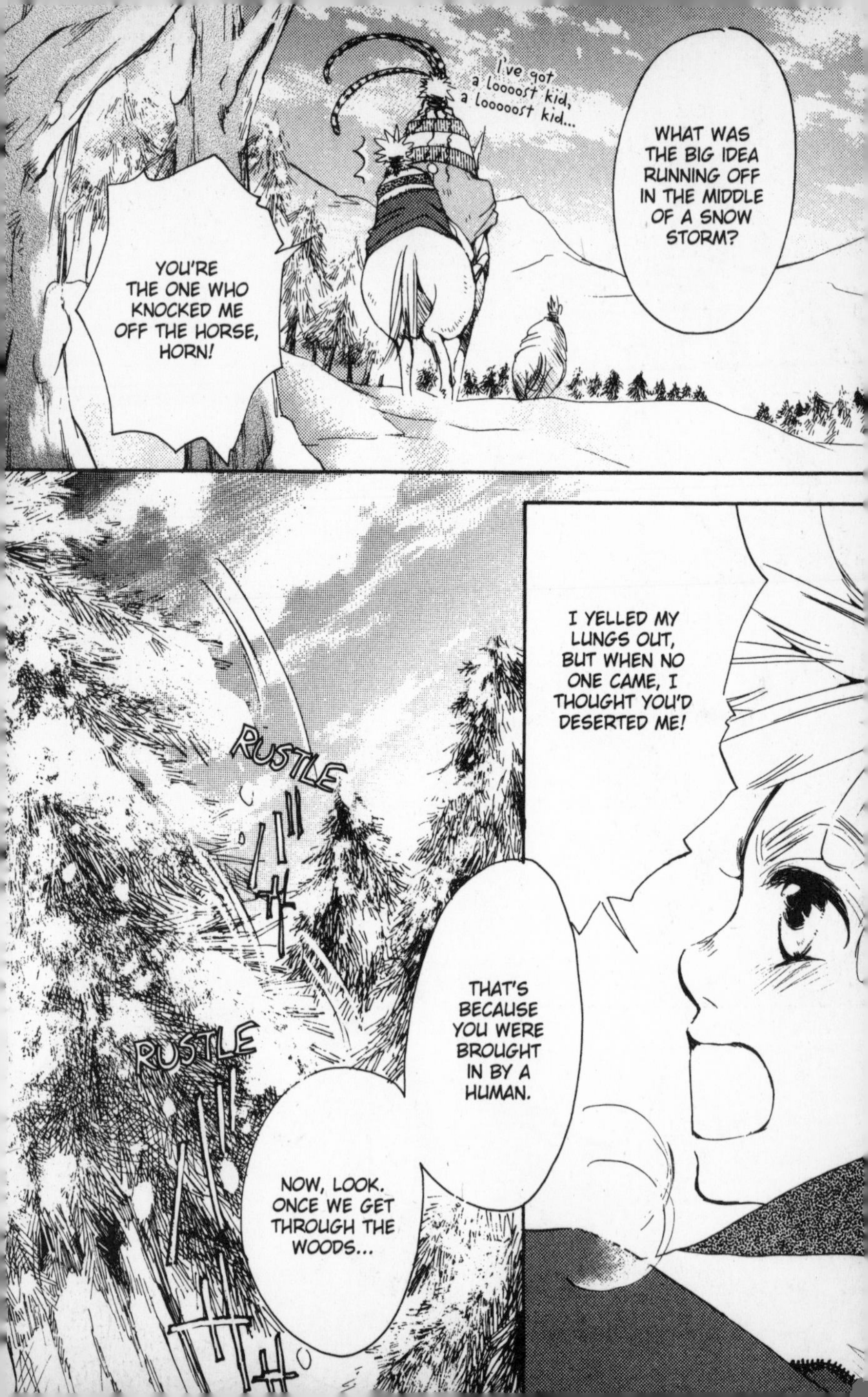
WHAT WAS THE BIG IDEA RUNNING OFF IN THE MIDDLE OF A SNOW STORM?
I've got a loooost kid, a looooost kid...
YOU'RE THE ONE WHO KNOCKED ME OFF THE HORSE, HORN!
I YELLED MY LUNGS OUT, BUT WHEN NO ONE CAME, I THOUGHT YOU'D DESERTED ME!
THAT'S BECAUSE YOU WERE BROUGHT IN BY A HUMAN.
NOW, LOOK. ONCE WE GET THROUGH THE WOODS...
RUSTLE
RUSTLE

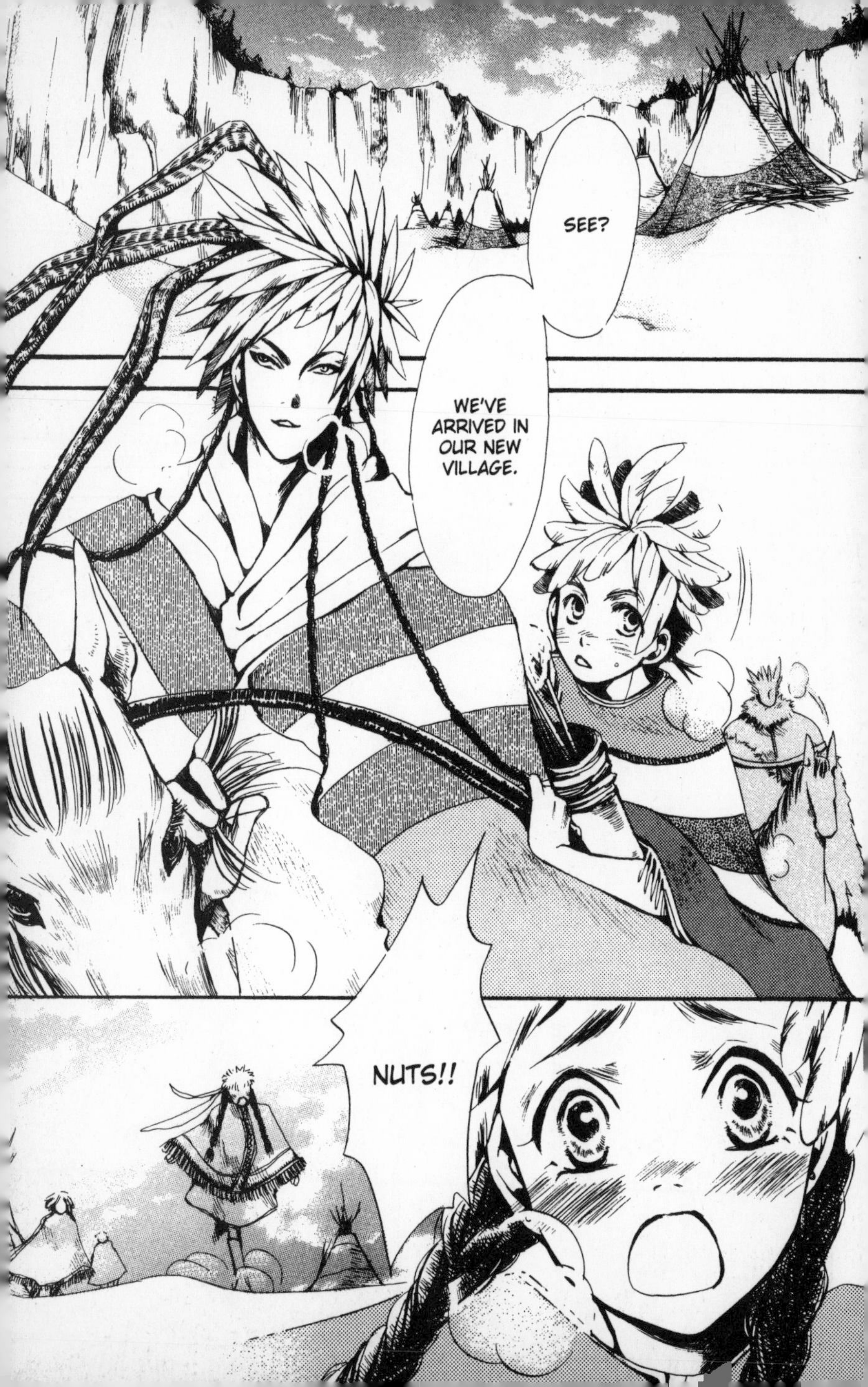
SEE?
WE'VE ARRIVED IN OUR NEW VILLAGE.
NUTS!!

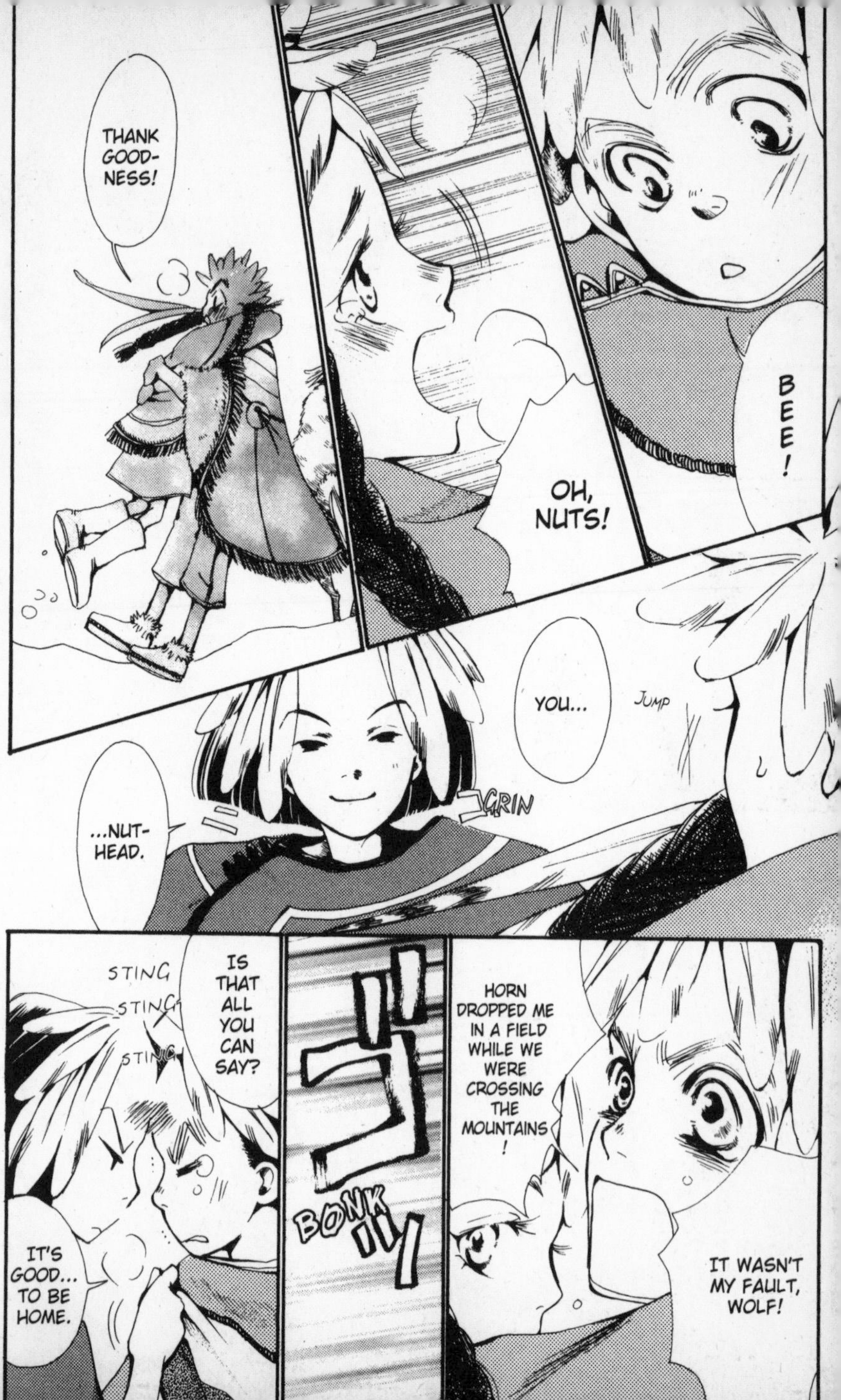
BEE!
OH, NUTS!
THANK GOODNESS!
YOU...
JUMP
GRIN
...NUT-HEAD.
HORN DROPPED ME IN A FIELD WHILE WE WERE CROSSING THE MOUNTAINS!
IT WASN'T MY FAULT, WOLF!
BONK
IS THAT ALL YOU CAN SAY?
STING
STING
STING
IT'S GOOD... TO BE HOME.

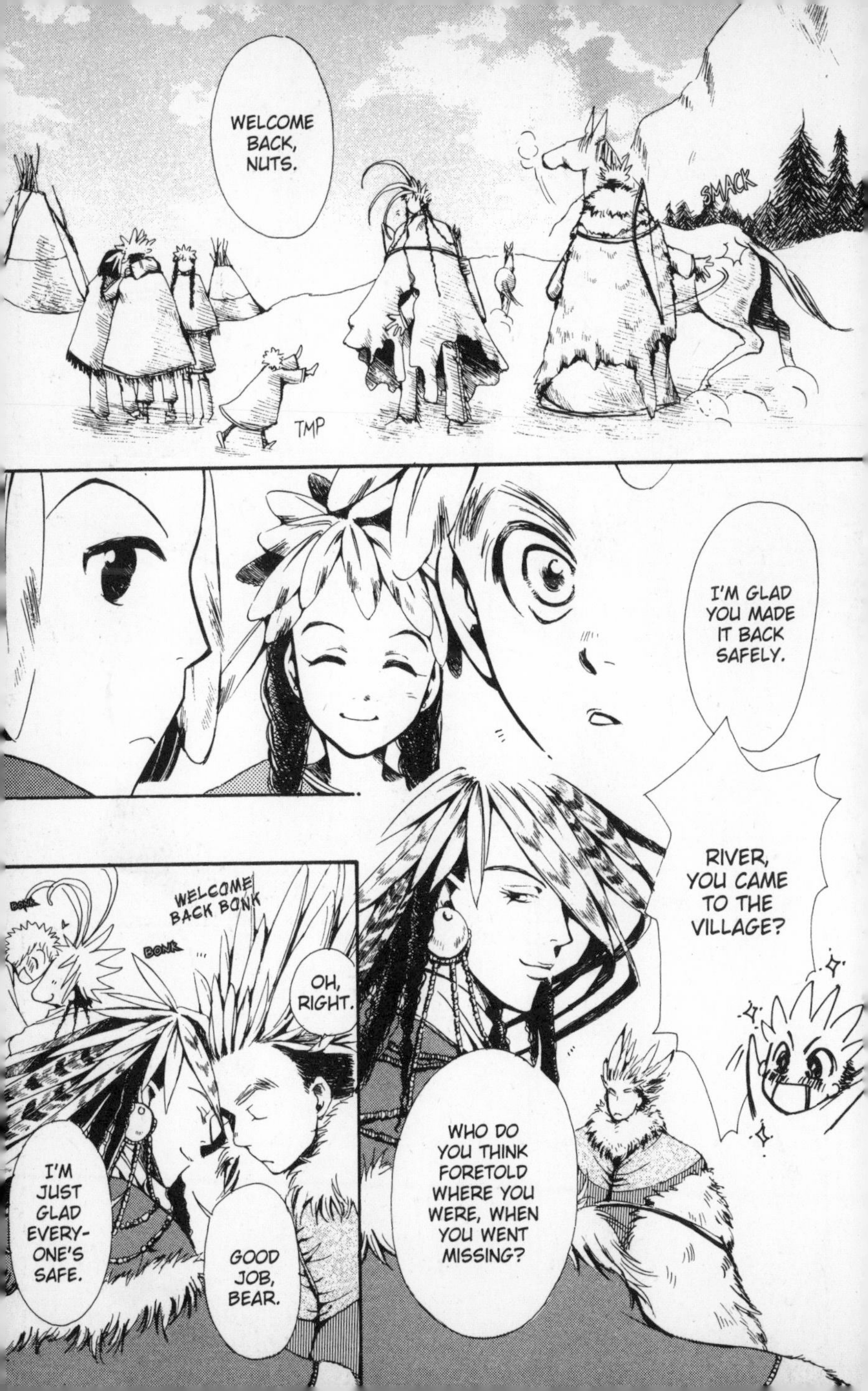
SMACK
WELCOME BACK, NUTS.
TMP
I'M GLAD YOU MADE IT BACK SAFELY.
RIVER, YOU CAME TO THE VILLAGE?
WHO DO YOU THINK FORETOLD WHERE YOU WERE, WHEN YOU WENT MISSING?
OH, RIGHT.
WELCOME BACK BONK
BONK
BONK
GOOD JOB, BEAR.
I'M JUST GLAD EVERY-ONE'S SAFE.

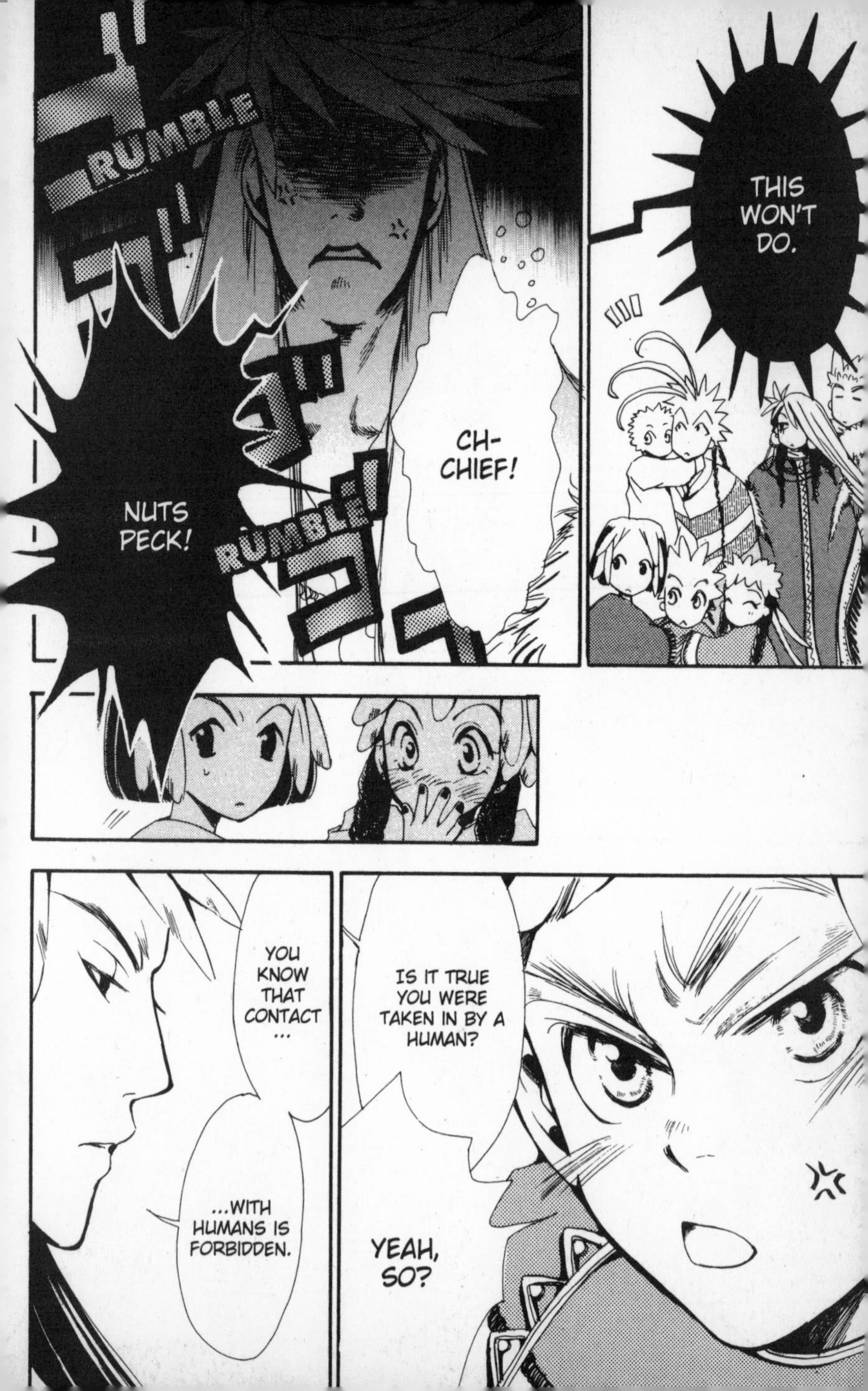
THIS WON'T DO.
CH-CHIEF!
RUMBLE
NUTS PECK!
RUMBLE
IS IT TRUE YOU WERE TAKEN IN BY A HUMAN?
YEAH, SO?
YOU KNOW THAT CONTACT ...
...WITH HUMANS IS FORBIDDEN.

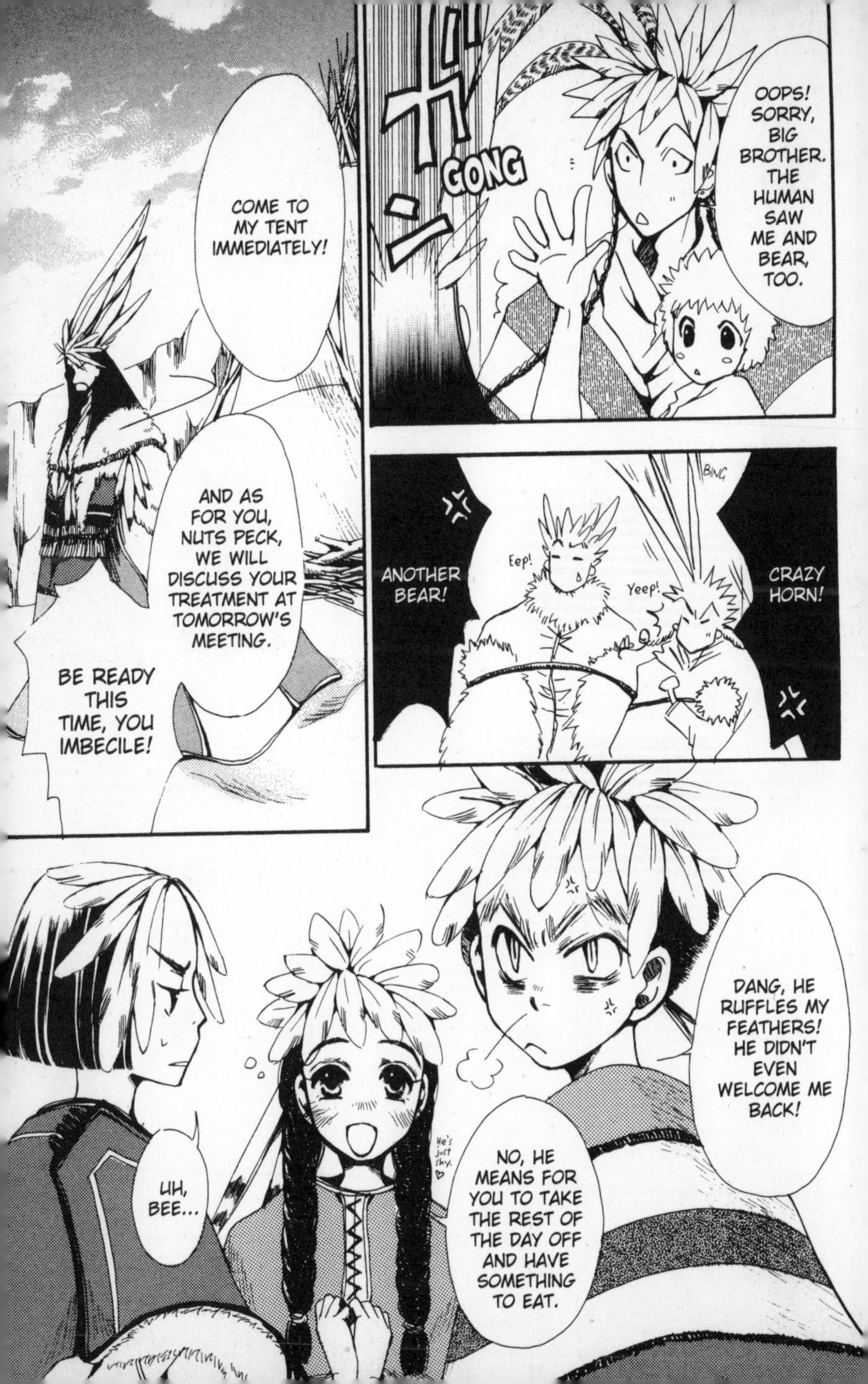
OOPS! SORRY, BIG BROTHER. THE HUMAN SAW ME AND BEAR, TOO.
GONG
BING
CRAZY HORN!
Yeep!
Eep!
ANOTHER BEAR!
COME TO MY TENT IMMEDIATELY!
AND AS FOR YOU, NUTS PECK, WE WILL DISCUSS YOUR TREATMENT AT TOMORROW'S MEETING.
BE READY THIS TIME, YOU IMBECILE!
DANG, HE RUFFLES MY FEATHERS! HE DIDN'T EVEN WELCOME ME BACK!
NO, HE MEANS FOR YOU TO TAKE THE REST OF THE DAY OFF AND HAVE SOMETHING TO EAT.
He's just shy. ♡
UH, BEE...

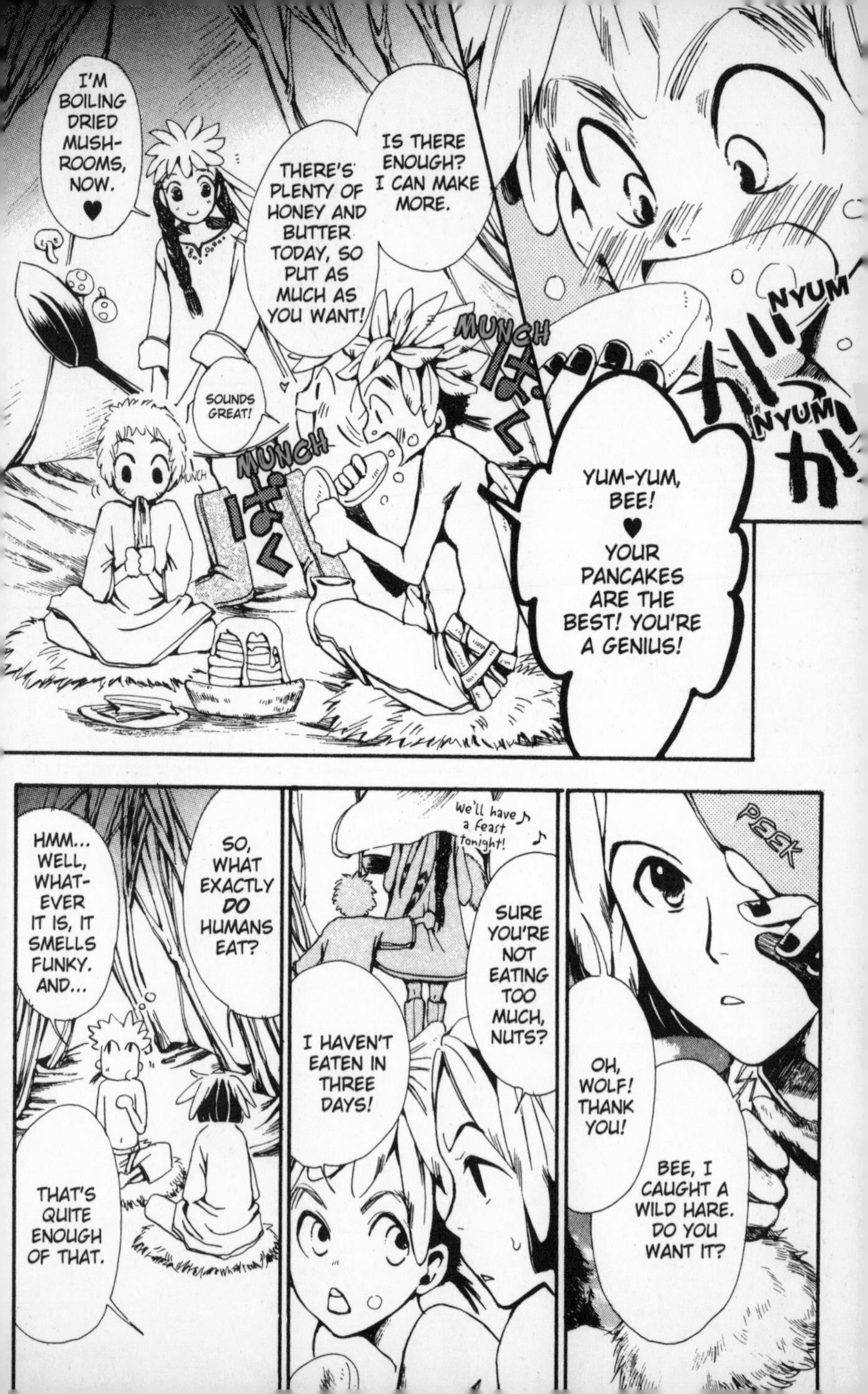

NYUM
NYUM
YUM-YUM, BEE! ♥ YOUR PANCAKES ARE THE BEST! YOU'RE A GENIUS!
IS THERE ENOUGH? I CAN MAKE MORE.
THERE'S PLENTY OF HONEY AND BUTTER TODAY, SO PUT AS MUCH AS YOU WANT!
I'M BOILING DRIED MUSH-ROOMS, NOW. ♥
MUNCH
SOUNDS GREAT!
MUNCH
MUNCH
PEEK
BEE, I CAUGHT A WILD HARE. DO YOU WANT IT?
OH, WOLF! THANK YOU!
We'll have a feast tonight! ♪
SURE YOU'RE NOT EATING TOO MUCH, NUTS?
I HAVEN'T EATEN IN THREE DAYS!
SO, WHAT EXACTLY DO HUMANS EAT?
HMM... WELL, WHAT-EVER IT IS, IT SMELLS FUNKY. AND...
THAT'S QUITE ENOUGH OF THAT.

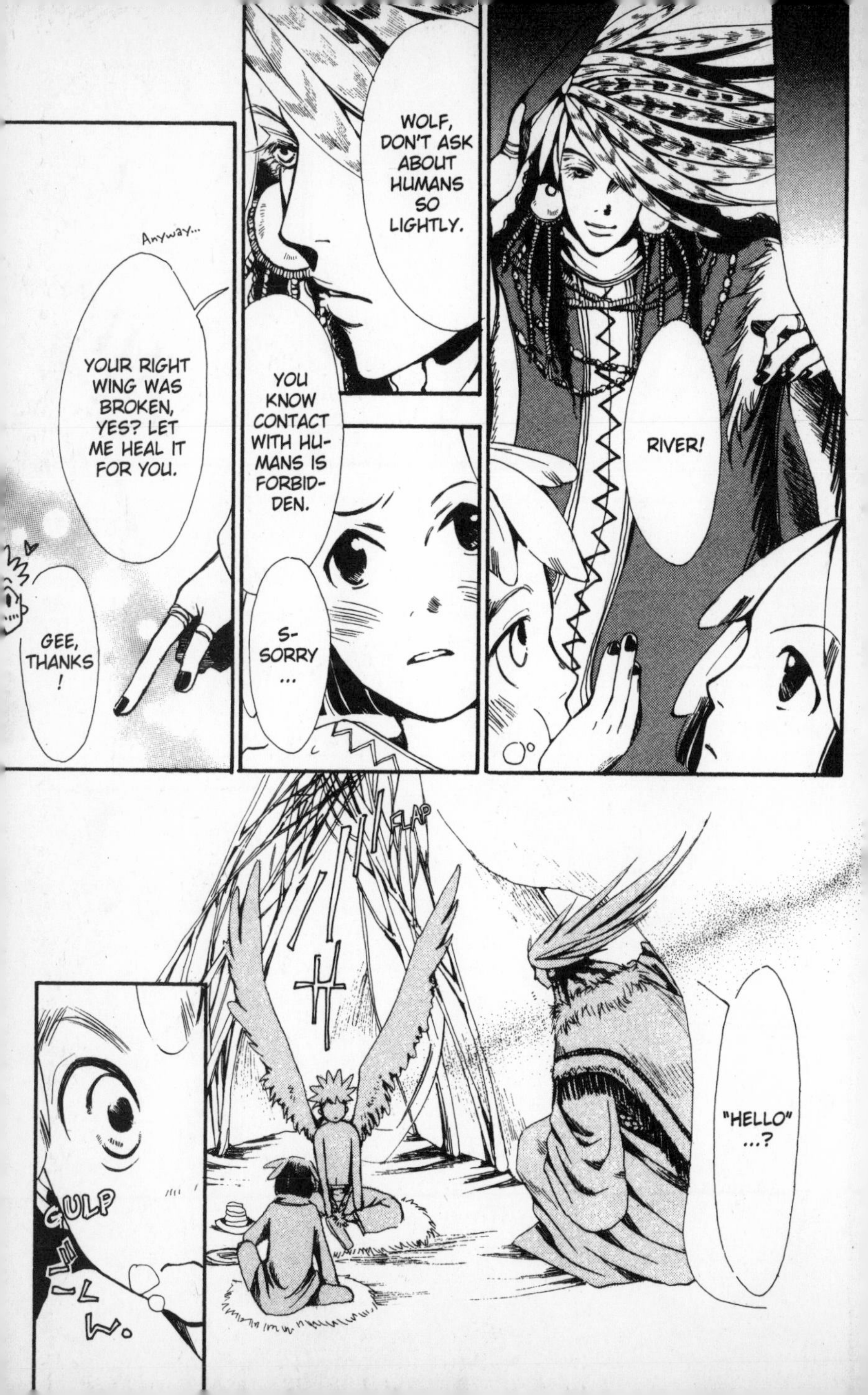
RIVER!
WOLF, DON'T ASK ABOUT HUMANS SO LIGHTLY.
YOU KNOW CONTACT WITH HUMANS IS FORBIDDEN.
S-SORRY...
Anyway...
YOUR RIGHT WING WAS BROKEN, YES? LET ME HEAL IT FOR YOU.
GEE, THANKS!
FLAP
"HELLO"...?
GULP

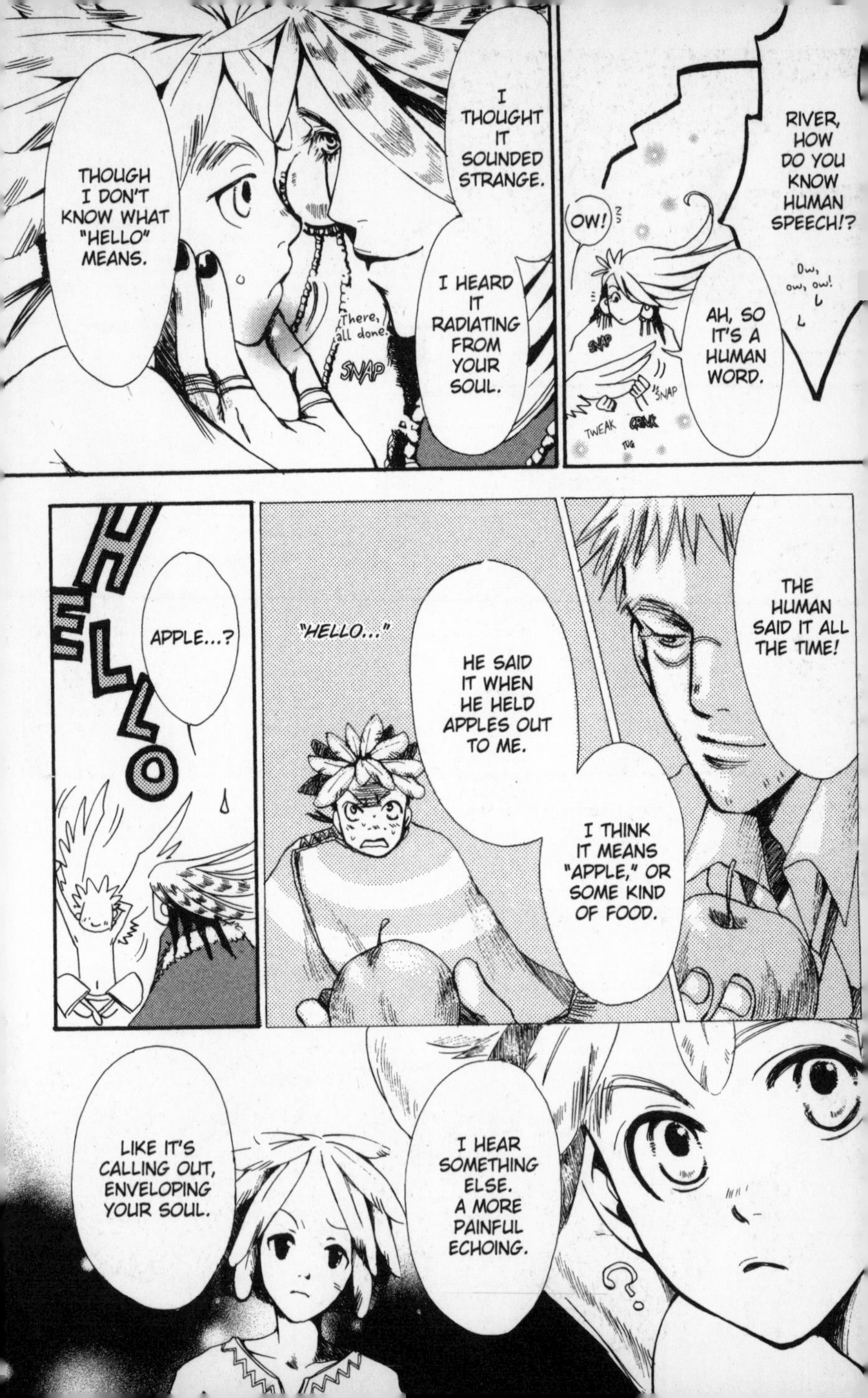
RIVER, HOW DO YOU KNOW HUMAN SPEECH!?
Ow, ow, ow!
OW!
AH, SO IT'S A HUMAN WORD.
SNAP
SNAP
TWEAK
CRNK
TUG
I THOUGHT IT SOUNDED STRANGE.
I HEARD IT RADIATING FROM YOUR SOUL.
There, all done.
SNAP
THOUGH I DON'T KNOW WHAT "HELLO" MEANS.
THE HUMAN SAID IT ALL THE TIME!
I THINK IT MEANS "APPLE," OR SOME KIND OF FOOD.
HE SAID IT WHEN HE HELD APPLES OUT TO ME.
"HELLO..."
APPLE...?
HELLO
I HEAR SOMETHING ELSE. A MORE PAINFUL ECHOING.
LIKE IT'S CALLING OUT, ENVELOPING YOUR SOUL.

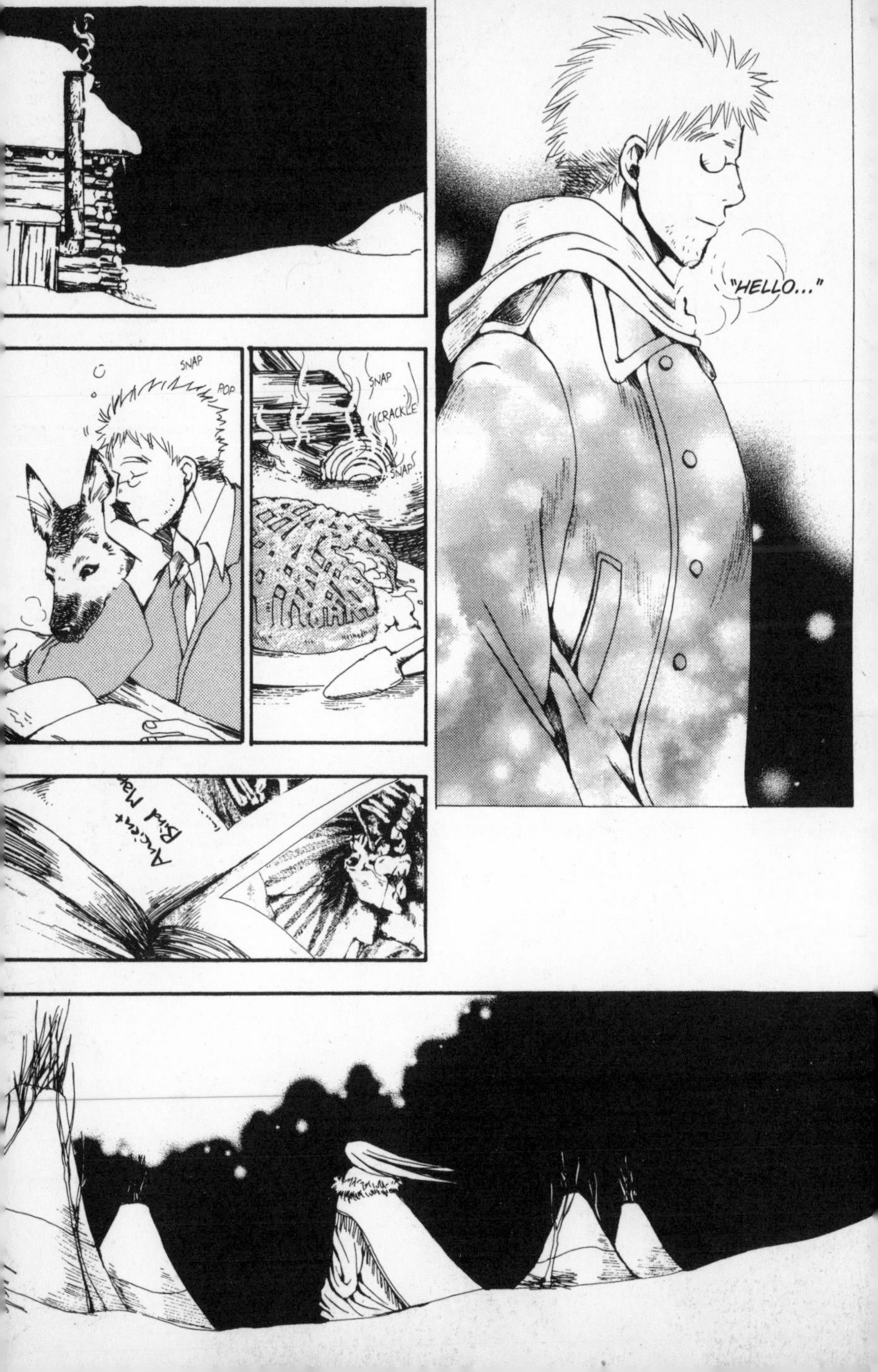
"HELLO..."
SNAP
CRACKLE
SNAP
SNAP
POP

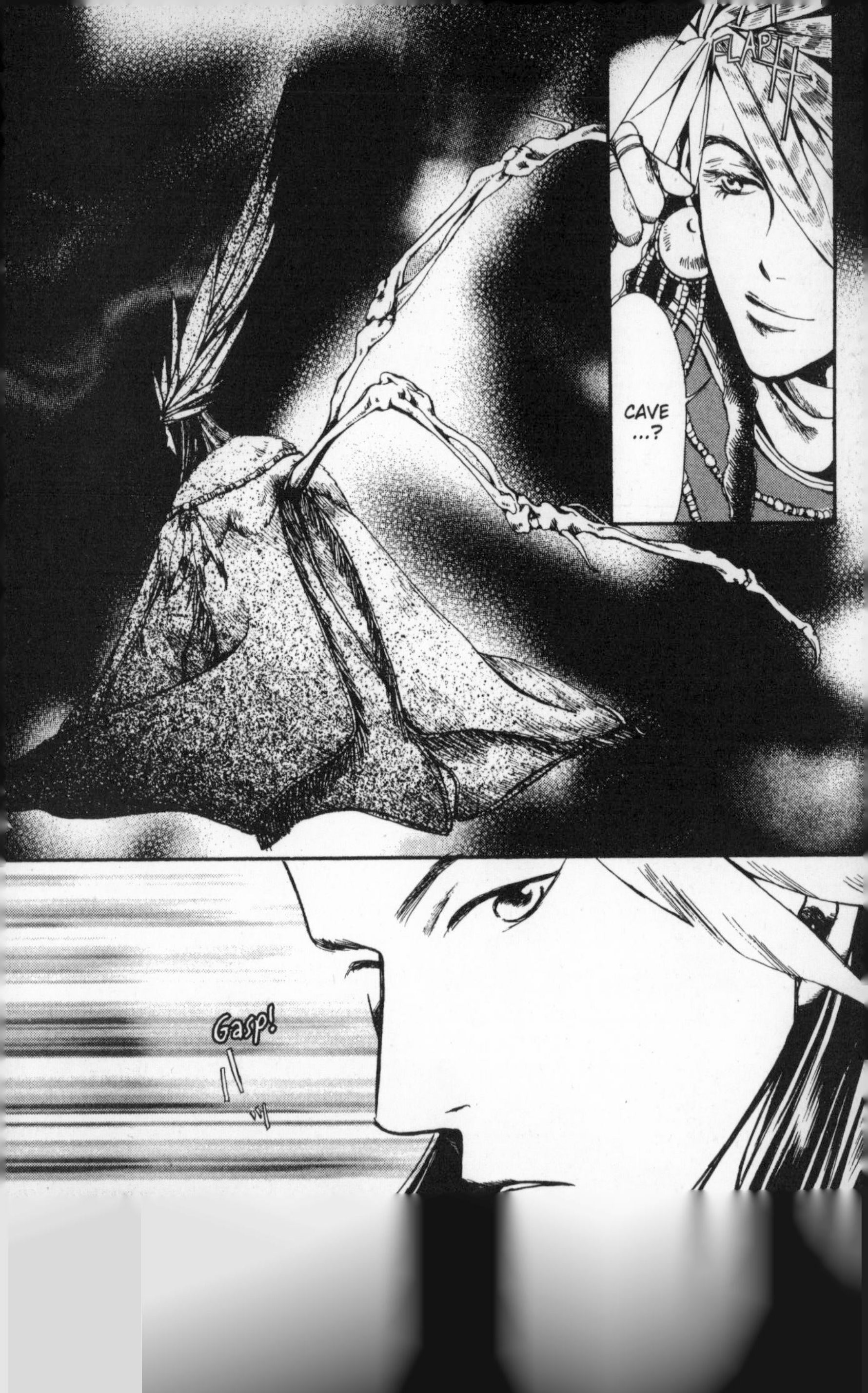
FLAP
CAVE ...?
Gasp!

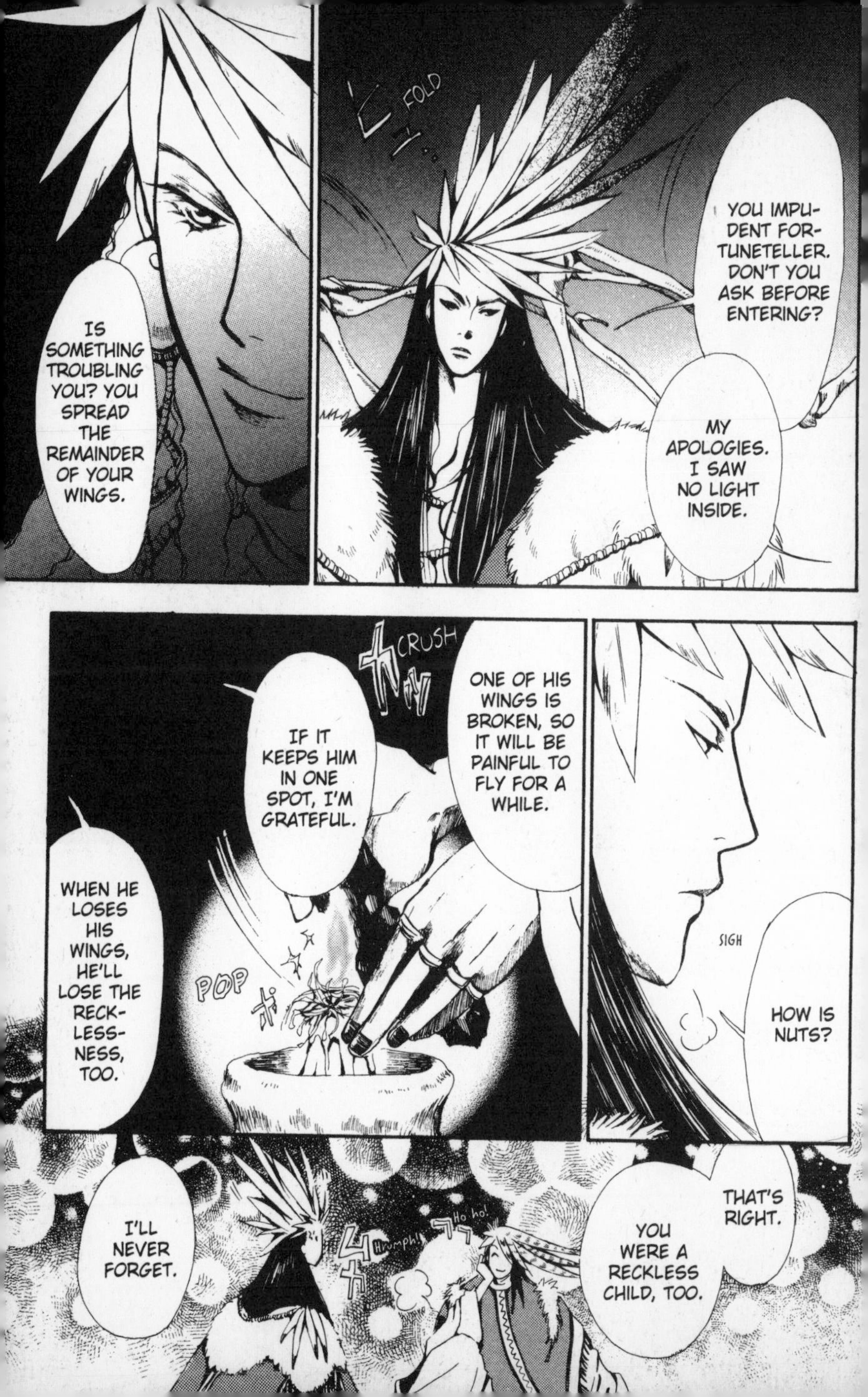
FOLD
YOU IMPUDENT FORTUNETELLER. DON'T YOU ASK BEFORE ENTERING?
MY APOLOGIES. I SAW NO LIGHT INSIDE.
IS SOMETHING TROUBLING YOU? YOU SPREAD THE REMAINDER OF YOUR WINGS.
SIGH
HOW IS NUTS?
CRUSH
ONE OF HIS WINGS IS BROKEN, SO IT WILL BE PAINFUL TO FLY FOR A WHILE.
IF IT KEEPS HIM IN ONE SPOT, I'M GRATEFUL.
POP
WHEN HE LOSES HIS WINGS, HE'LL LOSE THE RECKLESSNESS, TOO.
THAT'S RIGHT.
YOU WERE A RECKLESS CHILD, TOO.
Ho ho!
Hmmph!
I'LL NEVER FORGET.

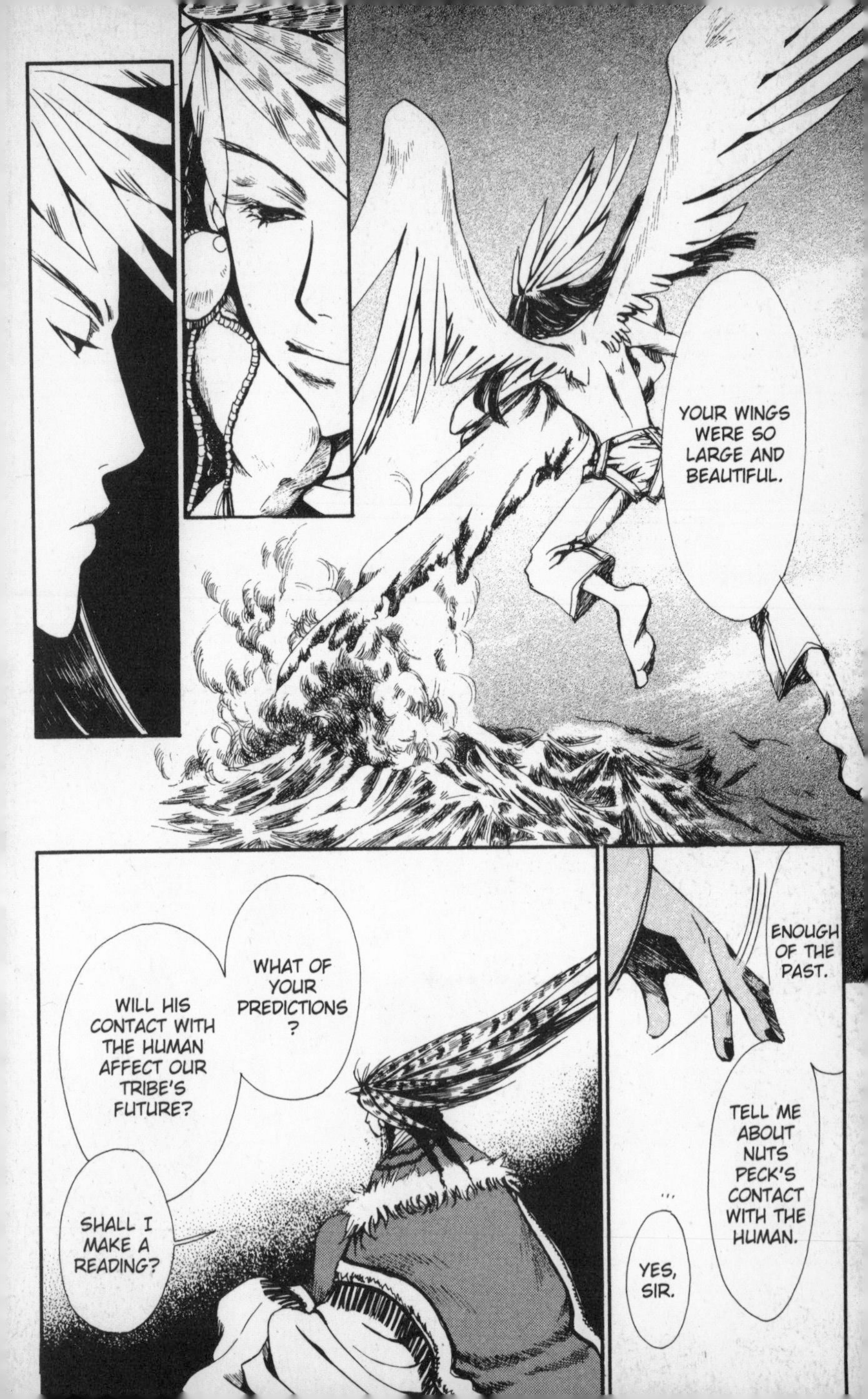
YOUR WINGS WERE SO LARGE AND BEAUTIFUL.
ENOUGH OF THE PAST.
TELL ME ABOUT NUTS PECK'S CONTACT WITH THE HUMAN.
...
YES, SIR.
WHAT OF YOUR PREDICTIONS?
WILL HIS CONTACT WITH THE HUMAN AFFECT OUR TRIBE'S FUTURE?
SHALL I MAKE A READING?

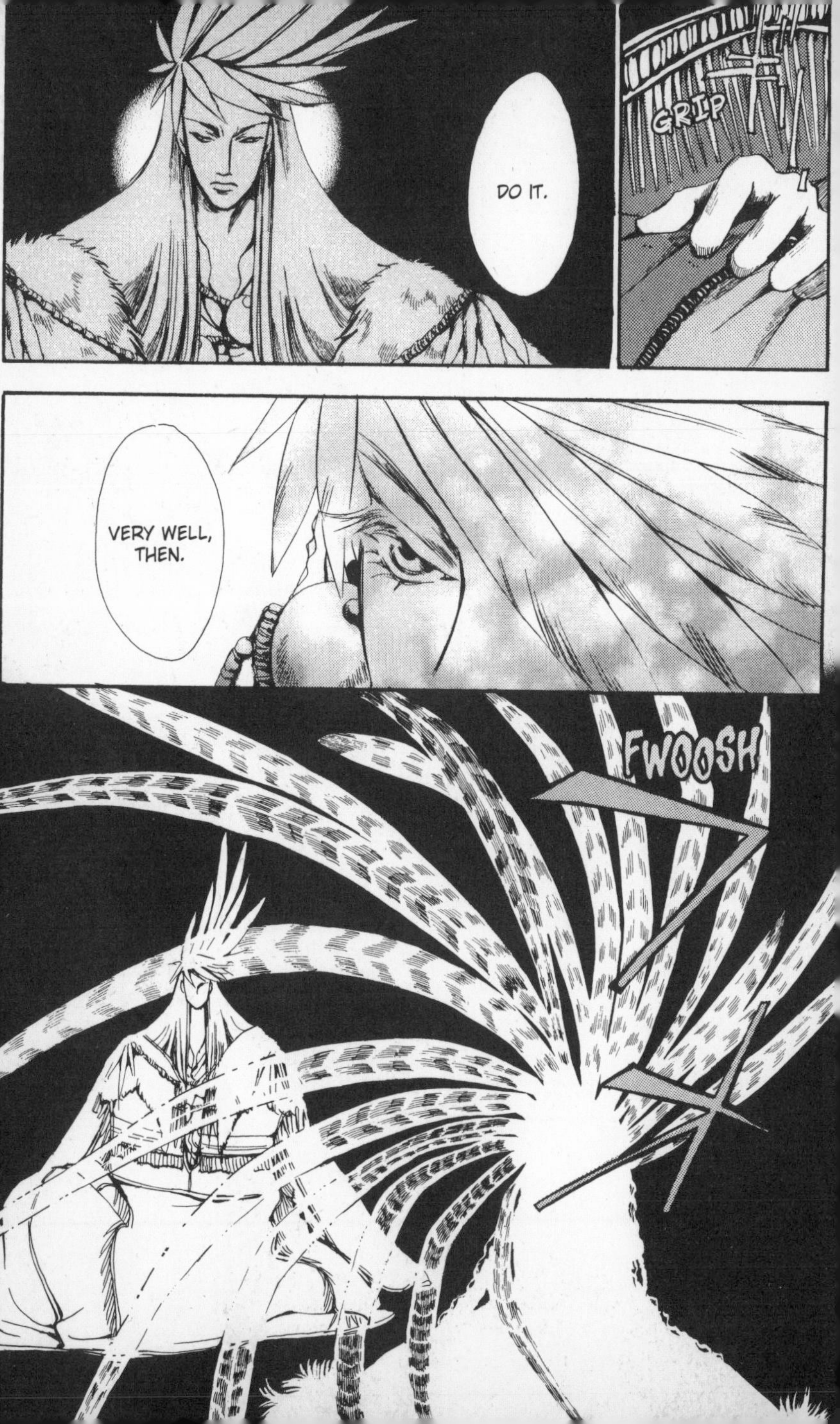
GRIP
DO IT.
VERY WELL, THEN.
FWOOSH

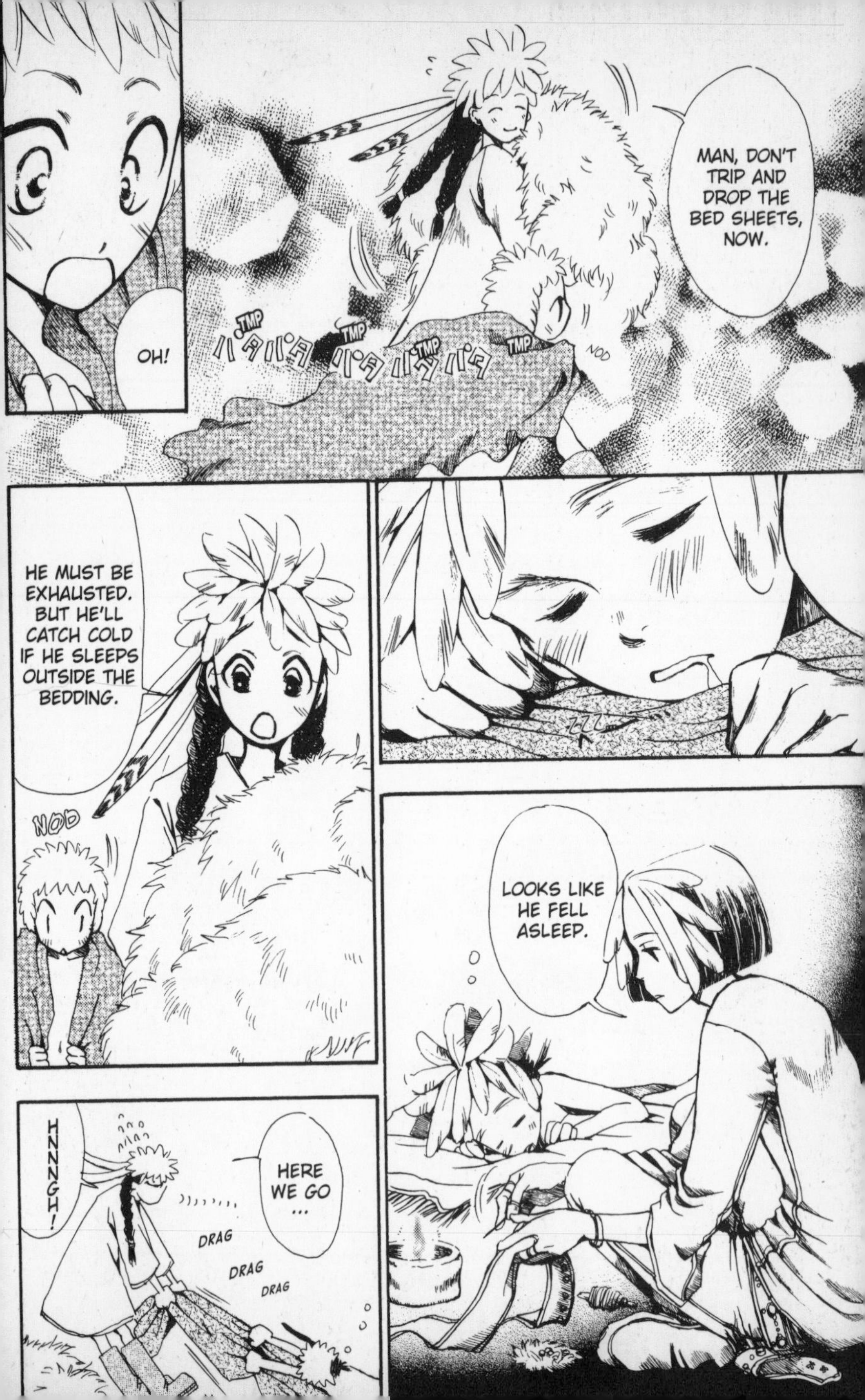
MAN, DON'T TRIP AND DROP THE BED SHEETS, NOW.
TMP TMP TMP TMP
パタパタ パタパタ
NOD
OH!
ZZZ
HE MUST BE EXHAUSTED. BUT HE'LL CATCH COLD IF HE SLEEPS OUTSIDE THE BEDDING.
NOD
LOOKS LIKE HE FELL ASLEEP.
HERE WE GO ...
HNNNGH!
DRAG
DRAG
DRAG

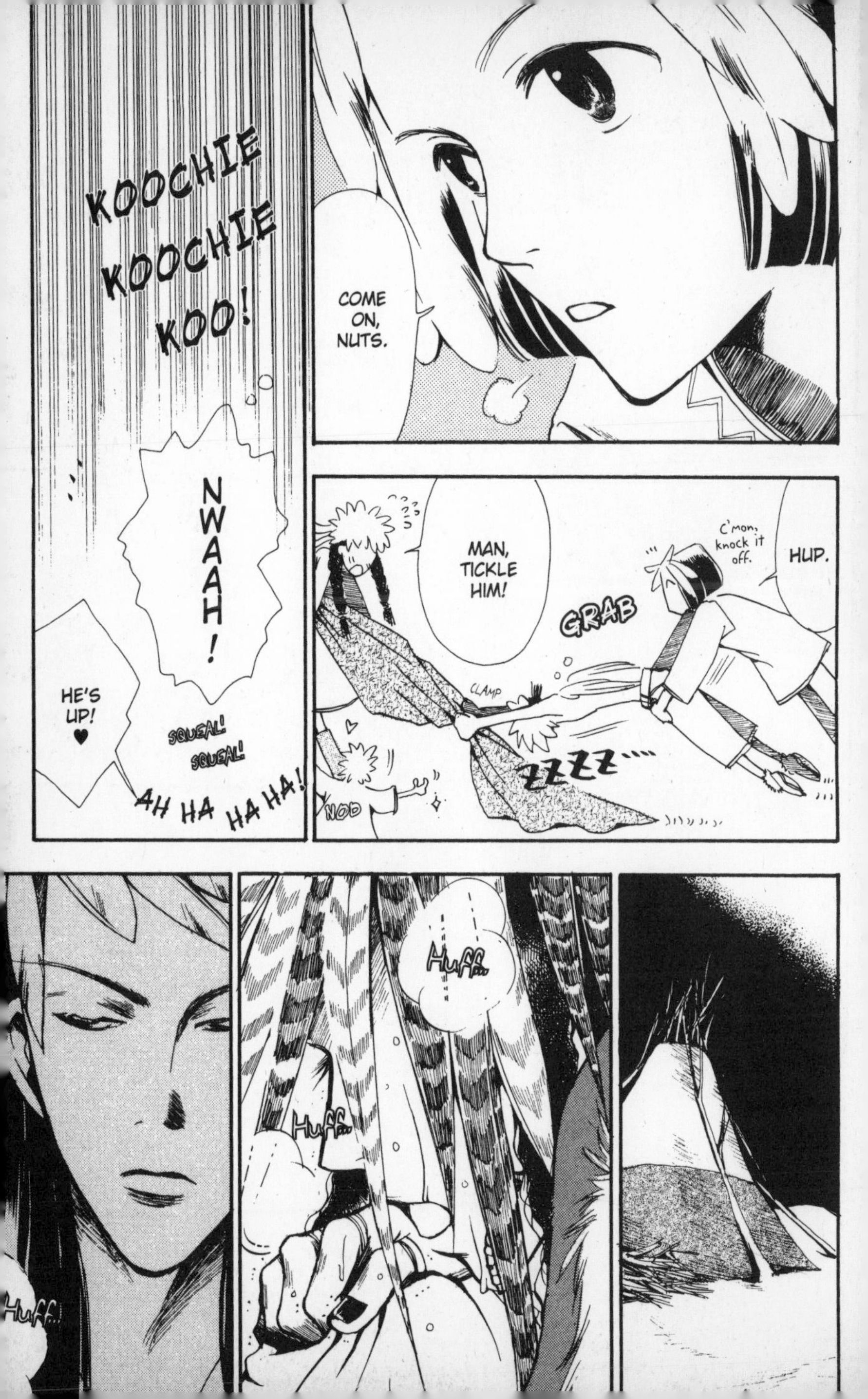
COME ON, NUTS.
HUP.
C'mon, knock it off.
GRAB
MAN, TICKLE HIM!
CLAMP
ZZZZ
NOD
KOOCHIE KOOCHIE KOOCHIE KOO!
NWAAAH!
HE'S UP! ♥
SQUEAL! SQUEAL!
AH HA HA HA!
Huff...
Huff...
Huff...

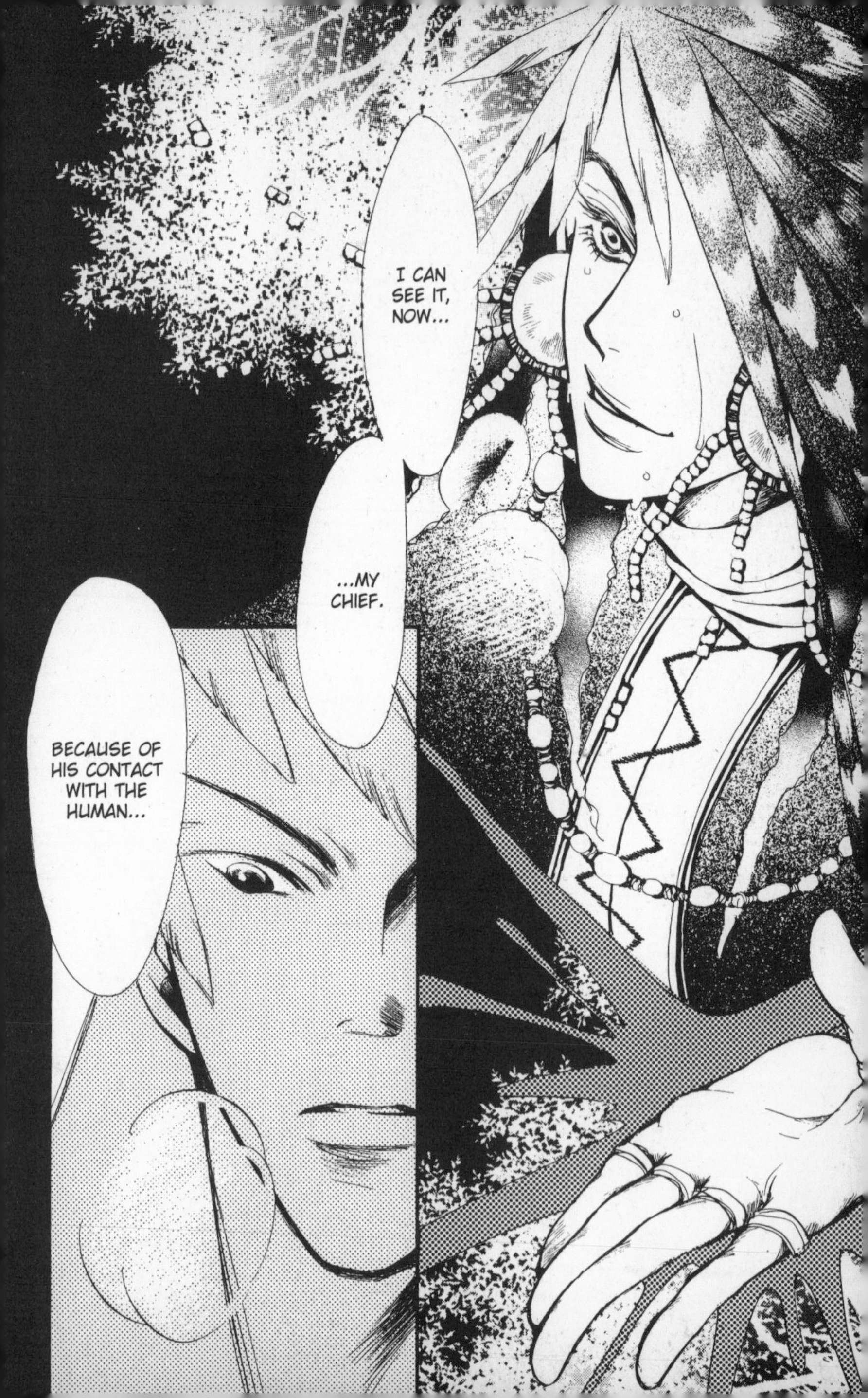
I CAN SEE IT, NOW...
...MY CHIEF.
BECAUSE OF HIS CONTACT WITH THE HUMAN...

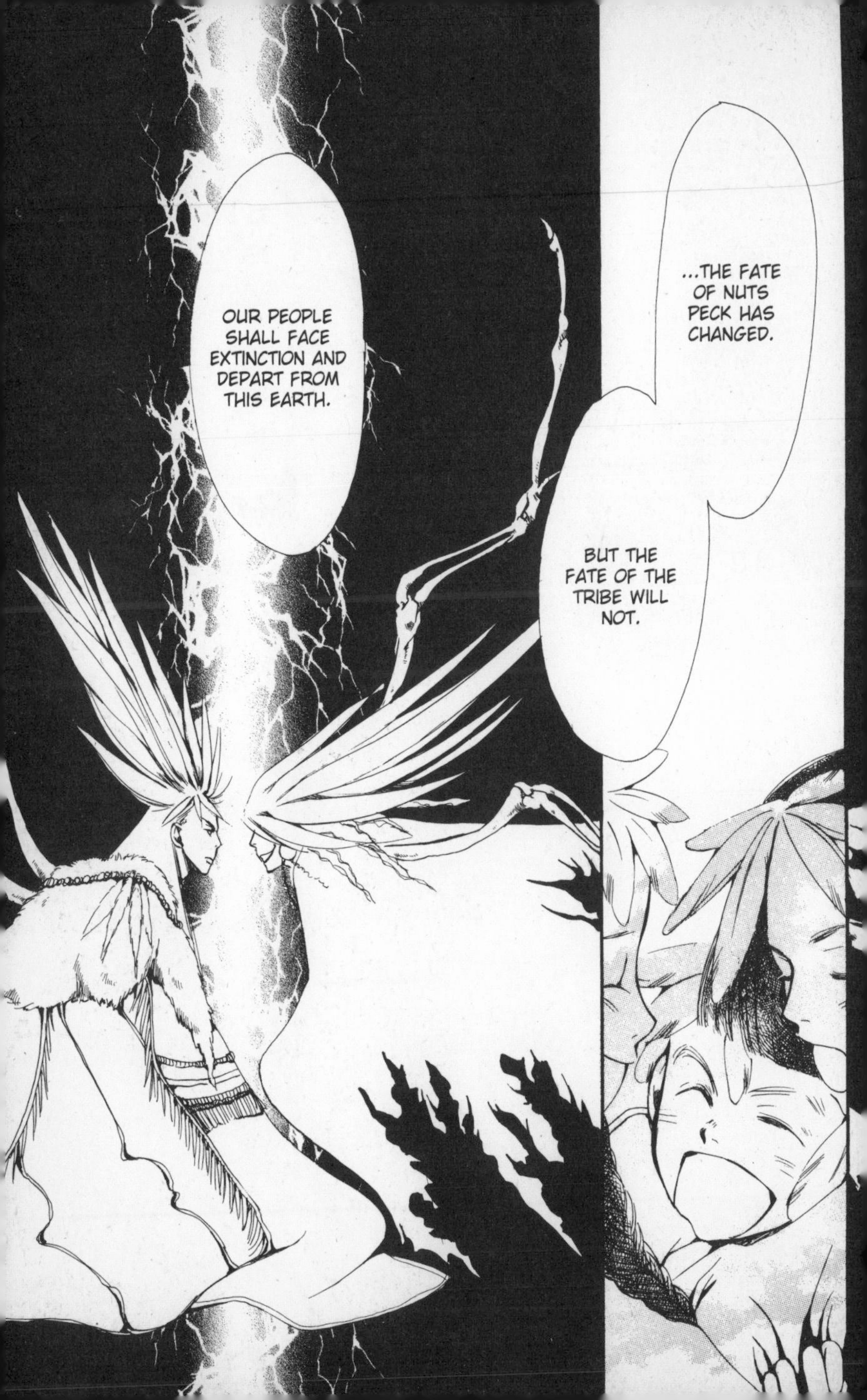
...THE FATE OF NUTS PECK HAS CHANGED.
BUT THE FATE OF THE TRIBE WILL NOT.
OUR PEOPLE SHALL FACE EXTINCTION AND DEPART FROM THIS EARTH.

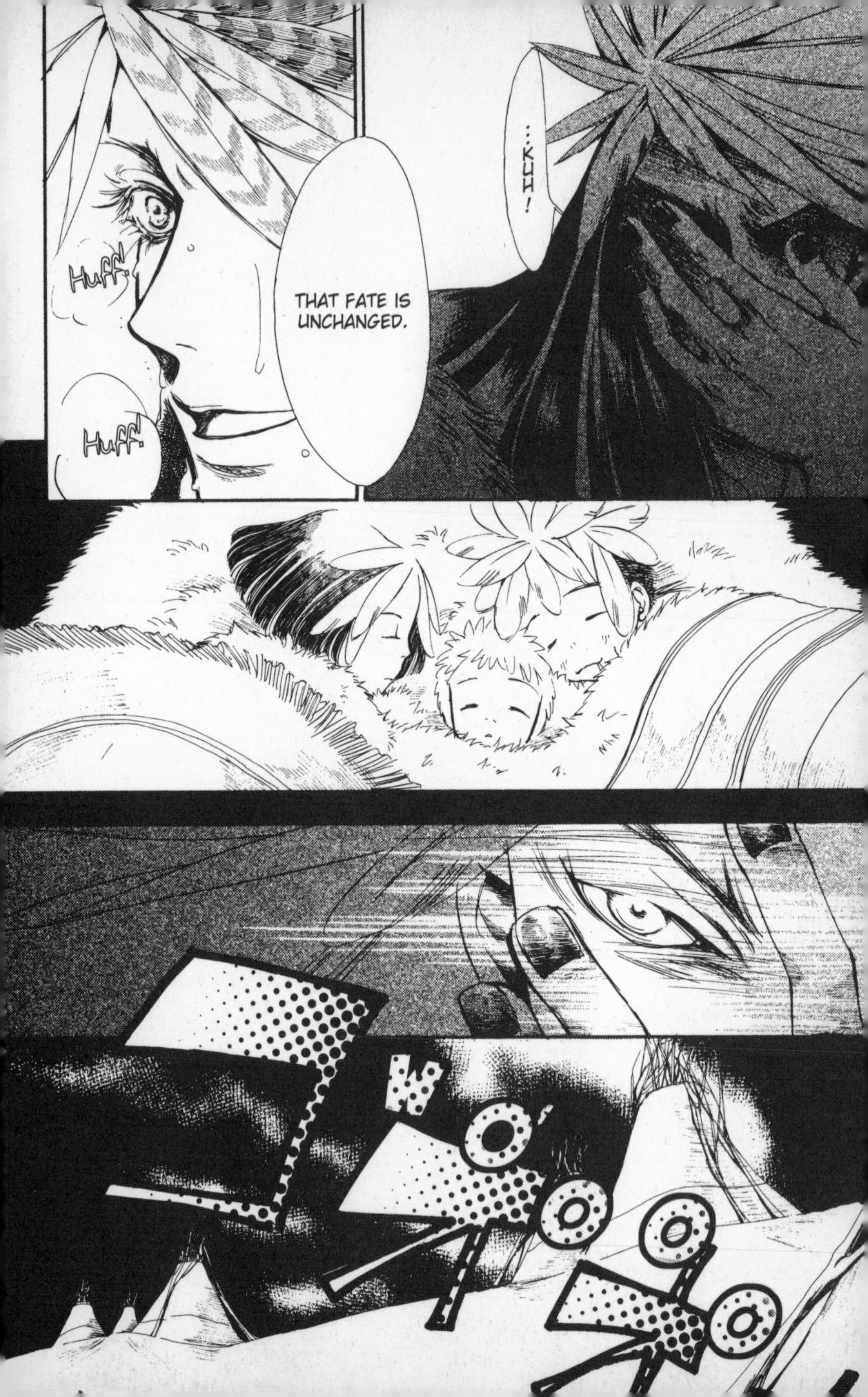
...KUH!
THAT FATE IS UNCHANGED.
Huff!
Huff!
WOOOO

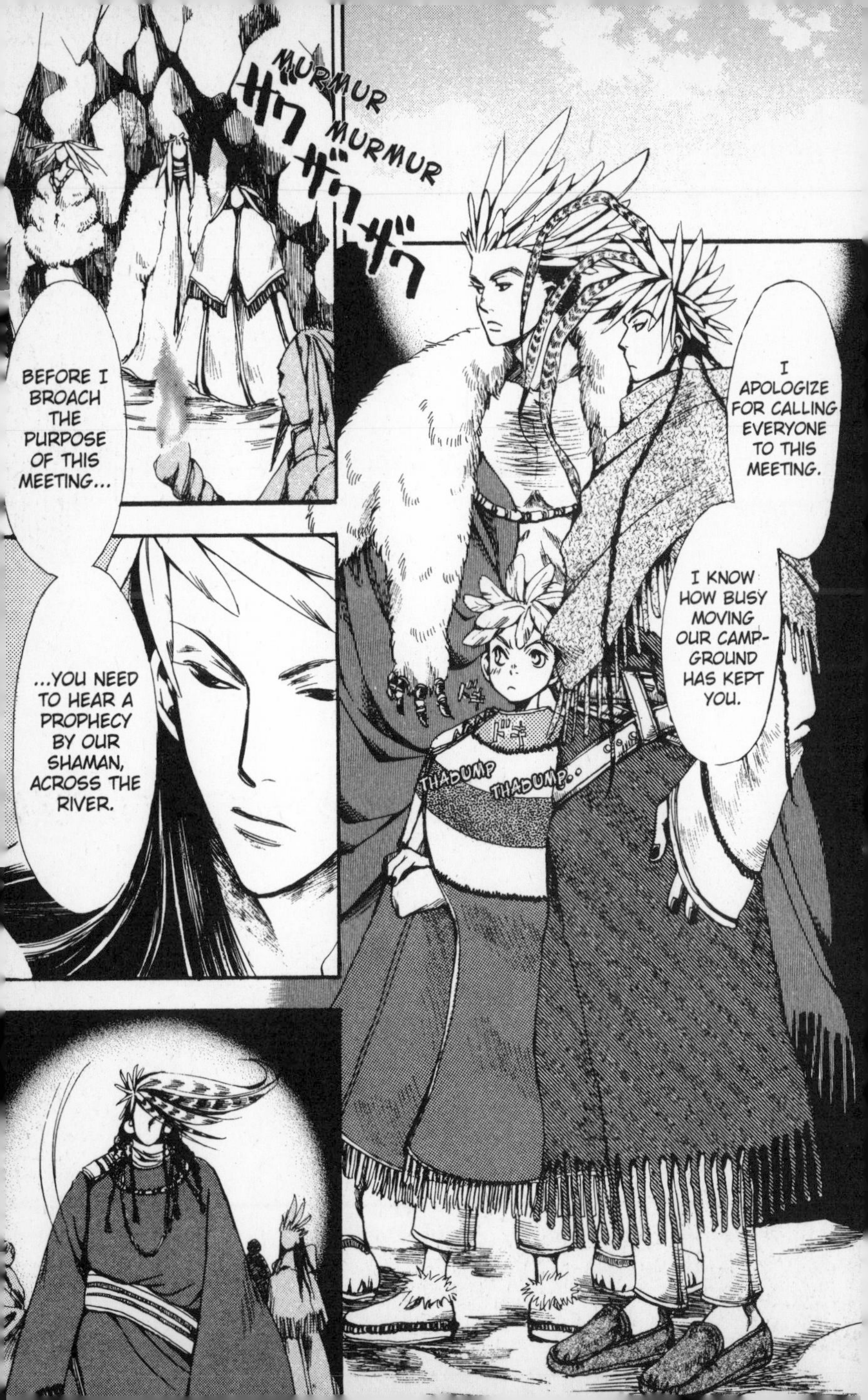
I APOLOGIZE FOR CALLING EVERYONE TO THIS MEETING.
I KNOW HOW BUSY MOVING OUR CAMP-GROUND HAS KEPT YOU.
ドキ
THADUMP THADUMP...
MURMUR MURMUR
ザワザワザワ
BEFORE I BROACH THE PURPOSE OF THIS MEETING...
...YOU NEED TO HEAR A PROPHECY BY OUR SHAMAN, ACROSS THE RIVER.

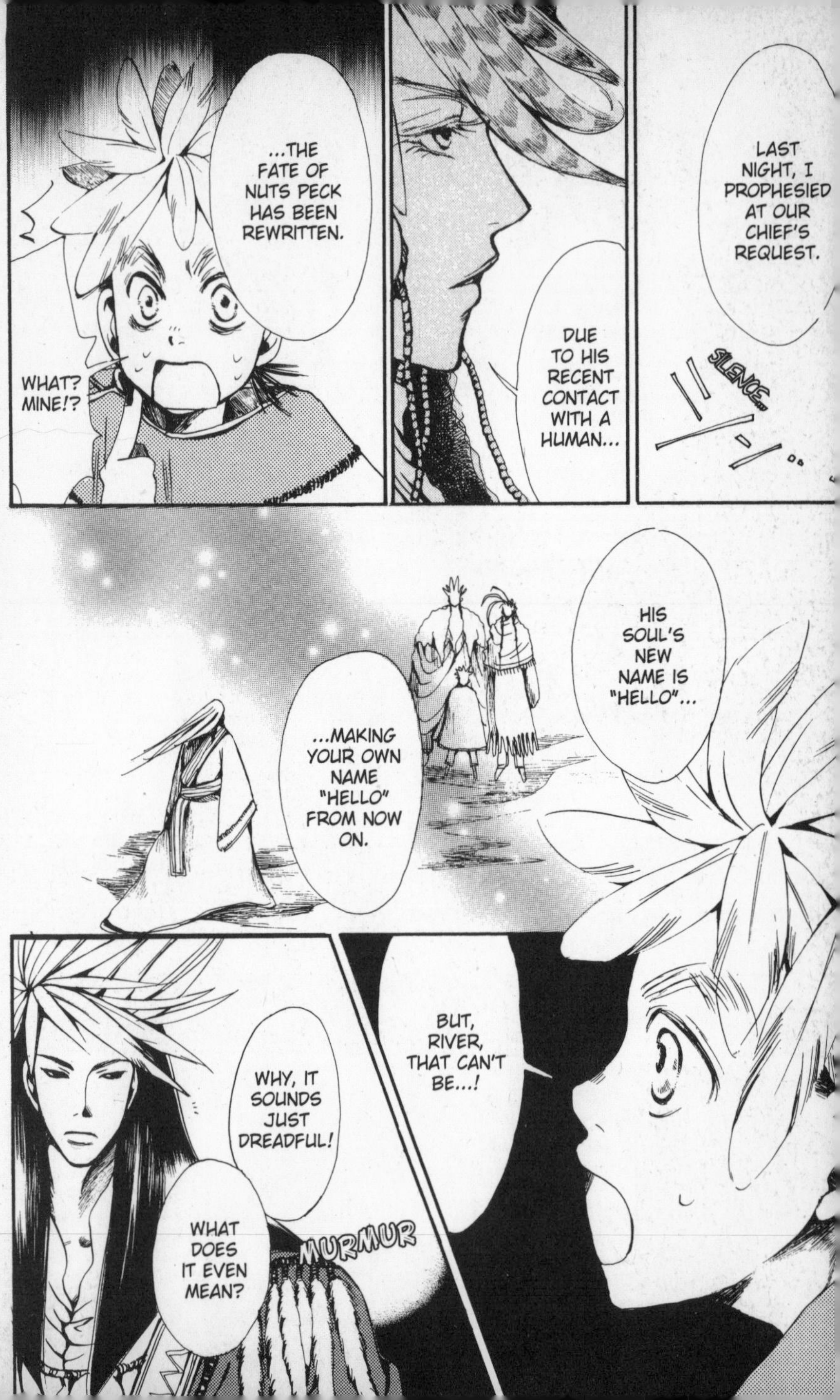
LAST NIGHT, I PROPHESIED AT OUR CHIEF'S REQUEST.
SILENCE...
DUE TO HIS RECENT CONTACT WITH A HUMAN...
...THE FATE OF NUTS PECK HAS BEEN REWRITTEN.
WHAT? MINE!?
HIS SOUL'S NEW NAME IS "HELLO"...
...MAKING YOUR OWN NAME "HELLO" FROM NOW ON.
BUT, RIVER, THAT CAN'T BE...!
WHY, IT SOUNDS JUST DREADFUL!
WHAT DOES IT EVEN MEAN?
MURMUR

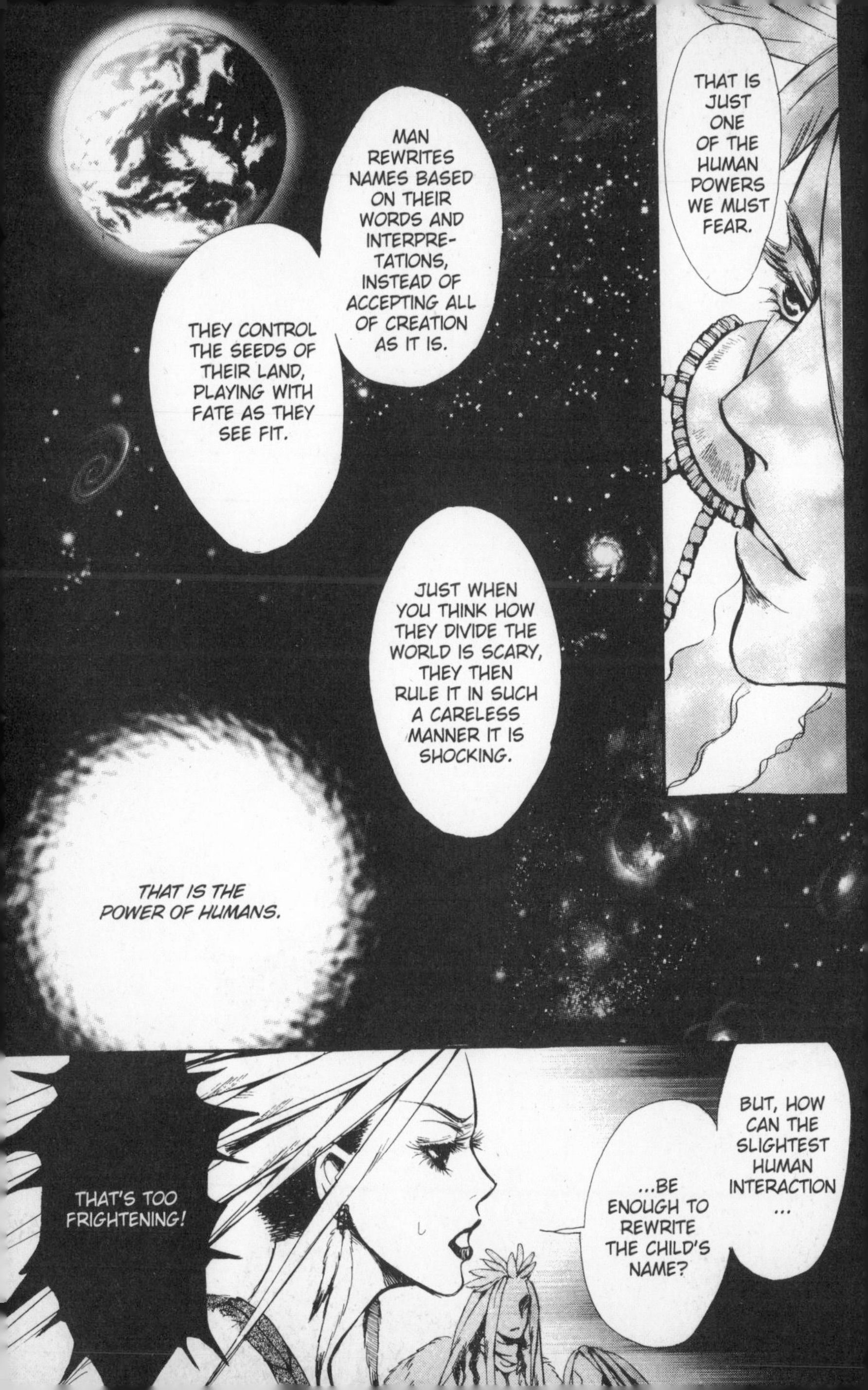
THAT IS JUST ONE OF THE HUMAN POWERS WE MUST FEAR.
MAN REWRITES NAMES BASED ON THEIR WORDS AND INTERPRE-TATIONS, INSTEAD OF ACCEPTING ALL OF CREATION AS IT IS.
THEY CONTROL THE SEEDS OF THEIR LAND, PLAYING WITH FATE AS THEY SEE FIT.
JUST WHEN YOU THINK HOW THEY DIVIDE THE WORLD IS SCARY, THEY THEN RULE IT IN SUCH A CARELESS MANNER IT IS SHOCKING.
THAT IS THE POWER OF HUMANS.
BUT, HOW CAN THE SLIGHTEST HUMAN INTERACTION ...
...BE ENOUGH TO REWRITE THE CHILD'S NAME?
THAT'S TOO FRIGHTENING!

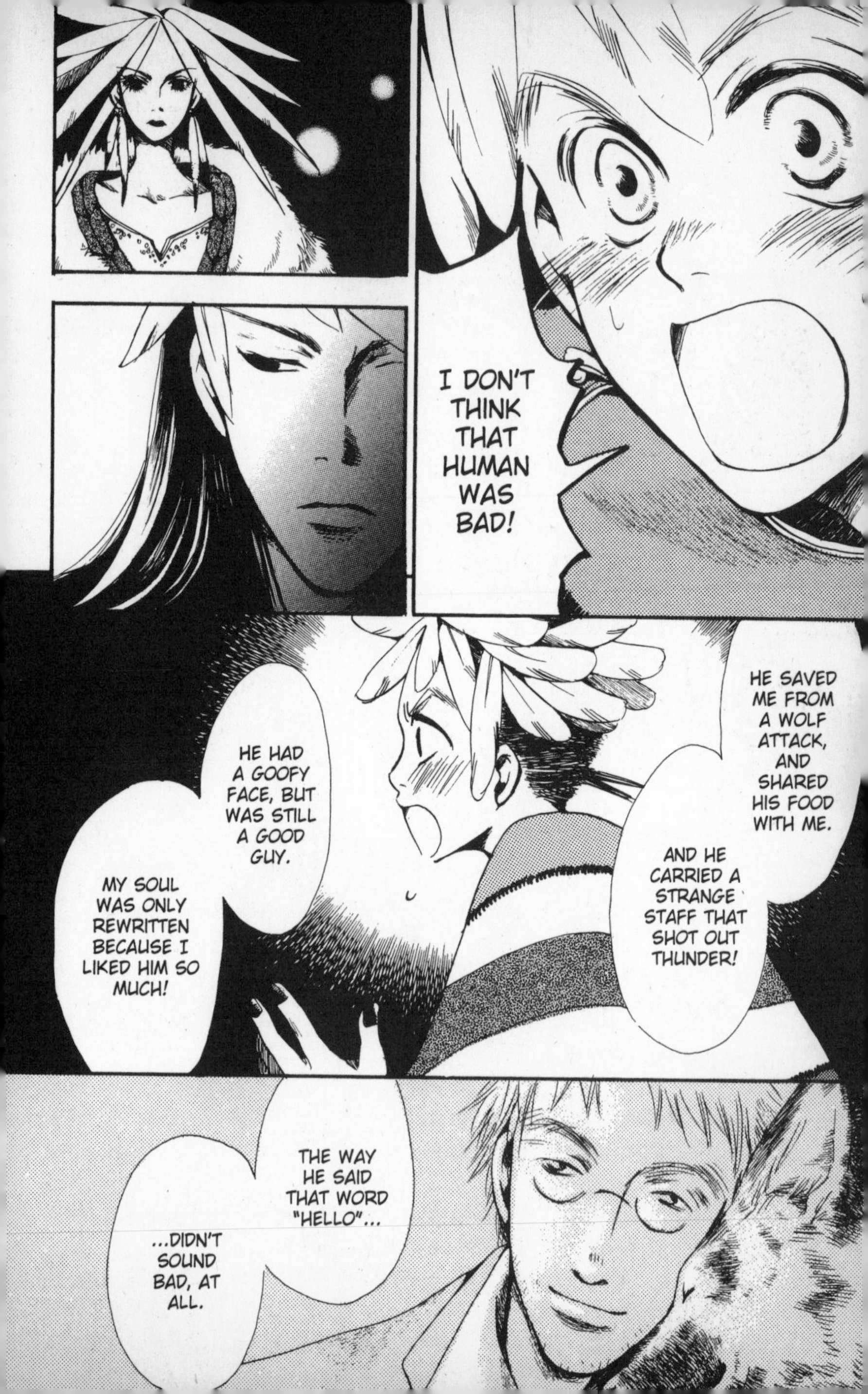
I DON'T THINK THAT HUMAN WAS BAD!
HE SAVED ME FROM A WOLF ATTACK, AND SHARED HIS FOOD WITH ME.
AND HE CARRIED A STRANGE STAFF THAT SHOT OUT THUNDER!
HE HAD A GOOFY FACE, BUT WAS STILL A GOOD GUY.
MY SOUL WAS ONLY REWRITTEN BECAUSE I LIKED HIM SO MUCH!
THE WAY HE SAID THAT WORD "HELLO"...
...DIDN'T SOUND BAD, AT ALL.

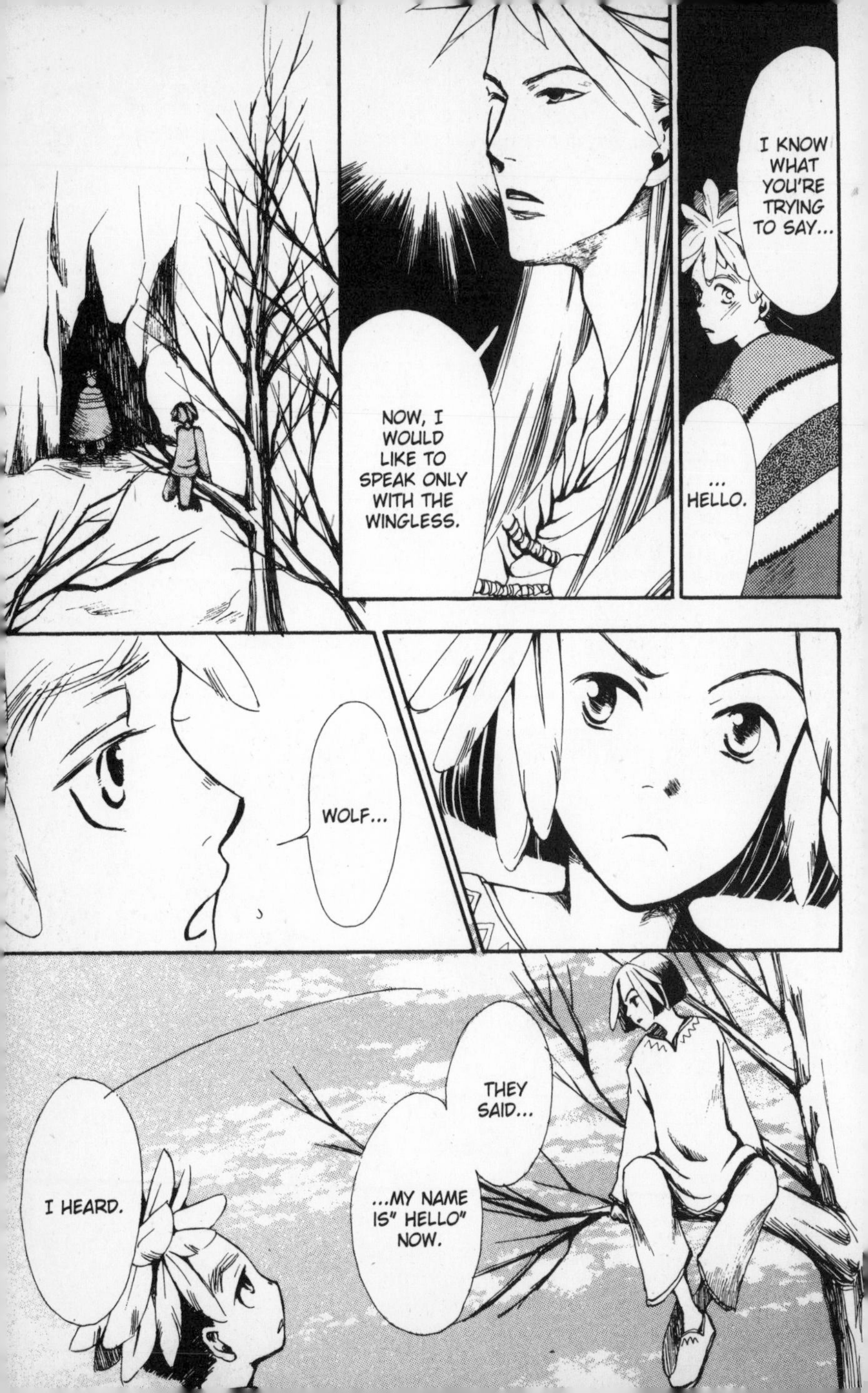
I KNOW WHAT YOU'RE TRYING TO SAY...
... HELLO.
NOW, I WOULD LIKE TO SPEAK ONLY WITH THE WINGLESS.
WOLF...
THEY SAID...
...MY NAME IS" HELLO" NOW.
I HEARD.

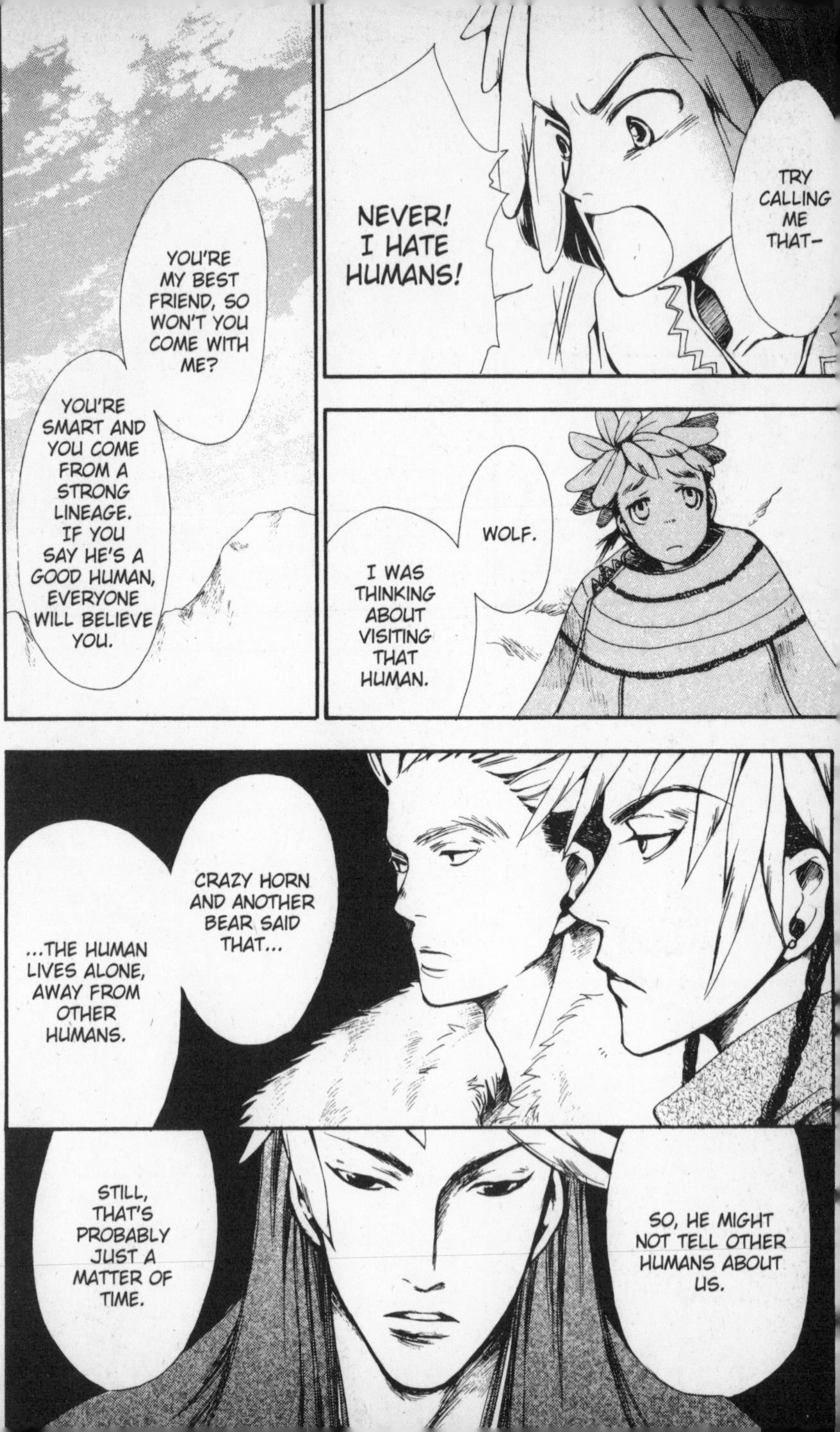
TRY CALLING ME THAT-
NEVER! I HATE HUMANS!
WOLF.
I WAS THINKING ABOUT VISITING THAT HUMAN.
YOU'RE MY BEST FRIEND, SO WON'T YOU COME WITH ME?
YOU'RE SMART AND YOU COME FROM A STRONG LINEAGE. IF YOU SAY HE'S A GOOD HUMAN, EVERYONE WILL BELIEVE YOU.
CRAZY HORN AND ANOTHER BEAR SAID THAT...
...THE HUMAN LIVES ALONE, AWAY FROM OTHER HUMANS.
SO, HE MIGHT NOT TELL OTHER HUMANS ABOUT US.
STILL, THAT'S PROBABLY JUST A MATTER OF TIME.

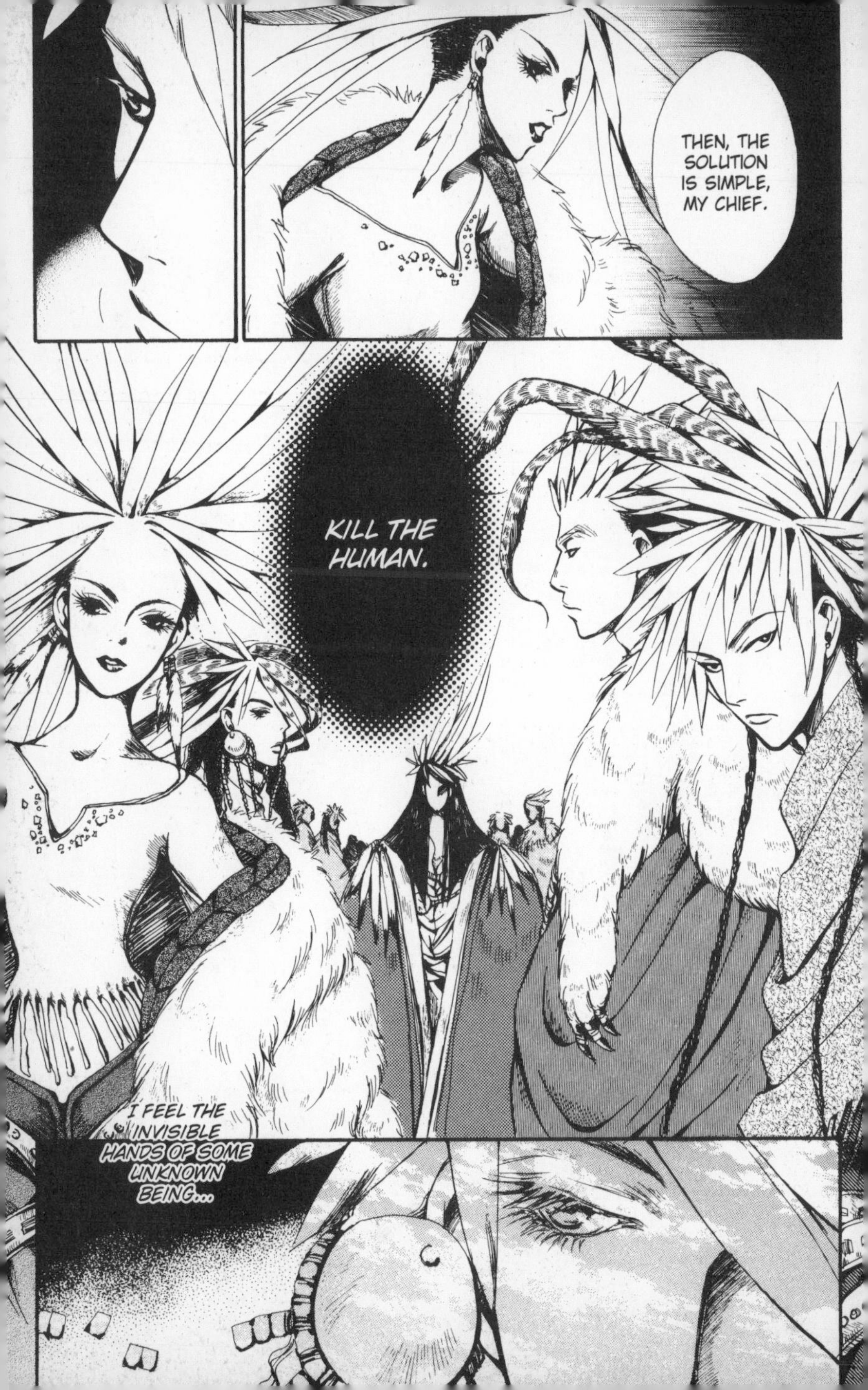
THEN, THE SOLUTION IS SIMPLE, MY CHIEF.
KILL THE HUMAN.
I FEEL THE INVISIBLE HANDS OF SOME UNKNOWN BEING...

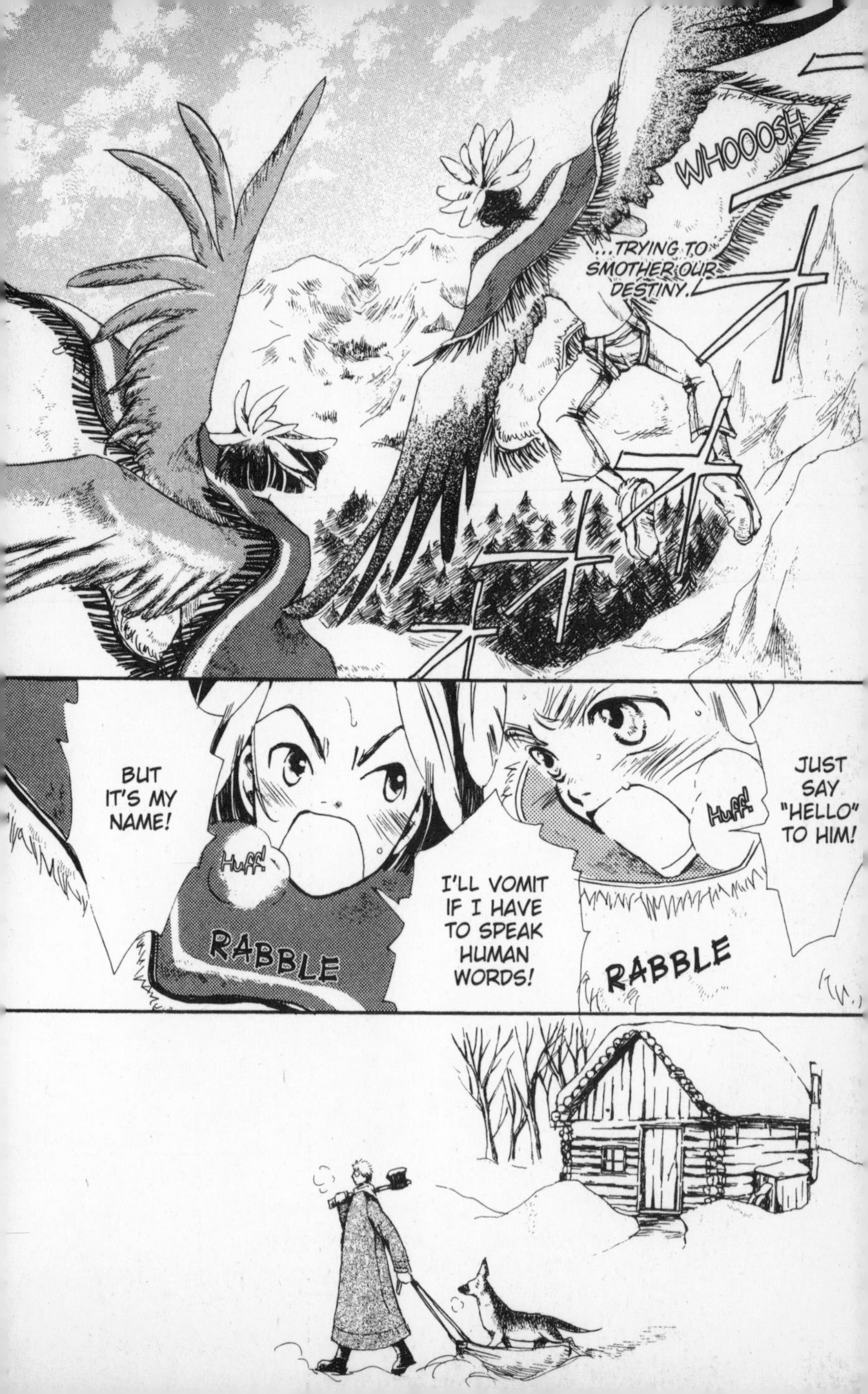
WHOOOSH
...TRYING TO SMOTHER OUR DESTINY.
JUST SAY "HELLO" TO HIM!
Huff!
RABBLE
I'LL VOMIT IF I HAVE TO SPEAK HUMAN WORDS!
BUT IT'S MY NAME!
Huff!
RABBLE

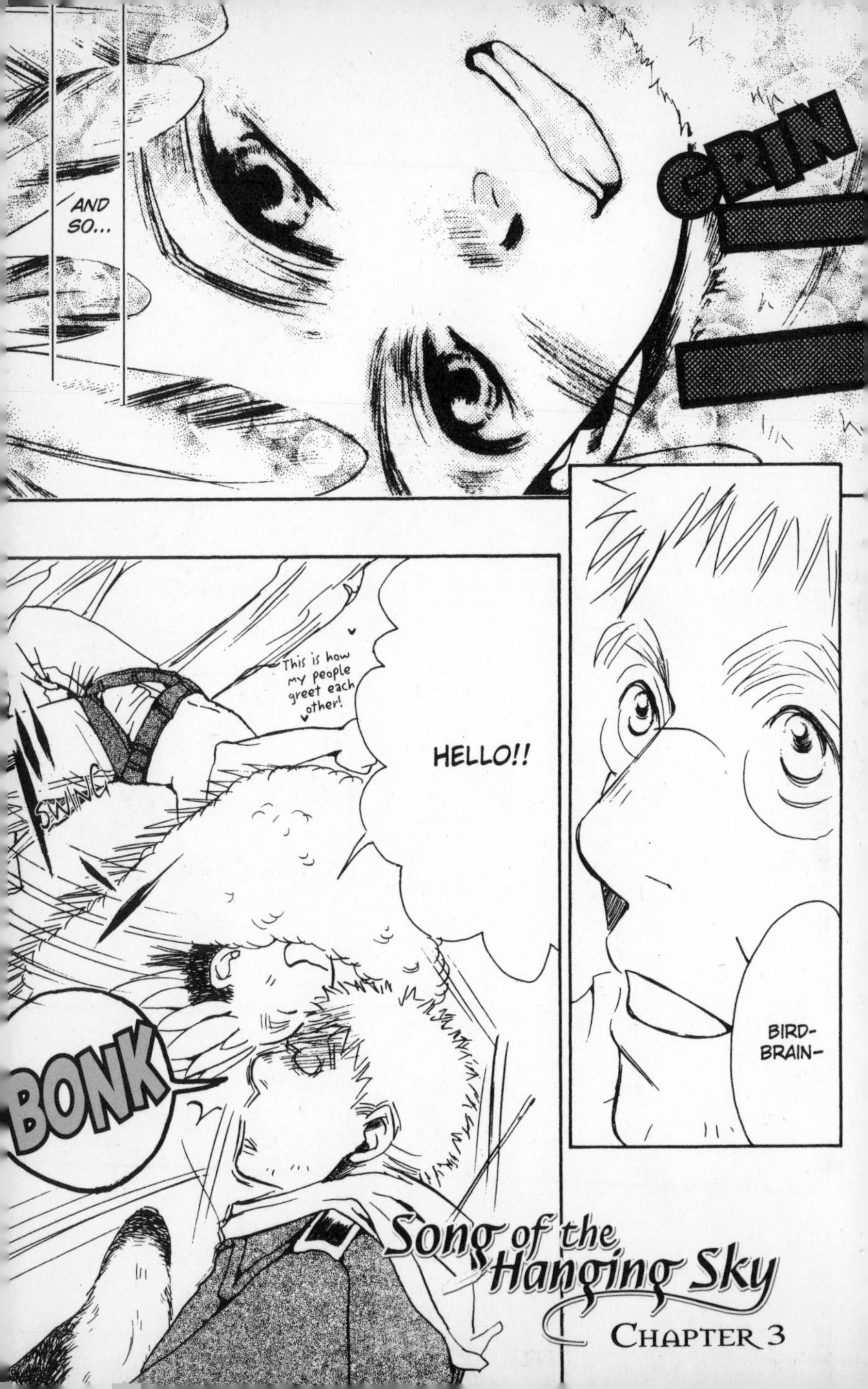
GRIN
AND SO...
BIRD-BRAIN-
HELLO!!
This is how my people greet each other!
SWING
BONK
Song of the Hanging Sky
CHAPTER 3

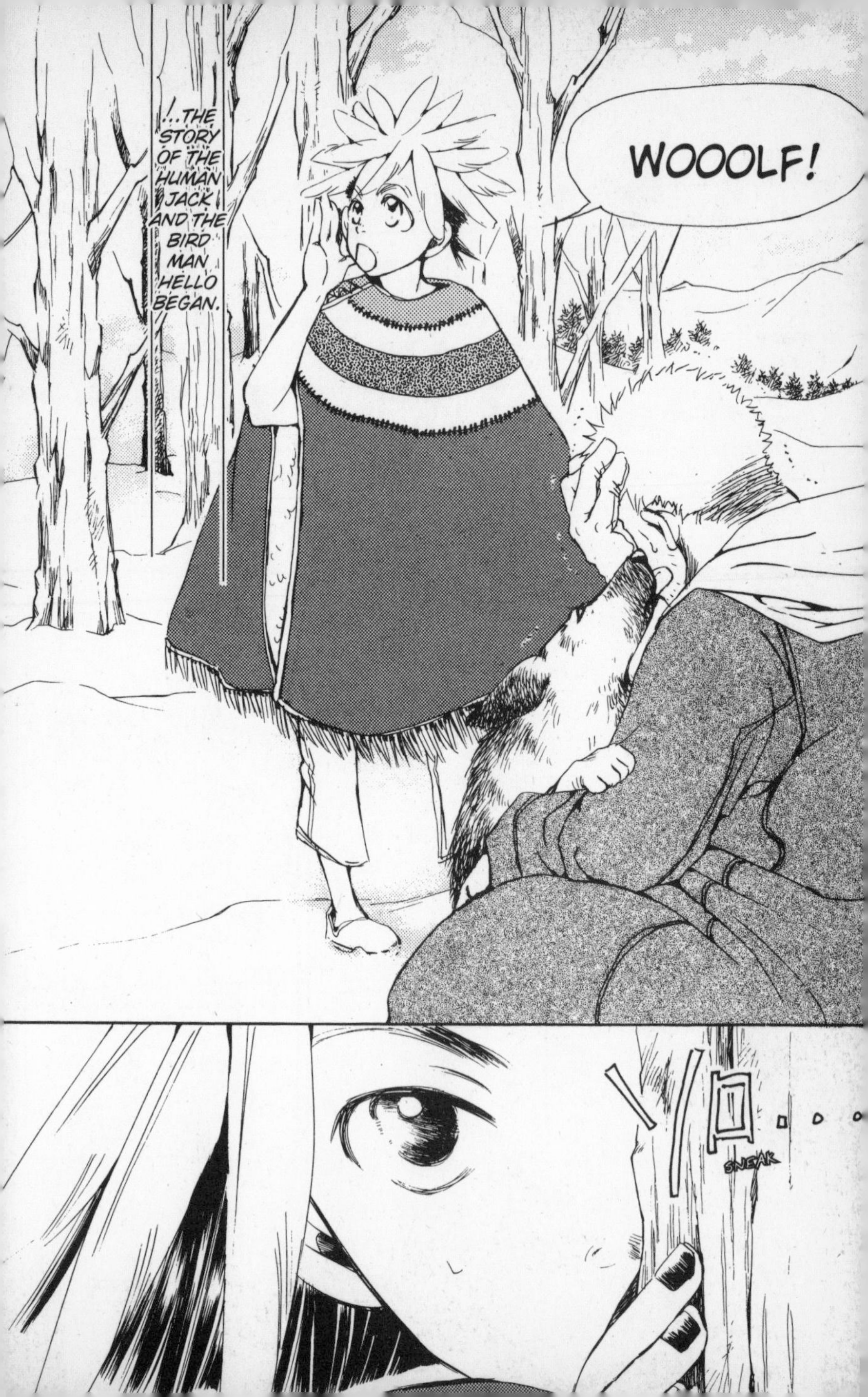
WOOOLF!
!..THE STORY OF THE HUMAN JACK AND THE BIRD MAN HELLO BEGAN.
SNEAK

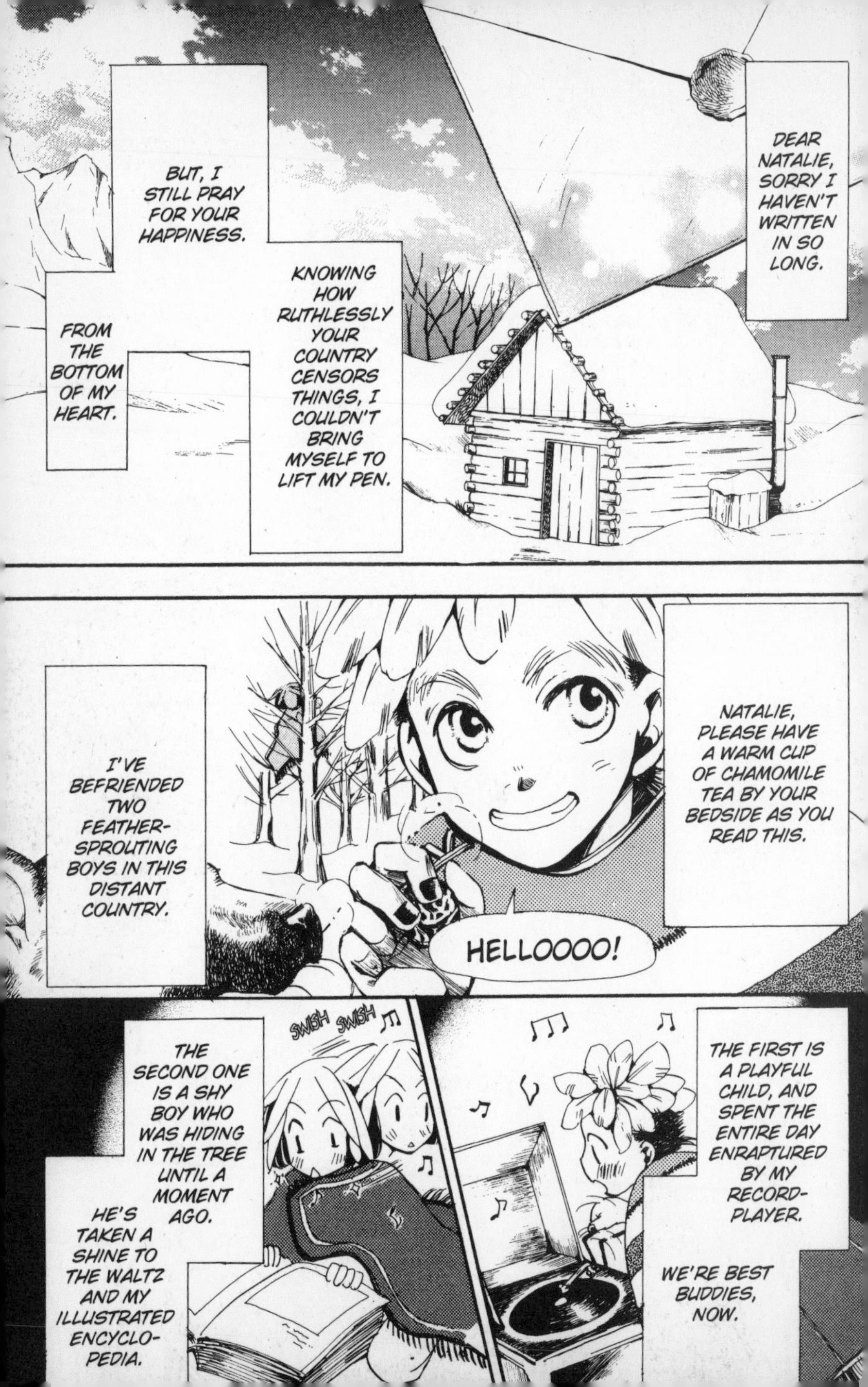
DEAR NATALIE, SORRY I HAVEN'T WRITTEN IN SO LONG.
KNOWING HOW RUTHLESSLY YOUR COUNTRY CENSORS THINGS, I COULDN'T BRING MYSELF TO LIFT MY PEN.
BUT, I STILL PRAY FOR YOUR HAPPINESS.
FROM THE BOTTOM OF MY HEART.
NATALIE, PLEASE HAVE A WARM CUP OF CHAMOMILE TEA BY YOUR BEDSIDE AS YOU READ THIS.
HELLOOOO!
I'VE BEFRIENDED TWO FEATHER-SPROUTING BOYS IN THIS DISTANT COUNTRY.
THE FIRST IS A PLAYFUL CHILD, AND SPENT THE ENTIRE DAY ENRAPTURED BY MY RECORD-PLAYER.
WE'RE BEST BUDDIES, NOW.
SWISH SWISH
THE SECOND ONE IS A SHY BOY WHO WAS HIDING IN THE TREE UNTIL A MOMENT AGO.
HE'S TAKEN A SHINE TO THE WALTZ AND MY ILLUSTRATED ENCYCLO-PEDIA.

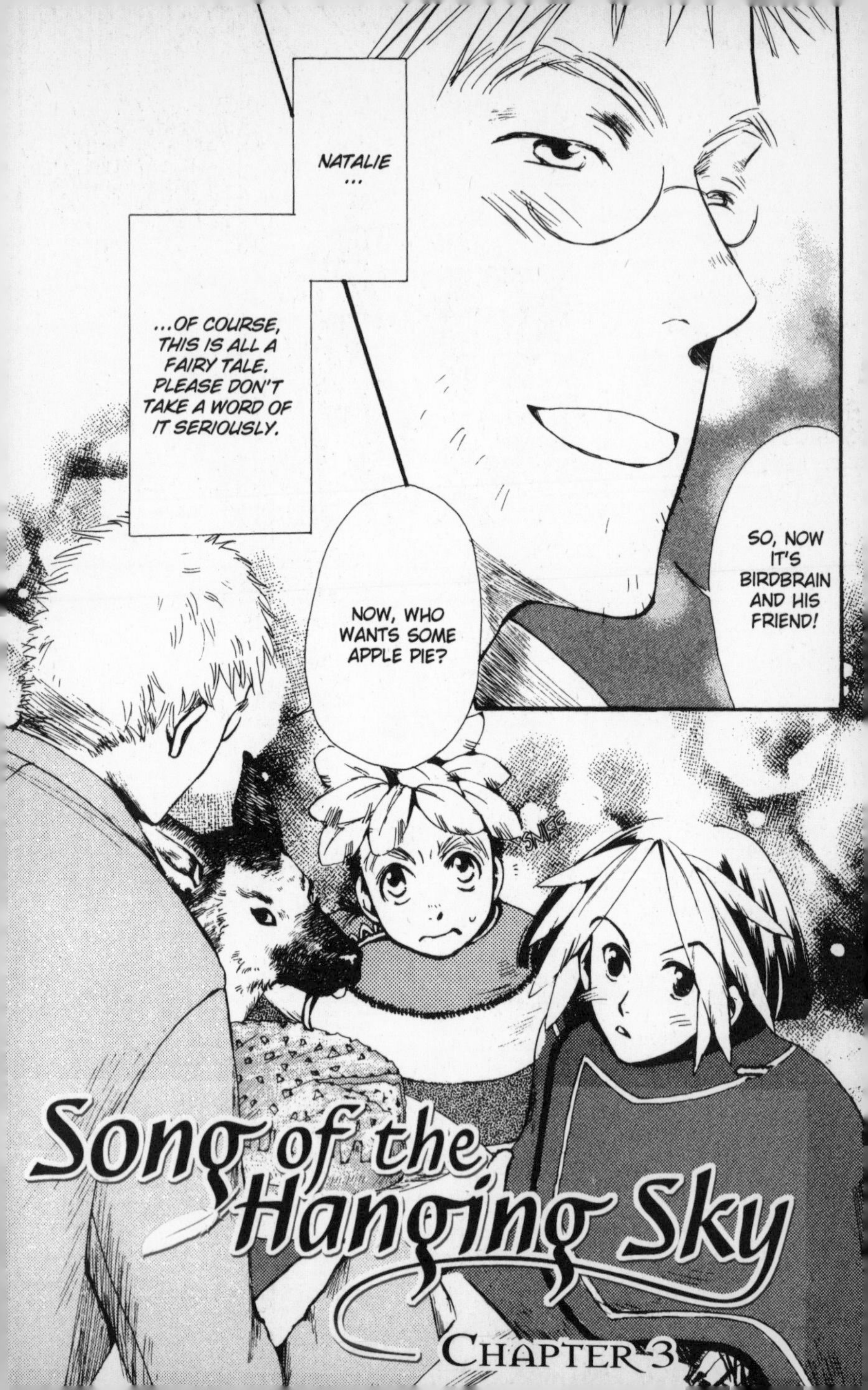
NATALIE ...
...OF COURSE, THIS IS ALL A FAIRY TALE. PLEASE DON'T TAKE A WORD OF IT SERIOUSLY.
NOW, WHO WANTS SOME APPLE PIE?
SO, NOW IT'S BIRDBRAIN AND HIS FRIEND!
Song of the Hanging Sky
CHAPTER 3

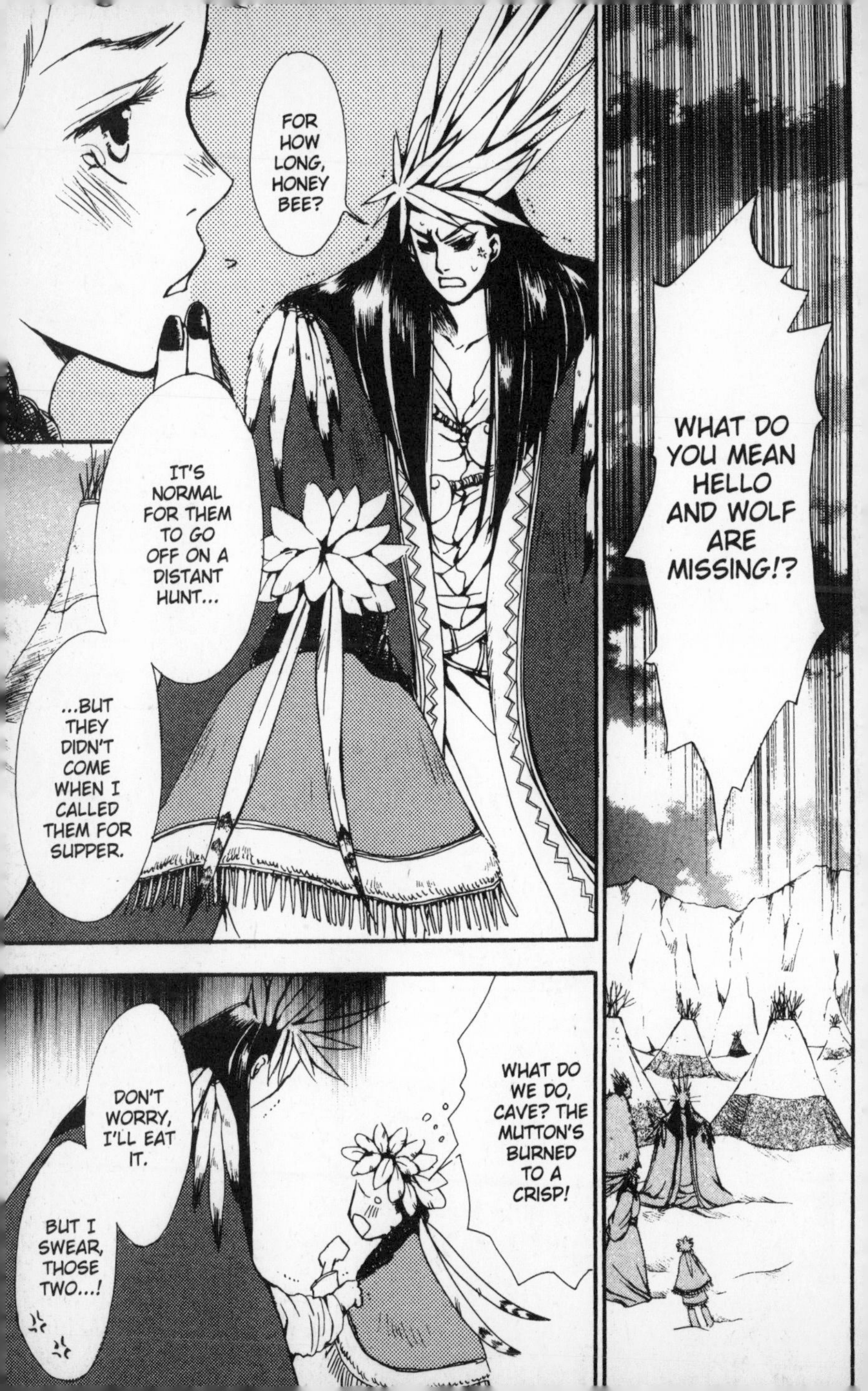
WHAT DO YOU MEAN HELLO AND WOLF ARE MISSING!?
IT'S NORMAL FOR THEM TO GO OFF ON A DISTANT HUNT...
...BUT THEY DIDN'T COME WHEN I CALLED THEM FOR SUPPER.
FOR HOW LONG, HONEY BEE?
WHAT DO WE DO, CAVE? THE MUTTON'S BURNED TO A CRISP!
DON'T WORRY, I'LL EAT IT.
BUT I SWEAR, THOSE TWO...!

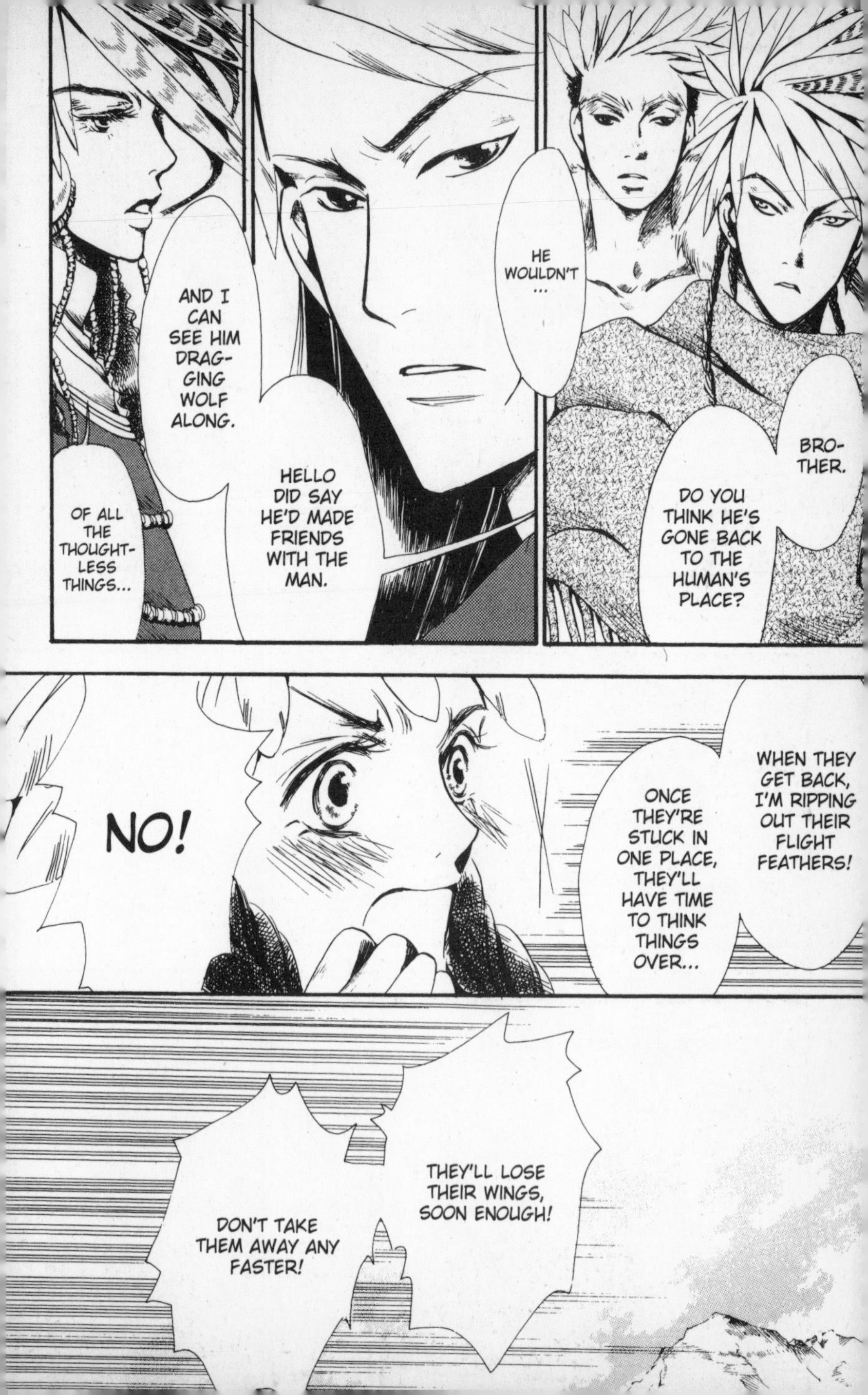
BRO-THER.
DO YOU THINK HE'S GONE BACK TO THE HUMAN'S PLACE?
HE WOULDN'T ...
HELLO DID SAY HE'D MADE FRIENDS WITH THE MAN.
AND I CAN SEE HIM DRAG-GING WOLF ALONG.
OF ALL THE THOUGHT-LESS THINGS...
WHEN THEY GET BACK, I'M RIPPING OUT THEIR FLIGHT FEATHERS!
ONCE THEY'RE STUCK IN ONE PLACE, THEY'LL HAVE TIME TO THINK THINGS OVER...
NO!
THEY'LL LOSE THEIR WINGS, SOON ENOUGH!
DON'T TAKE THEM AWAY ANY FASTER!

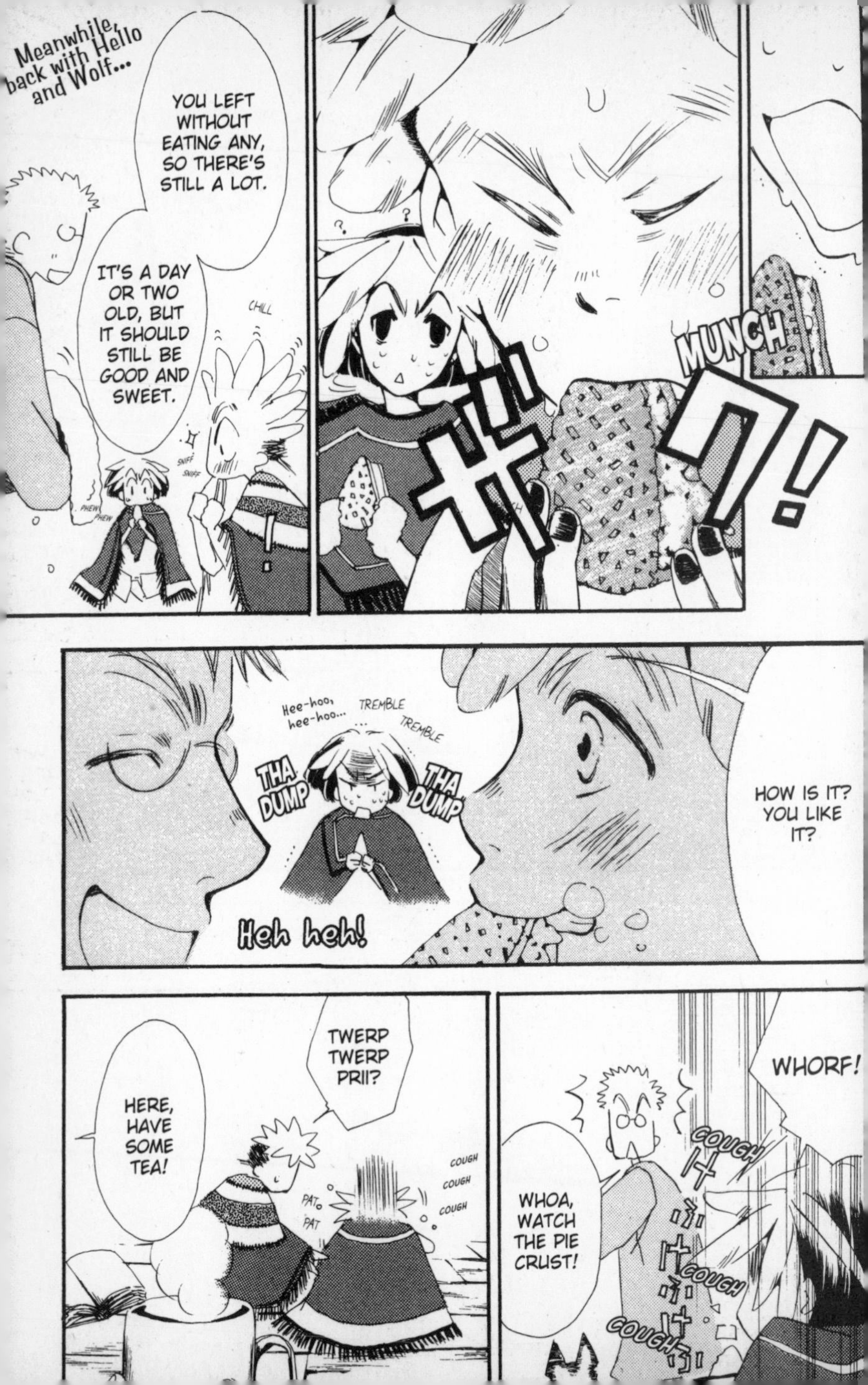
MUNCH
? ?
Meanwhile, back with Hello and Wolf...
YOU LEFT WITHOUT EATING ANY, SO THERE'S STILL A LOT.
IT'S A DAY OR TWO OLD, BUT IT SHOULD STILL BE GOOD AND SWEET.
CHILL
SNIFF SNIFF
PHEW PHEW
HOW IS IT? YOU LIKE IT?
THA DUMP
TREMBLE TREMBLE
Hee-hoo, hee-hoo...
THA DUMP
Heh heh!
WHORF!
COUGH
COUGH
COUGH
WHOA, WATCH THE PIE CRUST!
TWERP TWERP PRII?
HERE, HAVE SOME TEA!
COUGH COUGH COUGH
PAT PAT

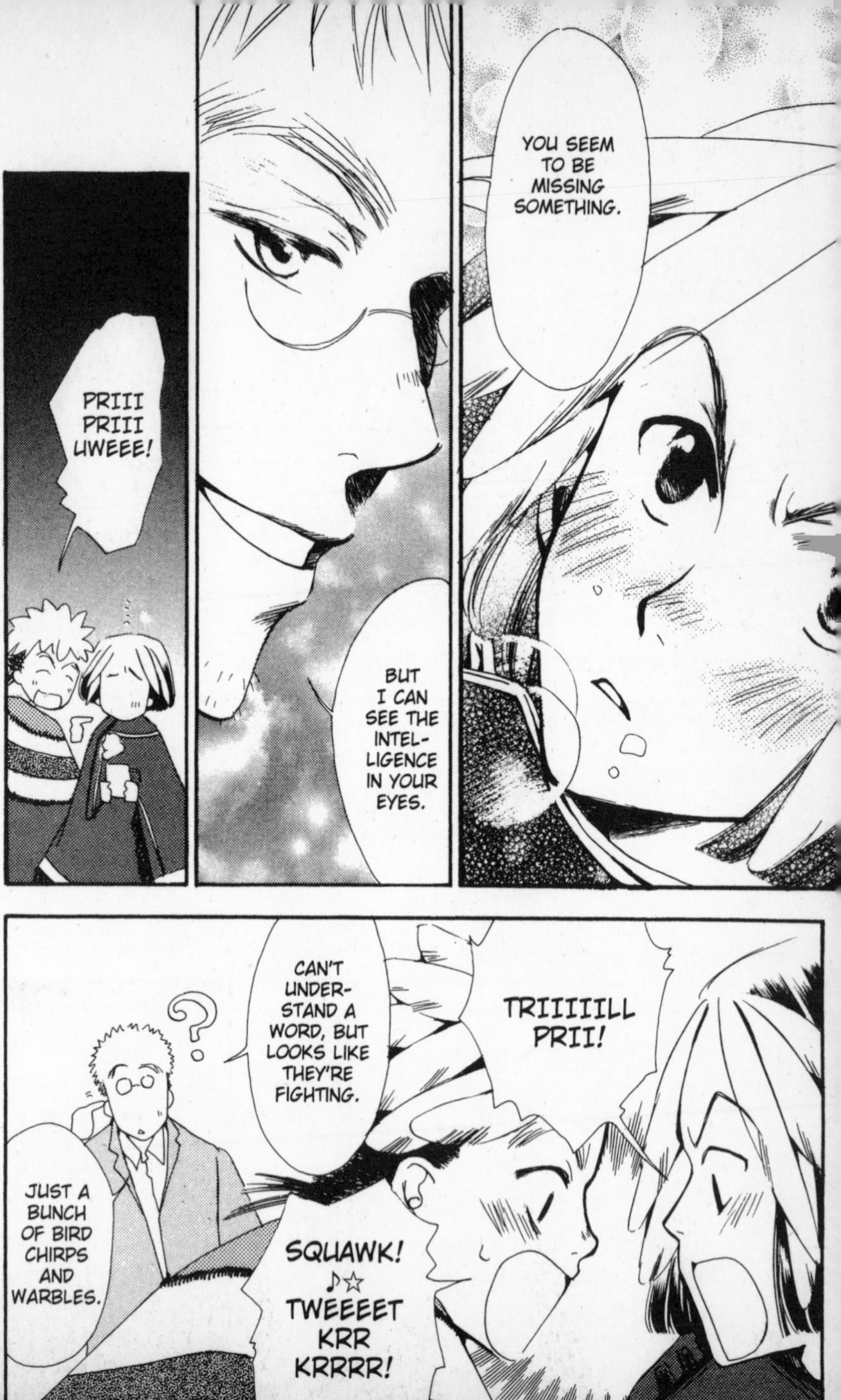
YOU SEEM TO BE MISSING SOMETHING.
BUT I CAN SEE THE INTEL-LIGENCE IN YOUR EYES.
PRIII PRIII UWEEE!
TRIIIIILL PRII!
CAN'T UNDER-STAND A WORD, BUT LOOKS LIKE THEY'RE FIGHTING.
SQUAWK! ♪☆ TWEEEET KRR KRRRR!
JUST A BUNCH OF BIRD CHIRPS AND WARBLES.

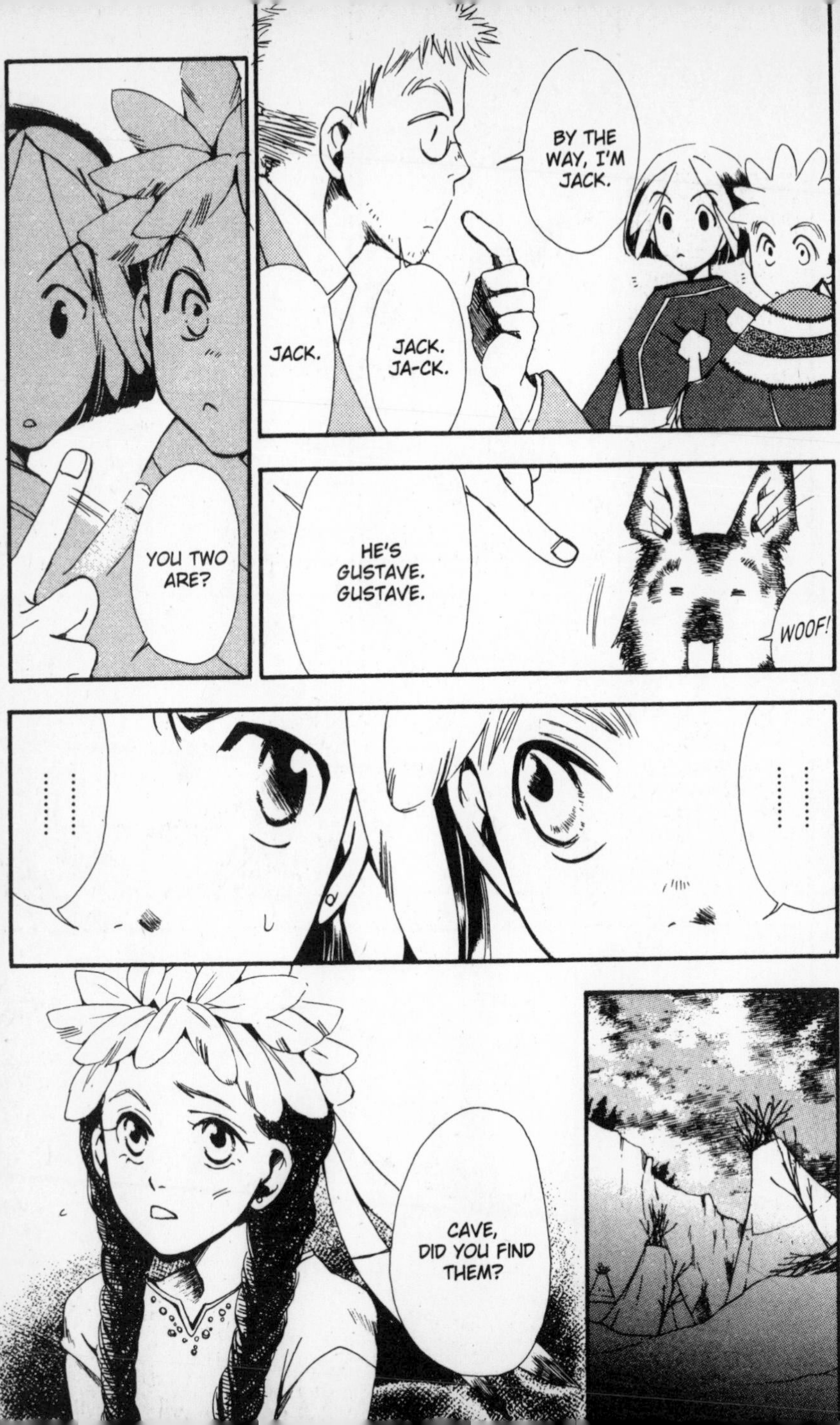
BY THE WAY, I'M JACK.
JACK. JA-CK.
JACK.
HE'S GUSTAVE. GUSTAVE.
WOOF!
YOU TWO ARE?
......
......
CAVE, DID YOU FIND THEM?

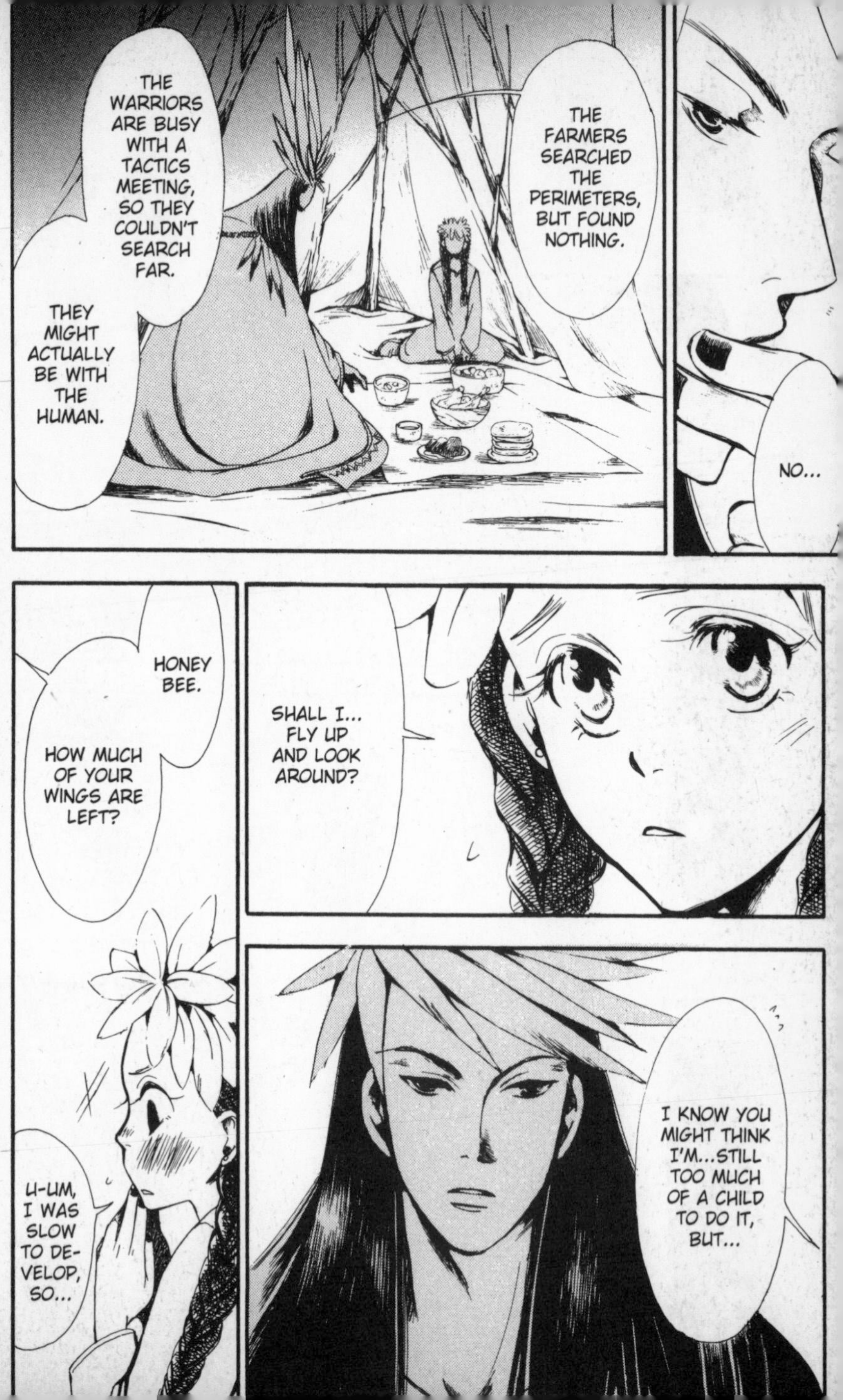
NO...
THE FARMERS SEARCHED THE PERIMETERS, BUT FOUND NOTHING.
THE WARRIORS ARE BUSY WITH A TACTICS MEETING, SO THEY COULDN'T SEARCH FAR.
THEY MIGHT ACTUALLY BE WITH THE HUMAN.
SHALL I... FLY UP AND LOOK AROUND?
I KNOW YOU MIGHT THINK I'M...STILL TOO MUCH OF A CHILD TO DO IT, BUT...
HONEY BEE.
HOW MUCH OF YOUR WINGS ARE LEFT?
U-UM, I WAS SLOW TO DE-VELOP, SO...

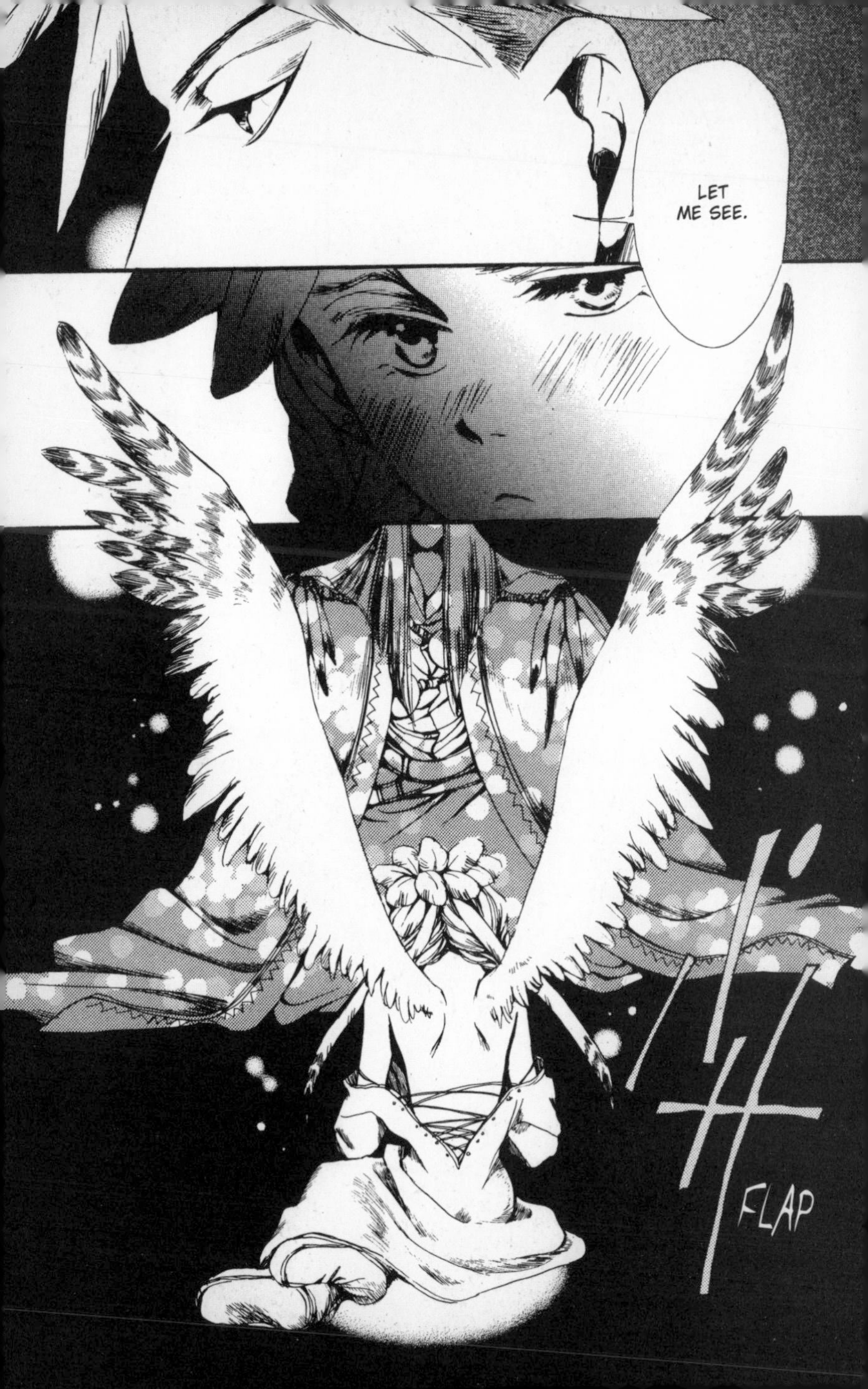
LET ME SEE.
FLAP

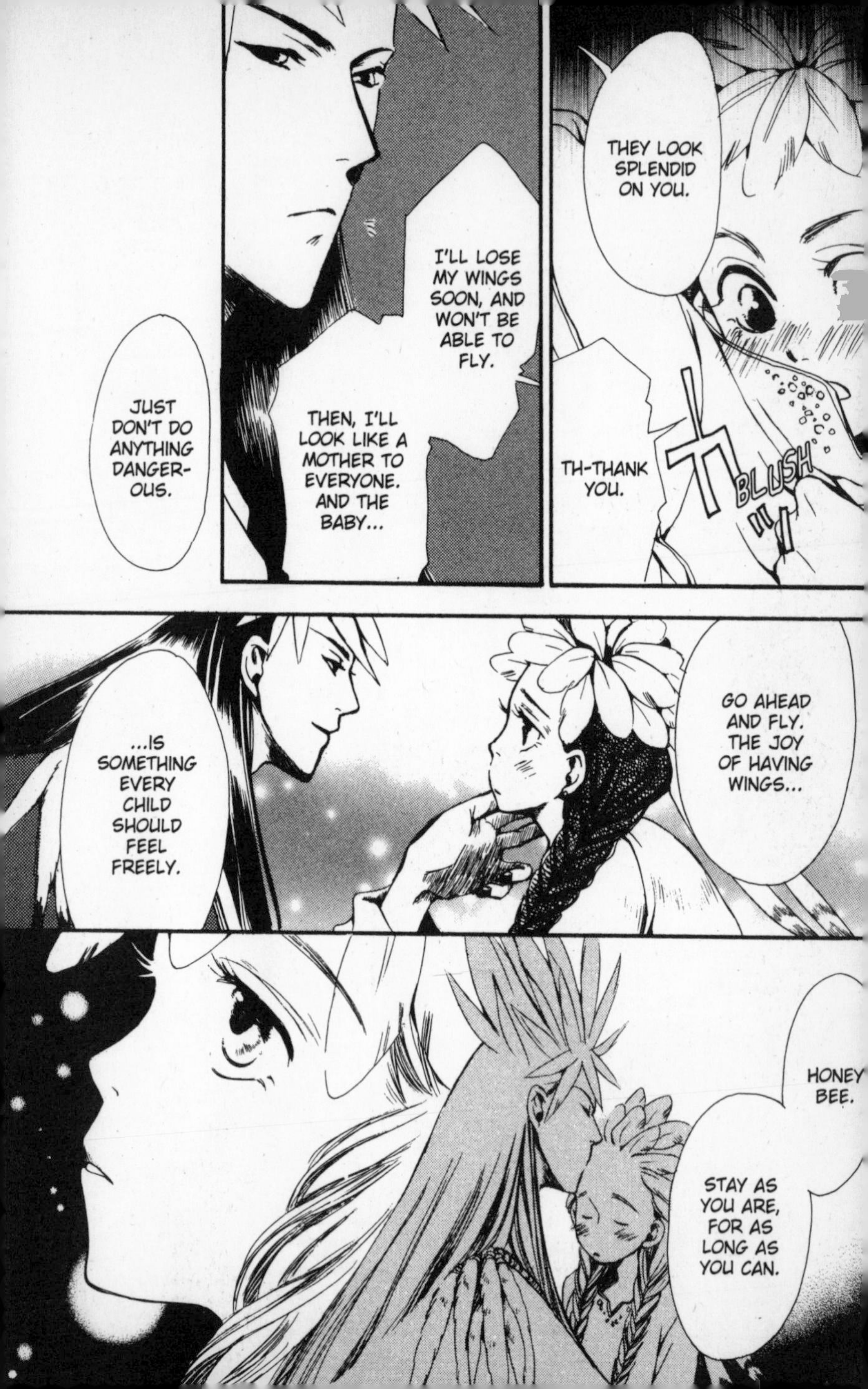
THEY LOOK SPLENDID ON YOU.
TH-THANK YOU.
BLUSH
I'LL LOSE MY WINGS SOON, AND WON'T BE ABLE TO FLY.
THEN, I'LL LOOK LIKE A MOTHER TO EVERYONE. AND THE BABY...
JUST DON'T DO ANYTHING DANGER-OUS.
GO AHEAD AND FLY. THE JOY OF HAVING WINGS...
...IS SOMETHING EVERY CHILD SHOULD FEEL FREELY.
HONEY BEE.
STAY AS YOU ARE, FOR AS LONG AS YOU CAN.

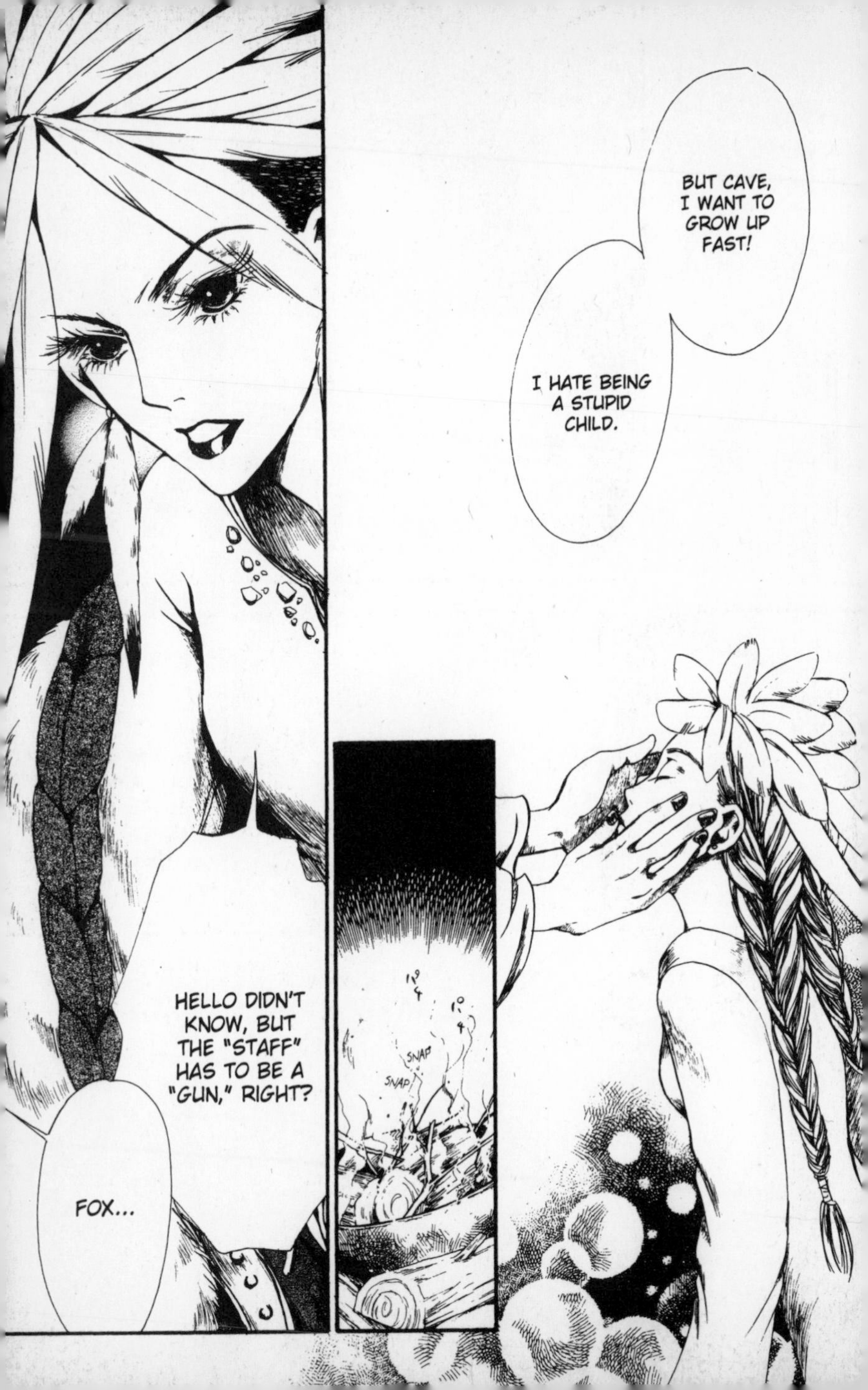
BUT CAVE, I WANT TO GROW UP FAST!
I HATE BEING A STUPID CHILD.
SNAP
SNAP
HELLO DIDN'T KNOW, BUT THE "STAFF" HAS TO BE A "GUN," RIGHT?
FOX...

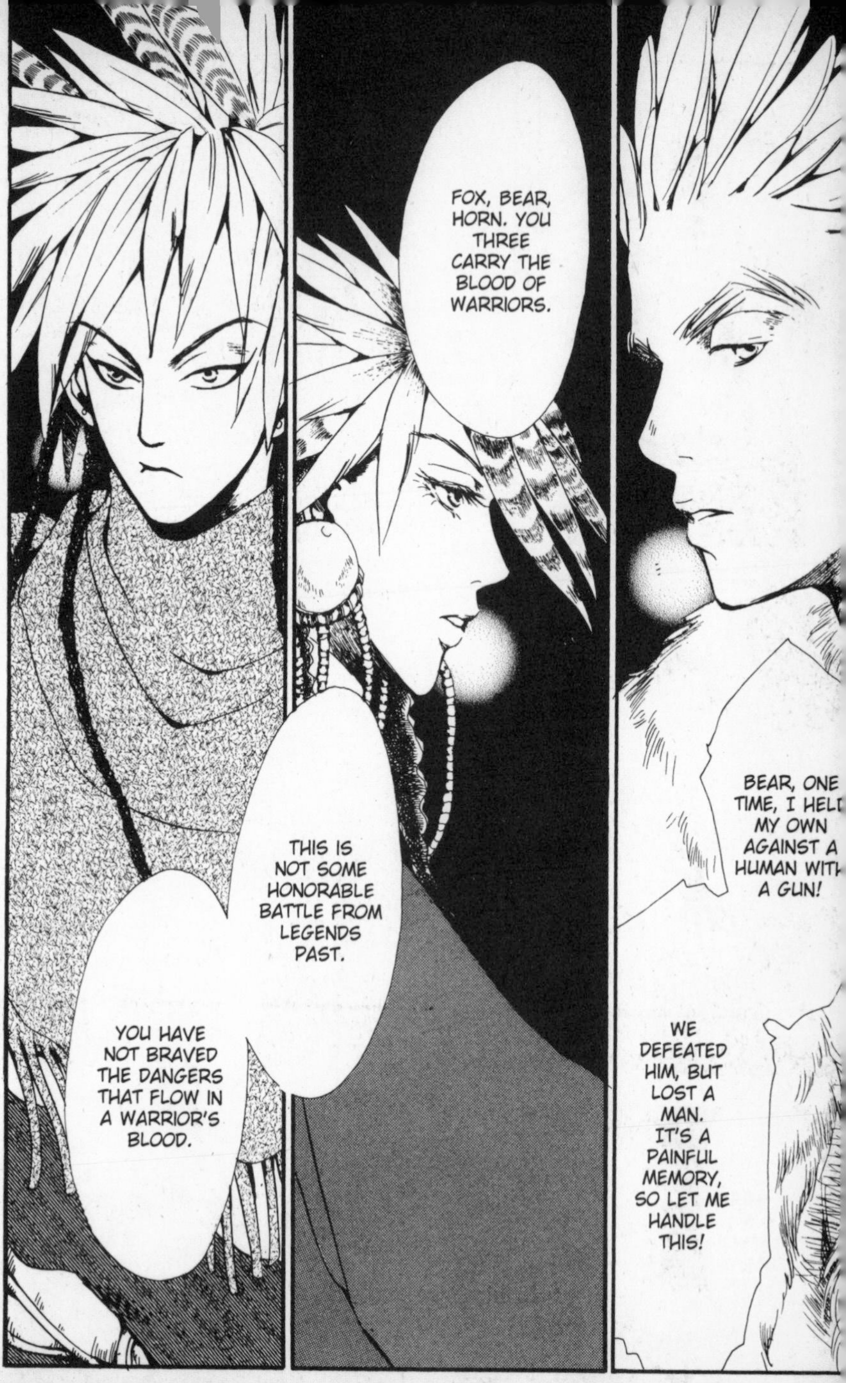
BEAR, ONE TIME, I HELD MY OWN AGAINST A HUMAN WITH A GUN!
WE DEFEATED HIM, BUT LOST A MAN. IT'S A PAINFUL MEMORY, SO LET ME HANDLE THIS!
FOX, BEAR, HORN. YOU THREE CARRY THE BLOOD OF WARRIORS.
THIS IS NOT SOME HONORABLE BATTLE FROM LEGENDS PAST.
YOU HAVE NOT BRAVED THE DANGERS THAT FLOW IN A WARRIOR'S BLOOD.

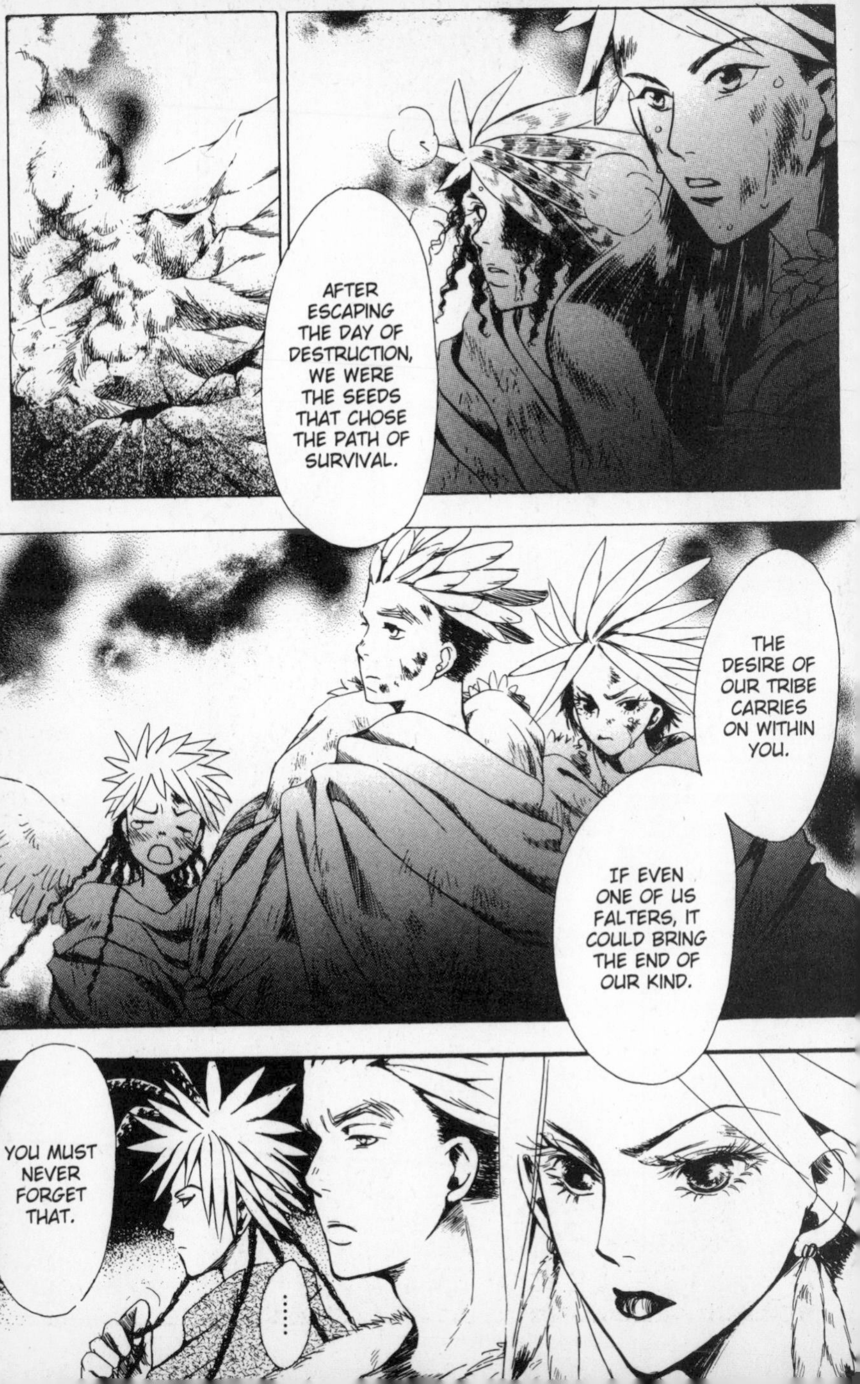
AFTER ESCAPING THE DAY OF DESTRUCTION, WE WERE THE SEEDS THAT CHOSE THE PATH OF SURVIVAL.
THE DESIRE OF OUR TRIBE CARRIES ON WITHIN YOU.
IF EVEN ONE OF US FALTERS, IT COULD BRING THE END OF OUR KIND.
YOU MUST NEVER FORGET THAT.
......

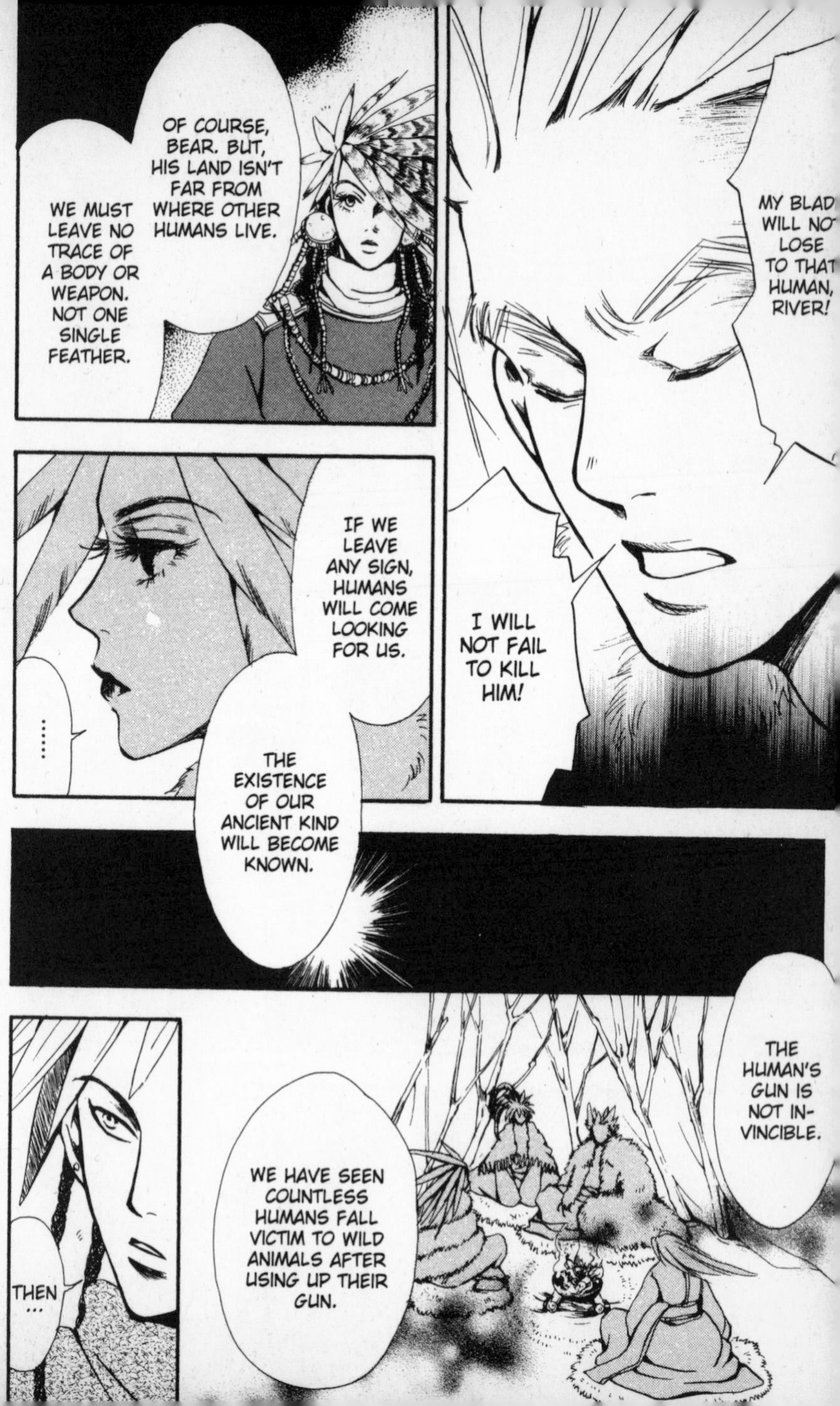
MY BLAD WILL NO LOSE TO THAT HUMAN, RIVER!
I WILL NOT FAIL TO KILL HIM!
OF COURSE, BEAR. BUT, HIS LAND ISN'T FAR FROM WHERE OTHER HUMANS LIVE.
WE MUST LEAVE NO TRACE OF A BODY OR WEAPON. NOT ONE SINGLE FEATHER.
IF WE LEAVE ANY SIGN, HUMANS WILL COME LOOKING FOR US.
THE EXISTENCE OF OUR ANCIENT KIND WILL BECOME KNOWN.
......
THE HUMAN'S GUN IS NOT IN-VINCIBLE.
WE HAVE SEEN COUNTLESS HUMANS FALL VICTIM TO WILD ANIMALS AFTER USING UP THEIR GUN.
THEN ...

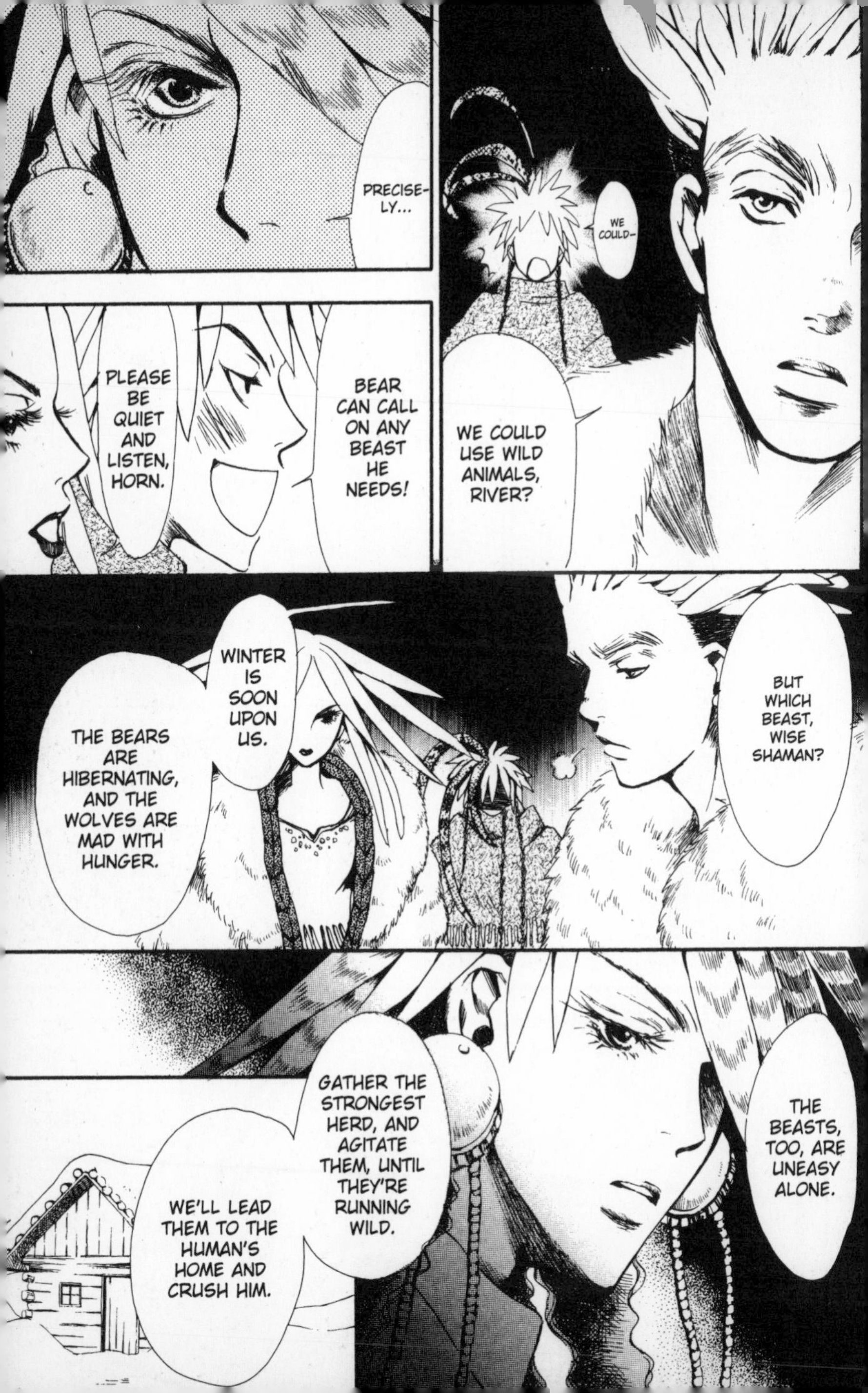
WE COULD—
WE COULD USE WILD ANIMALS, RIVER?
PRECISE-LY...
BEAR CAN CALL ON ANY BEAST HE NEEDS!
PLEASE BE QUIET AND LISTEN, HORN.
BUT WHICH BEAST, WISE SHAMAN?
WINTER IS SOON UPON US.
THE BEARS ARE HIBERNATING, AND THE WOLVES ARE MAD WITH HUNGER.
THE BEASTS, TOO, ARE UNEASY ALONE.
GATHER THE STRONGEST HERD, AND AGITATE THEM, UNTIL THEY'RE RUNNING WILD.
WE'LL LEAD THEM TO THE HUMAN'S HOME AND CRUSH HIM.

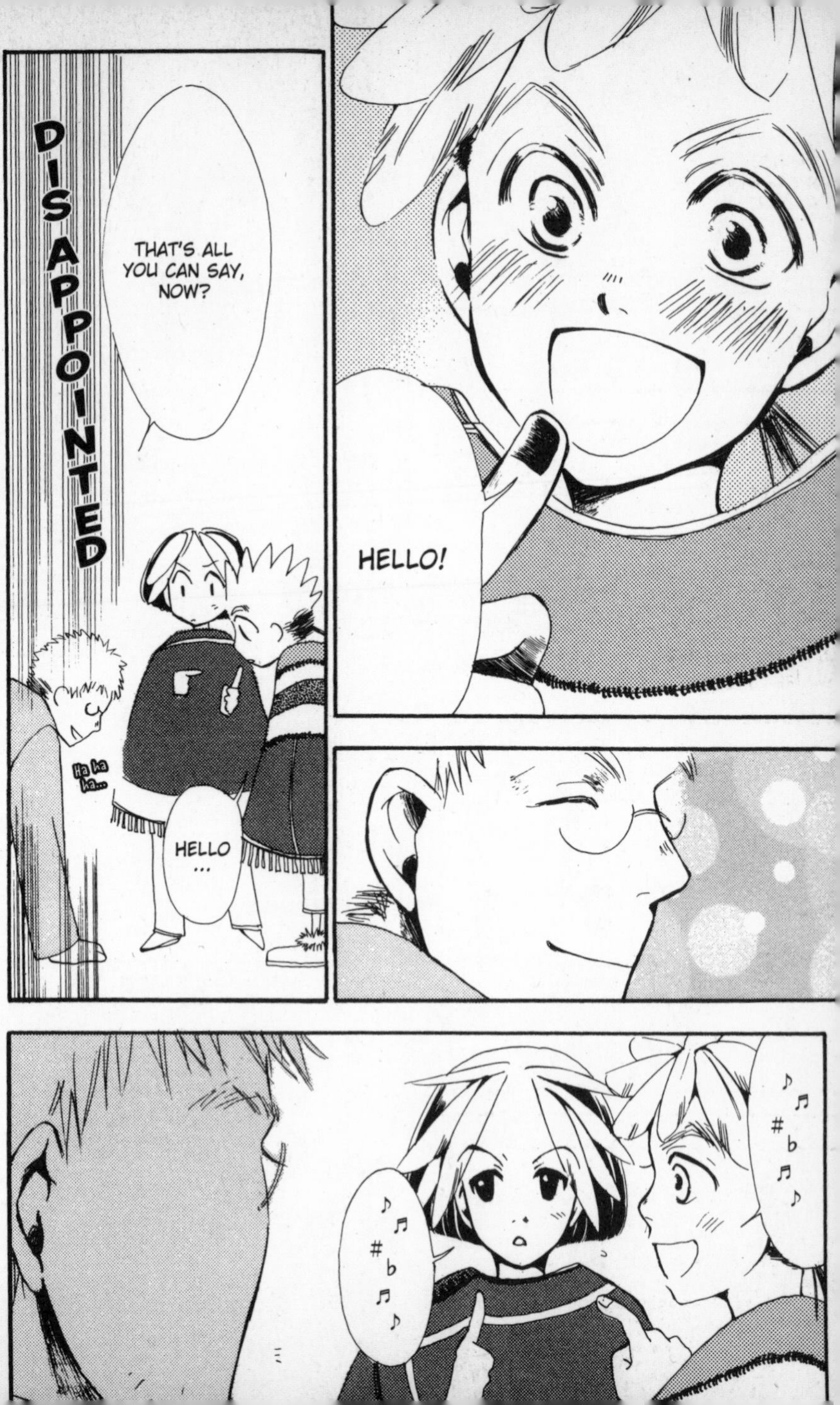
HELLO!
THAT'S ALL YOU CAN SAY, NOW?
DISAPPOINTED
HELLO ...
Ha ha ha...
♪ ♬ # b ♬ ♪
♪ ♬ # b ♬ ♪

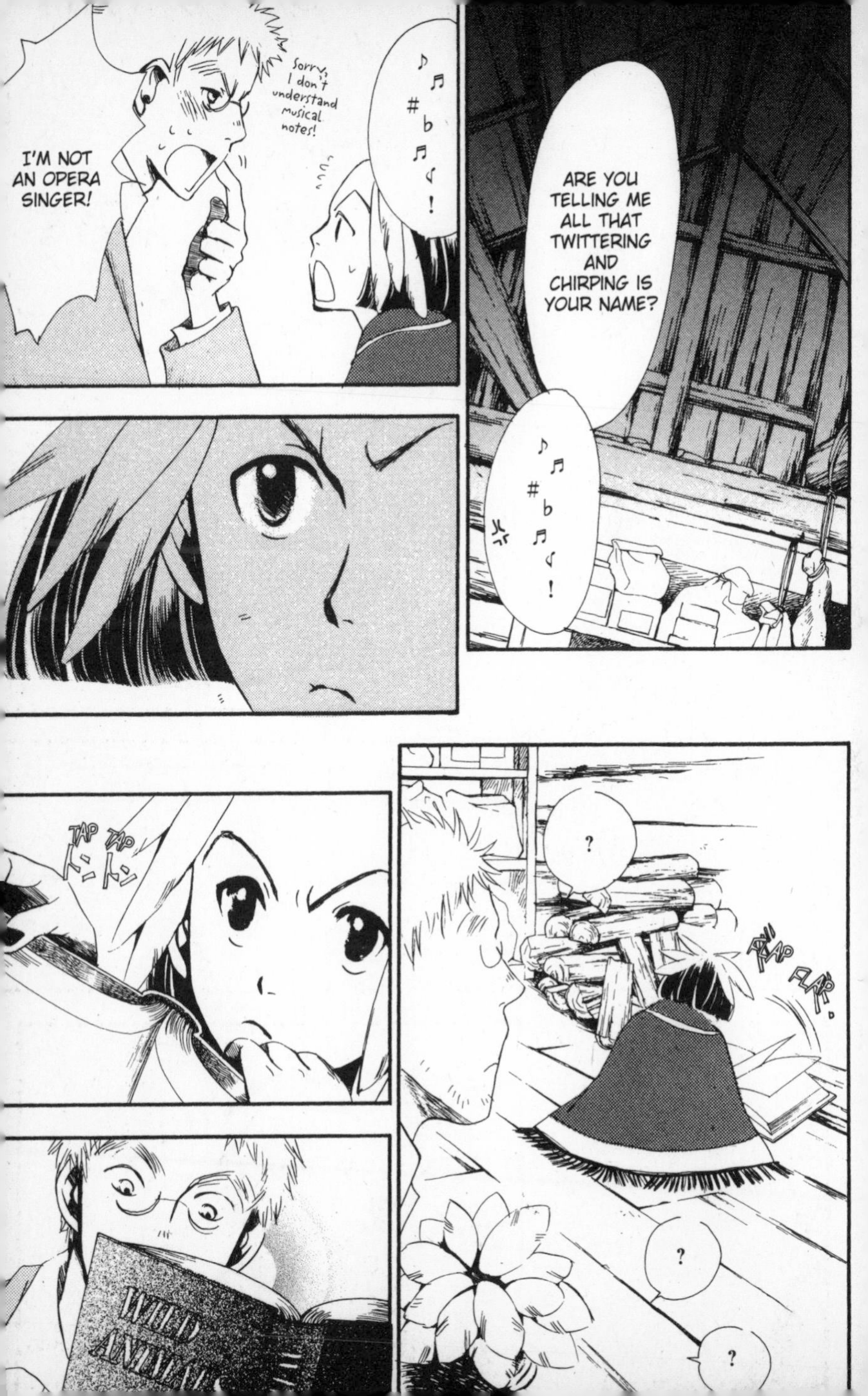

ARE YOU TELLING ME ALL THAT TWITTERING AND CHIRPING IS YOUR NAME?
♪♫#b♫♩!
♪♫#b♫♩!
Sorry, I don't understand musical notes!
I'M NOT AN OPERA SINGER!
?
FLAP FLAP
?
?
TAP TAP
トン トン

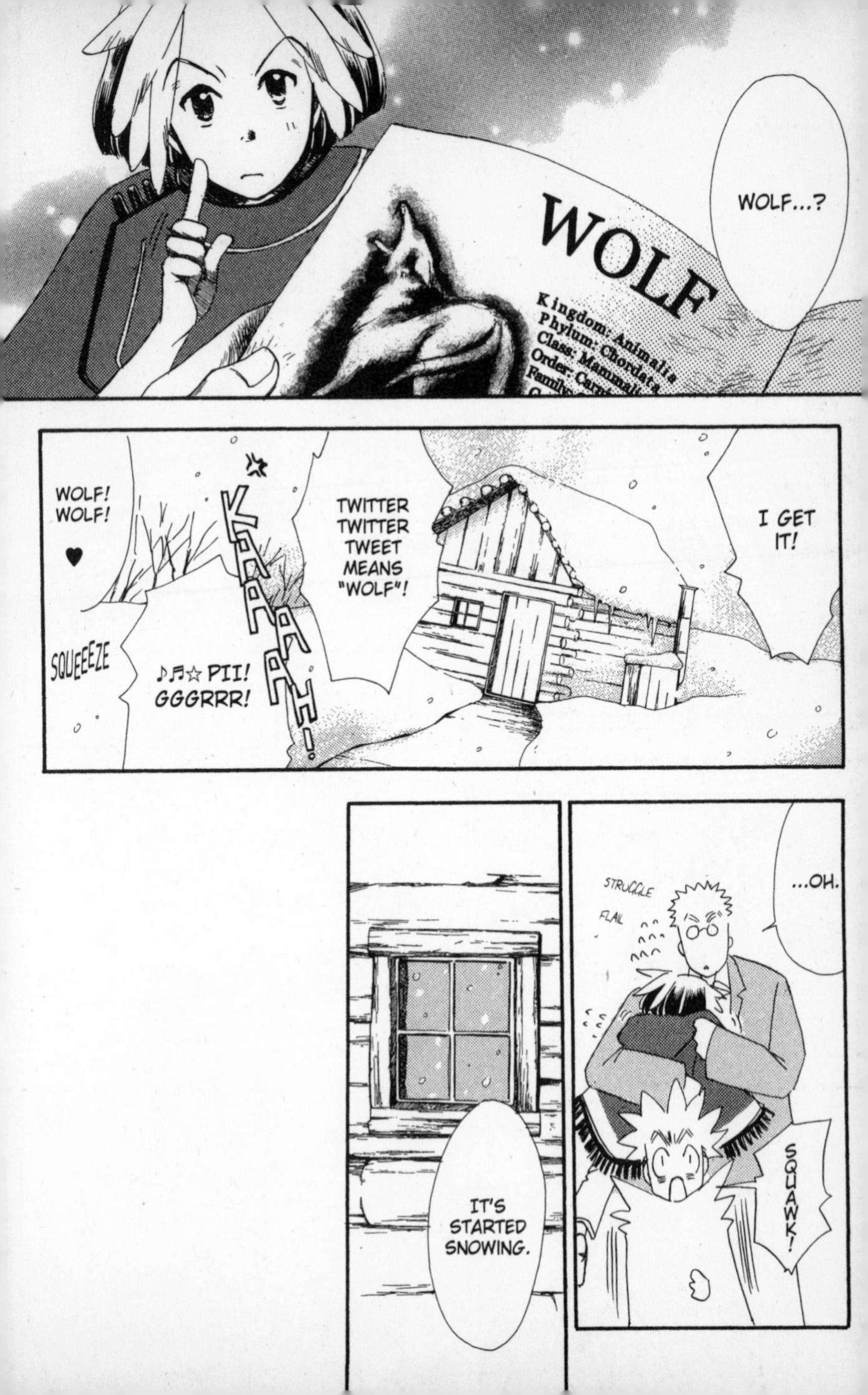
WOLF...?
WOLF
Kingdom: Animalia
Phylum: Chordata
Class: Mammalia
I GET IT!
TWITTER TWITTER TWEET MEANS "WOLF"!
KAAAAAAH!
♪♬☆ PII! GGGRRR!
WOLF! WOLF! ♥
SQUEEEZE
...OH.
STRUGGLE
FLAIL
SQUAWK!
IT'S STARTED SNOWING.

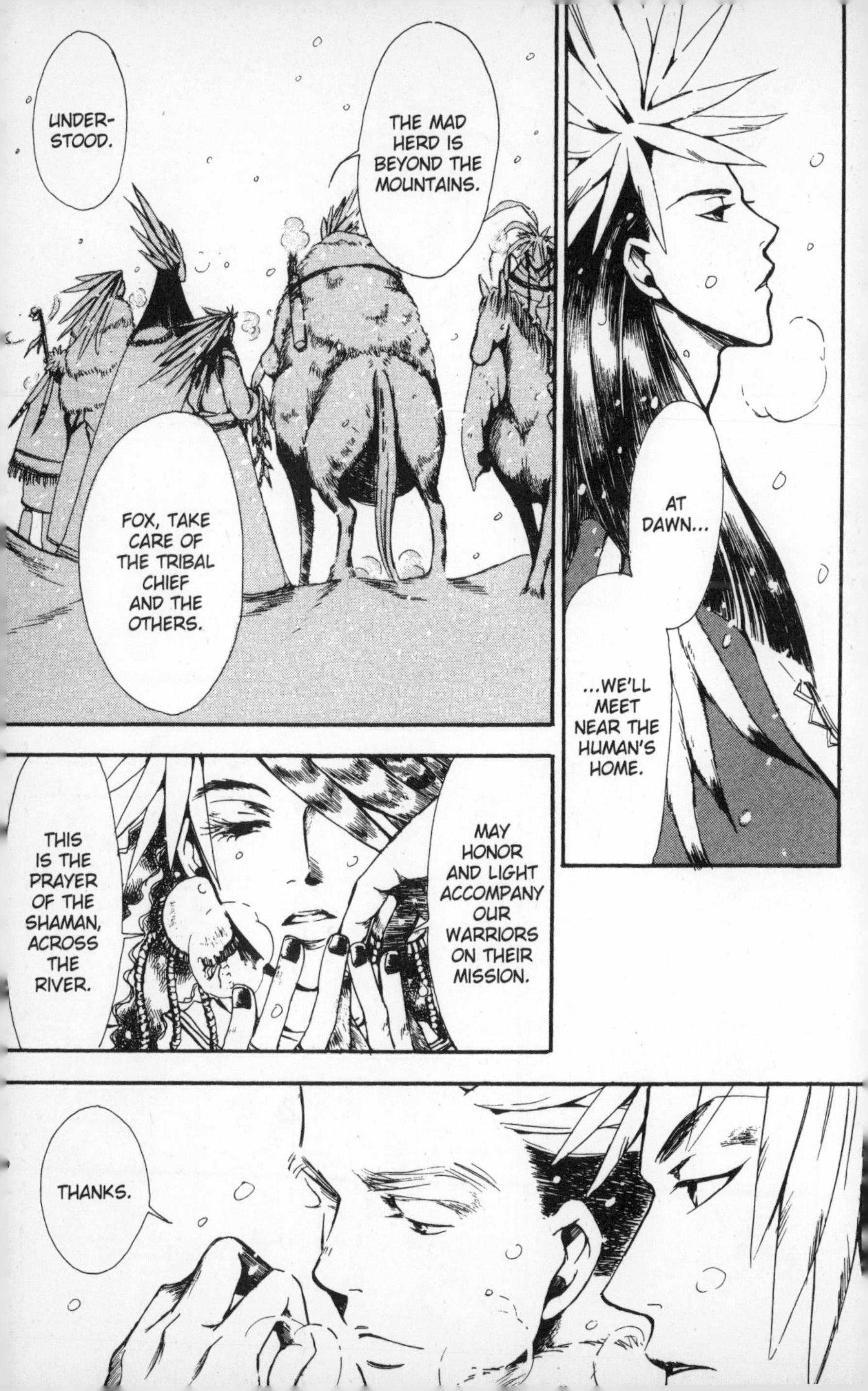
AT DAWN...
...WE'LL MEET NEAR THE HUMAN'S HOME.
THE MAD HERD IS BEYOND THE MOUNTAINS.
UNDER-STOOD.
FOX, TAKE CARE OF THE TRIBAL CHIEF AND THE OTHERS.
MAY HONOR AND LIGHT ACCOMPANY OUR WARRIORS ON THEIR MISSION.
THIS IS THE PRAYER OF THE SHAMAN, ACROSS THE RIVER.
THANKS.

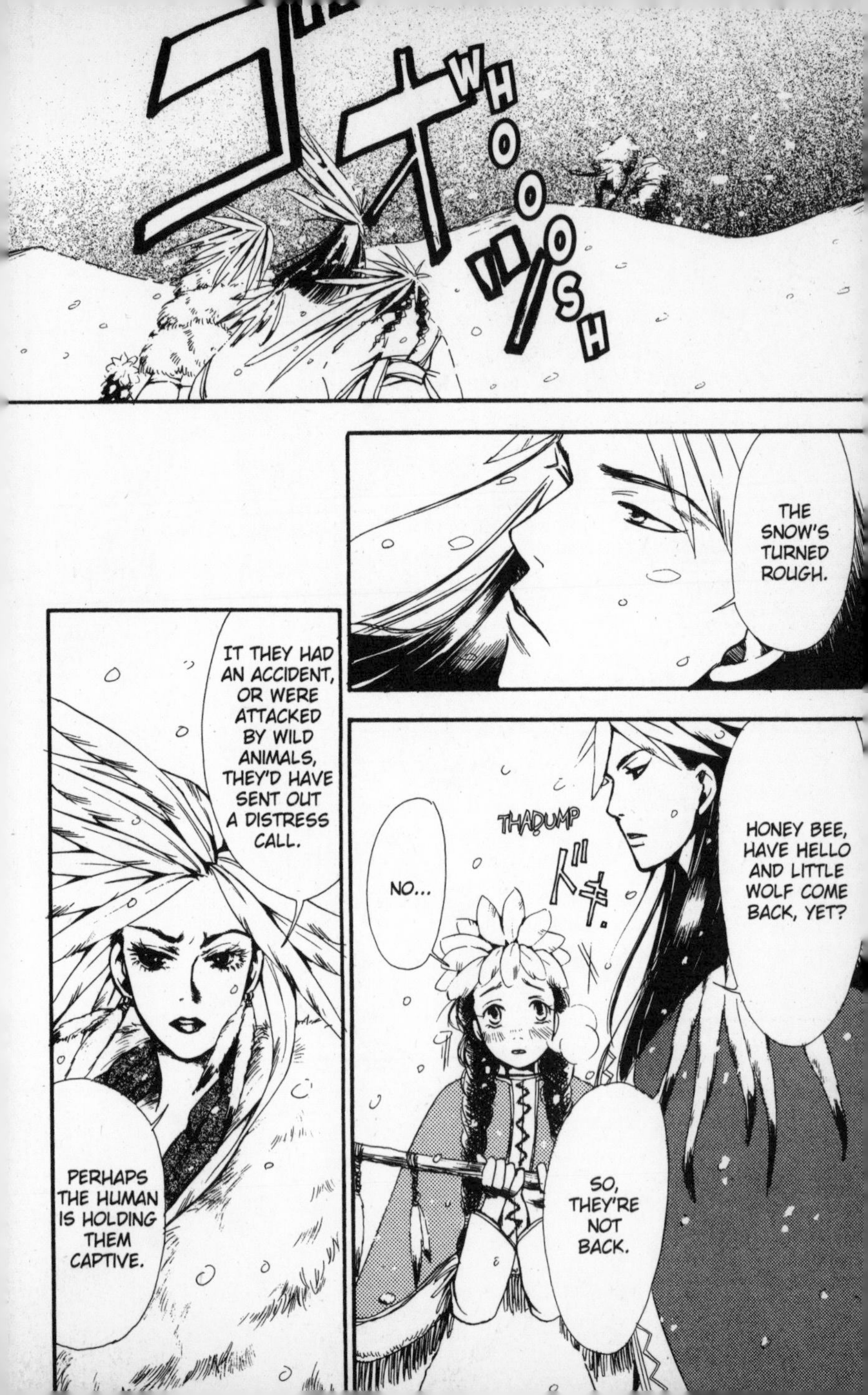
WHOOOOSH
THE SNOW'S TURNED ROUGH.
HONEY BEE, HAVE HELLO AND LITTLE WOLF COME BACK, YET?
THADUMP
NO...
SO, THEY'RE NOT BACK.
IT THEY HAD AN ACCIDENT, OR WERE ATTACKED BY WILD ANIMALS, THEY'D HAVE SENT OUT A DISTRESS CALL.
PERHAPS THE HUMAN IS HOLDING THEM CAPTIVE.

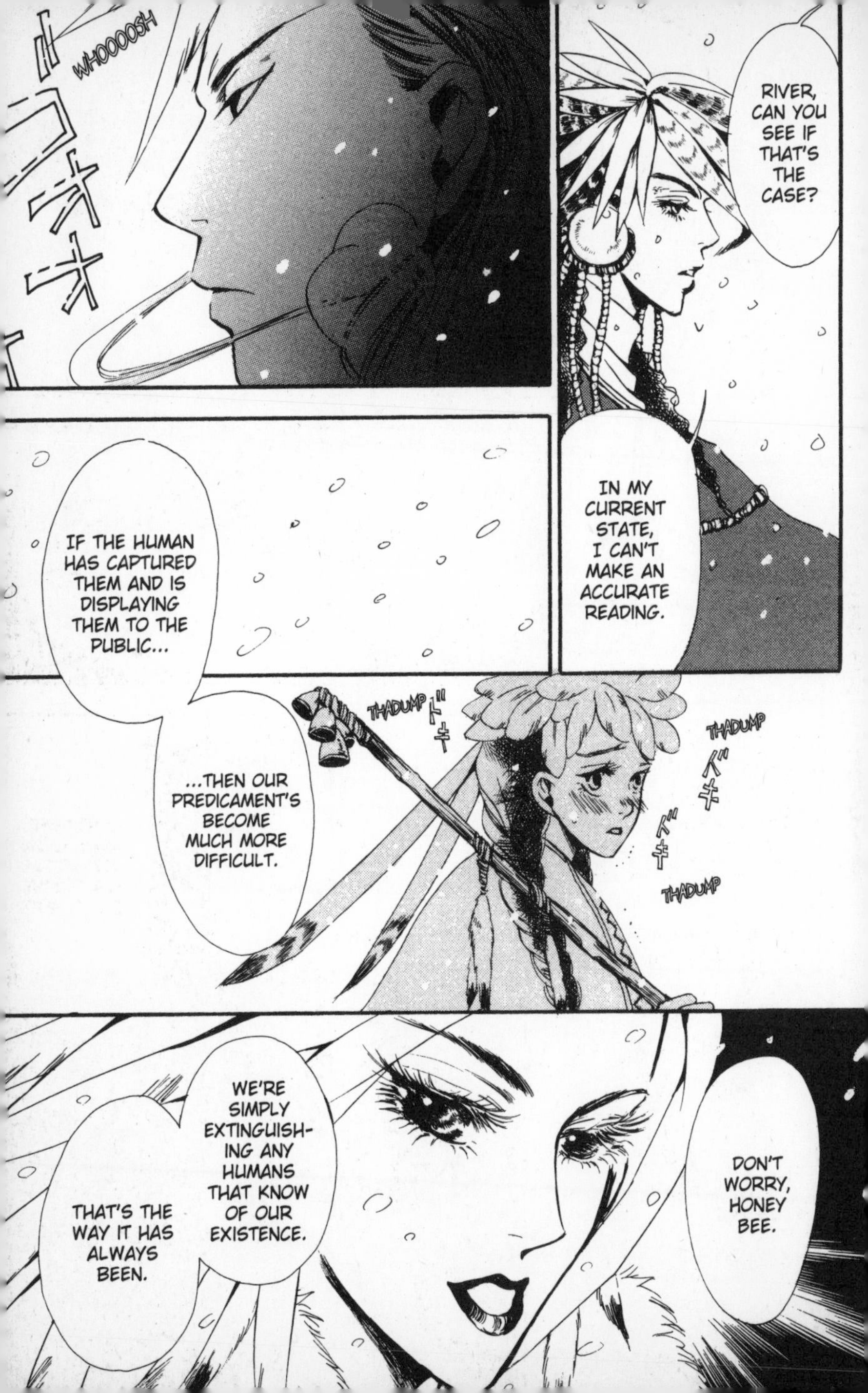
RIVER, CAN YOU SEE IF THAT'S THE CASE?
IN MY CURRENT STATE, I CAN'T MAKE AN ACCURATE READING.
WHOOOOSH
IF THE HUMAN HAS CAPTURED THEM AND IS DISPLAYING THEM TO THE PUBLIC...
...THEN OUR PREDICAMENT'S BECOME MUCH MORE DIFFICULT.
THADUMP
THADUMP
THADUMP
DON'T WORRY, HONEY BEE.
WE'RE SIMPLY EXTINGUISH-ING ANY HUMANS THAT KNOW OF OUR EXISTENCE.
THAT'S THE WAY IT HAS ALWAYS BEEN.

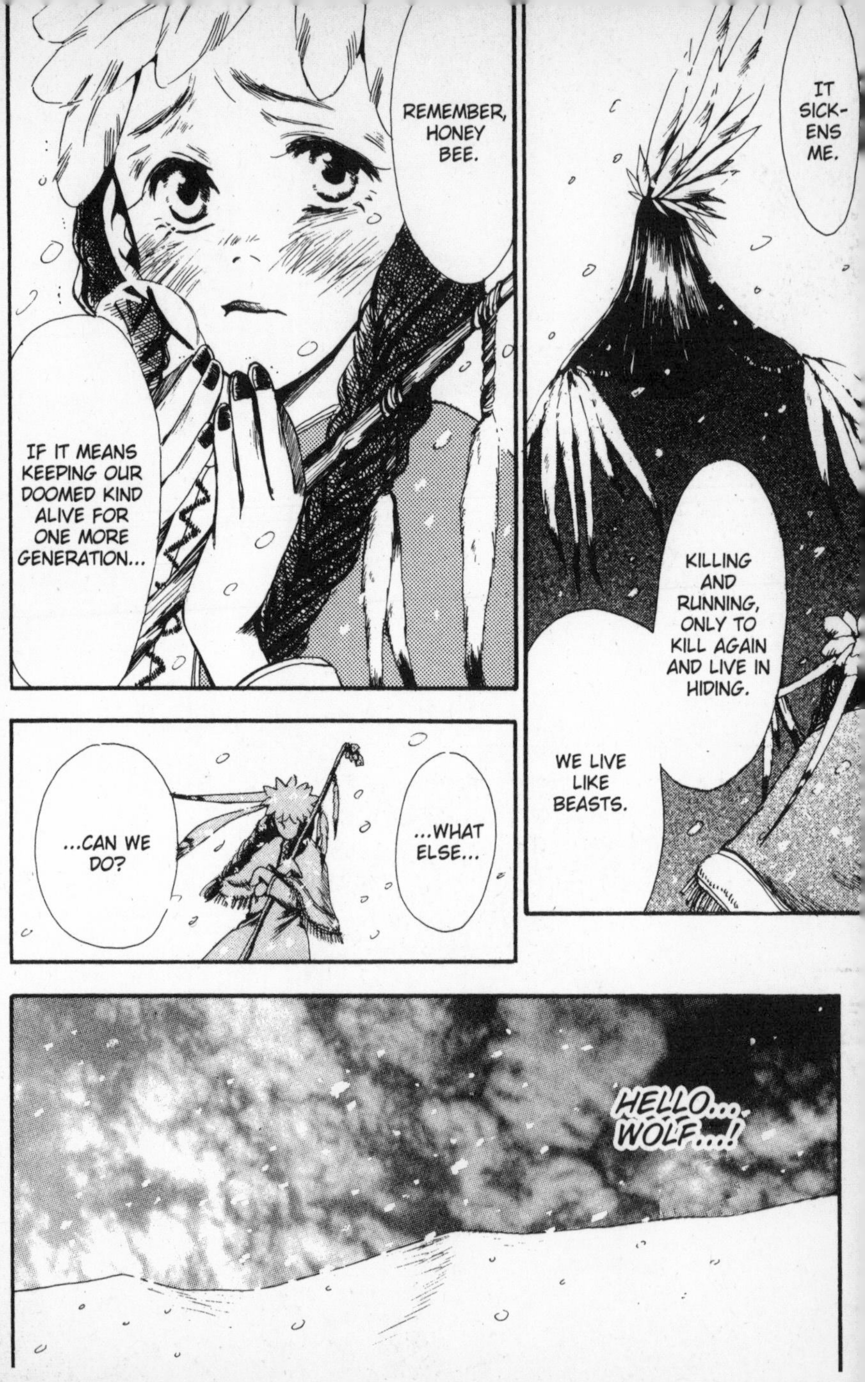
IT SICK-ENS ME.
KILLING AND RUNNING, ONLY TO KILL AGAIN AND LIVE IN HIDING.
WE LIVE LIKE BEASTS.
REMEMBER, HONEY BEE.
IF IT MEANS KEEPING OUR DOOMED KIND ALIVE FOR ONE MORE GENERATION...
...WHAT ELSE...
...CAN WE DO?
HELLO... WOLF...!

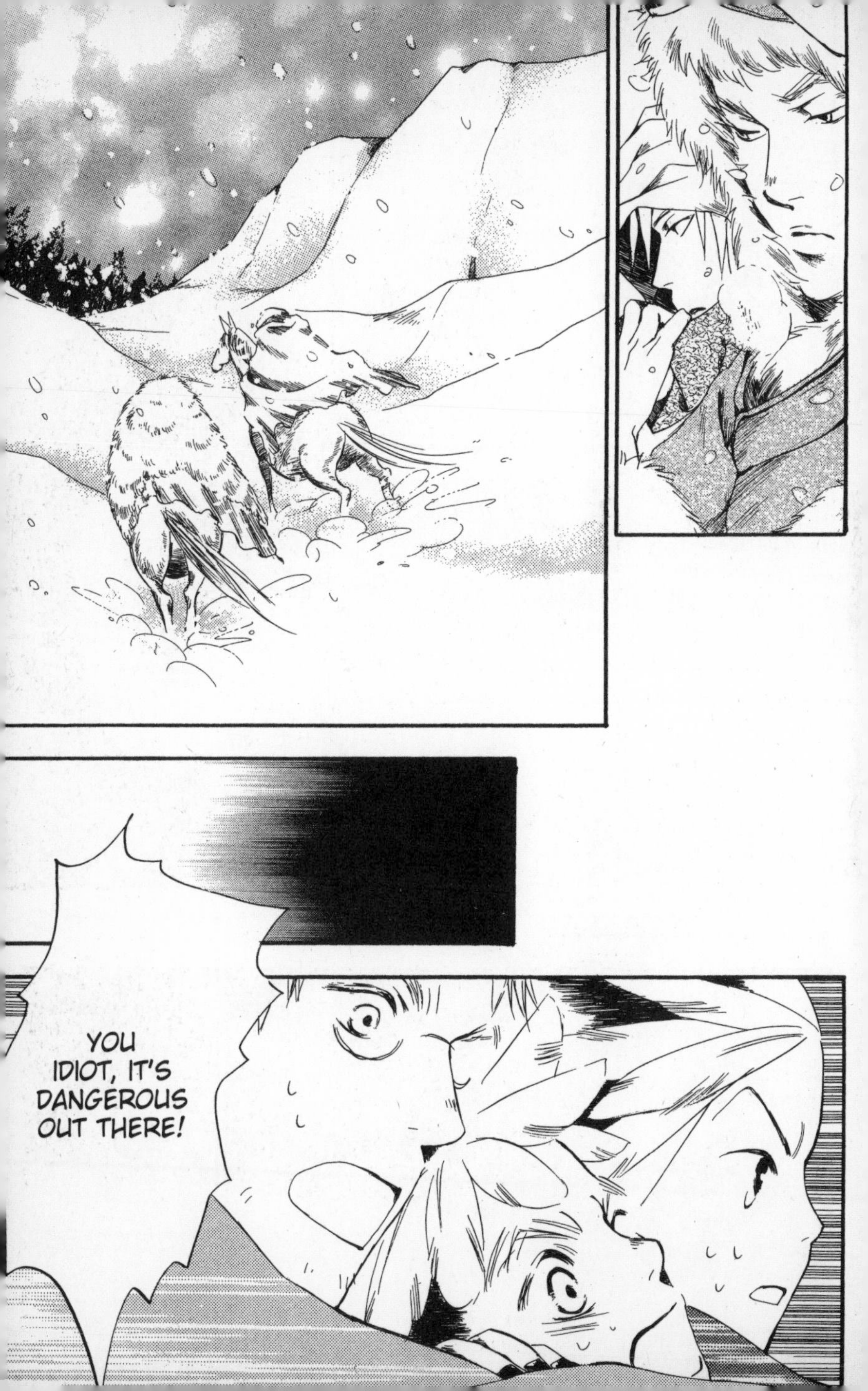
YOU IDIOT, IT'S DANGEROUS OUT THERE!

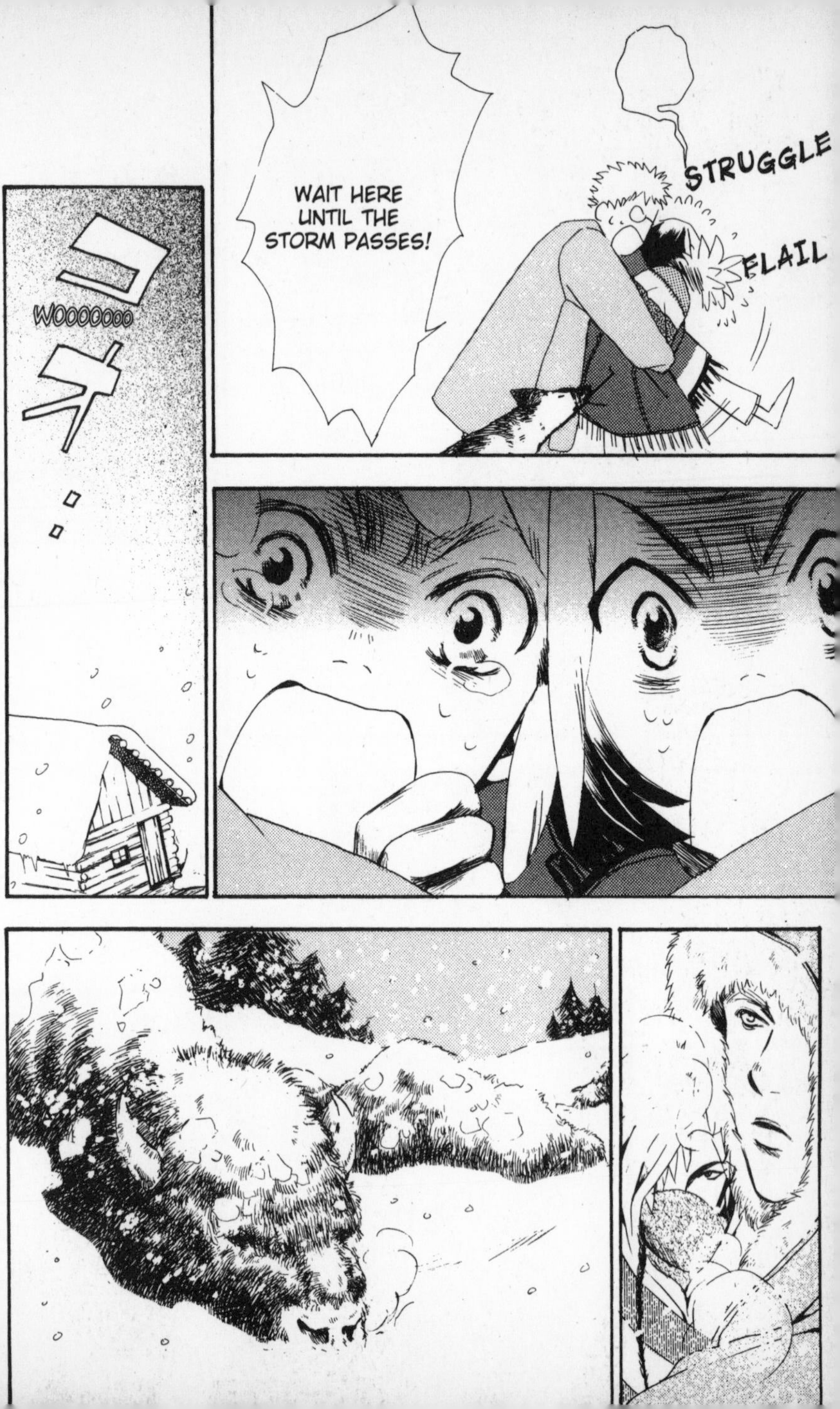
STRUGGLE
FLAIL
WAIT HERE UNTIL THE STORM PASSES!
WOOOOOOO

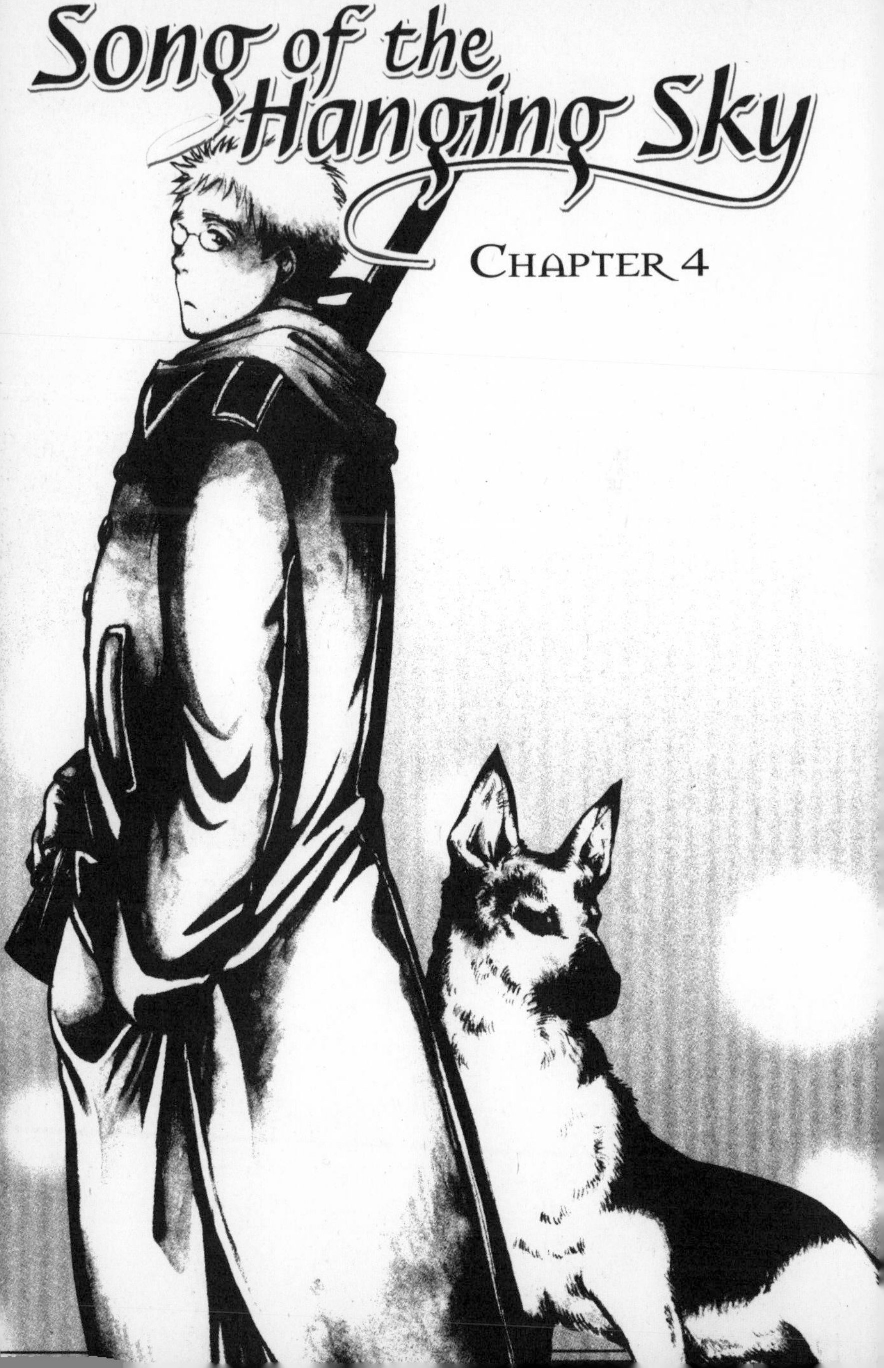
Song of the Hanging Sky
Chapter 4

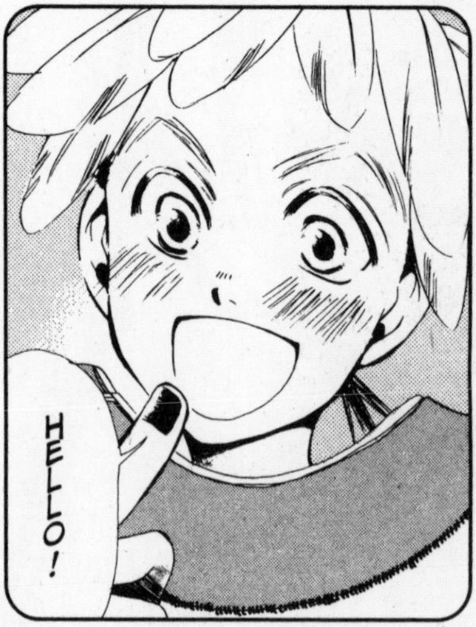
HELLO!

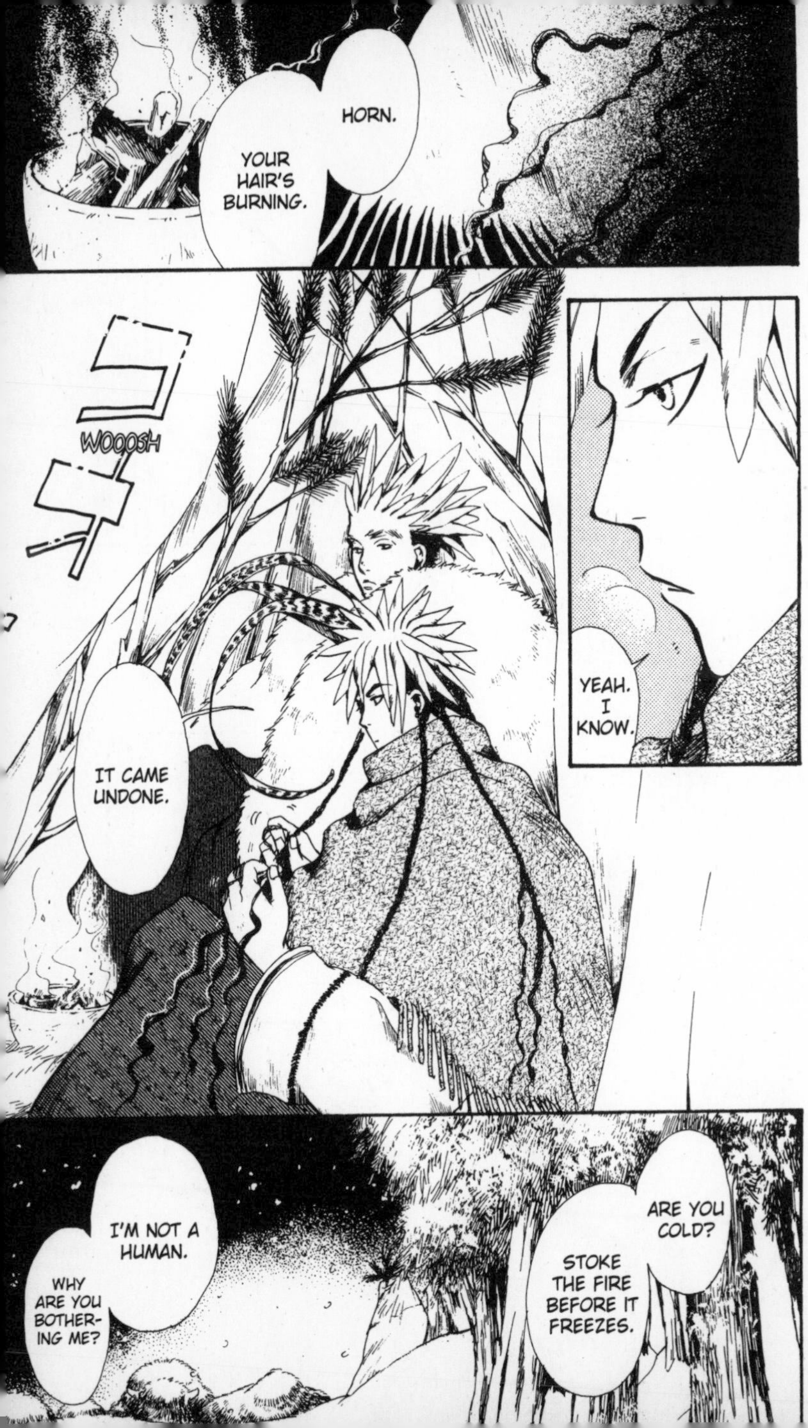
HORN.
YOUR HAIR'S BURNING.
YEAH. I KNOW.
WOOOSH
IT CAME UNDONE.
ARE YOU COLD?
STOKE THE FIRE BEFORE IT FREEZES.
I'M NOT A HUMAN.
WHY ARE YOU BOTHERING ME?

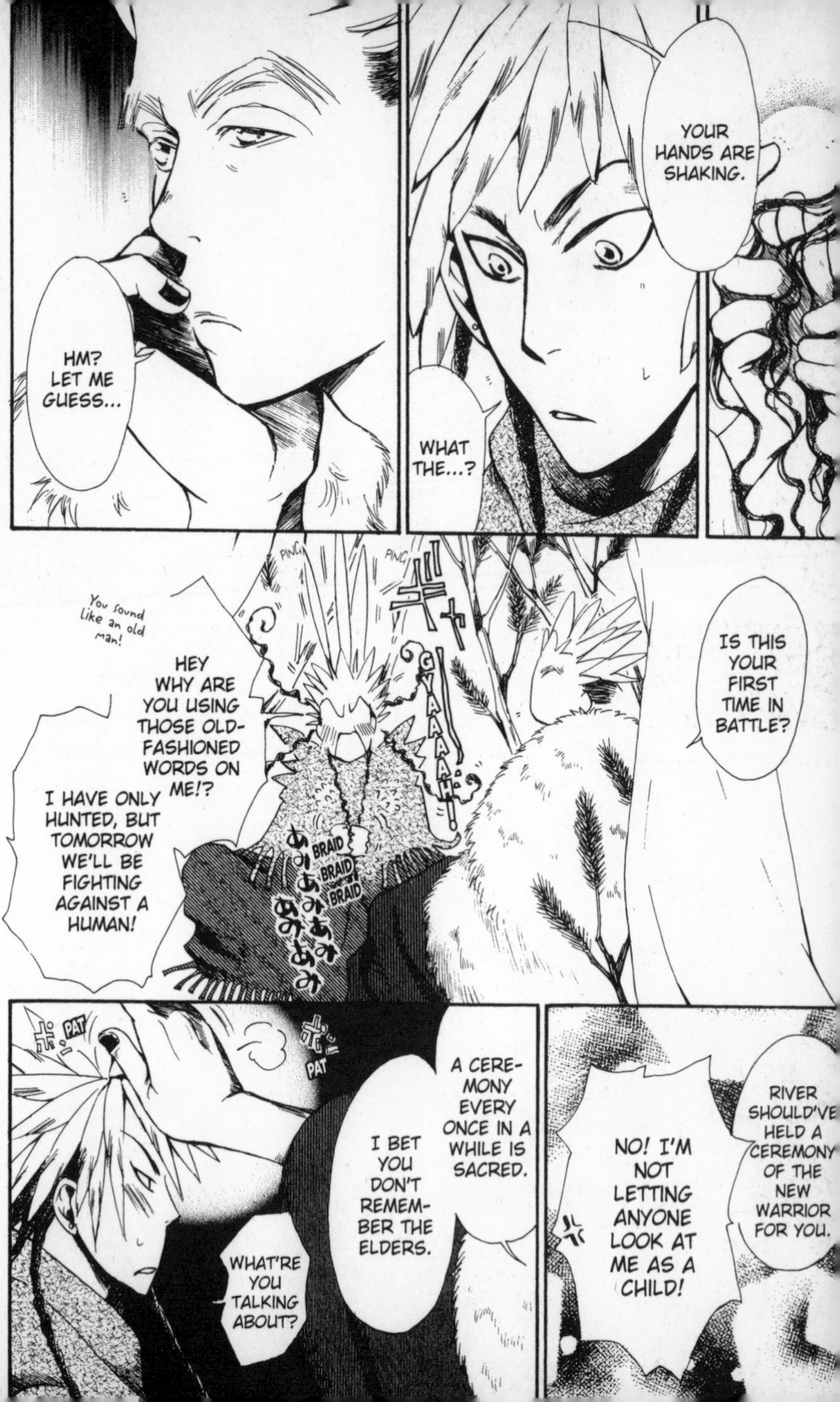
YOUR HANDS ARE SHAKING.
WHAT THE...?
HM? LET ME GUESS...
IS THIS YOUR FIRST TIME IN BATTLE?
PING
PING
GYAAAAAH!
HEY WHY ARE YOU USING THOSE OLD-FASHIONED WORDS ON ME!?
You sound like an old man!
I HAVE ONLY HUNTED, BUT TOMORROW WE'LL BE FIGHTING AGAINST A HUMAN!
BRAID BRAID BRAID
RIVER SHOULD'VE HELD A CEREMONY OF THE NEW WARRIOR FOR YOU.
NO! I'M NOT LETTING ANYONE LOOK AT ME AS A CHILD!
A CERE-MONY EVERY ONCE IN A WHILE IS SACRED.
I BET YOU DON'T REMEM-BER THE ELDERS.
PAT
PAT
WHAT'RE YOU TALKING ABOUT?

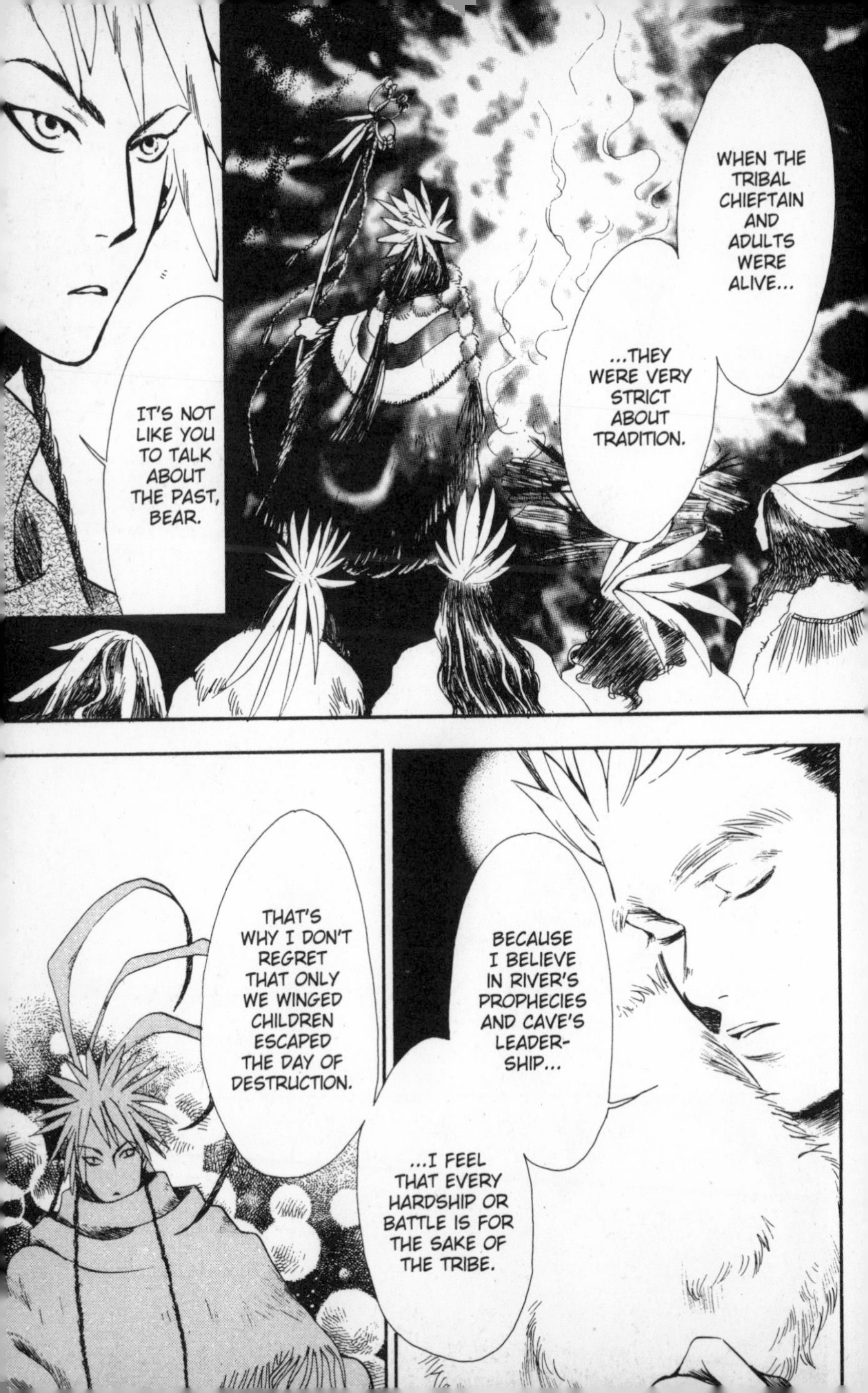
WHEN THE TRIBAL CHIEFTAIN AND ADULTS WERE ALIVE...
...THEY WERE VERY STRICT ABOUT TRADITION.
IT'S NOT LIKE YOU TO TALK ABOUT THE PAST, BEAR.
BECAUSE I BELIEVE IN RIVER'S PROPHECIES AND CAVE'S LEADER-SHIP...
...I FEEL THAT EVERY HARDSHIP OR BATTLE IS FOR THE SAKE OF THE TRIBE.
THAT'S WHY I DON'T REGRET THAT ONLY WE WINGED CHILDREN ESCAPED THE DAY OF DESTRUCTION.

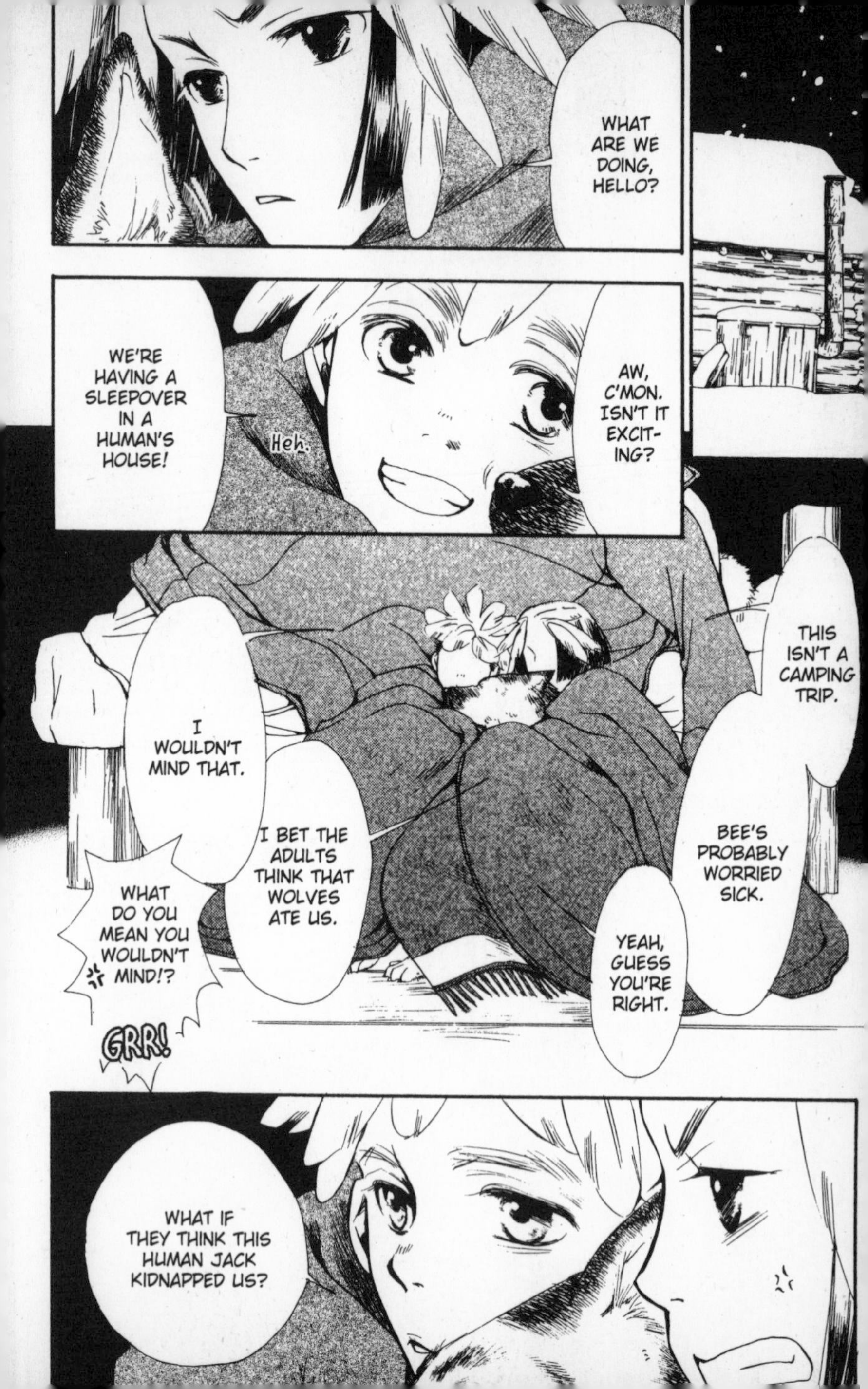
WHAT ARE WE DOING, HELLO?
AW, C'MON. ISN'T IT EXCIT-ING?
WE'RE HAVING A SLEEPOVER IN A HUMAN'S HOUSE!
Heh.
THIS ISN'T A CAMPING TRIP.
I WOULDN'T MIND THAT.
BEE'S PROBABLY WORRIED SICK.
YEAH, GUESS YOU'RE RIGHT.
I BET THE ADULTS THINK THAT WOLVES ATE US.
WHAT DO YOU MEAN YOU WOULDN'T MIND!?
GRR!
WHAT IF THEY THINK THIS HUMAN JACK KIDNAPPED US?

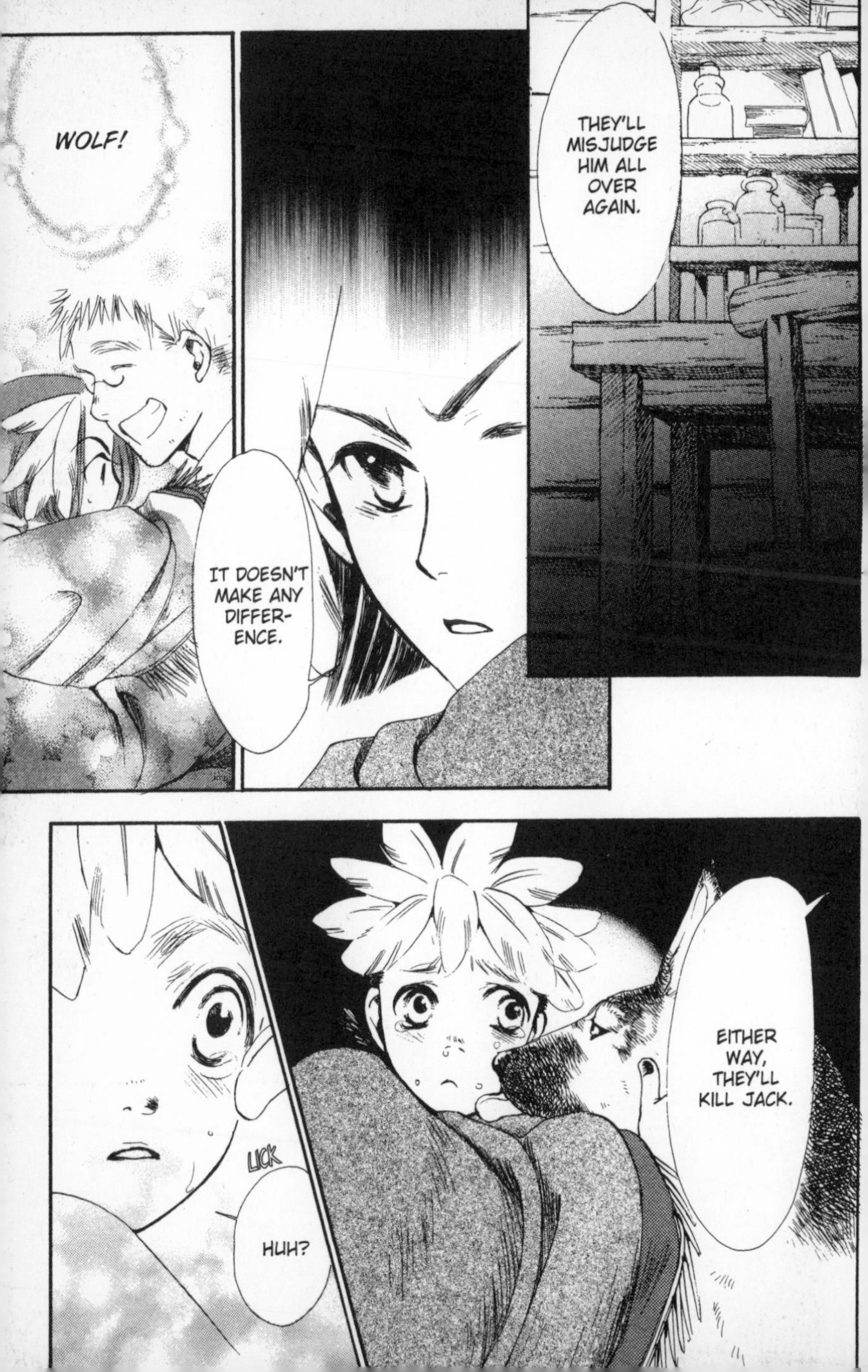
THEY'LL MISJUDGE HIM ALL OVER AGAIN.
IT DOESN'T MAKE ANY DIFFER-ENCE.
WOLF!
EITHER WAY, THEY'LL KILL JACK.
LICK
HUH?

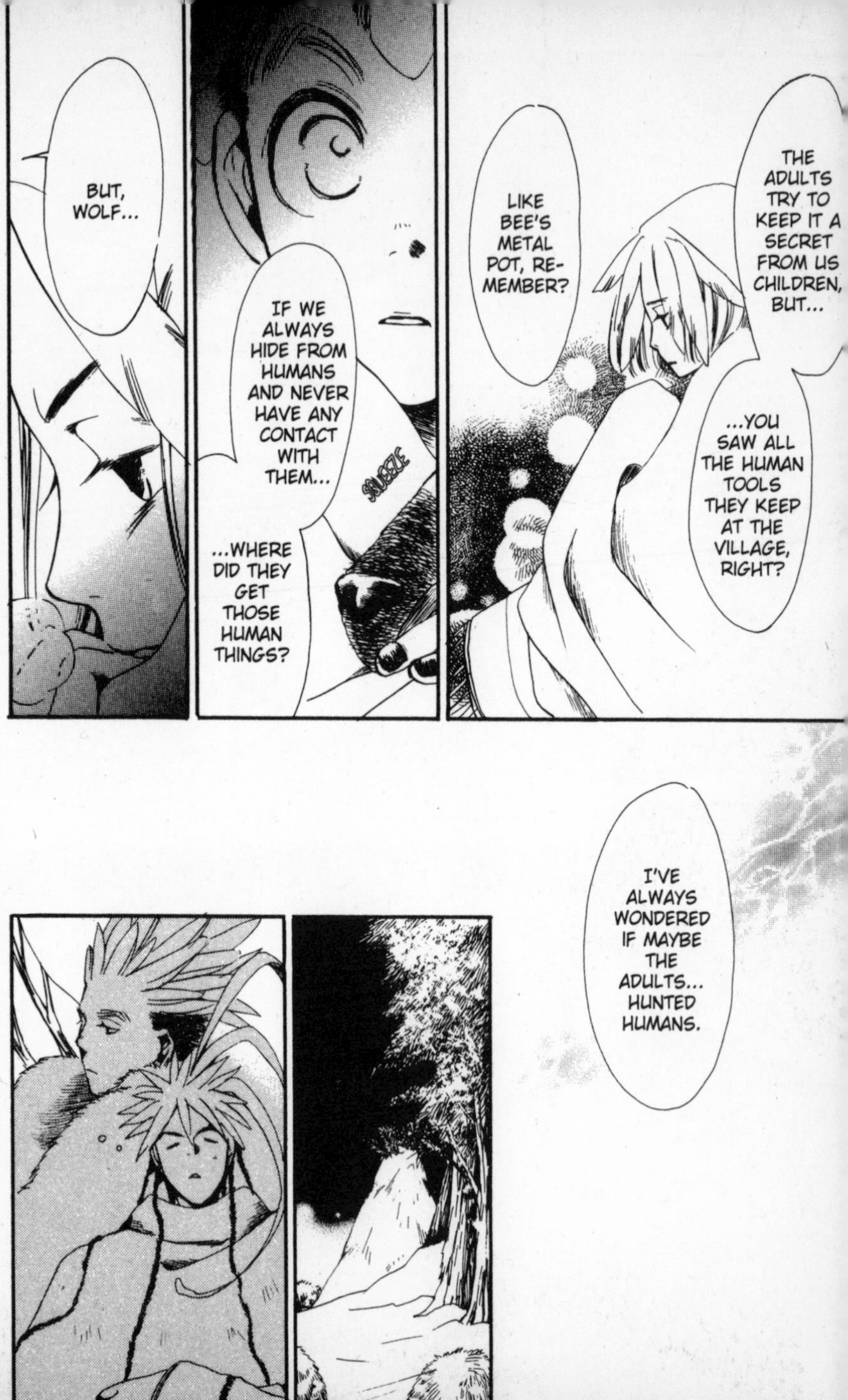
THE ADULTS TRY TO KEEP IT A SECRET FROM US CHILDREN, BUT...
...YOU SAW ALL THE HUMAN TOOLS THEY KEEP AT THE VILLAGE, RIGHT?
LIKE BEE'S METAL POT, RE-MEMBER?
IF WE ALWAYS HIDE FROM HUMANS AND NEVER HAVE ANY CONTACT WITH THEM...
SQUEEZE
...WHERE DID THEY GET THOSE HUMAN THINGS?
BUT, WOLF...
I'VE ALWAYS WONDERED IF MAYBE THE ADULTS... HUNTED HUMANS.

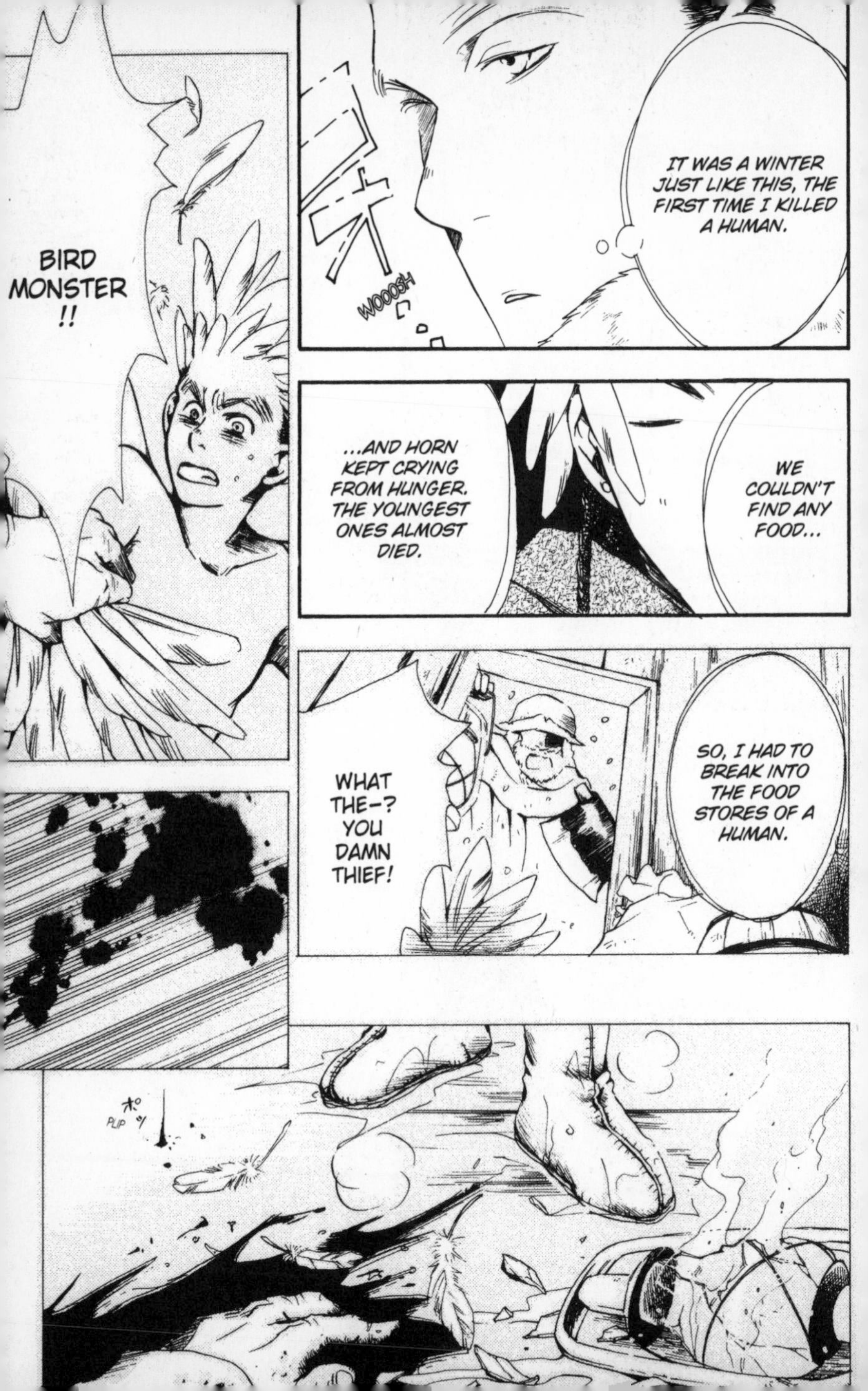
IT WAS A WINTER JUST LIKE THIS, THE FIRST TIME I KILLED A HUMAN.
WOOOSH
WE COULDN'T FIND ANY FOOD...
...AND HORN KEPT CRYING FROM HUNGER. THE YOUNGEST ONES ALMOST DIED.
SO, I HAD TO BREAK INTO THE FOOD STORES OF A HUMAN.
WHAT THE-? YOU DAMN THIEF!
BIRD MONSTER !!
PLIP

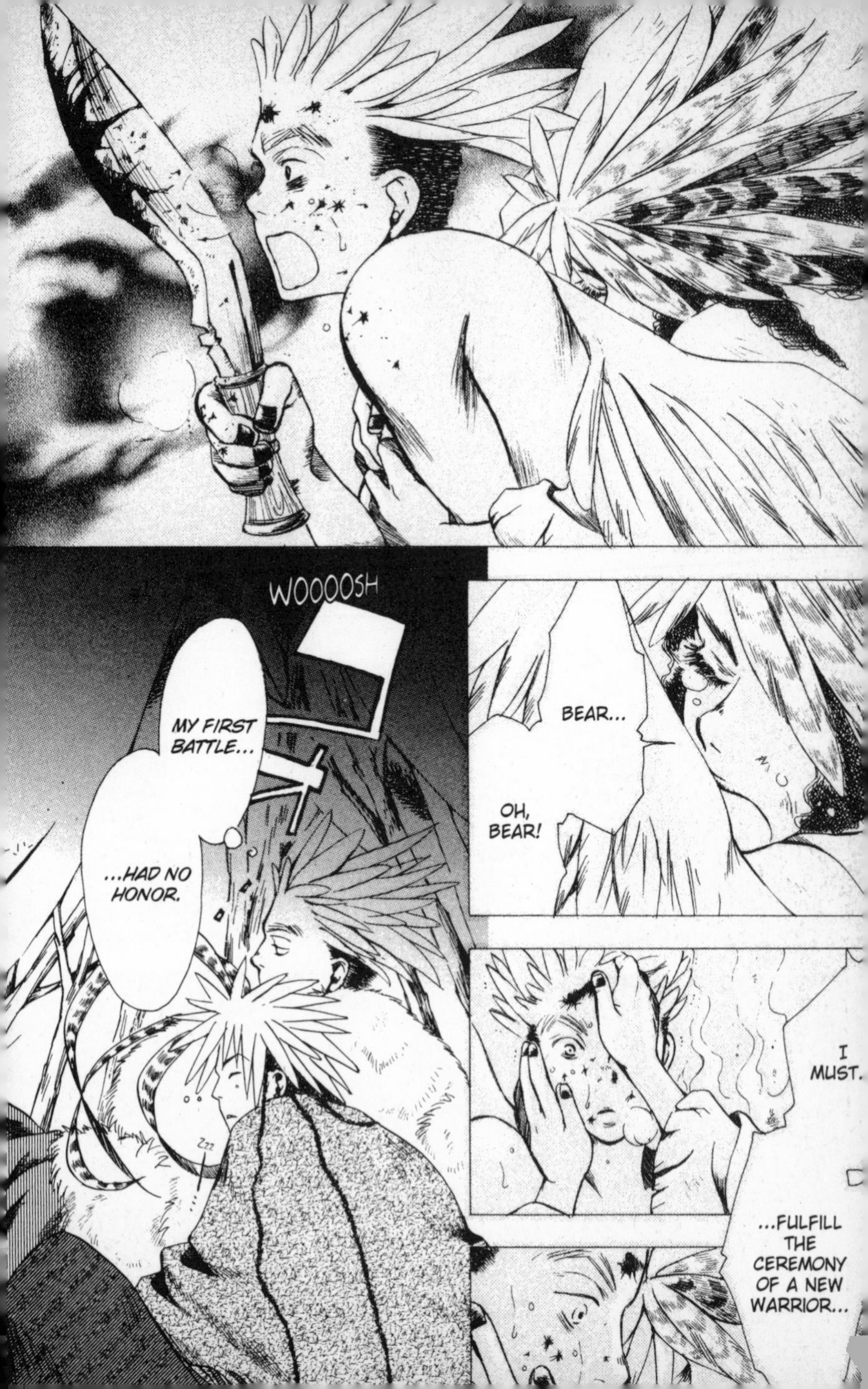
BEAR...
OH, BEAR!
I MUST.
...FULFILL THE CEREMONY OF A NEW WARRIOR...
WOOOOSH
MY FIRST BATTLE...
...HAD NO HONOR.

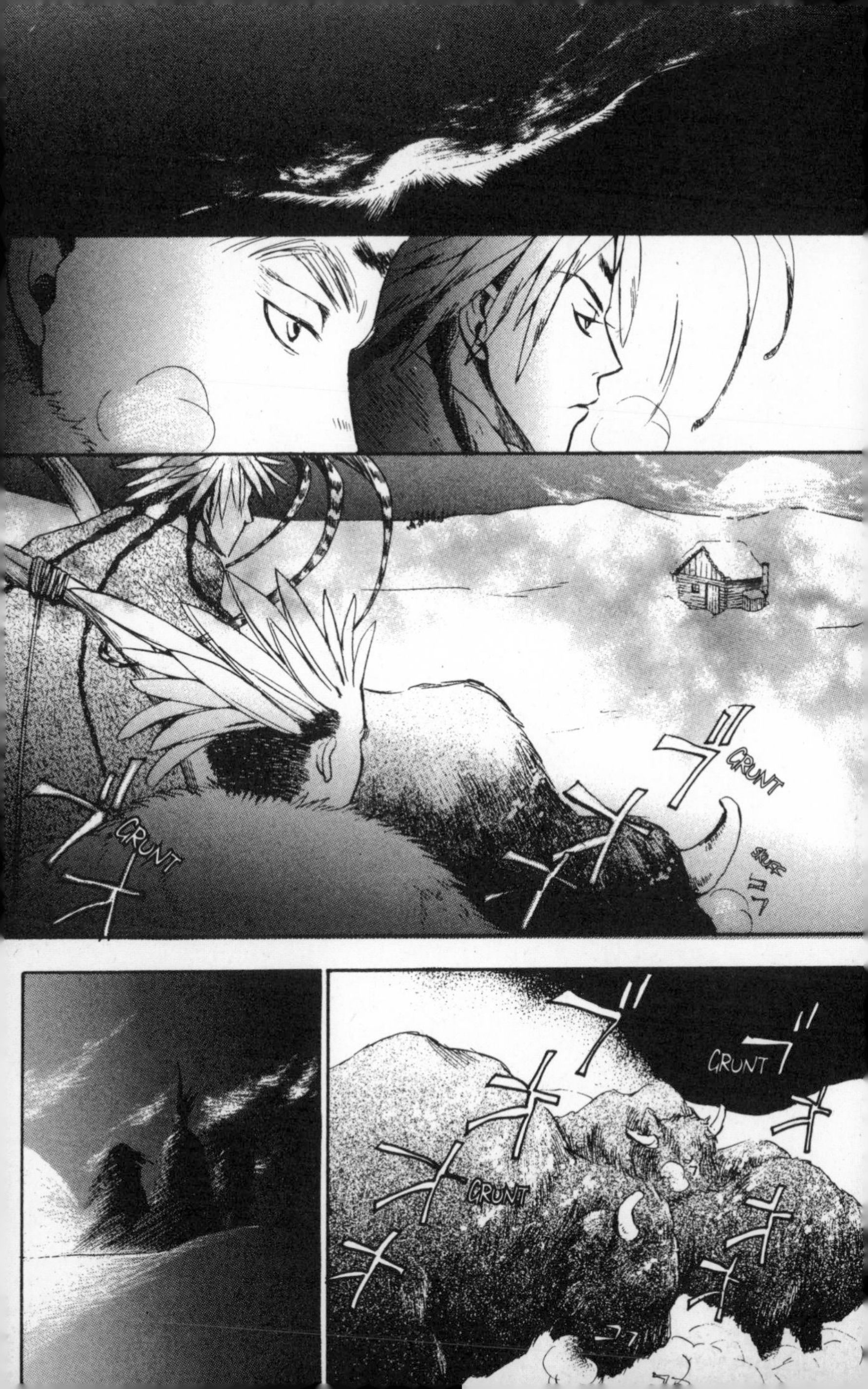
GRUNT
SNUFF
GRUNT
GRUNT
GRUNT

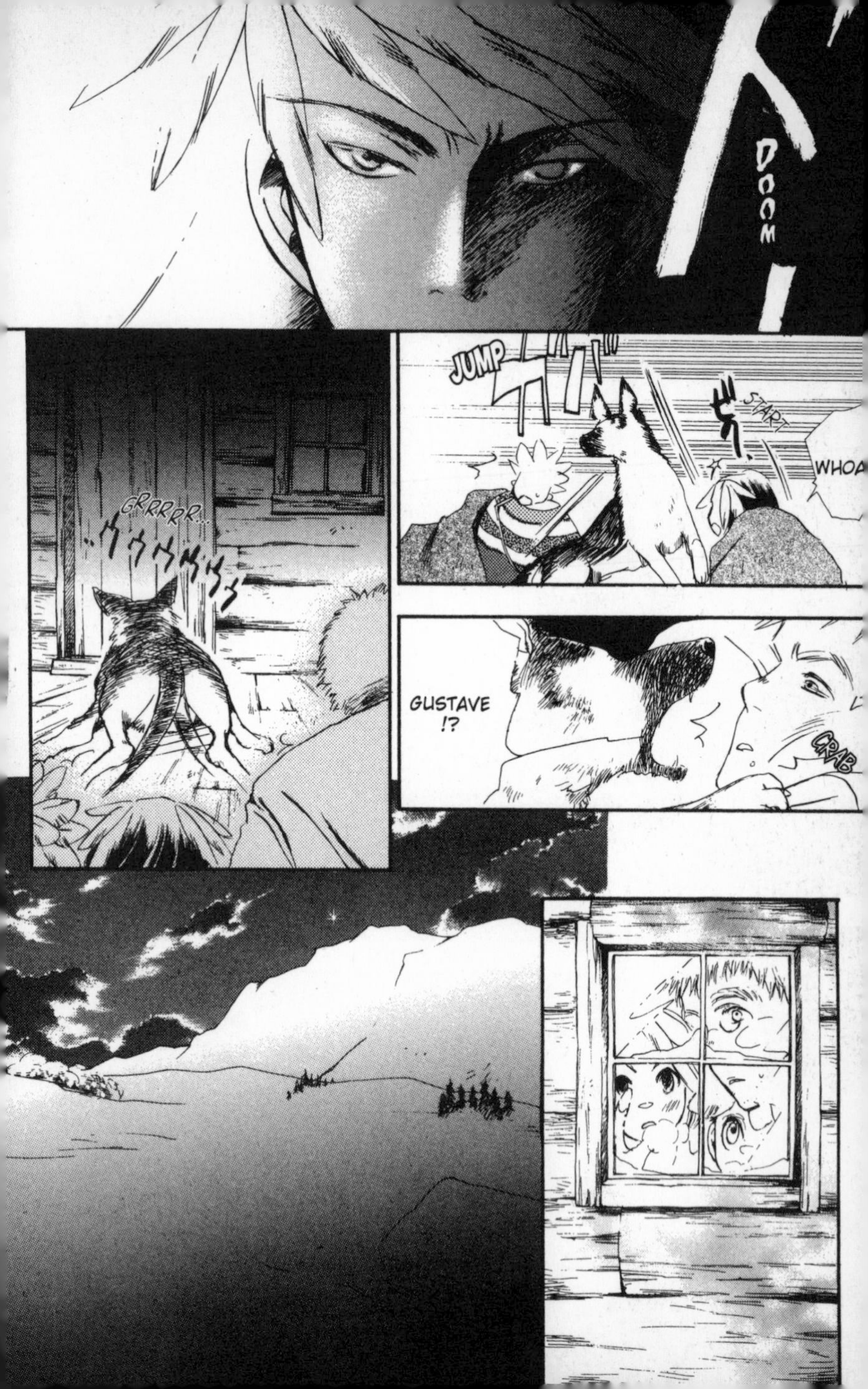
DOOM
JUMP
START
WHOA
GUSTAVE !?
GRAB
GRRRRR...

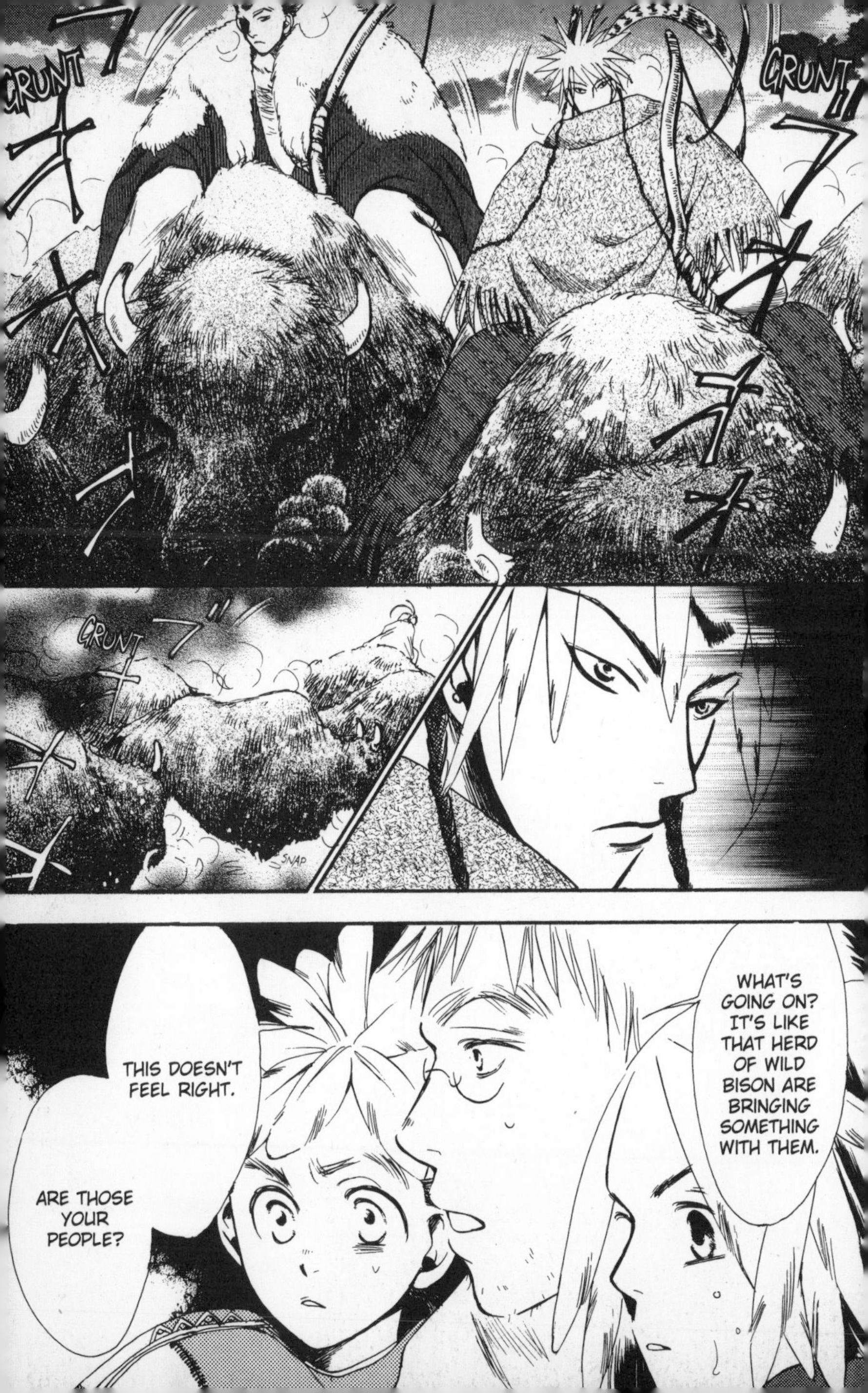
GRUNT
GRUNT
GRUNT
SNAP
WHAT'S GOING ON? IT'S LIKE THAT HERD OF WILD BISON ARE BRINGING SOMETHING WITH THEM.
THIS DOESN'T FEEL RIGHT.
ARE THOSE YOUR PEOPLE?

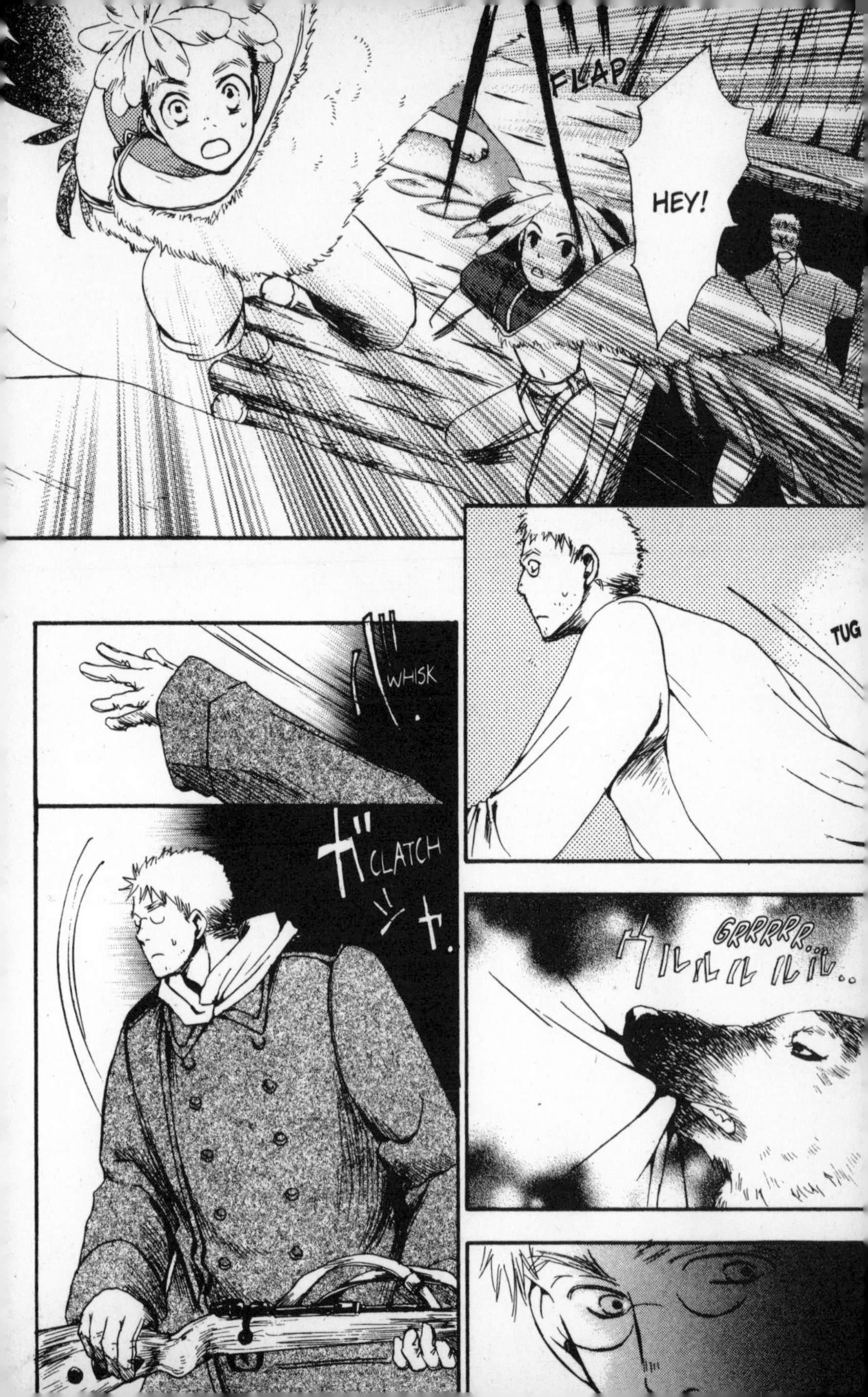
FLAP
HEY!
TUG
GRRRRR..
WHISK
CLATCH

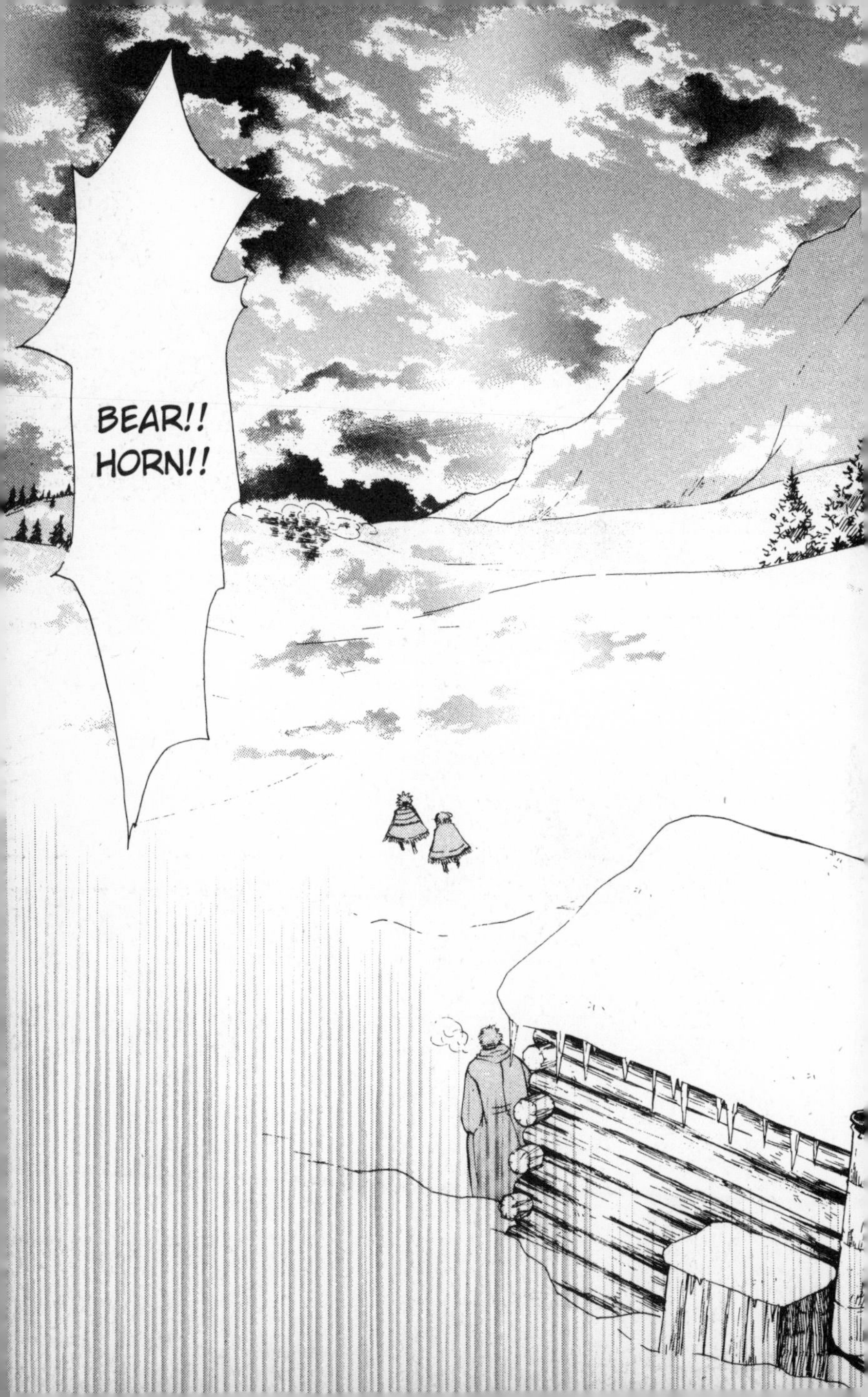
BEAR!! HORN!!

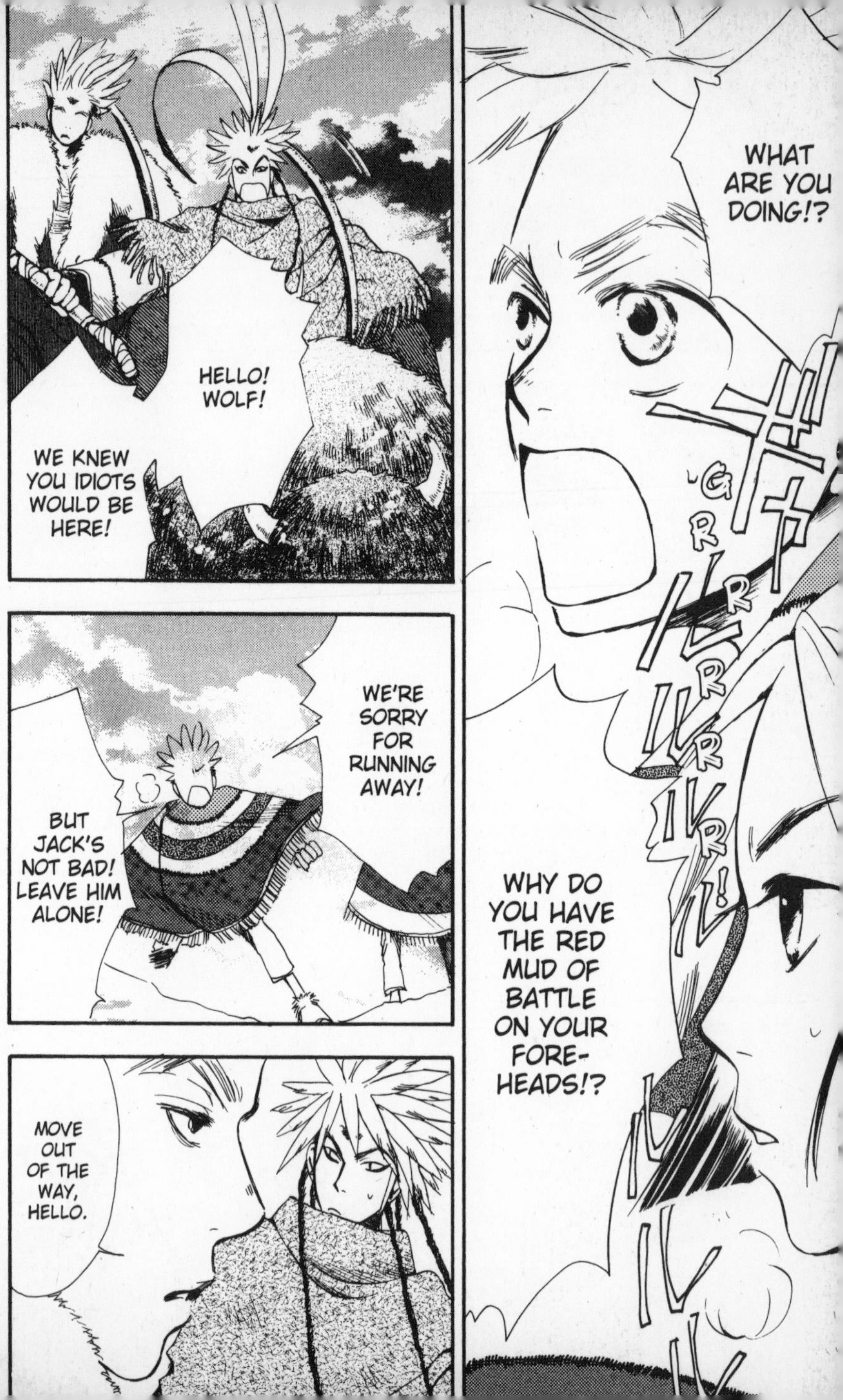
HELLO! WOLF!
WE KNEW YOU IDIOTS WOULD BE HERE!
WE'RE SORRY FOR RUNNING AWAY!
BUT JACK'S NOT BAD! LEAVE HIM ALONE!
MOVE OUT OF THE WAY, HELLO.
WHAT ARE YOU DOING!?
WHY DO YOU HAVE THE RED MUD OF BATTLE ON YOUR FORE-HEADS!?
GRRRRRRR!

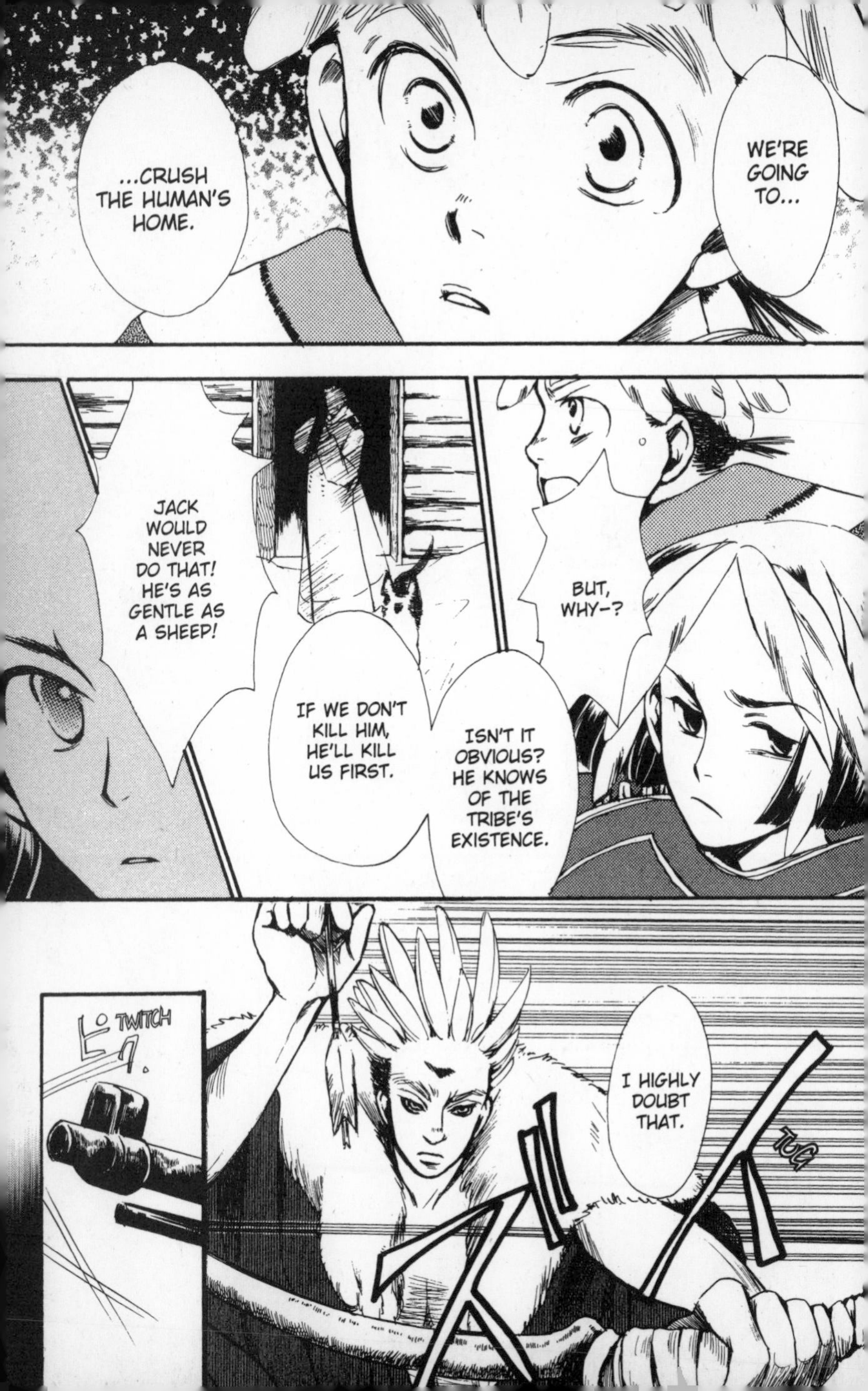
WE'RE GOING TO...
...CRUSH THE HUMAN'S HOME.
BUT, WHY-?
ISN'T IT OBVIOUS? HE KNOWS OF THE TRIBE'S EXISTENCE.
IF WE DON'T KILL HIM, HE'LL KILL US FIRST.
JACK WOULD NEVER DO THAT! HE'S AS GENTLE AS A SHEEP!
I HIGHLY DOUBT THAT.
TUG
TWITCH

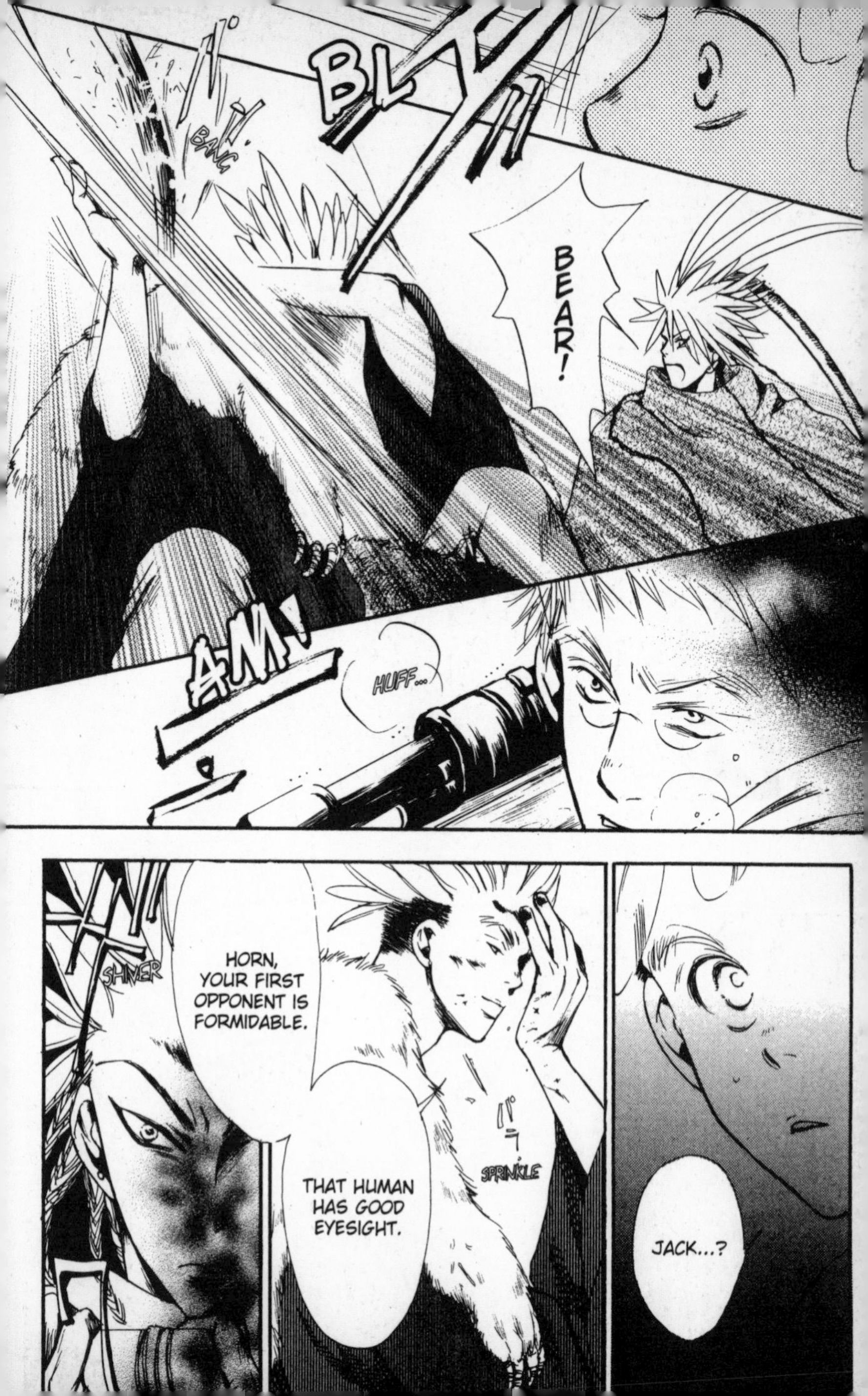
BLAM
BANG
BEAR!
HUFF...
JACK...?
SPRINKLE
HORN, YOUR FIRST OPPONENT IS FORMIDABLE.
THAT HUMAN HAS GOOD EYESIGHT.
SHIVER

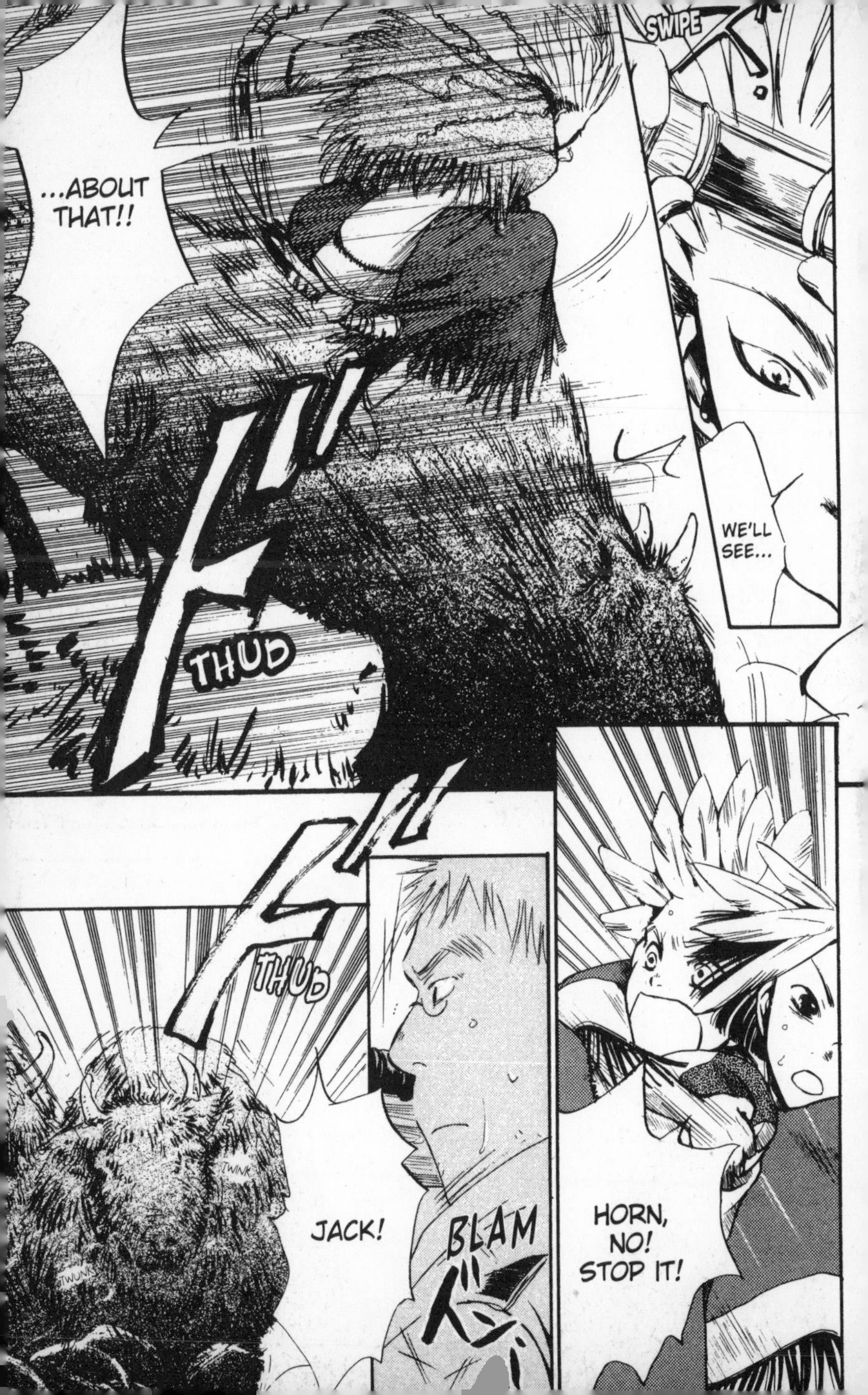
SWIPE
WE'LL SEE...
...ABOUT THAT!!
THUD
HORN, NO! STOP IT!
JACK!
BLAM
THUD
TWINK
TWUNK

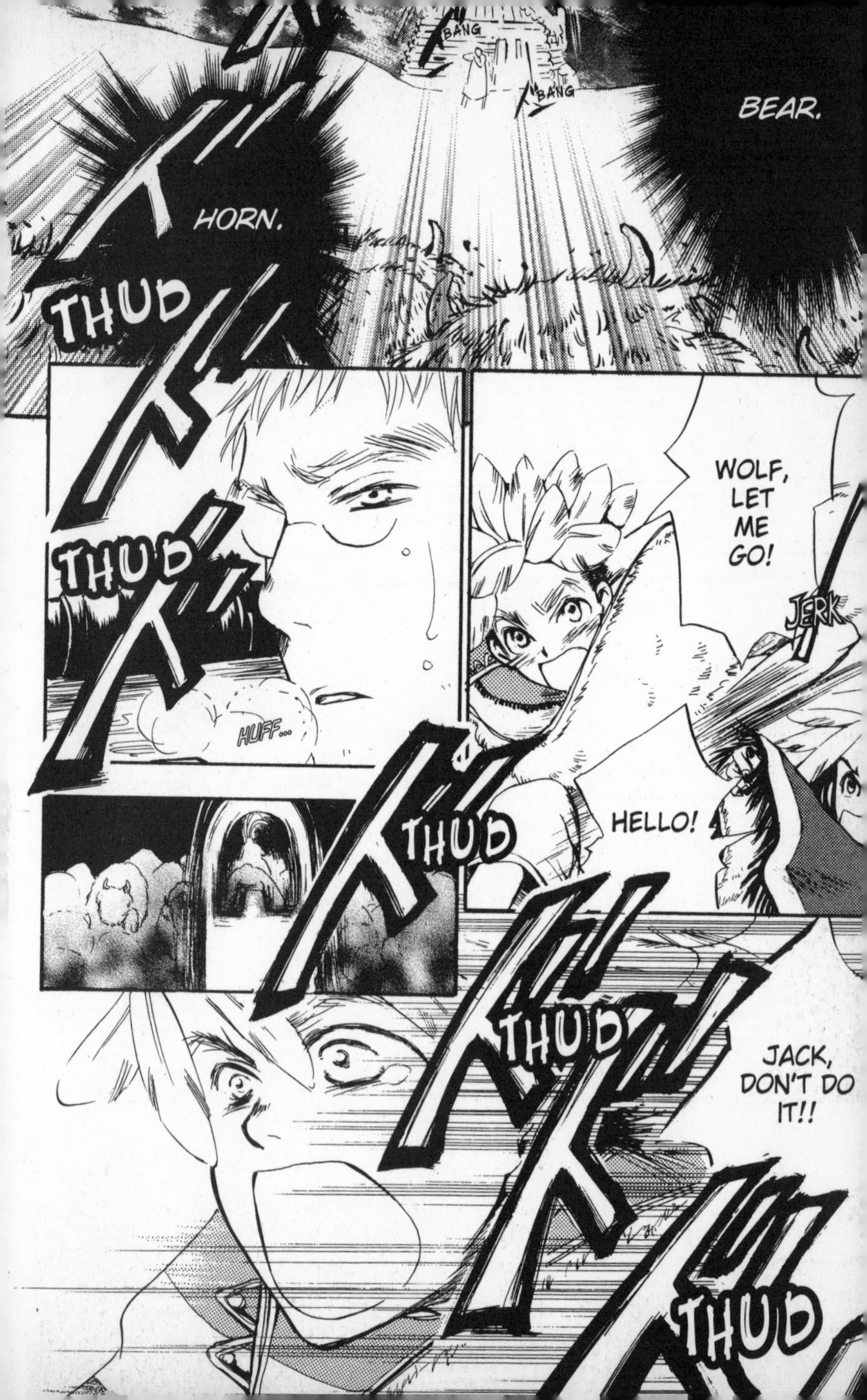
BANG
BANG
BEAR.
HORN.
THUD
WOLF, LET ME GO!
JERK
HELLO!
THUD
THUD
HUFF...
JACK, DON'T DO IT!!
THUD
THUD

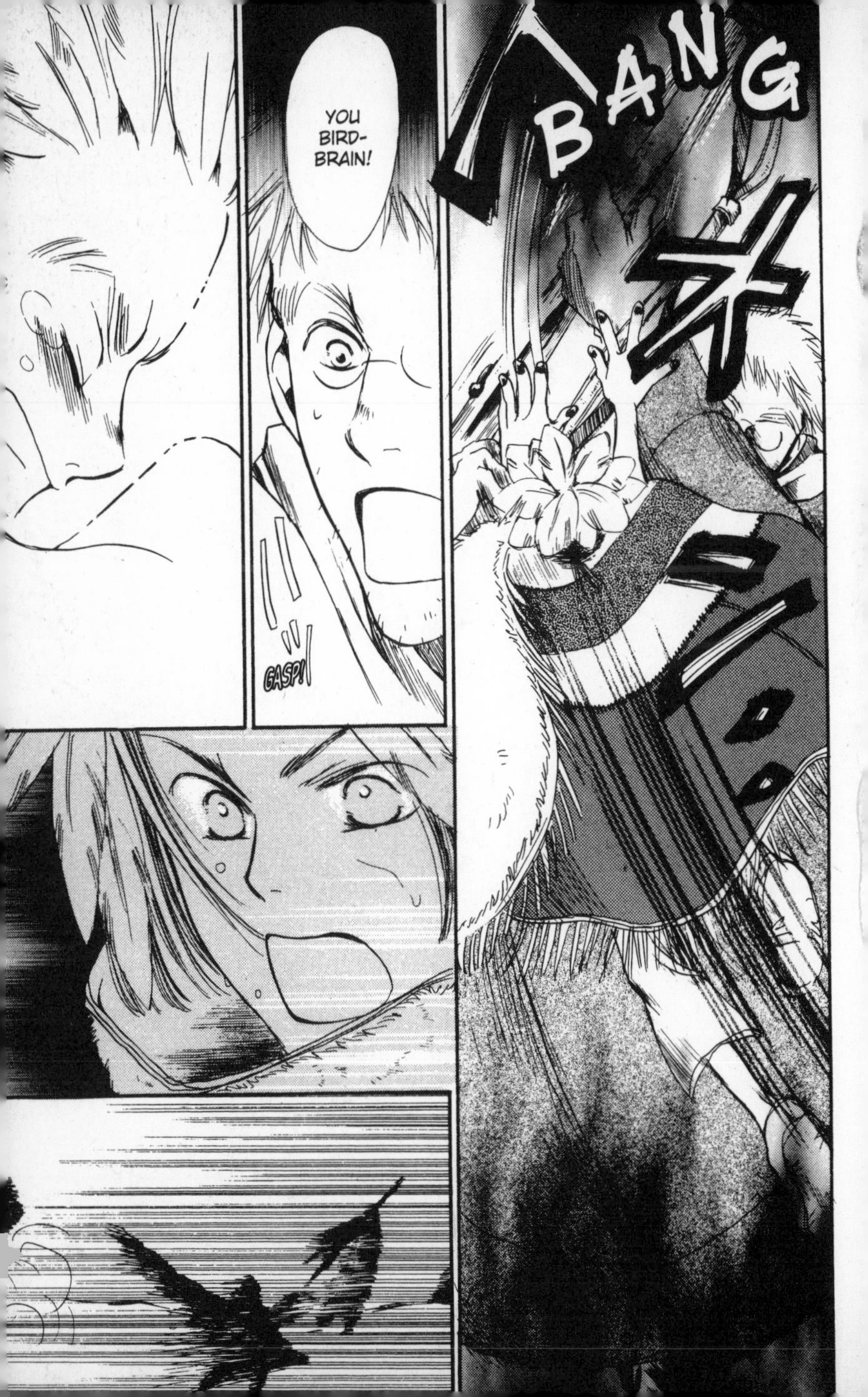
BANG
YOU BIRD-BRAIN!
GASP!

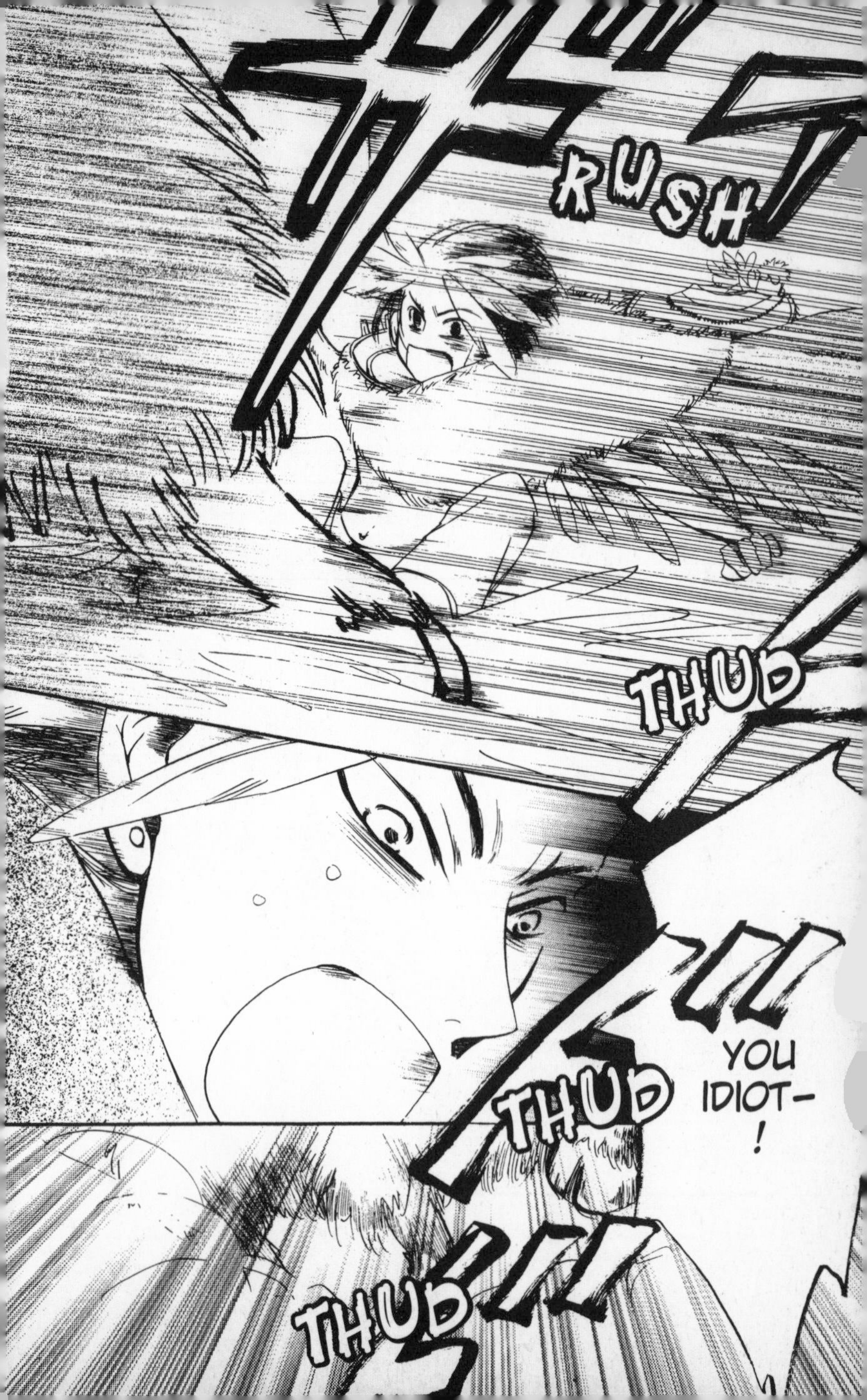
RUSH
THUD
YOU IDIOT-!
THUD
THUD

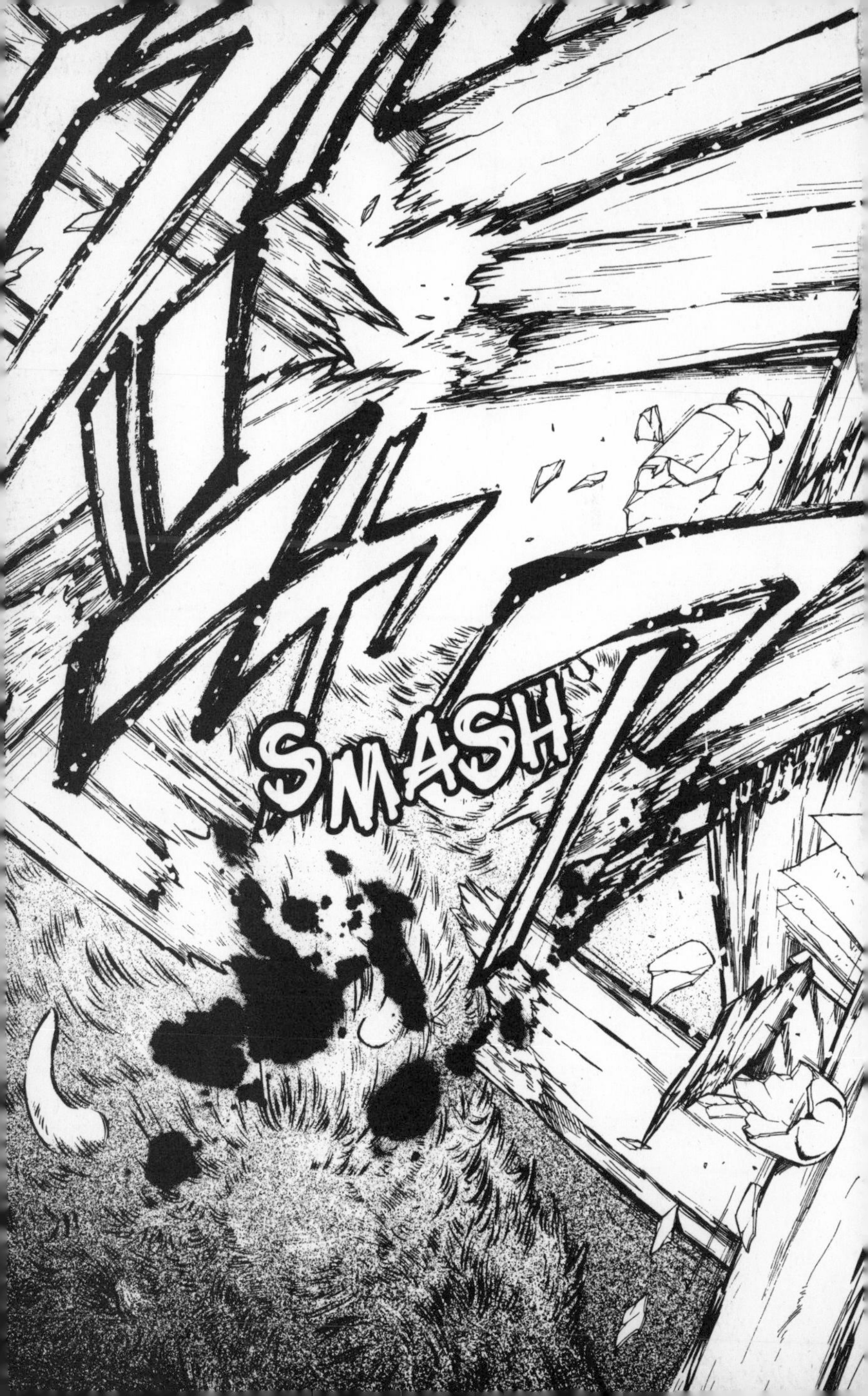
SMASH

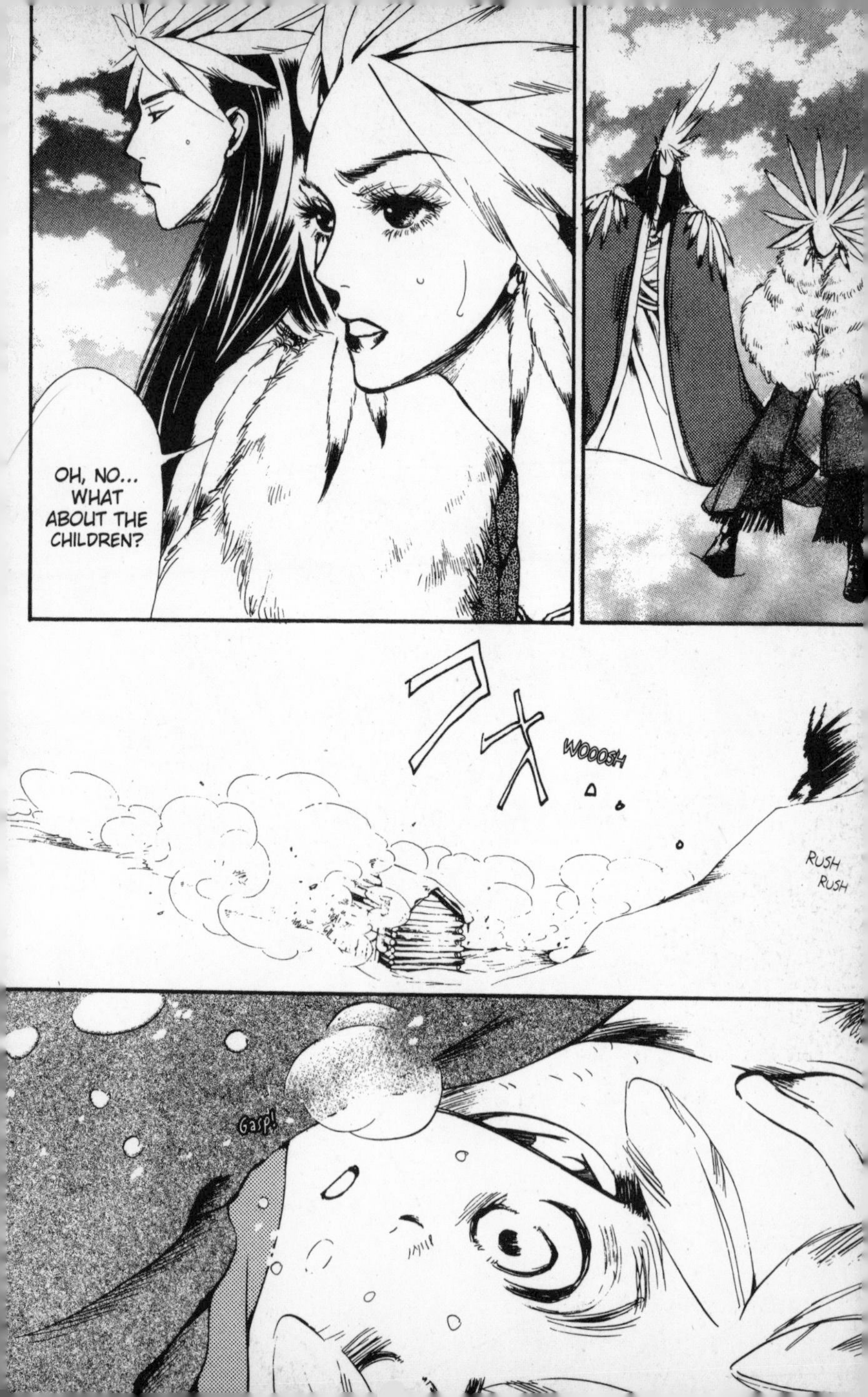
OH, NO... WHAT ABOUT THE CHILDREN?
RUSH RUSH
フォ
WOOOSH
Gasp!

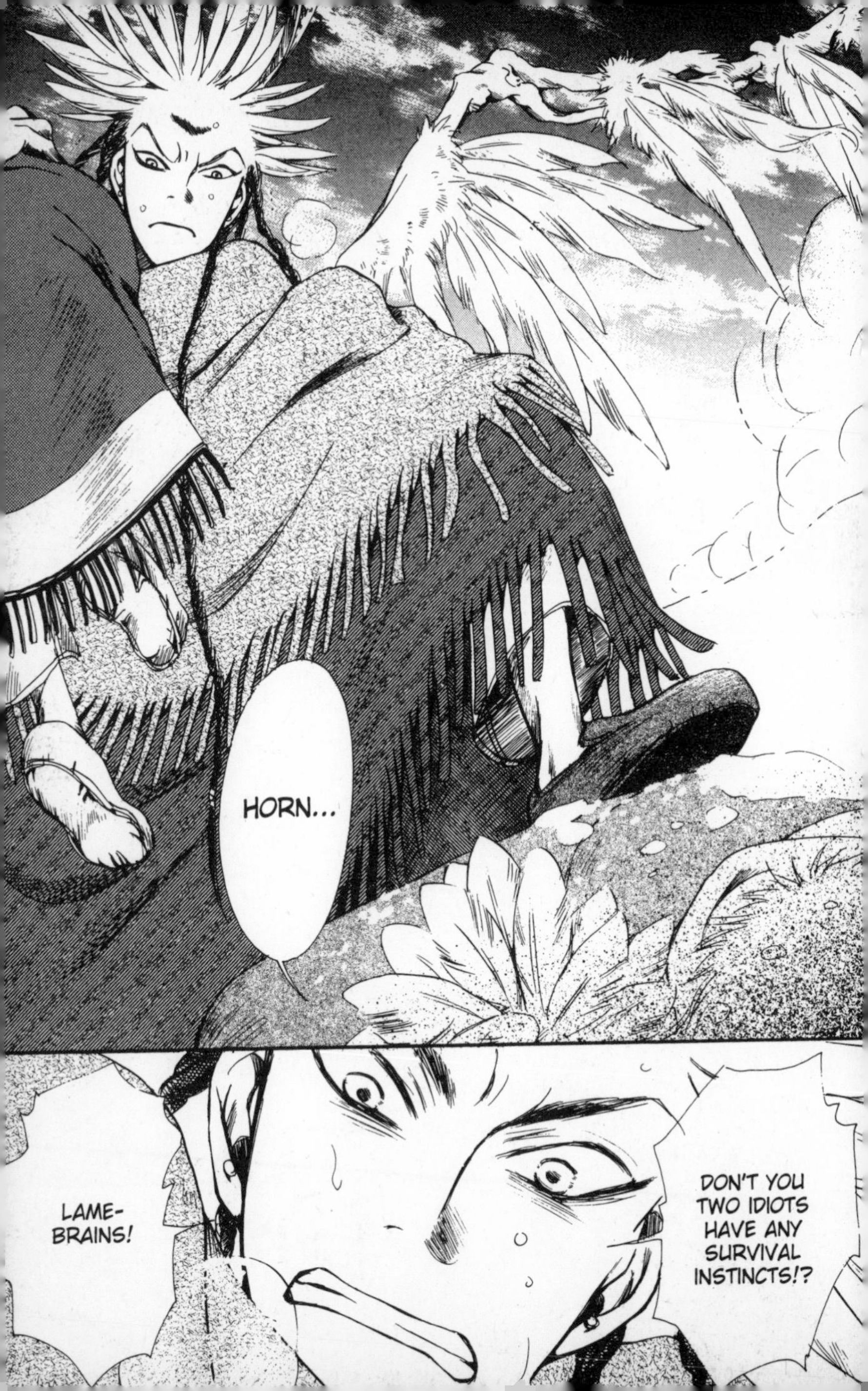
HORN...
DON'T YOU TWO IDIOTS HAVE ANY SURVIVAL INSTINCTS!?
LAME-BRAINS!

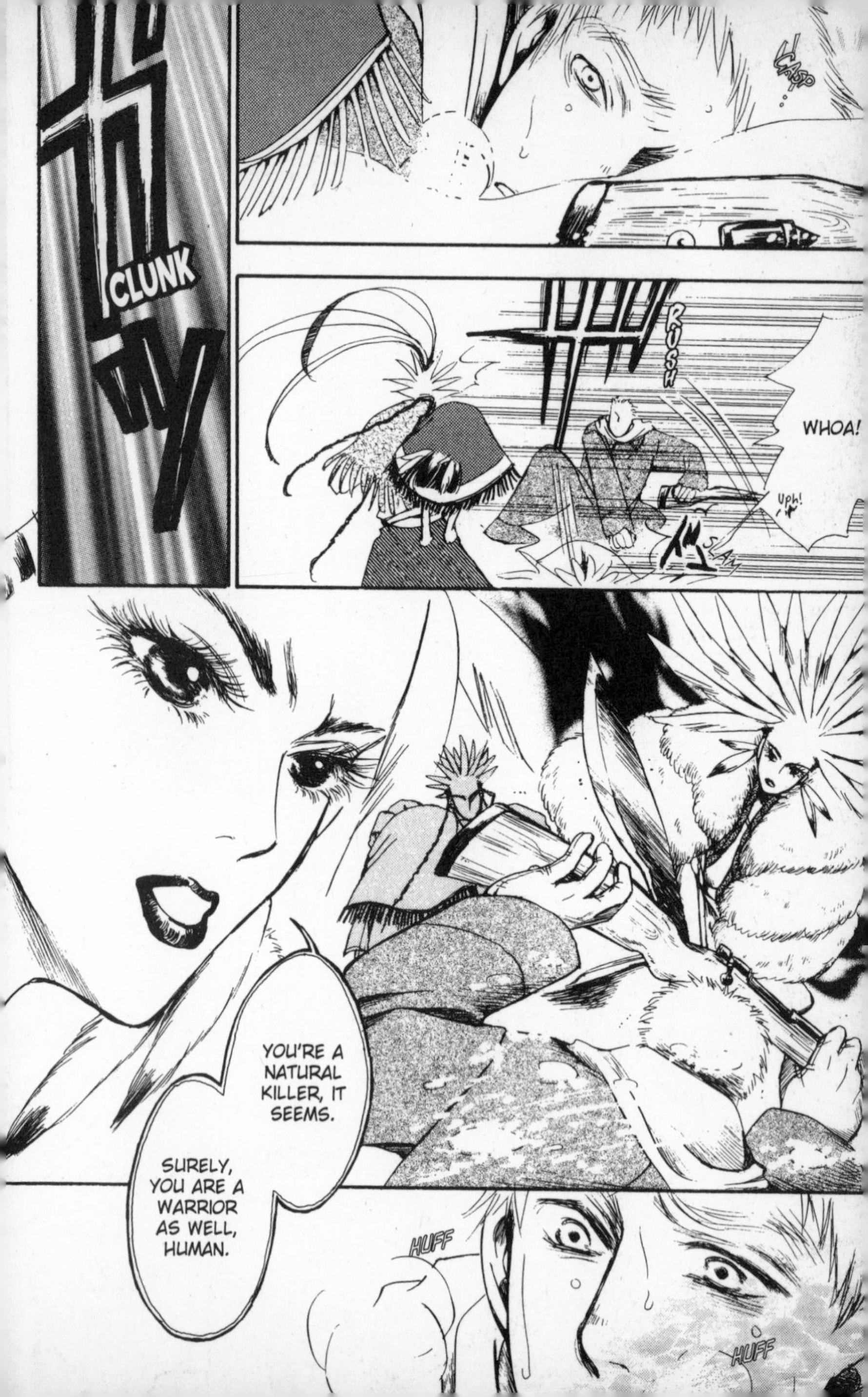
GASP!
RUSH
WHOA!
UPH!
SLAM
CLUNK
YOU'RE A NATURAL KILLER, IT SEEMS.
SURELY, YOU ARE A WARRIOR AS WELL, HUMAN.
HUFF
HUFF

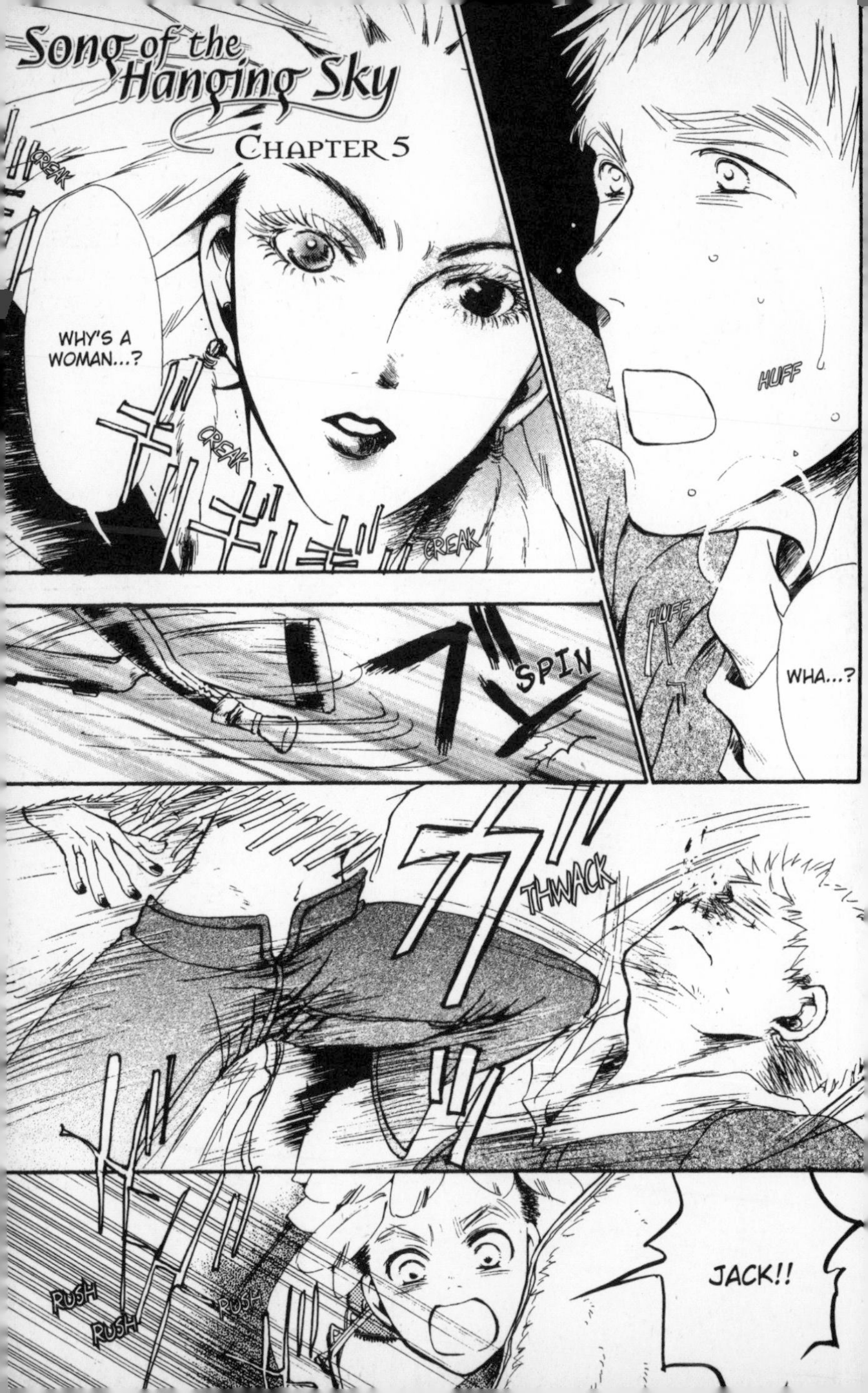
Song of the Hanging Sky
Chapter 5
HUFF
HUFF
WHA...?
CREAK
WHY'S A WOMAN...?
CREAK
CREAK
SPIN
THWACK
JACK!!
RUSH
RUSH
RUSH

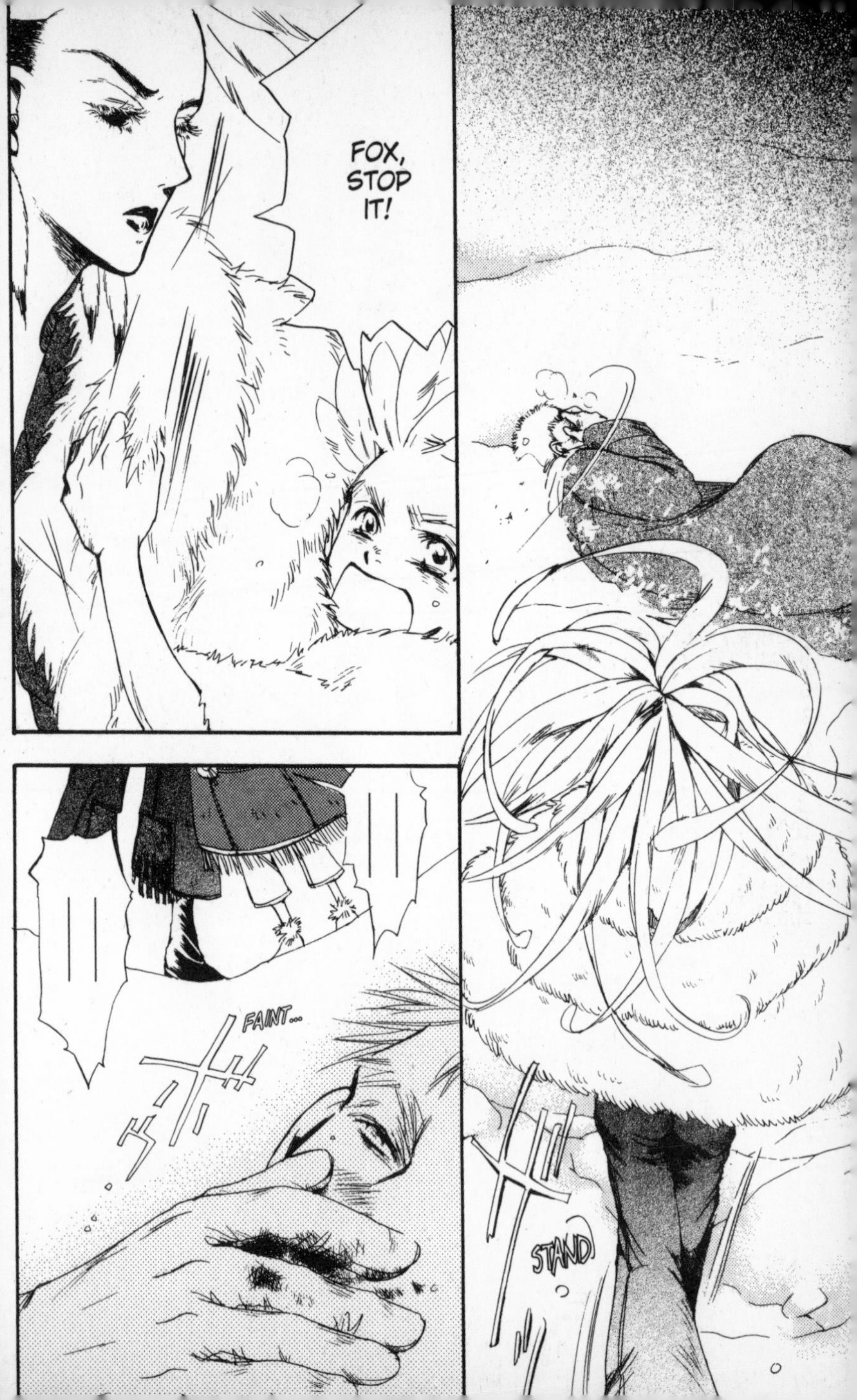
STAND
FOX, STOP IT!
FAINT...

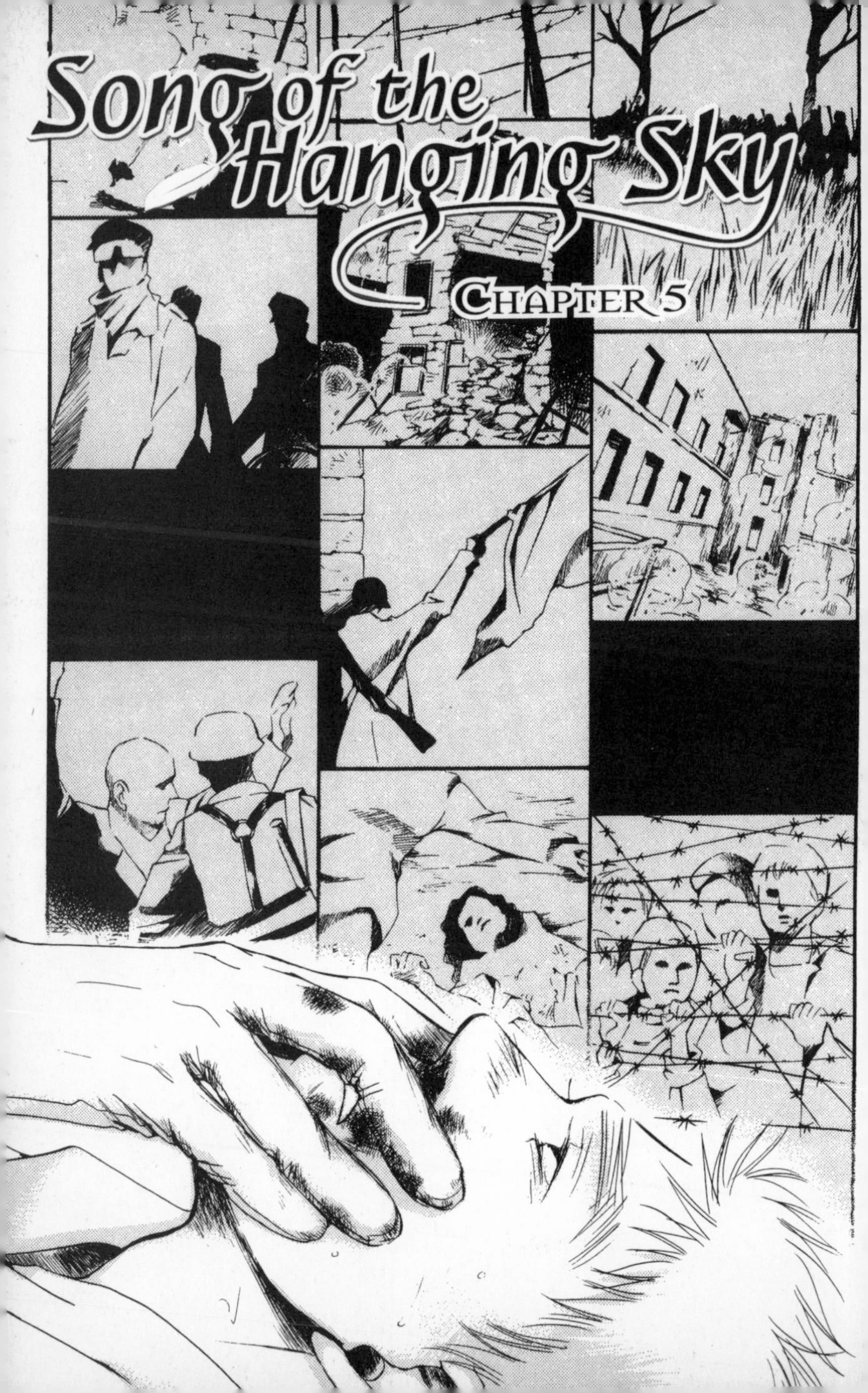
Song of the Hanging Sky
Chapter 5

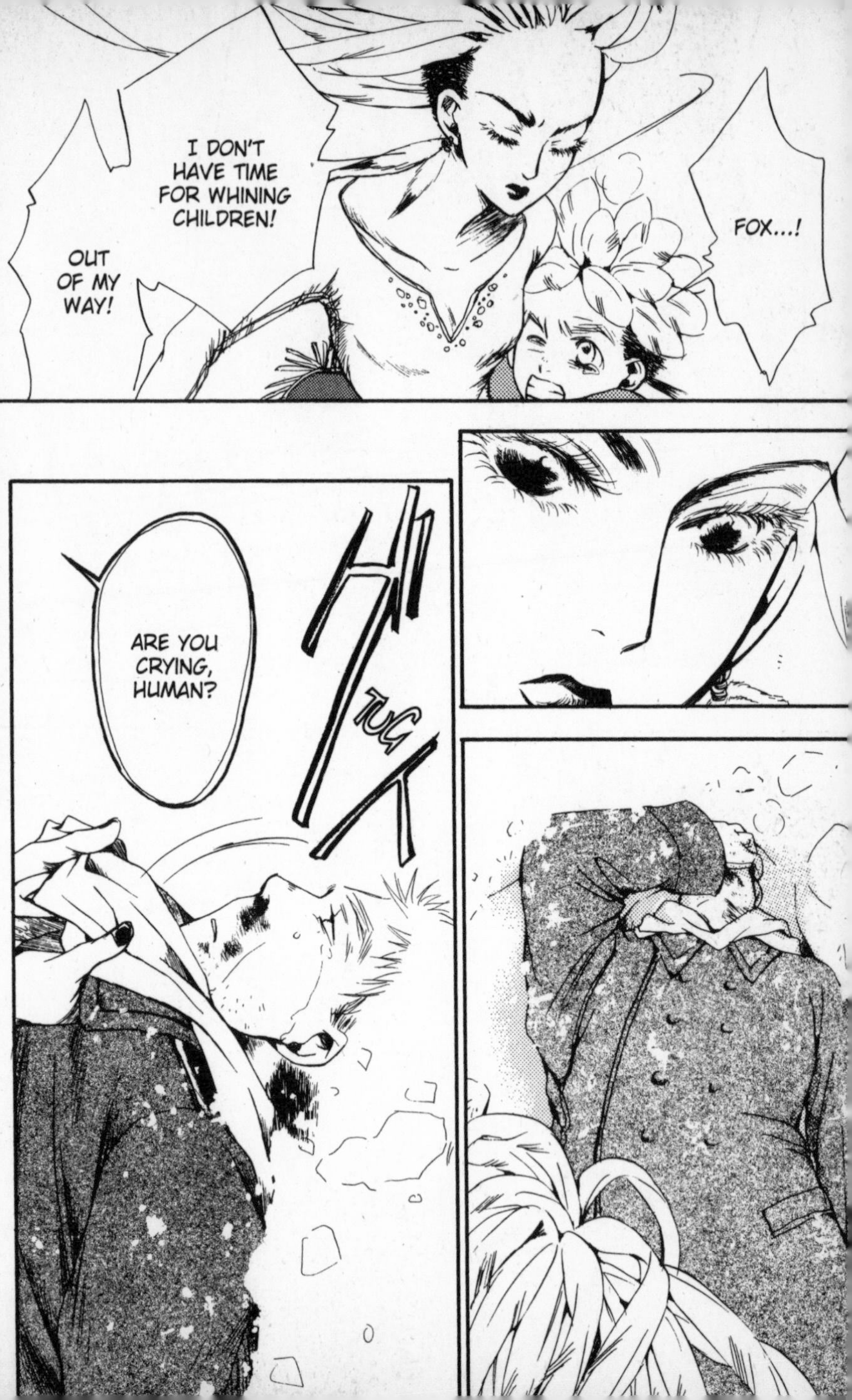
FOX...!
I DON'T HAVE TIME FOR WHINING CHILDREN!
OUT OF MY WAY!
TUG
ARE YOU CRYING, HUMAN?

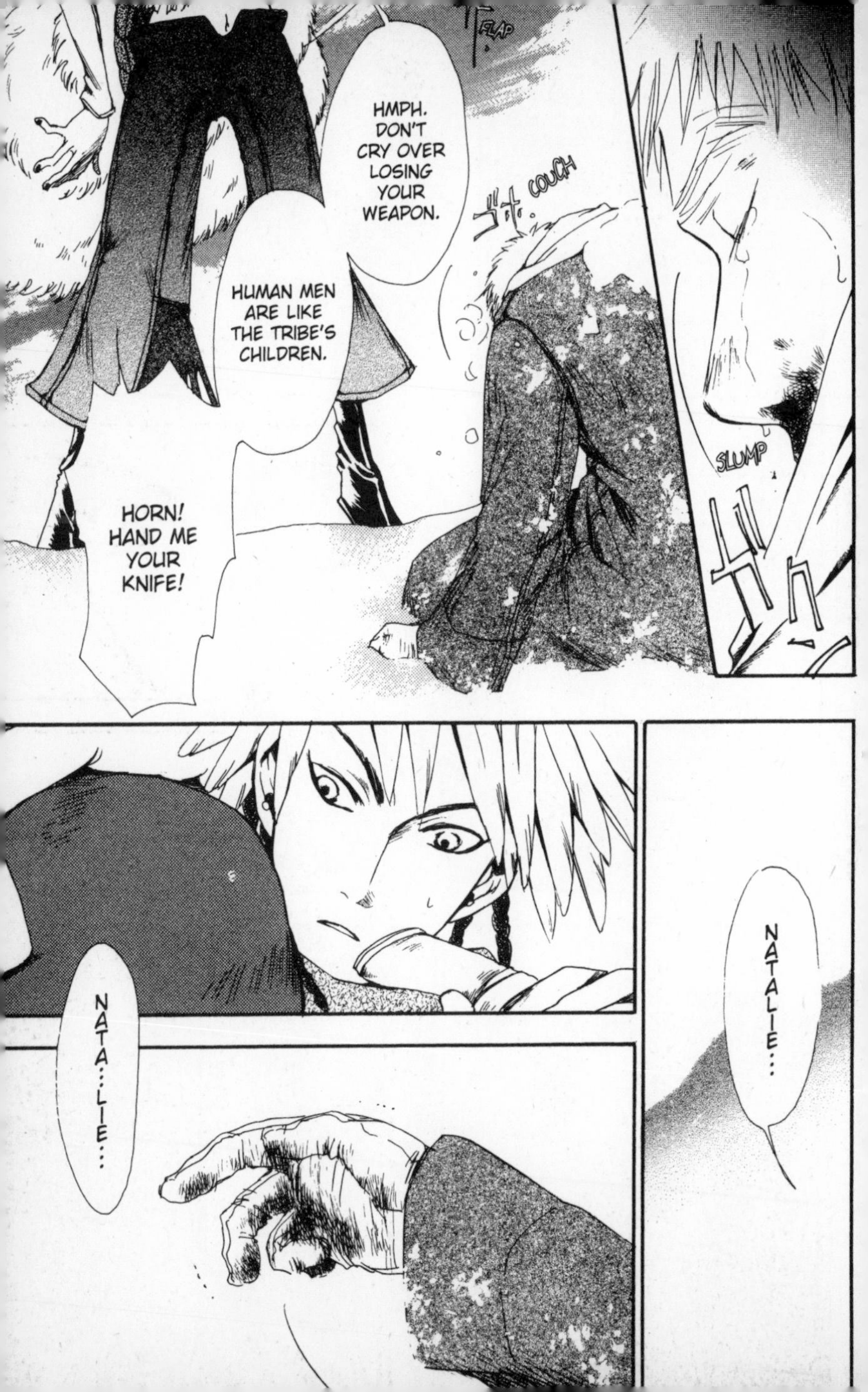
SLUMP
FLAP
COUGH
HMPH. DON'T CRY OVER LOSING YOUR WEAPON.
HUMAN MEN ARE LIKE THE TRIBE'S CHILDREN.
HORN! HAND ME YOUR KNIFE!
NATALIE...
NATA...LIE...

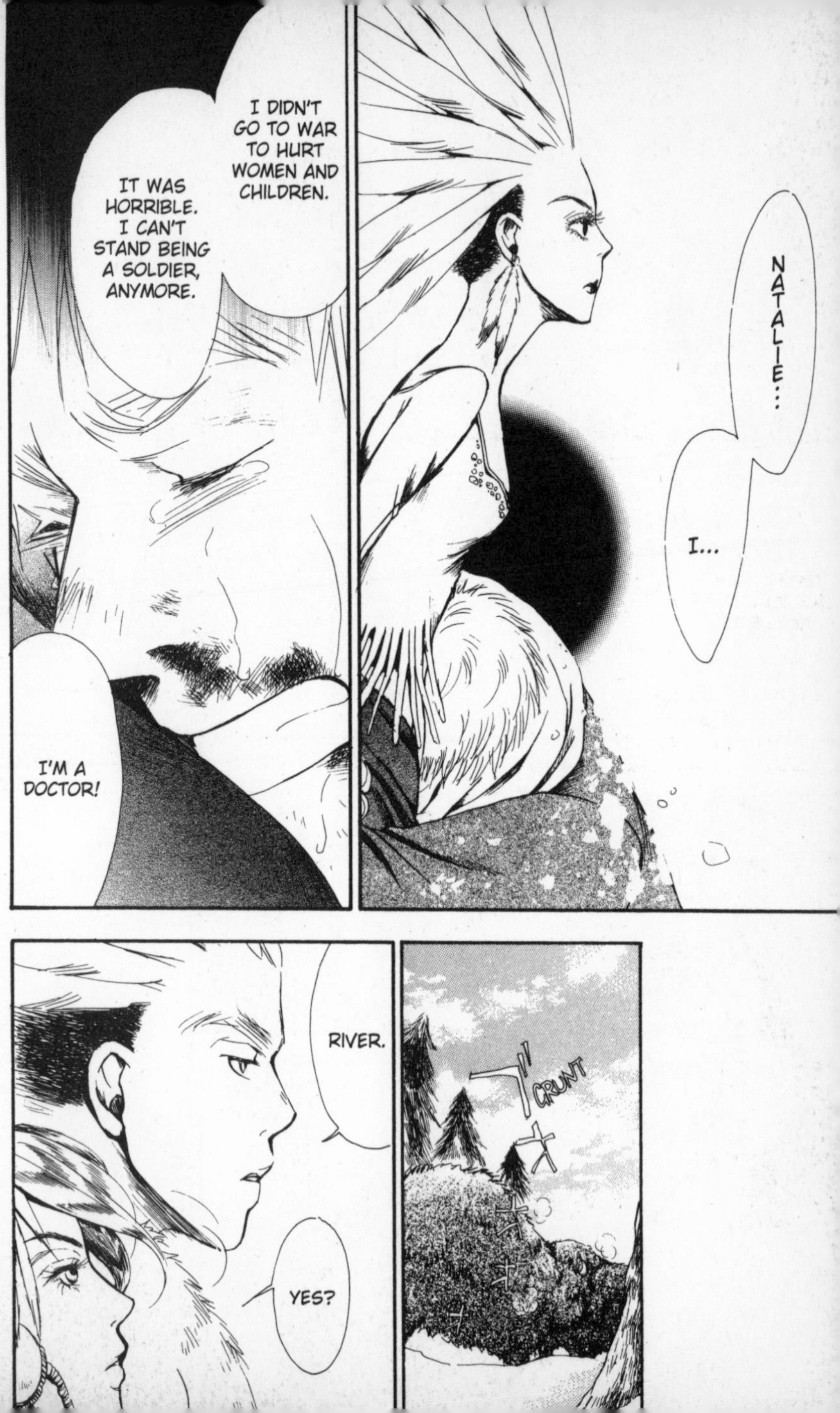
NATALIE...
I...
I DIDN'T GO TO WAR TO HURT WOMEN AND CHILDREN.
IT WAS HORRIBLE. I CAN'T STAND BEING A SOLDIER, ANYMORE.
I'M A DOCTOR!
GRUNT
RIVER.
YES?

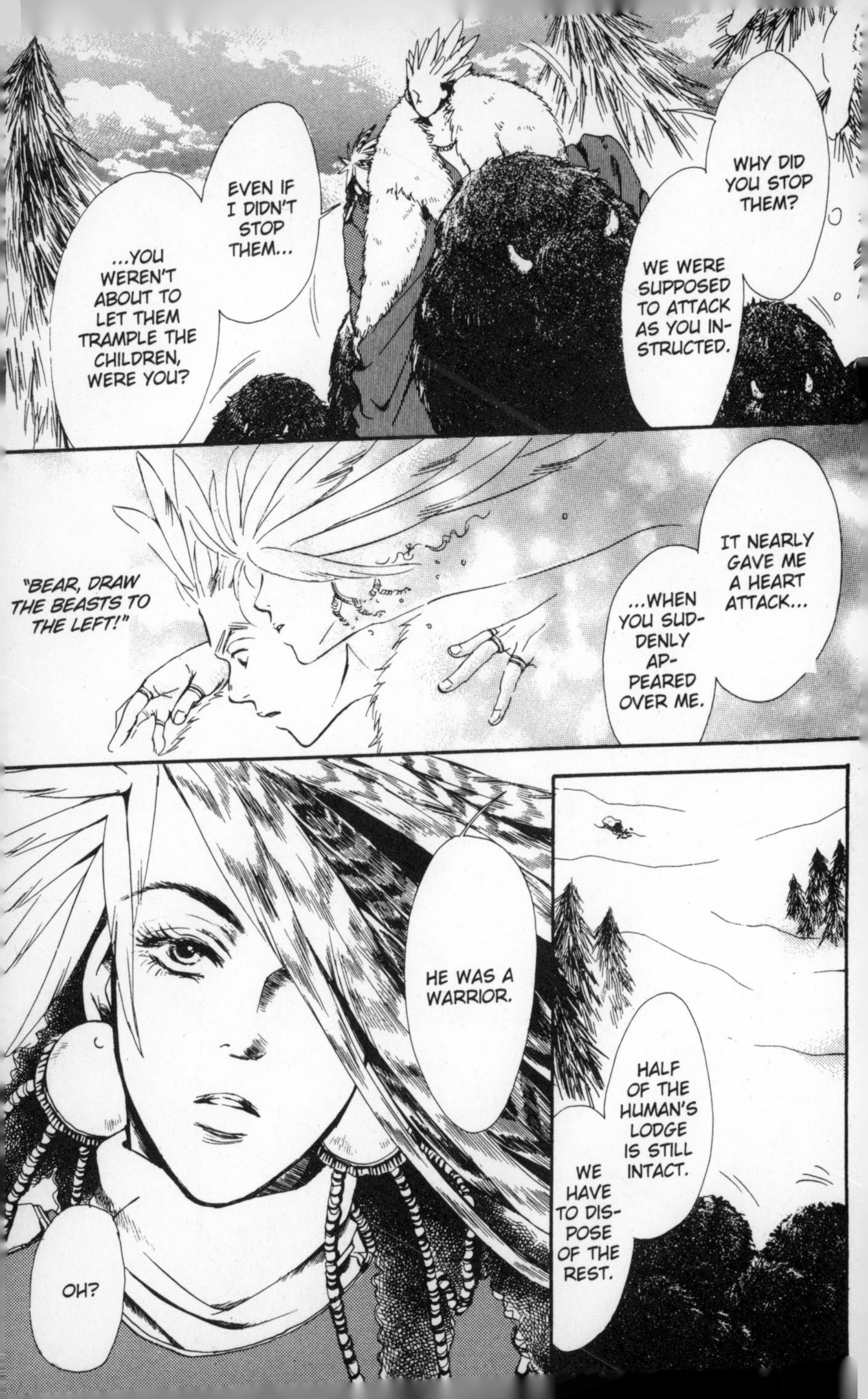
WHY DID YOU STOP THEM?
WE WERE SUPPOSED TO ATTACK AS YOU INSTRUCTED.
EVEN IF I DIDN'T STOP THEM...
...YOU WEREN'T ABOUT TO LET THEM TRAMPLE THE CHILDREN, WERE YOU?
IT NEARLY GAVE ME A HEART ATTACK...
...WHEN YOU SUDDENLY APPEARED OVER ME.
"BEAR, DRAW THE BEASTS TO THE LEFT!"
HALF OF THE HUMAN'S LODGE IS STILL INTACT.
WE HAVE TO DISPOSE OF THE REST.
HE WAS A WARRIOR.
OH?

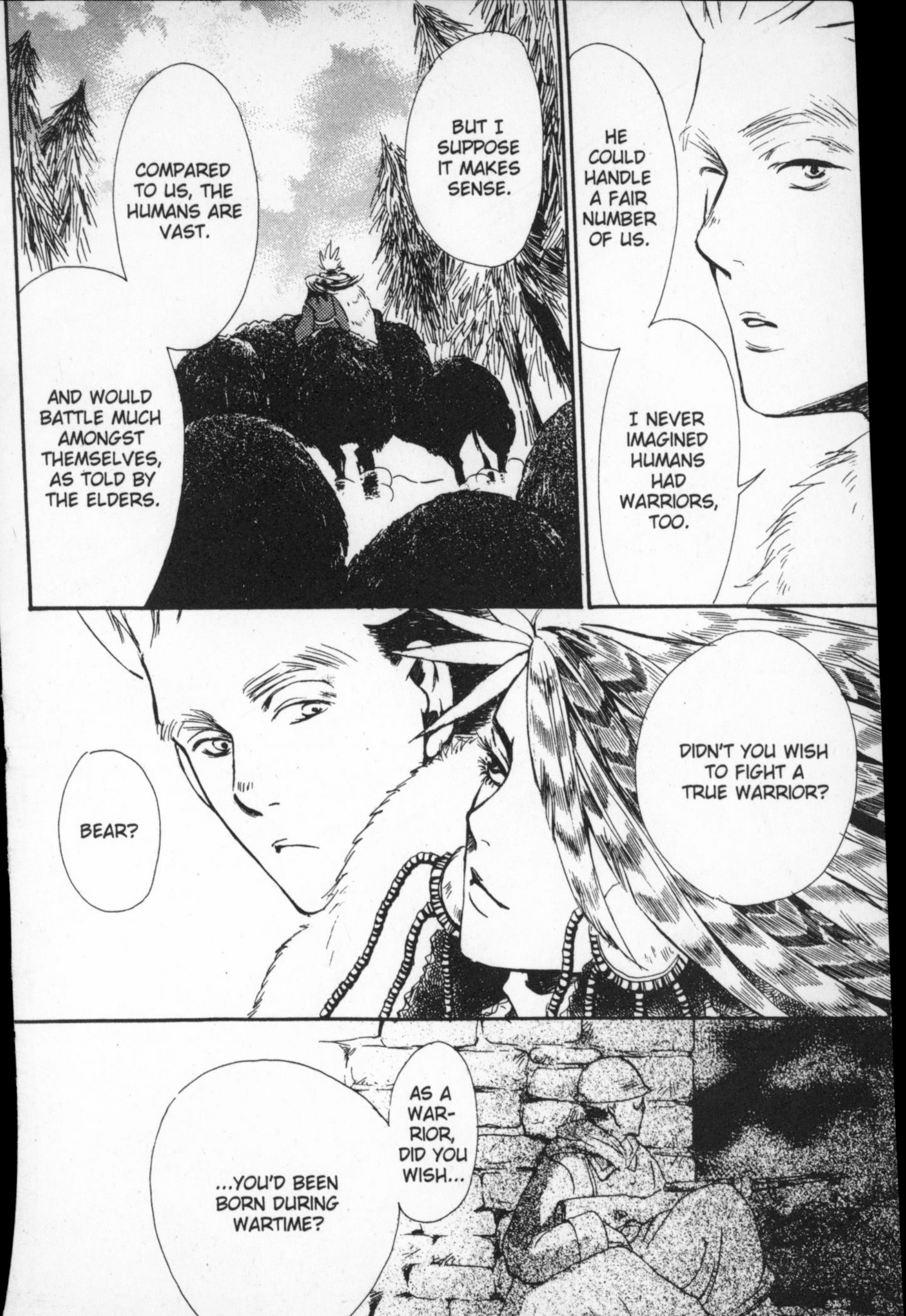
HE COULD HANDLE A FAIR NUMBER OF US.
I NEVER IMAGINED HUMANS HAD WARRIORS, TOO.
BUT I SUPPOSE IT MAKES SENSE.
COMPARED TO US, THE HUMANS ARE VAST.
AND WOULD BATTLE MUCH AMONGST THEMSELVES, AS TOLD BY THE ELDERS.
DIDN'T YOU WISH TO FIGHT A TRUE WARRIOR?
BEAR?
AS A WAR-RIOR, DID YOU WISH...
...YOU'D BEEN BORN DURING WARTIME?

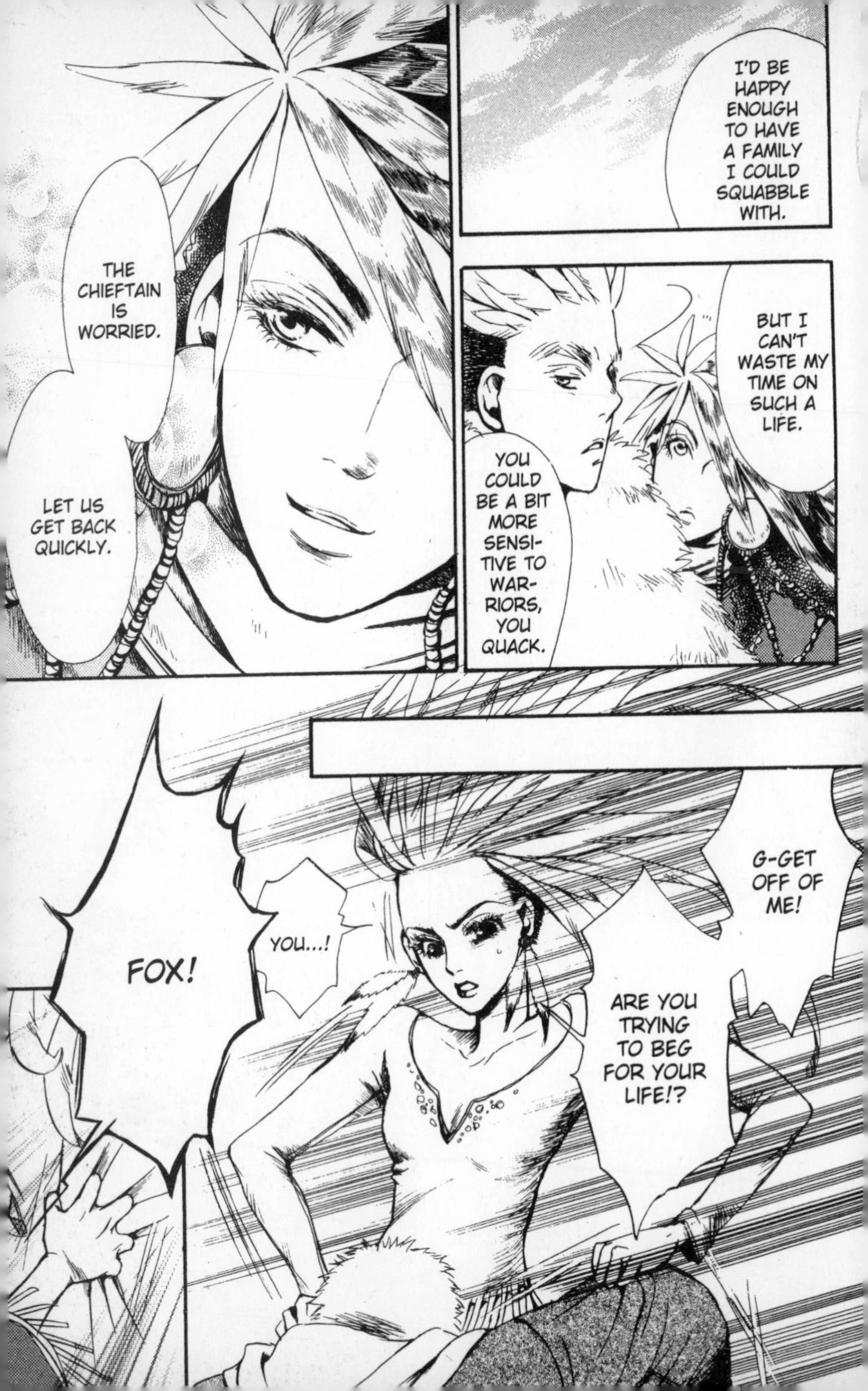
I'D BE HAPPY ENOUGH TO HAVE A FAMILY I COULD SQUABBLE WITH.
BUT I CAN'T WASTE MY TIME ON SUCH A LIFE.
YOU COULD BE A BIT MORE SENSI-TIVE TO WAR-RIORS, YOU QUACK.
THE CHIEFTAIN IS WORRIED.
LET US GET BACK QUICKLY.
G-GET OFF OF ME!
ARE YOU TRYING TO BEG FOR YOUR LIFE!?
YOU...!
FOX!

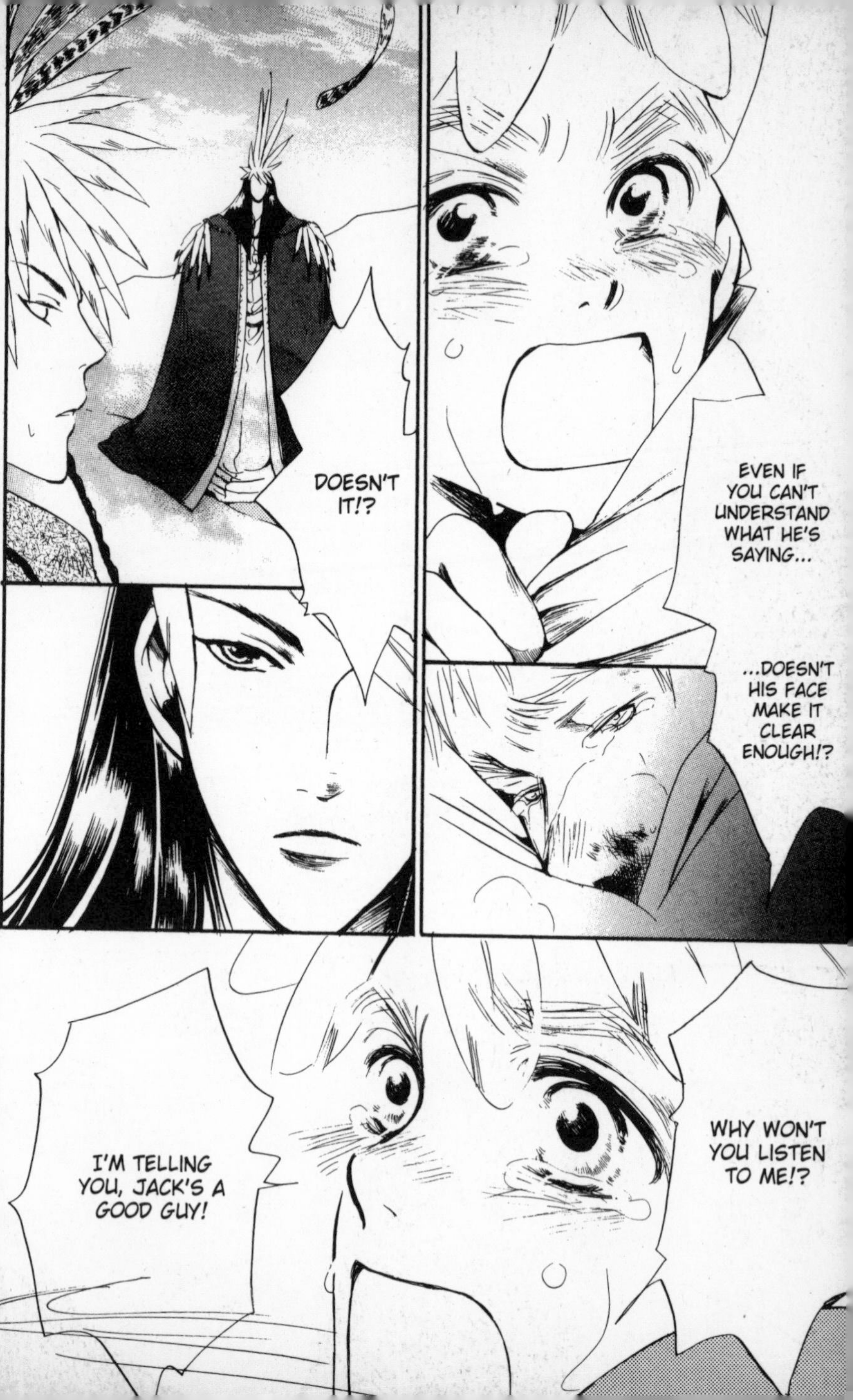
EVEN IF YOU CAN'T UNDERSTAND WHAT HE'S SAYING...
...DOESN'T HIS FACE MAKE IT CLEAR ENOUGH!?
DOESN'T IT!?
WHY WON'T YOU LISTEN TO ME!?
I'M TELLING YOU, JACK'S A GOOD GUY!

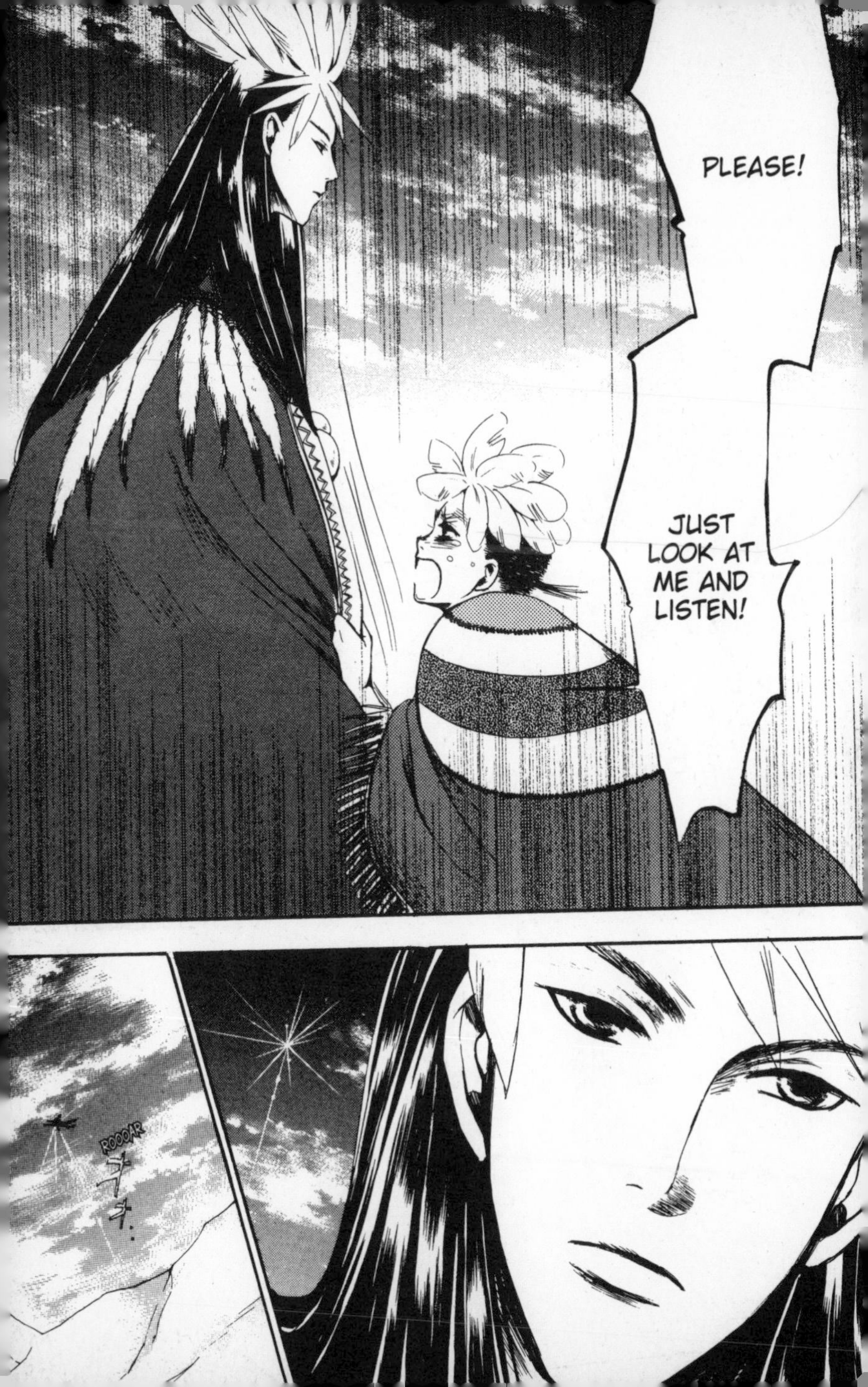
PLEASE!
JUST LOOK AT ME AND LISTEN!
ROOOAR

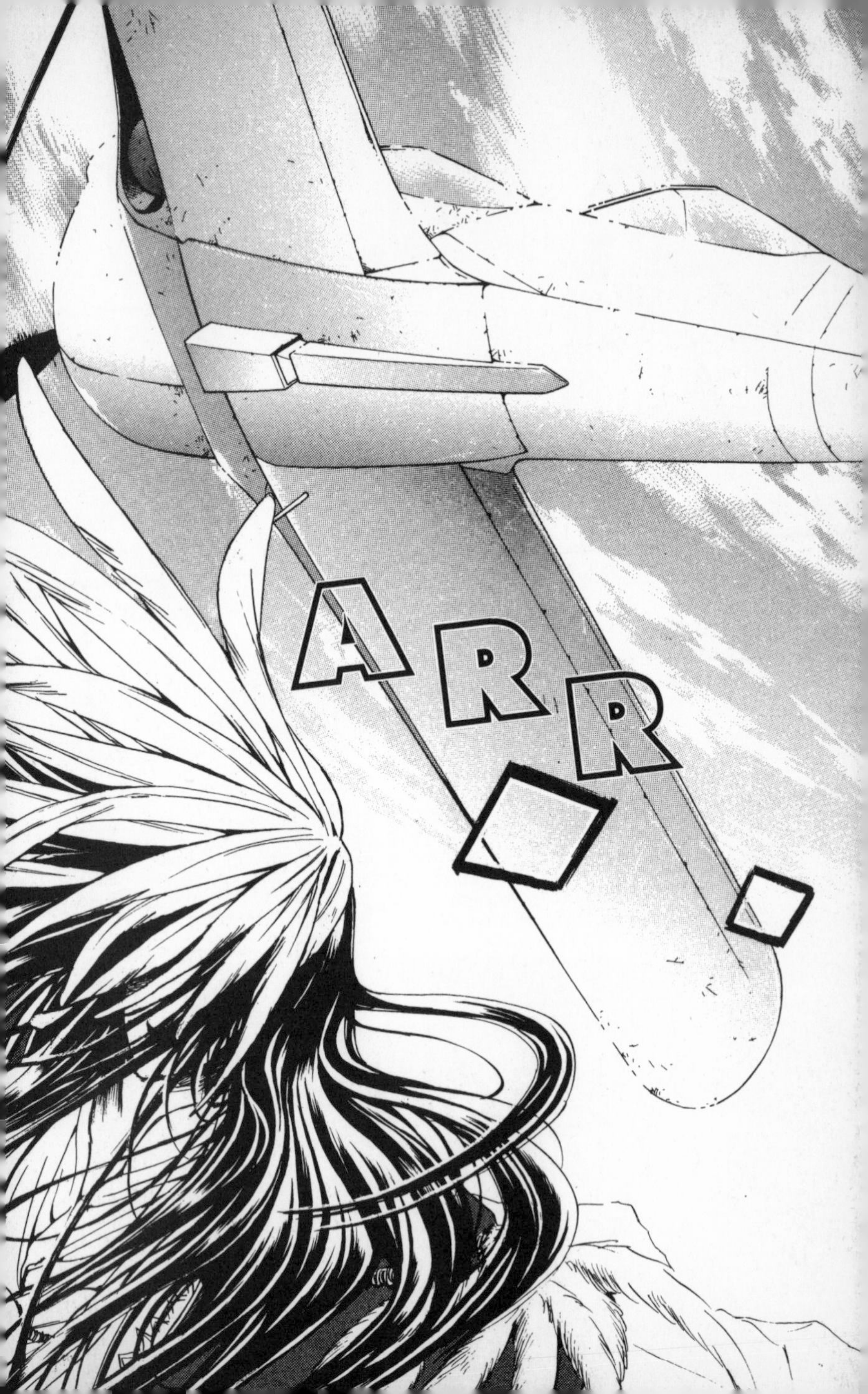
ARR..

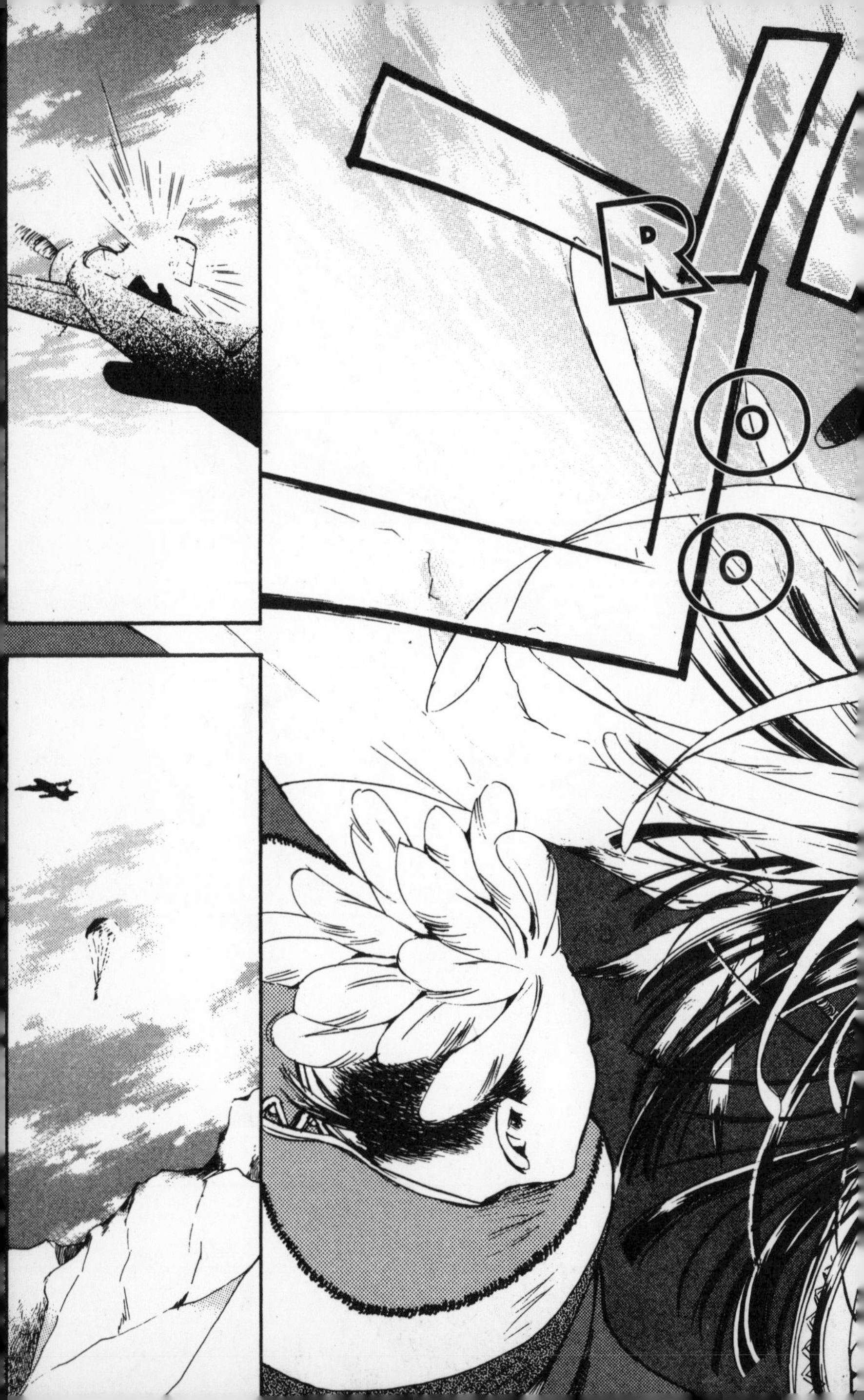
ROO

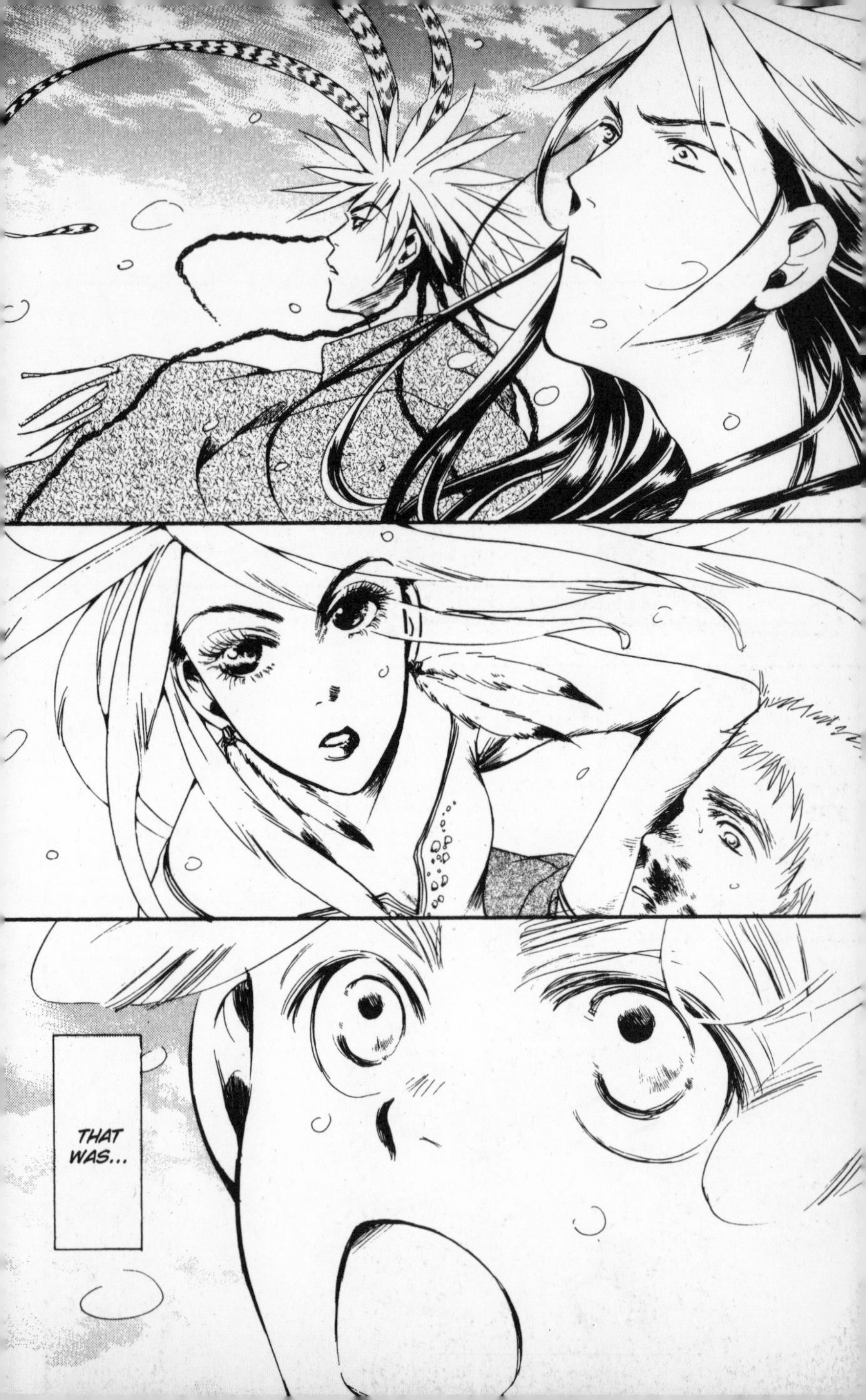
THAT WAS...

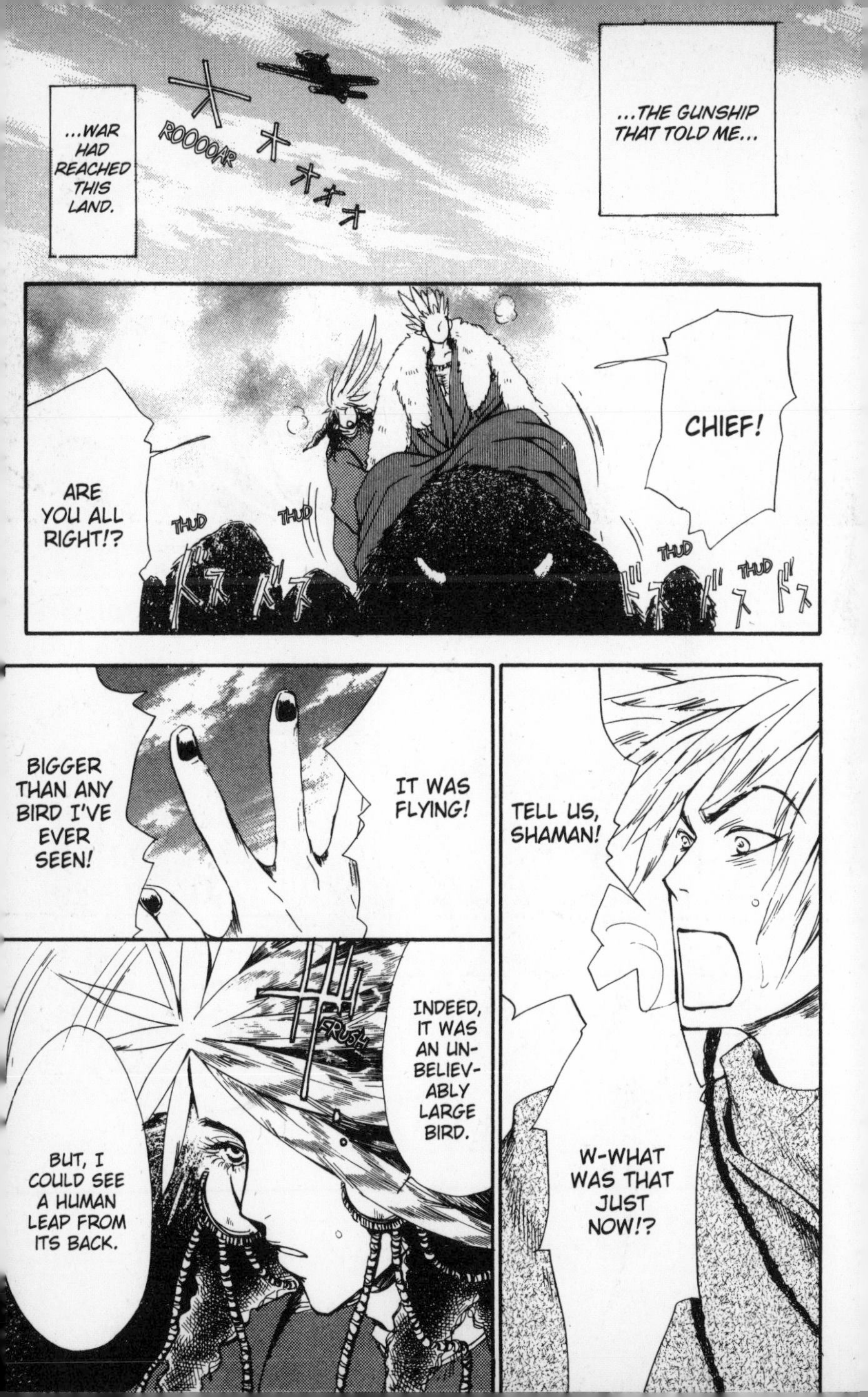
...THE GUNSHIP THAT TOLD ME...
ROOOOAR
...WAR HAD REACHED THIS LAND.
CHIEF!
THUD
THUD
ARE YOU ALL RIGHT!?
THUD
THUD
TELL US, SHAMAN!
W-WHAT WAS THAT JUST NOW!?
IT WAS FLYING!
BIGGER THAN ANY BIRD I'VE EVER SEEN!
FRUSH
INDEED, IT WAS AN UN-BELIEV-ABLY LARGE BIRD.
BUT, I COULD SEE A HUMAN LEAP FROM ITS BACK.

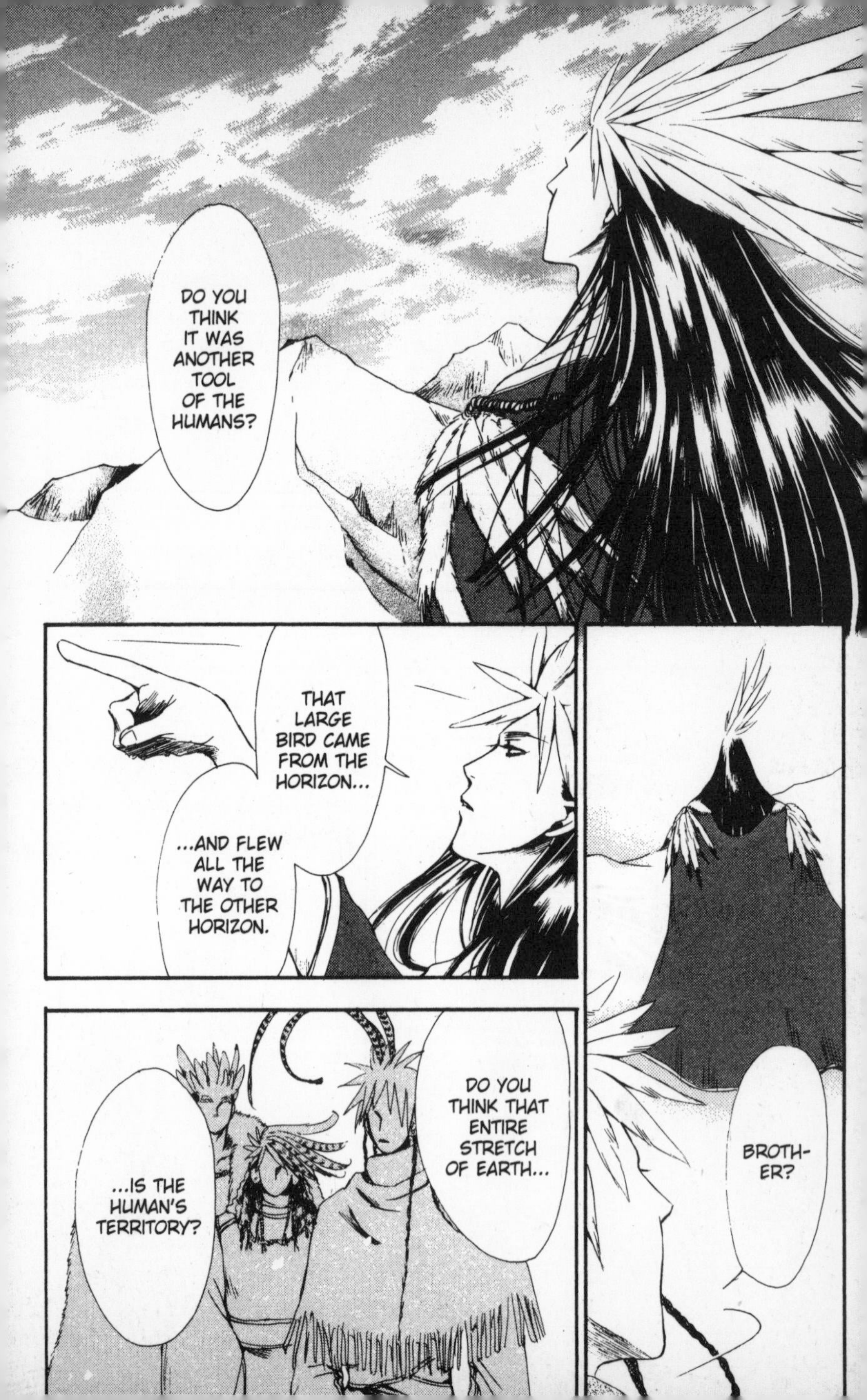
DO YOU THINK IT WAS ANOTHER TOOL OF THE HUMANS?
BROTH-ER?
THAT LARGE BIRD CAME FROM THE HORIZON...
...AND FLEW ALL THE WAY TO THE OTHER HORIZON.
DO YOU THINK THAT ENTIRE STRETCH OF EARTH...
...IS THE HUMAN'S TERRITORY?

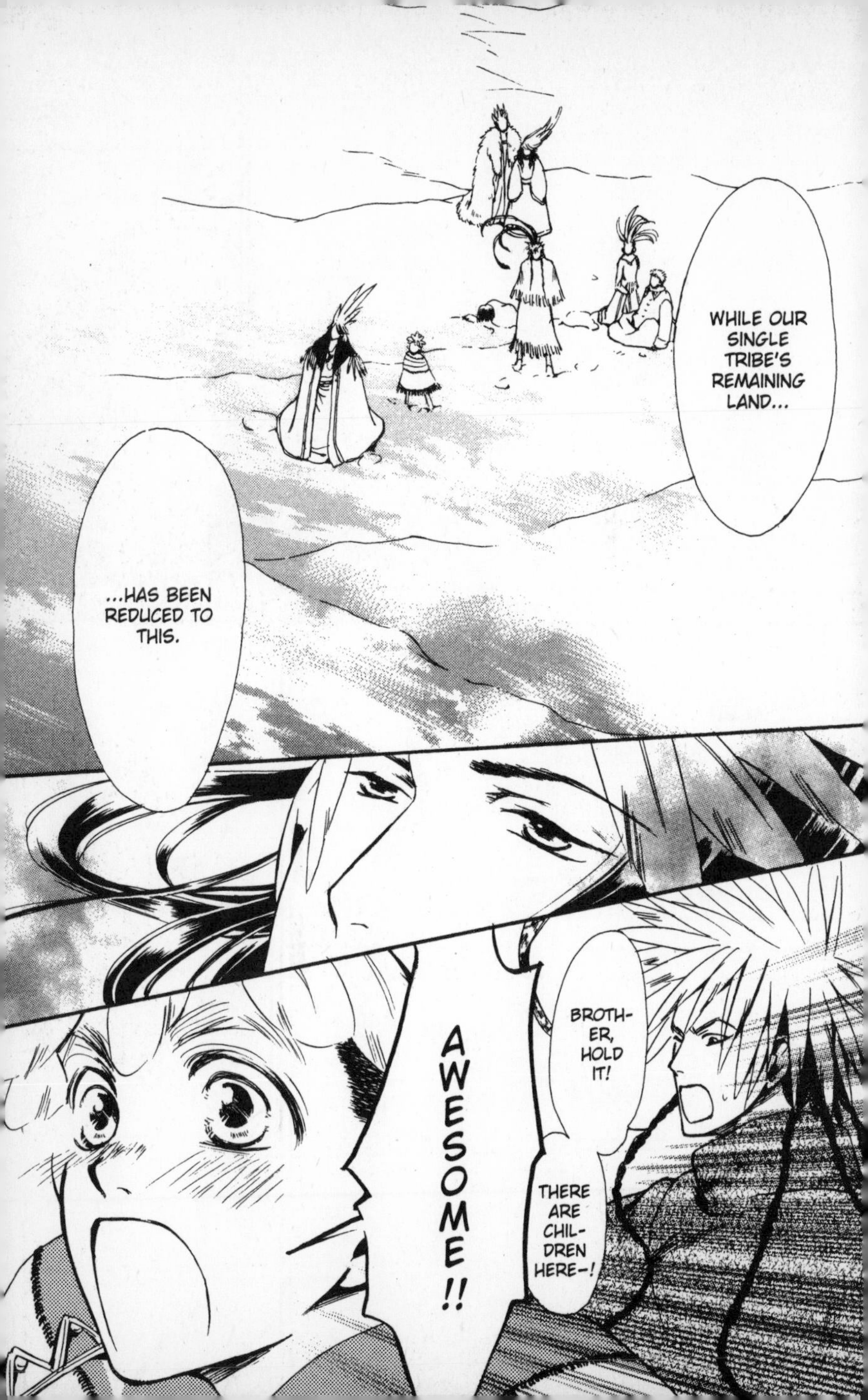
WHILE OUR SINGLE TRIBE'S REMAINING LAND...
...HAS BEEN REDUCED TO THIS.
BROTH-ER, HOLD IT!
THERE ARE CHIL-DREN HERE-!
AWESOME!!

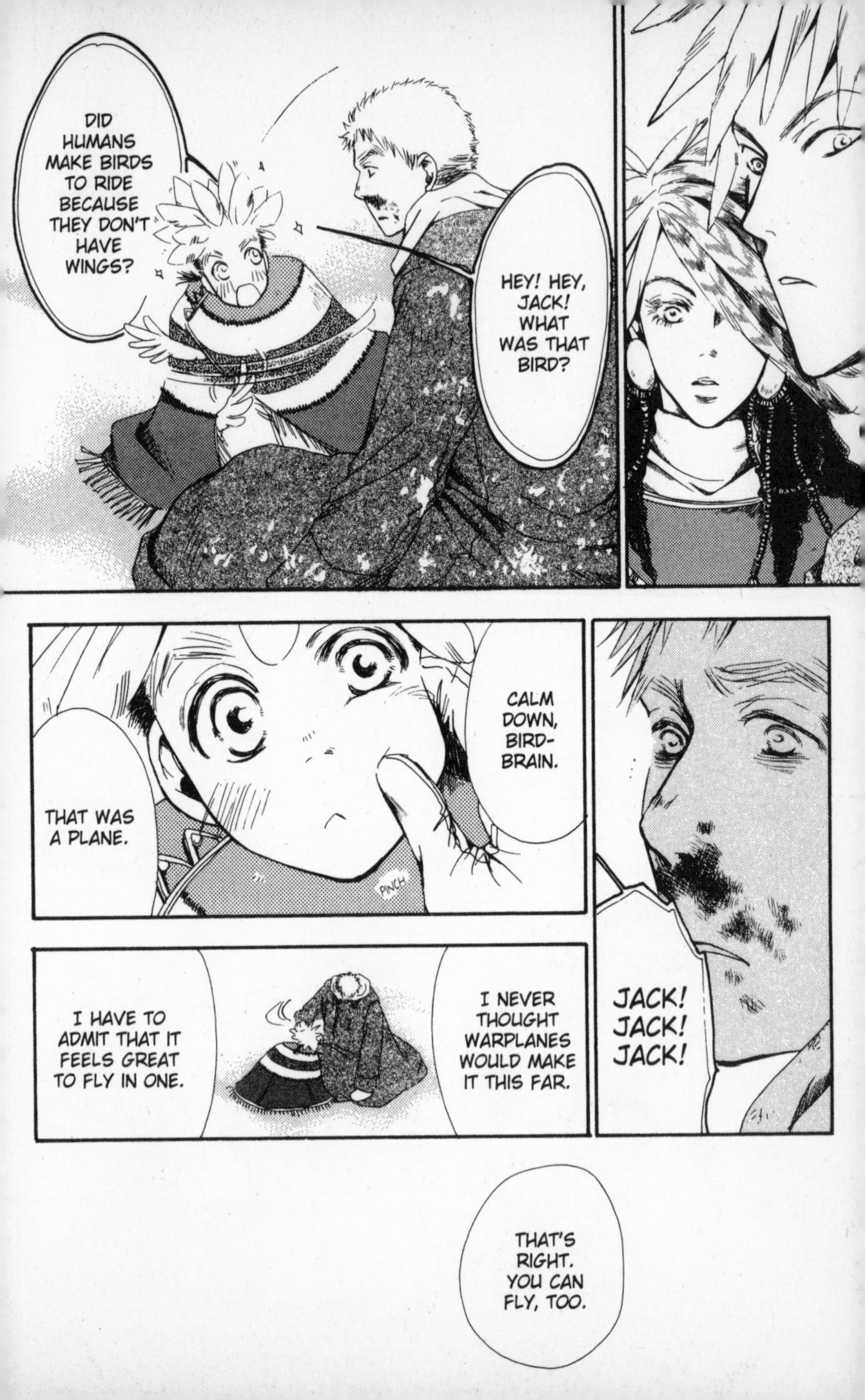
HEY! HEY, JACK! WHAT WAS THAT BIRD?
DID HUMANS MAKE BIRDS TO RIDE BECAUSE THEY DON'T HAVE WINGS?
JACK! JACK! JACK!
CALM DOWN, BIRD-BRAIN.
THAT WAS A PLANE.
PINCH
I NEVER THOUGHT WARPLANES WOULD MAKE IT THIS FAR.
I HAVE TO ADMIT THAT IT FEELS GREAT TO FLY IN ONE.
THAT'S RIGHT. YOU CAN FLY, TOO.

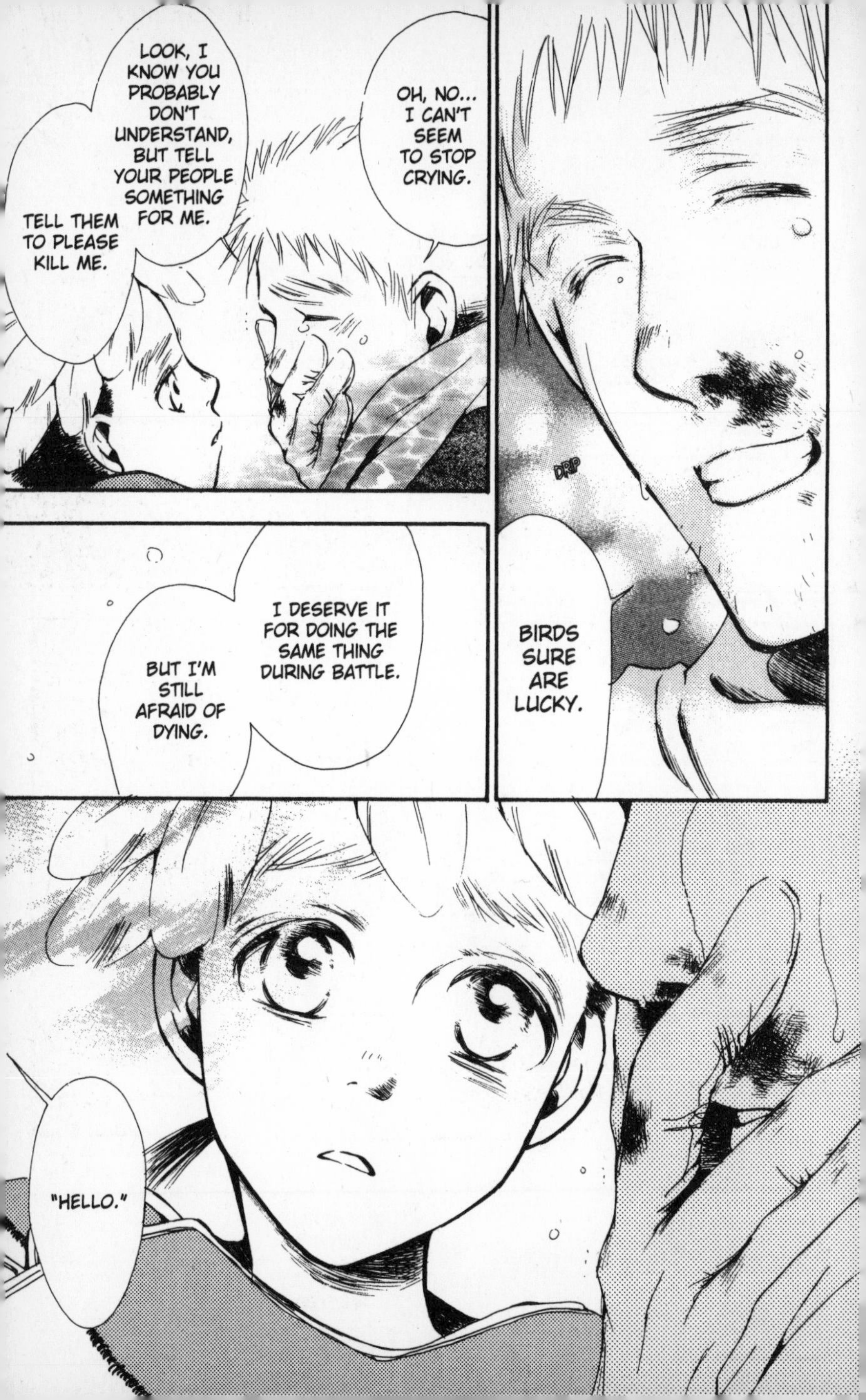
DRIP
BIRDS SURE ARE LUCKY.
OH, NO... I CAN'T SEEM TO STOP CRYING.
LOOK, I KNOW YOU PROBABLY DON'T UNDERSTAND, BUT TELL YOUR PEOPLE SOMETHING FOR ME.
TELL THEM TO PLEASE KILL ME.
I DESERVE IT FOR DOING THE SAME THING DURING BATTLE.
BUT I'M STILL AFRAID OF DYING.
"HELLO."

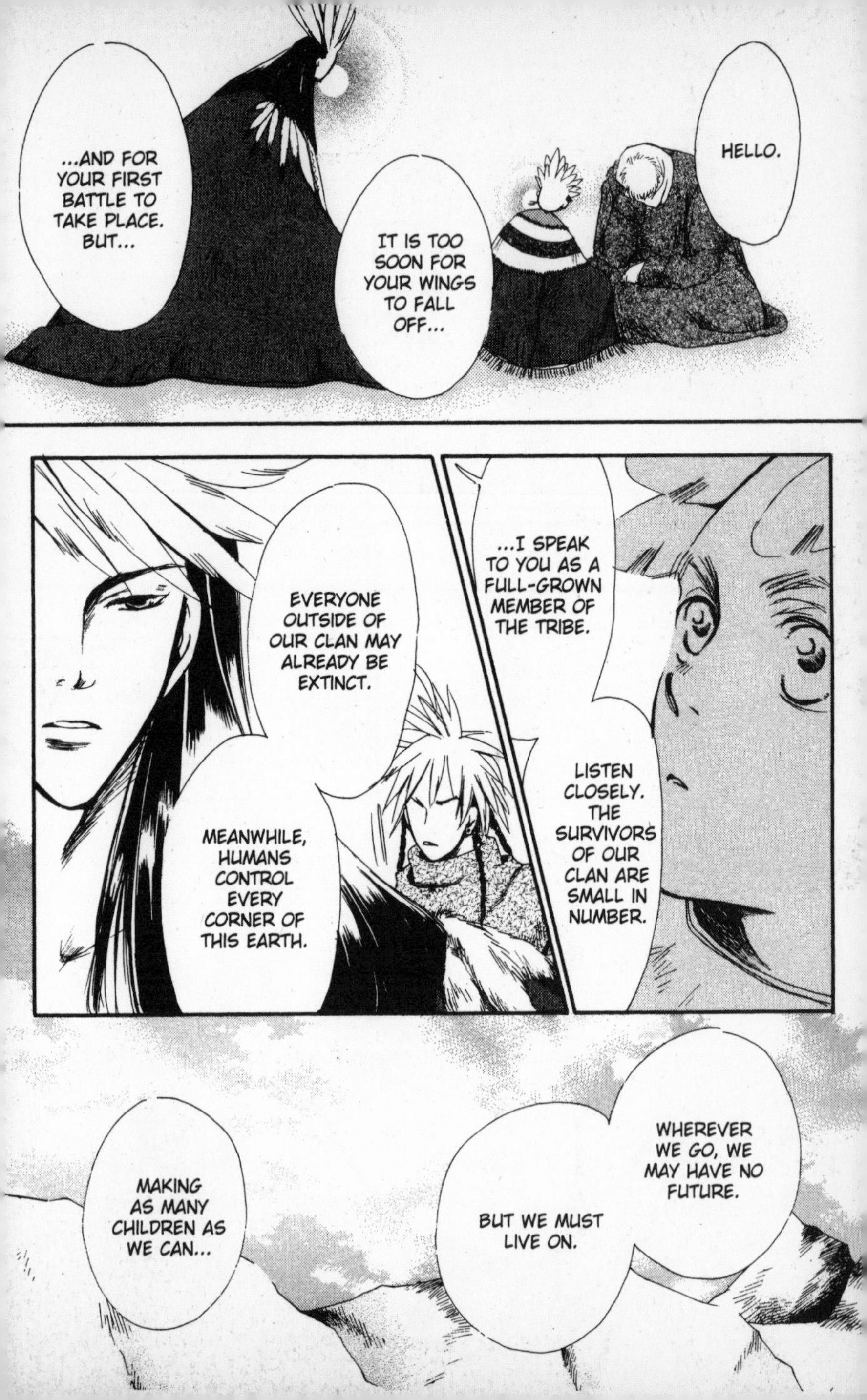
HELLO.
IT IS TOO SOON FOR YOUR WINGS TO FALL OFF...
...AND FOR YOUR FIRST BATTLE TO TAKE PLACE. BUT...
...I SPEAK TO YOU AS A FULL-GROWN MEMBER OF THE TRIBE.
LISTEN CLOSELY. THE SURVIVORS OF OUR CLAN ARE SMALL IN NUMBER.
EVERYONE OUTSIDE OF OUR CLAN MAY ALREADY BE EXTINCT.
MEANWHILE, HUMANS CONTROL EVERY CORNER OF THIS EARTH.
WHEREVER WE GO, WE MAY HAVE NO FUTURE.
BUT WE MUST LIVE ON.
MAKING AS MANY CHILDREN AS WE CAN...

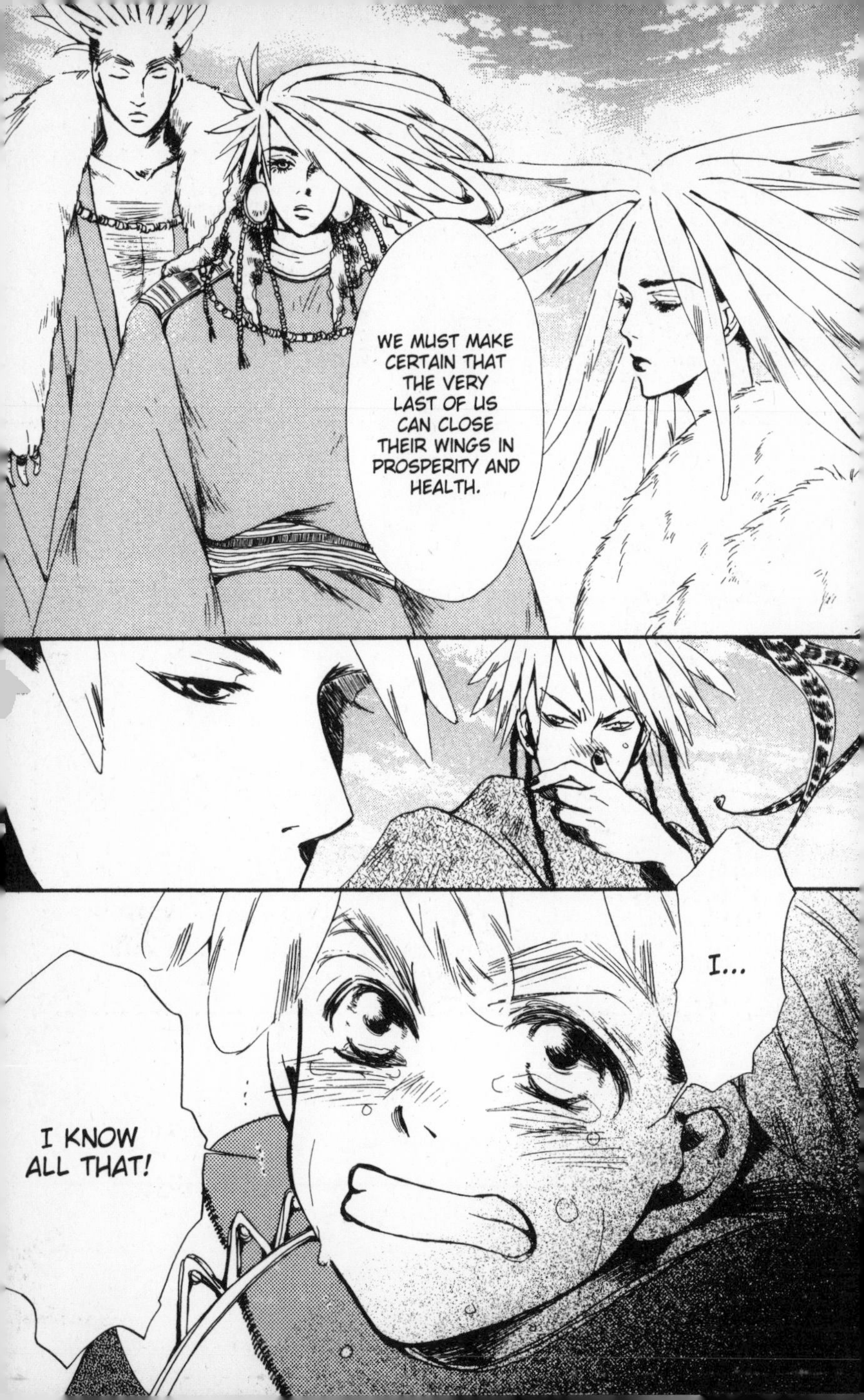
WE MUST MAKE CERTAIN THAT THE VERY LAST OF US CAN CLOSE THEIR WINGS IN PROSPERITY AND HEALTH.
I...
I KNOW ALL THAT!

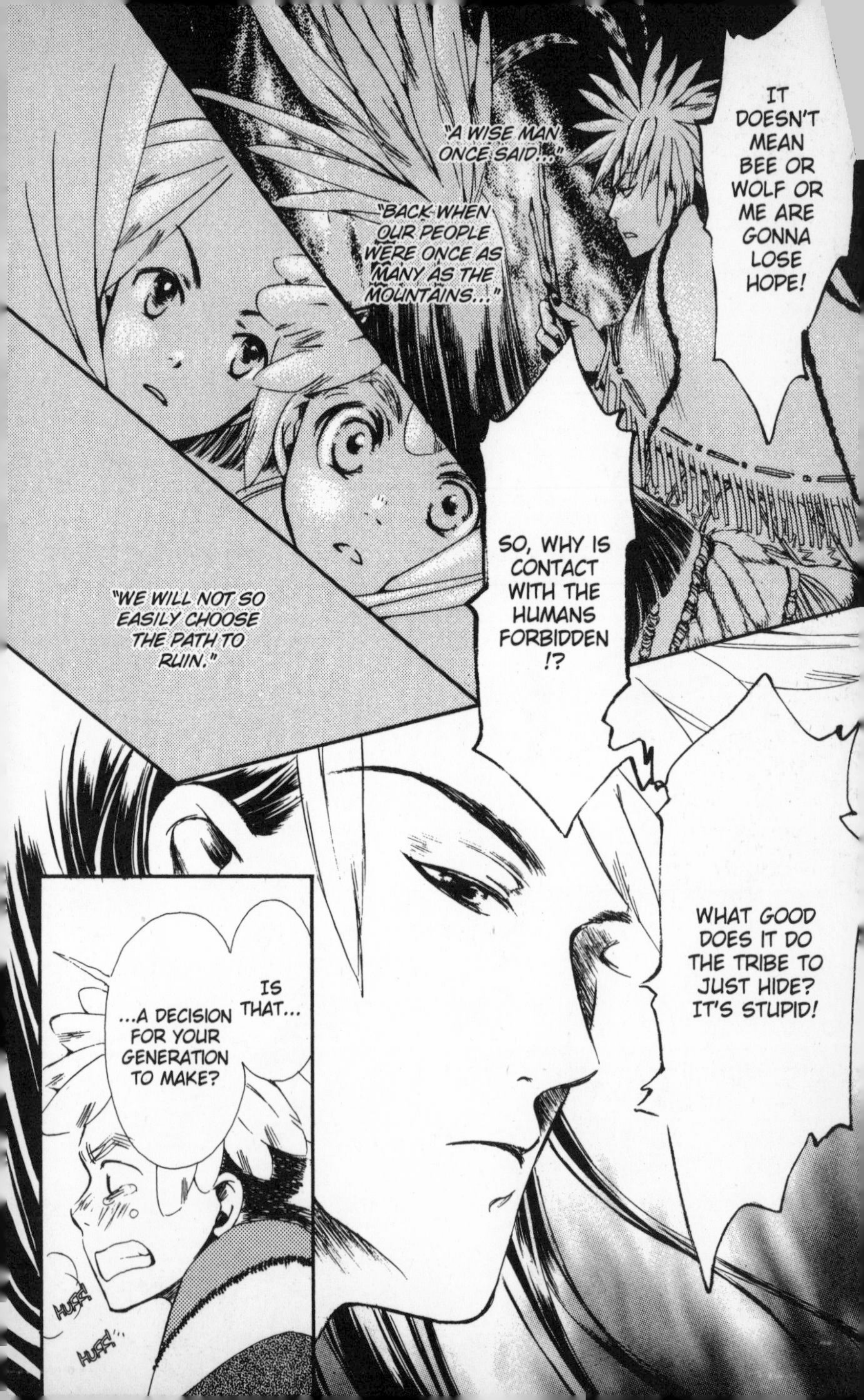
IT DOESN'T MEAN BEE OR WOLF OR ME ARE GONNA LOSE HOPE!
"A WISE MAN ONCE SAID..."
"BACK WHEN OUR PEOPLE WERE ONCE AS MANY AS THE MOUNTAINS..."
SO, WHY IS CONTACT WITH THE HUMANS FORBIDDEN!?
"WE WILL NOT SO EASILY CHOOSE THE PATH TO RUIN."
WHAT GOOD DOES IT DO THE TRIBE TO JUST HIDE? IT'S STUPID!
IS THAT...
...A DECISION FOR YOUR GENERATION TO MAKE?
HUFF!
HUFF!

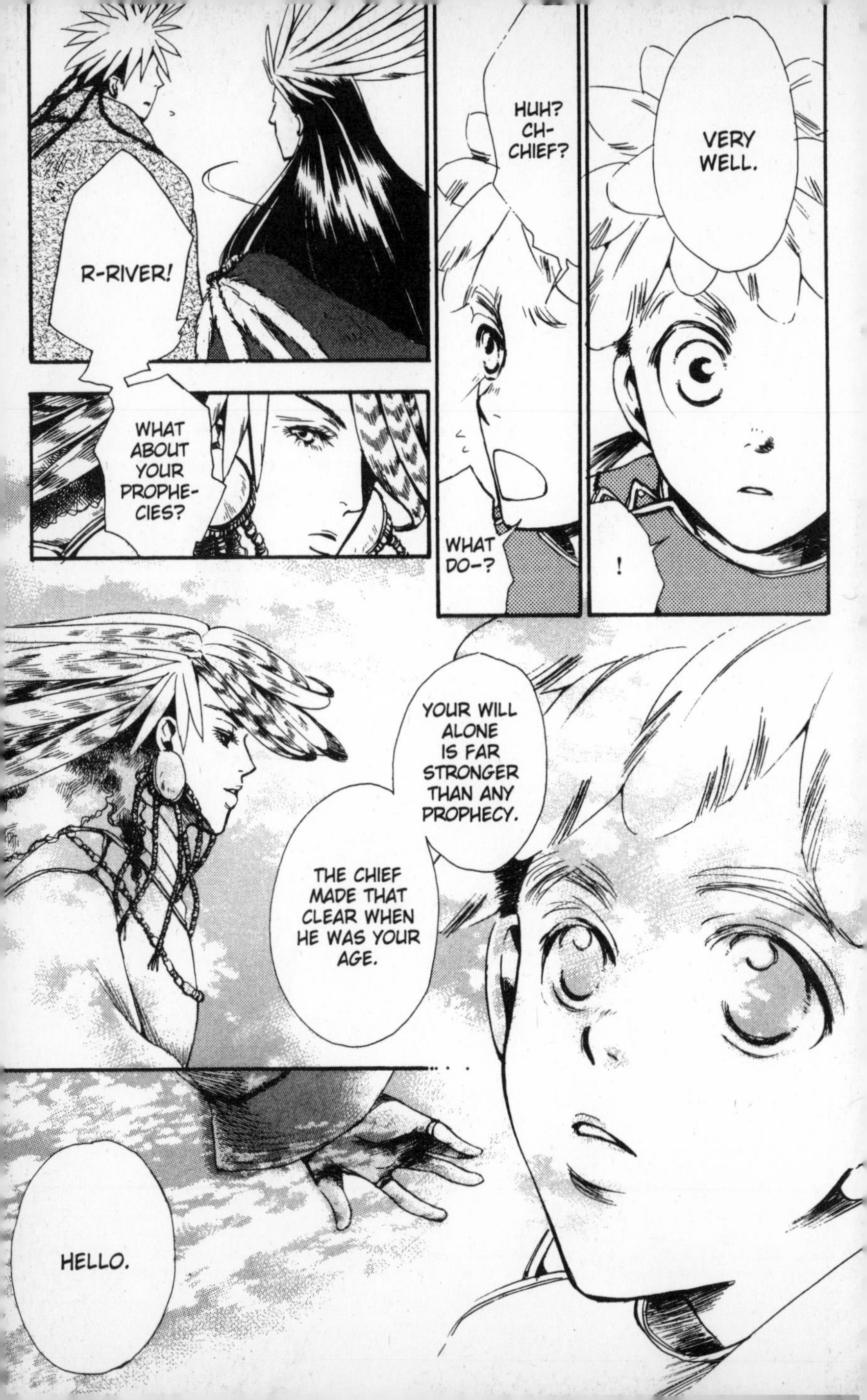
VERY WELL.
!
HUH? CH-CHIEF?
WHAT DO-?
R-RIVER!
WHAT ABOUT YOUR PROPHECIES?
YOUR WILL ALONE IS FAR STRONGER THAN ANY PROPHECY.
THE CHIEF MADE THAT CLEAR WHEN HE WAS YOUR AGE.
HELLO.

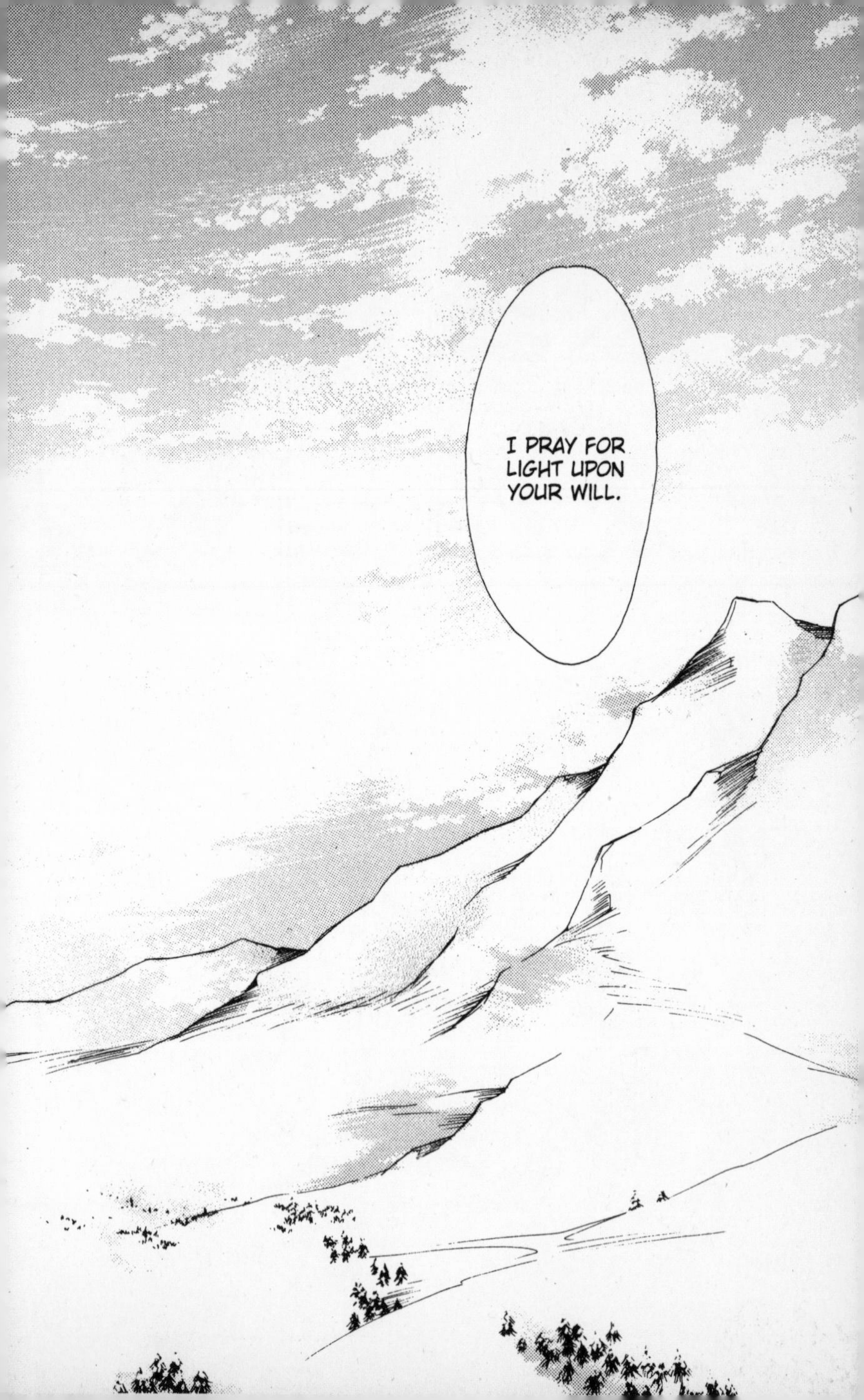
I PRAY FOR LIGHT UPON YOUR WILL.

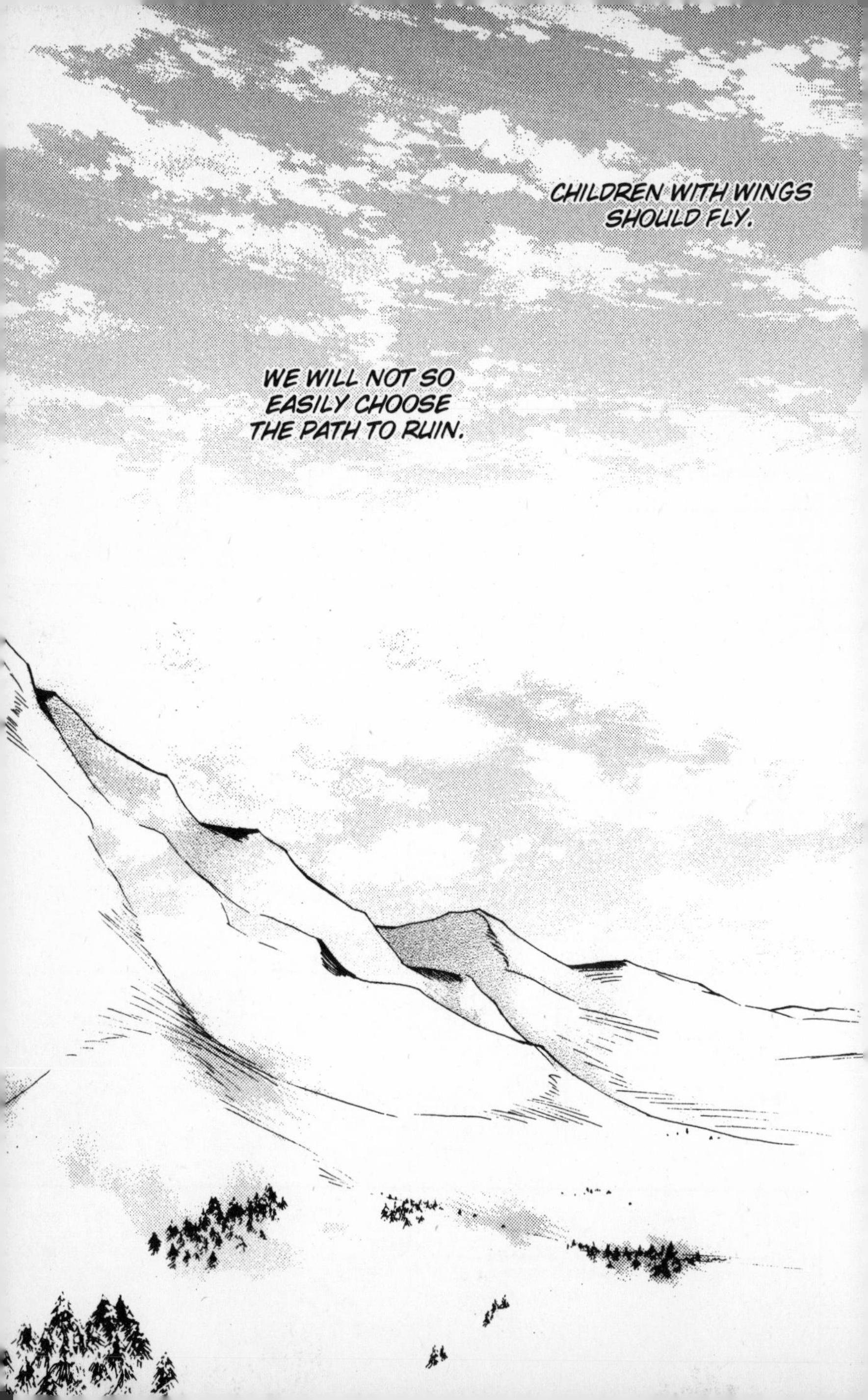
CHILDREN WITH WINGS SHOULD FLY.
WE WILL NOT SO EASILY CHOOSE THE PATH TO RUIN.

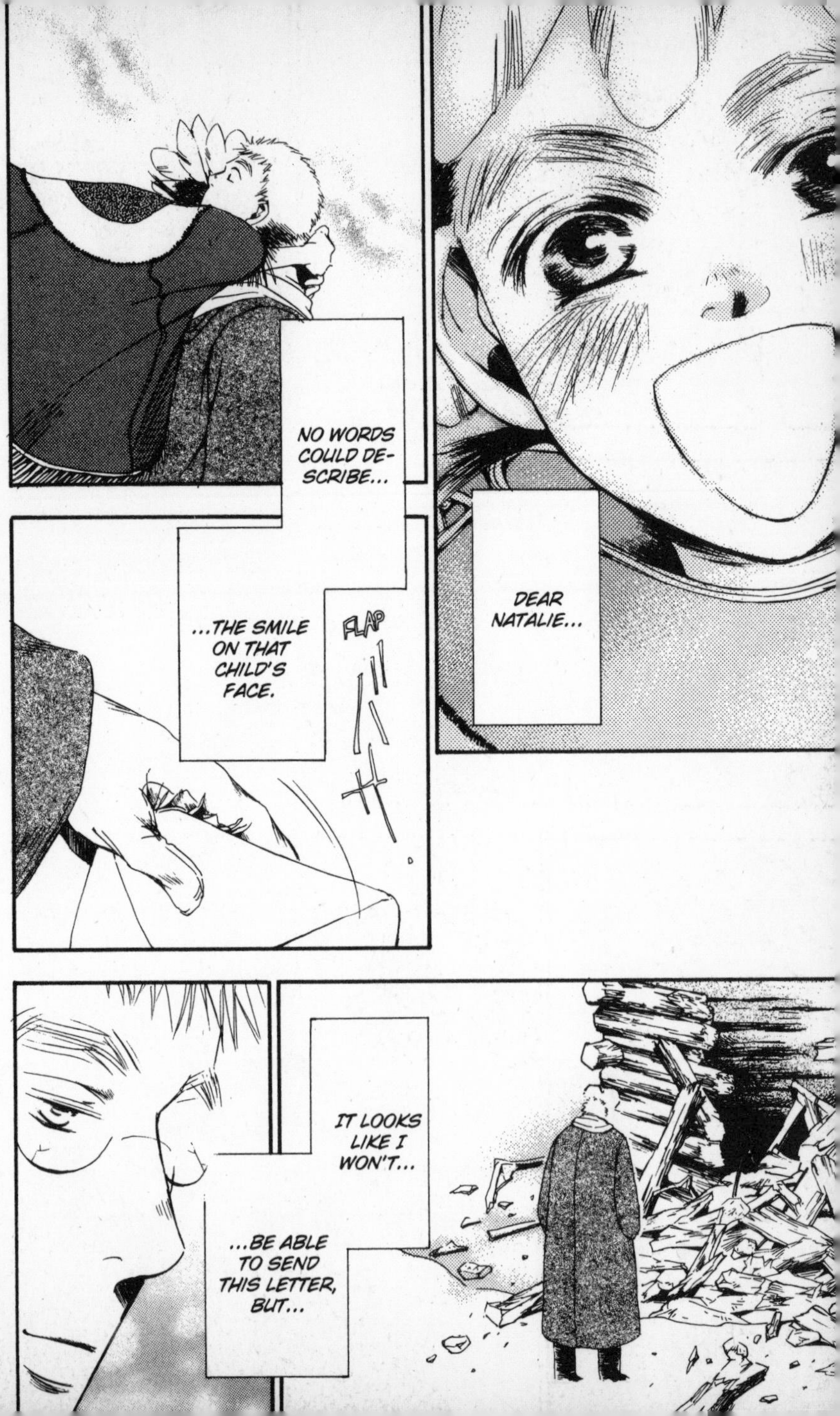
DEAR NATALIE...
NO WORDS COULD DE-SCRIBE...
...THE SMILE ON THAT CHILD'S FACE.
FLAP
IT LOOKS LIKE I WON'T...
...BE ABLE TO SEND THIS LETTER, BUT...

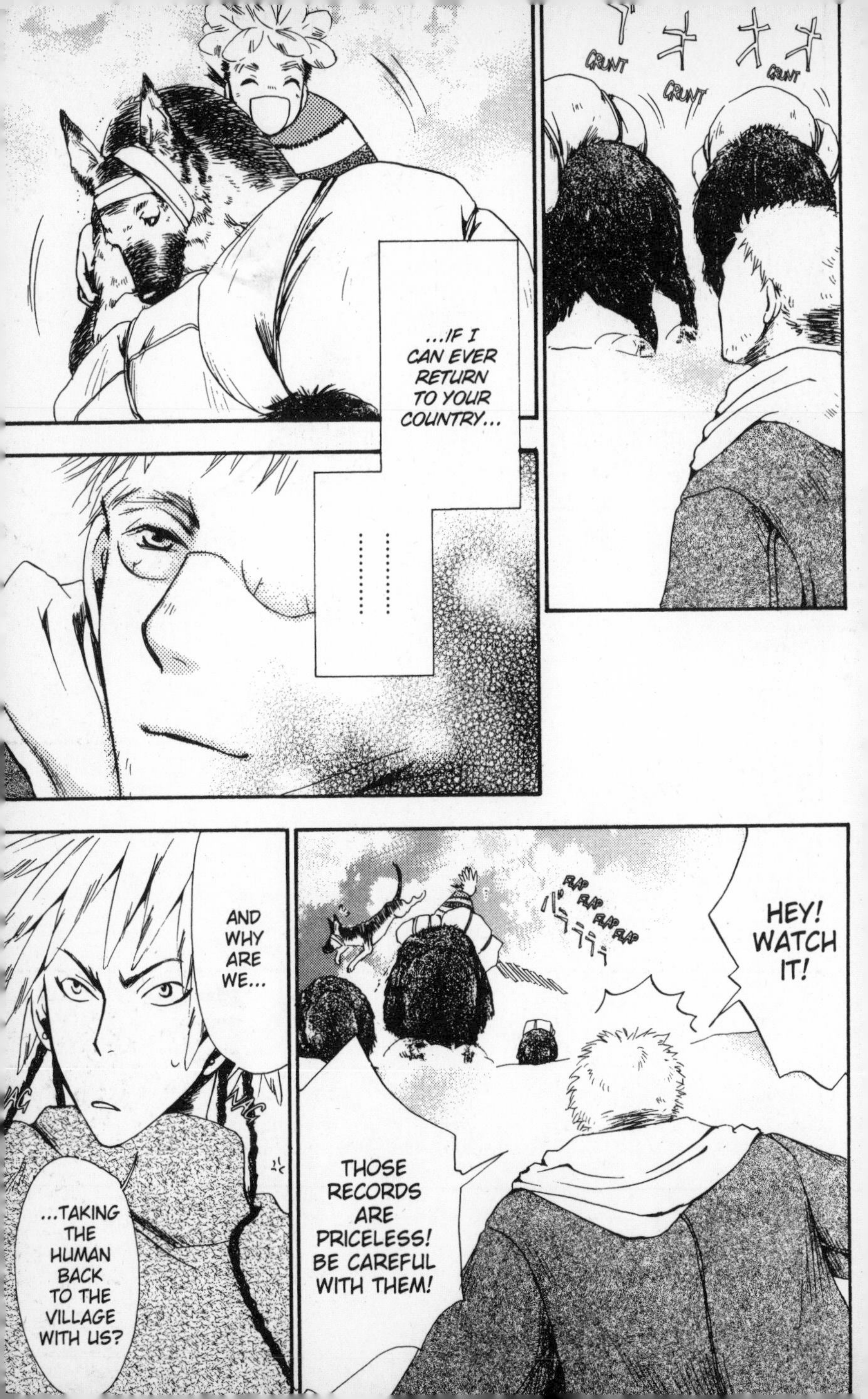
GRUNT
GRUNT
GRUNT
...IF I CAN EVER RETURN TO YOUR COUNTRY...
......
HEY! WATCH IT!
FLAP FLAP FLAP FLAP
THOSE RECORDS ARE PRICELESS! BE CAREFUL WITH THEM!
AND WHY ARE WE...
...TAKING THE HUMAN BACK TO THE VILLAGE WITH US?

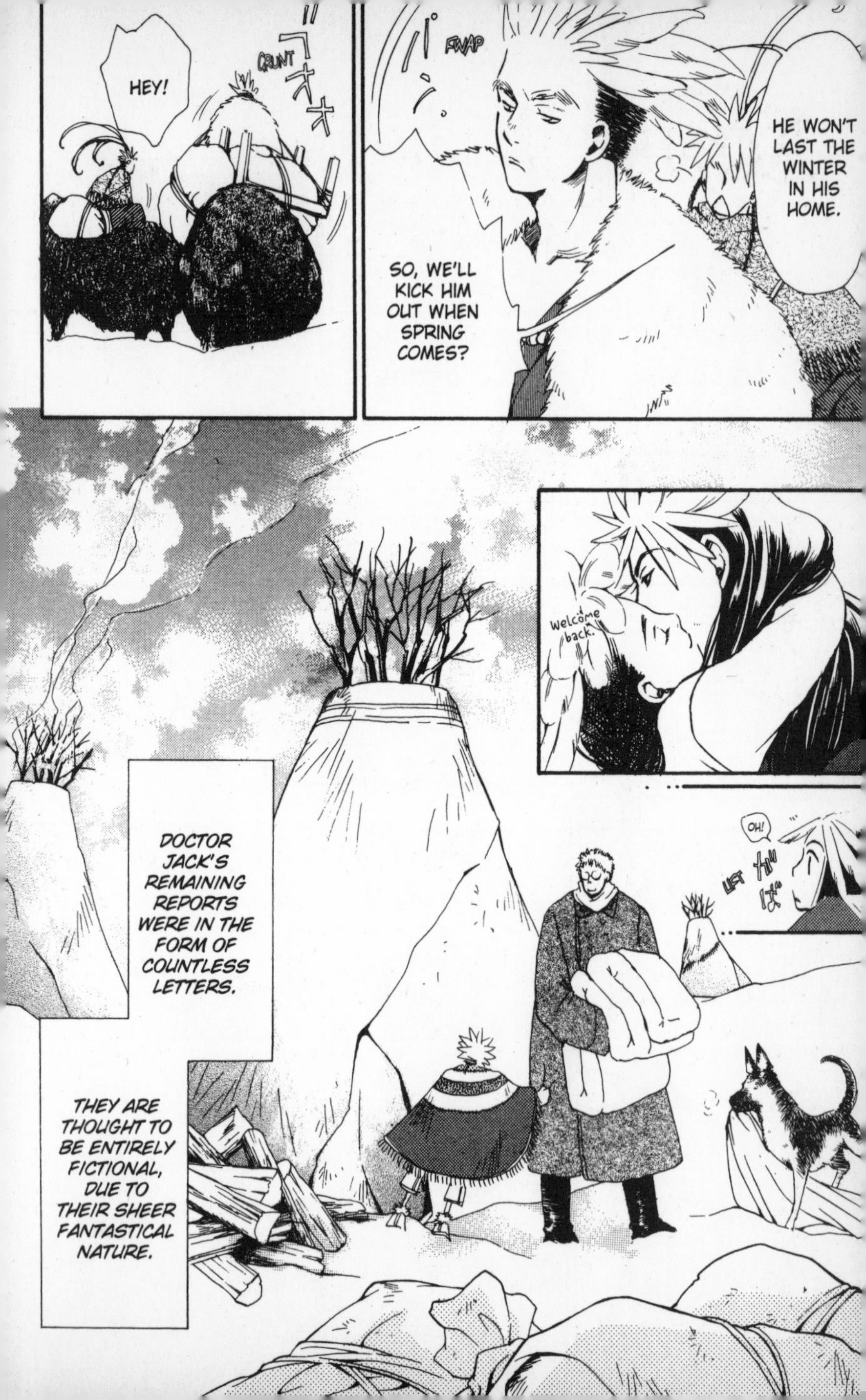
HE WON'T LAST THE WINTER IN HIS HOME.
FWAP
SO, WE'LL KICK HIM OUT WHEN SPRING COMES?
GRUNT
HEY!
Welcome back.
OH!
LIFT
DOCTOR JACK'S REMAINING REPORTS WERE IN THE FORM OF COUNTLESS LETTERS.
THEY ARE THOUGHT TO BE ENTIRELY FICTIONAL, DUE TO THEIR SHEER FANTASTICAL NATURE.

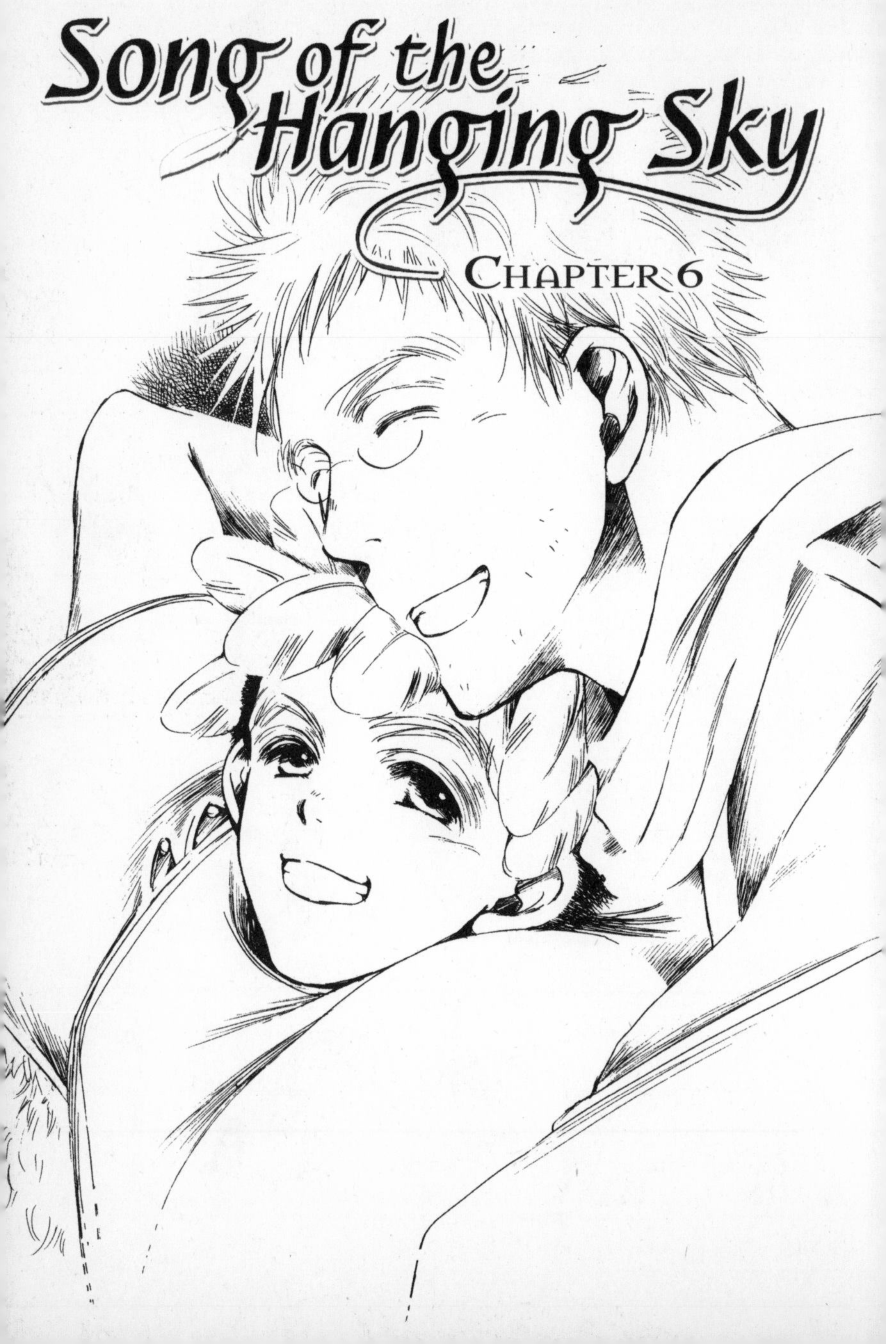
Song of the Hanging Sky
Chapter 6

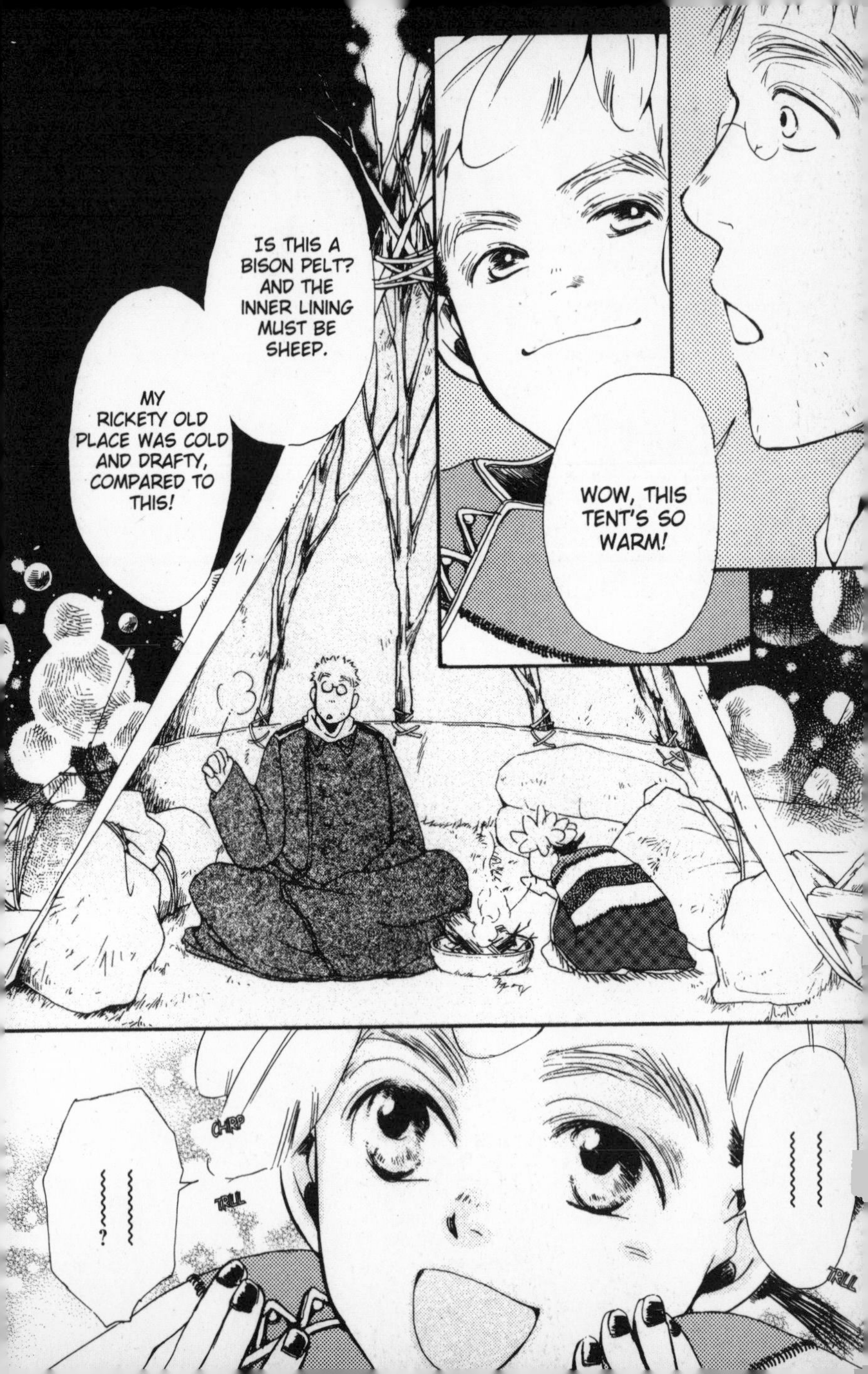
WOW, THIS TENT'S SO WARM!
IS THIS A BISON PELT? AND THE INNER LINING MUST BE SHEEP.
MY RICKETY OLD PLACE WAS COLD AND DRAFTY, COMPARED TO THIS!
TRLL
CHRP
TRLL

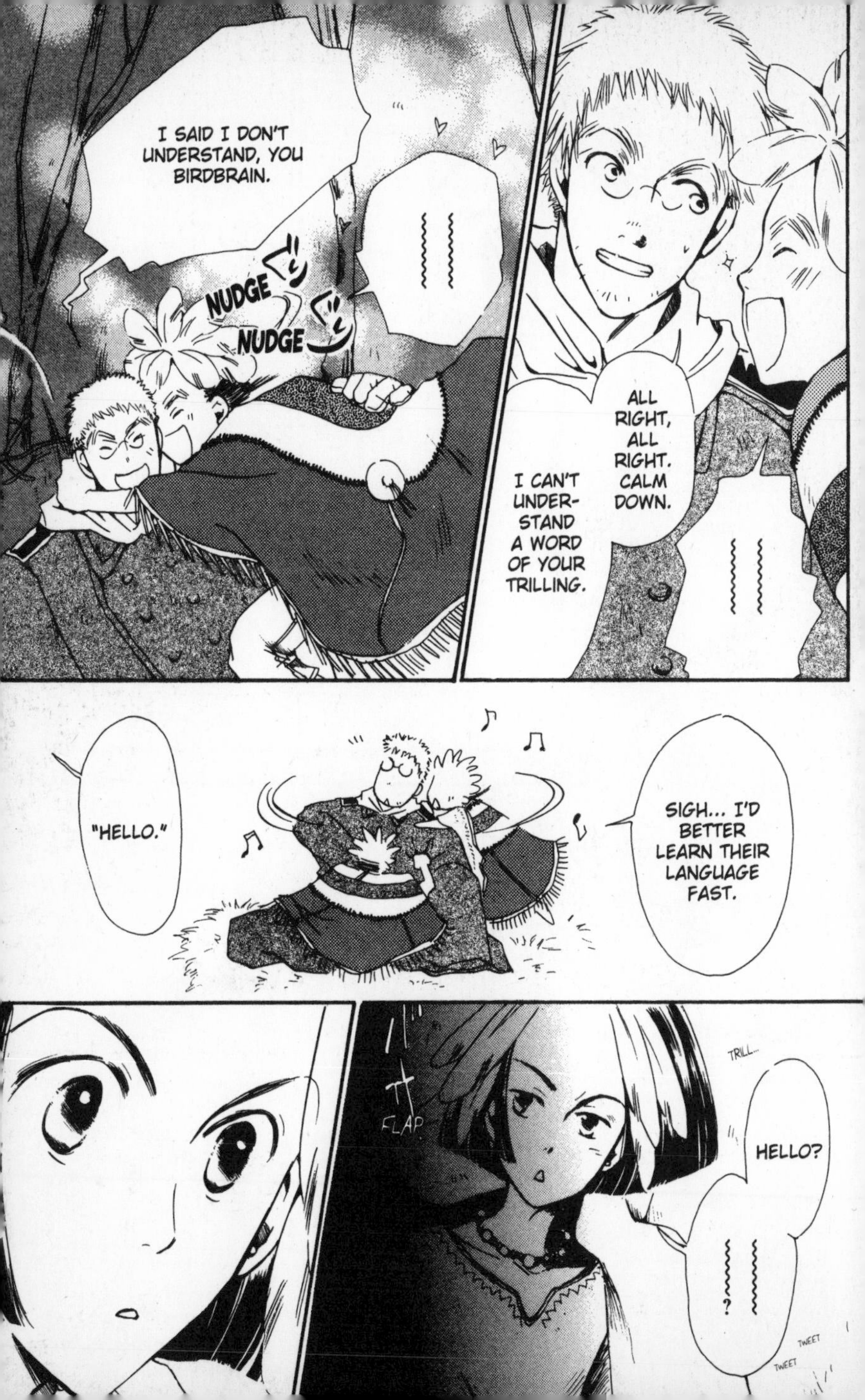
ALL RIGHT, ALL RIGHT. CALM DOWN.
I CAN'T UNDER-STAND A WORD OF YOUR TRILLING.
I SAID I DON'T UNDERSTAND, YOU BIRDBRAIN.
NUDGE
NUDGE
SIGH... I'D BETTER LEARN THEIR LANGUAGE FAST.
"HELLO."
TRILL...
HELLO?
TWEET
TWEET
FLAP

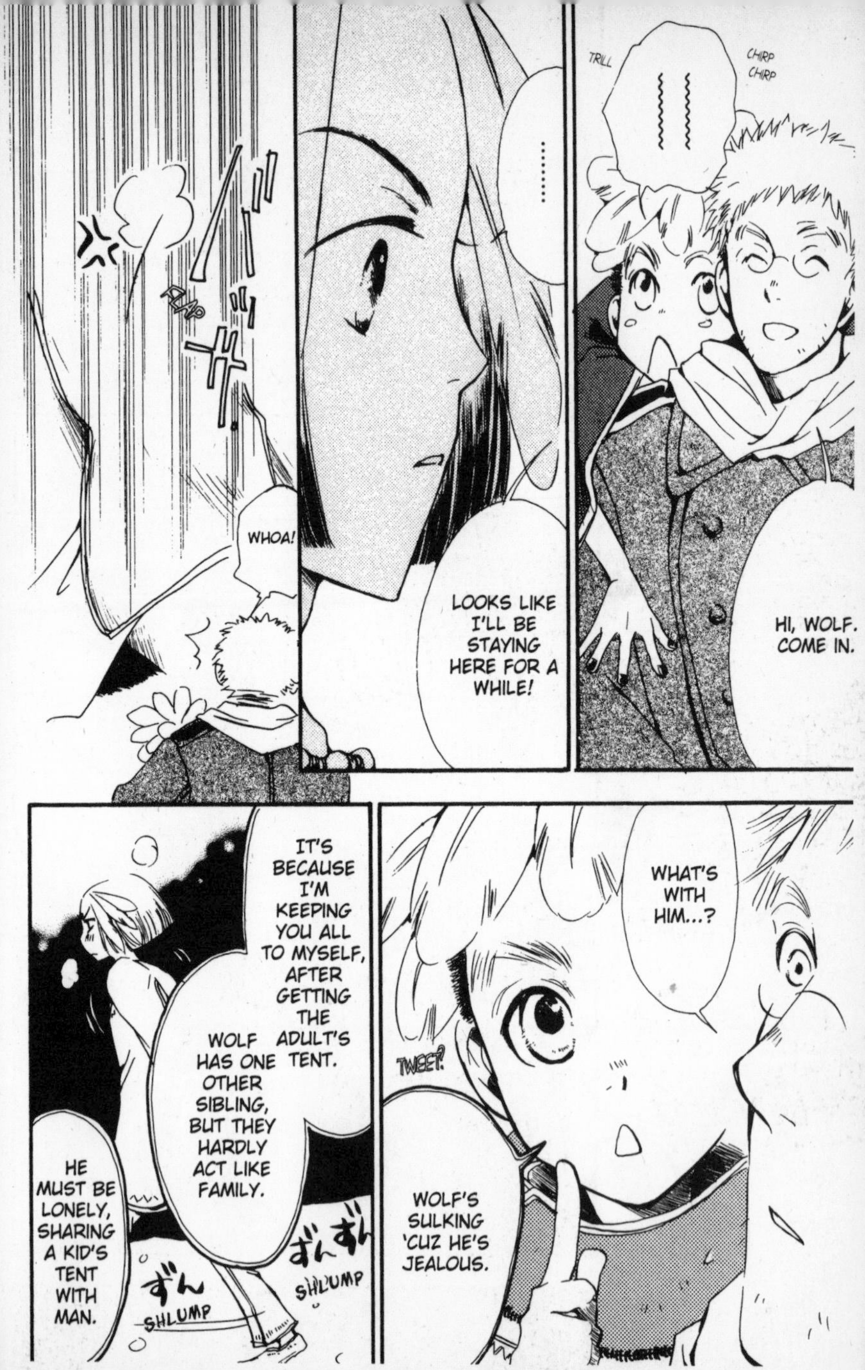
TRILL
CHIRP CHIRP
HI, WOLF. COME IN.
......
LOOKS LIKE I'LL BE STAYING HERE FOR A WHILE!
FLAP
WHOA!
WHAT'S WITH HIM...?
TWEET?
WOLF'S SULKING 'CUZ HE'S JEALOUS.
IT'S BECAUSE I'M KEEPING YOU ALL TO MYSELF, AFTER GETTING THE ADULT'S TENT.
WOLF HAS ONE OTHER SIBLING, BUT THEY HARDLY ACT LIKE FAMILY.
HE MUST BE LONELY, SHARING A KID'S TENT WITH MAN.
ずんずん
SHLUMP
ずん
SHLUMP

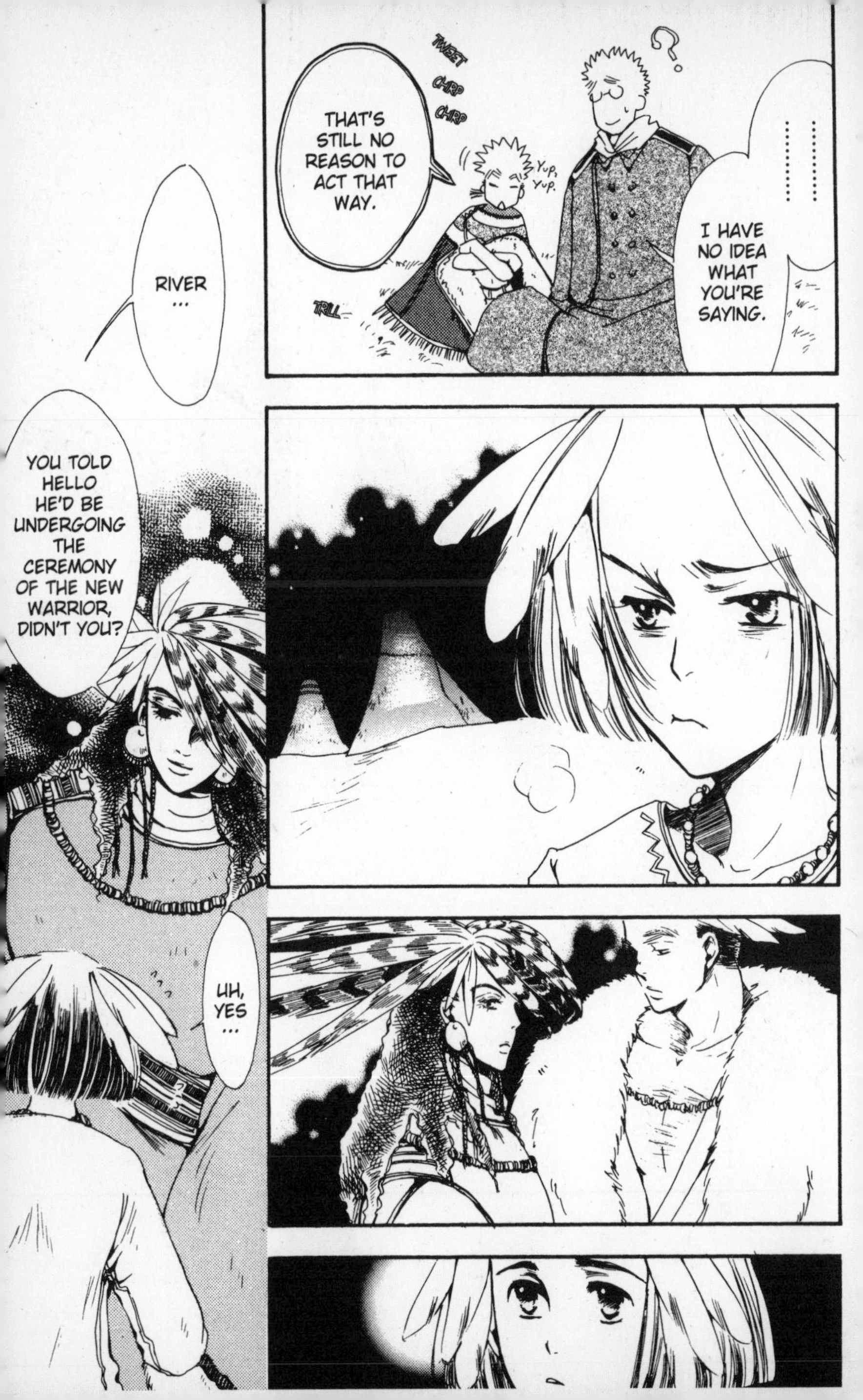
......
I HAVE NO IDEA WHAT YOU'RE SAYING.
TWEET
CHIRP
CHIRP
Yup, yup.
THAT'S STILL NO REASON TO ACT THAT WAY.
TRILL
RIVER ...
YOU TOLD HELLO HE'D BE UNDERGOING THE CEREMONY OF THE NEW WARRIOR, DIDN'T YOU?
UH, YES ...

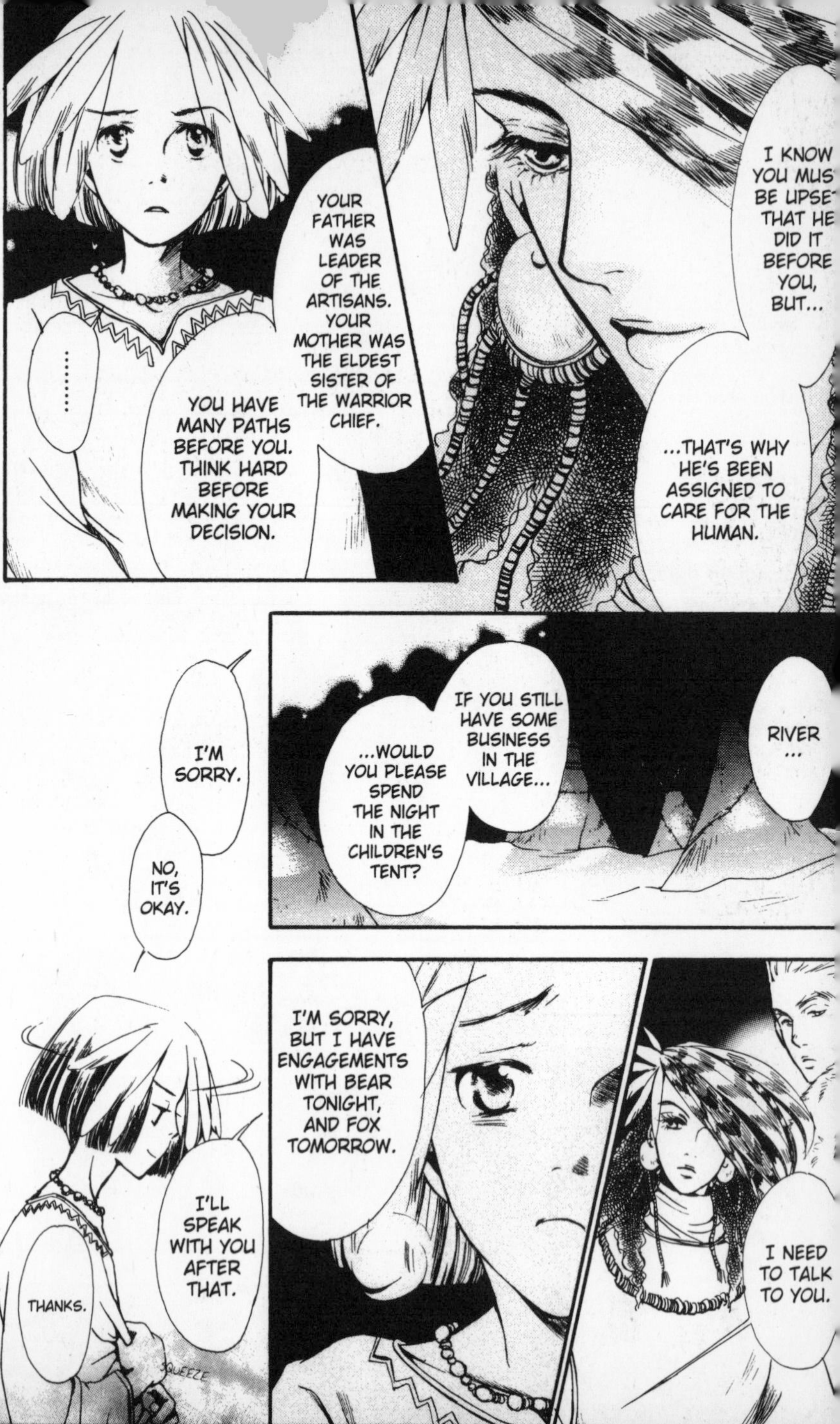
I KNOW YOU MUS BE UPSE THAT HE DID IT BEFORE YOU, BUT...
...THAT'S WHY HE'S BEEN ASSIGNED TO CARE FOR THE HUMAN.
YOUR FATHER WAS LEADER OF THE ARTISANS. YOUR MOTHER WAS THE ELDEST SISTER OF THE WARRIOR CHIEF.
YOU HAVE MANY PATHS BEFORE YOU. THINK HARD BEFORE MAKING YOUR DECISION.
......
RIVER ...
IF YOU STILL HAVE SOME BUSINESS IN THE VILLAGE...
...WOULD YOU PLEASE SPEND THE NIGHT IN THE CHILDREN'S TENT?
I'M SORRY.
NO, IT'S OKAY.
I NEED TO TALK TO YOU.
I'M SORRY, BUT I HAVE ENGAGEMENTS WITH BEAR TONIGHT, AND FOX TOMORROW.
I'LL SPEAK WITH YOU AFTER THAT.
THANKS.
SQUEEZE

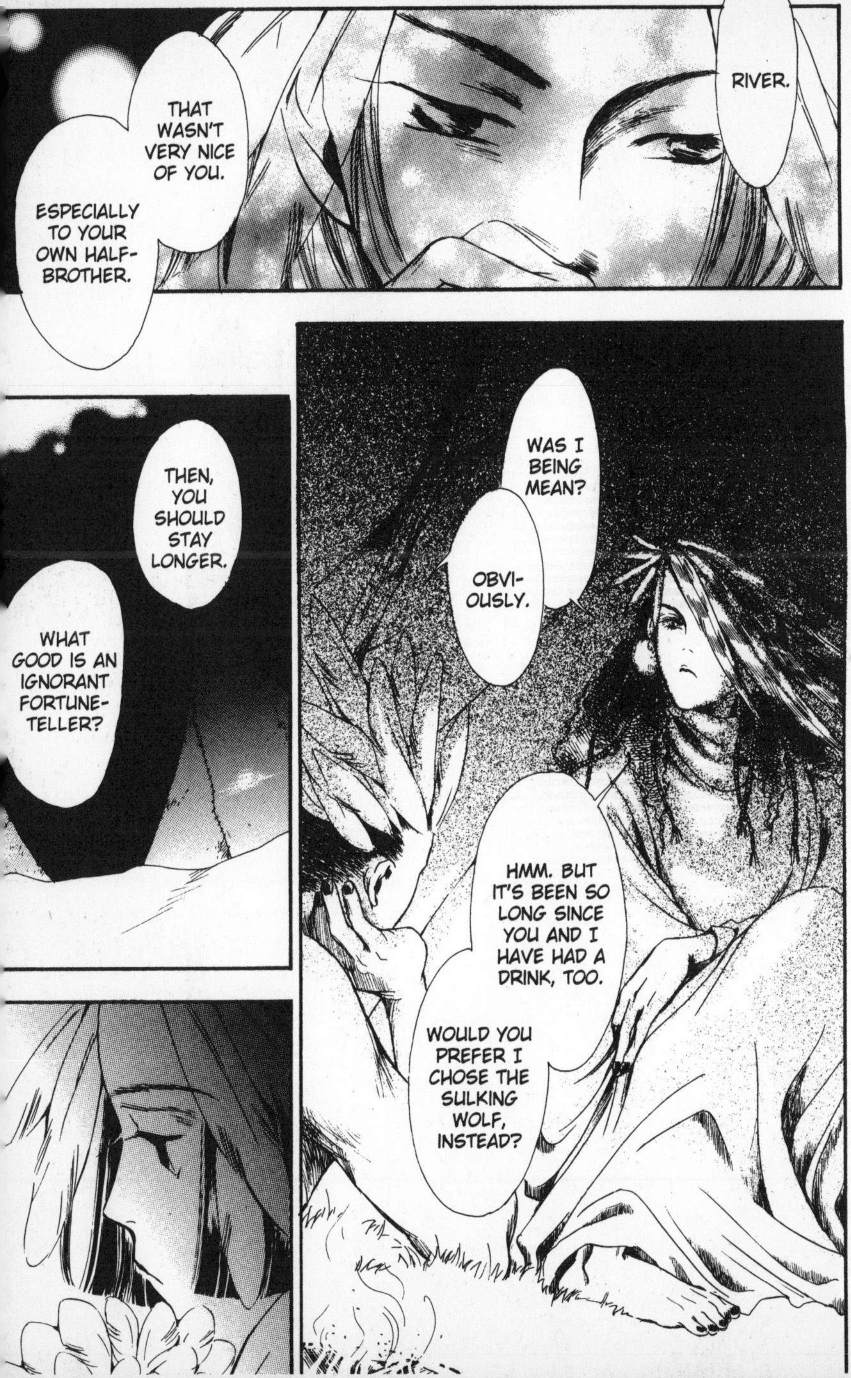
RIVER.
THAT WASN'T VERY NICE OF YOU.
ESPECIALLY TO YOUR OWN HALF-BROTHER.
WAS I BEING MEAN?
OBVI-OUSLY.
HMM. BUT IT'S BEEN SO LONG SINCE YOU AND I HAVE HAD A DRINK, TOO.
WOULD YOU PREFER I CHOSE THE SULKING WOLF, INSTEAD?
THEN, YOU SHOULD STAY LONGER.
WHAT GOOD IS AN IGNORANT FORTUNE-TELLER?

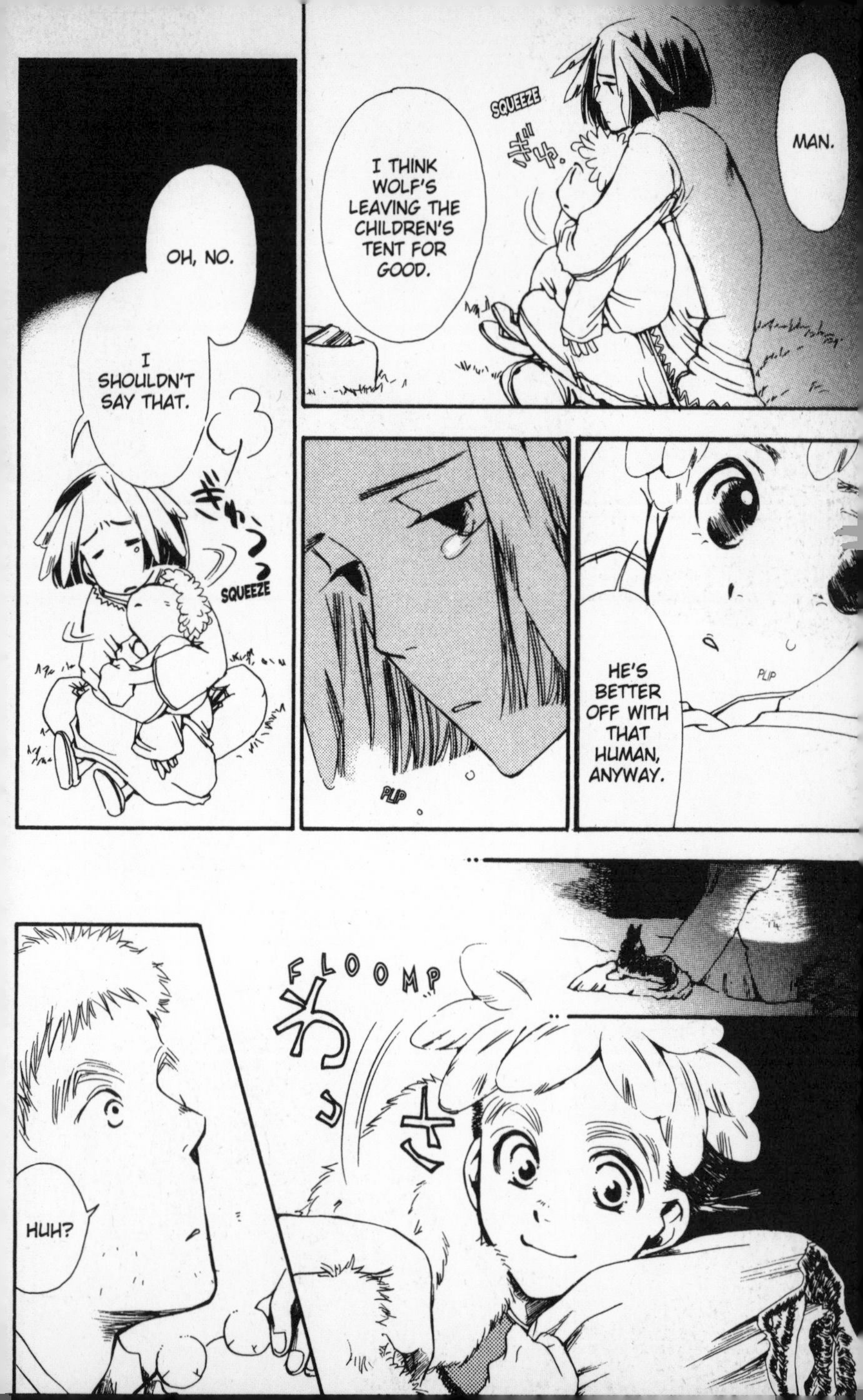
MAN.
I THINK WOLF'S LEAVING THE CHILDREN'S TENT FOR GOOD.
SQUEEZE
HE'S BETTER OFF WITH THAT HUMAN, ANYWAY.
PLIP
PLIP
OH, NO.
I SHOULDN'T SAY THAT.
SQUEEZE
FLOOMP
HUH?

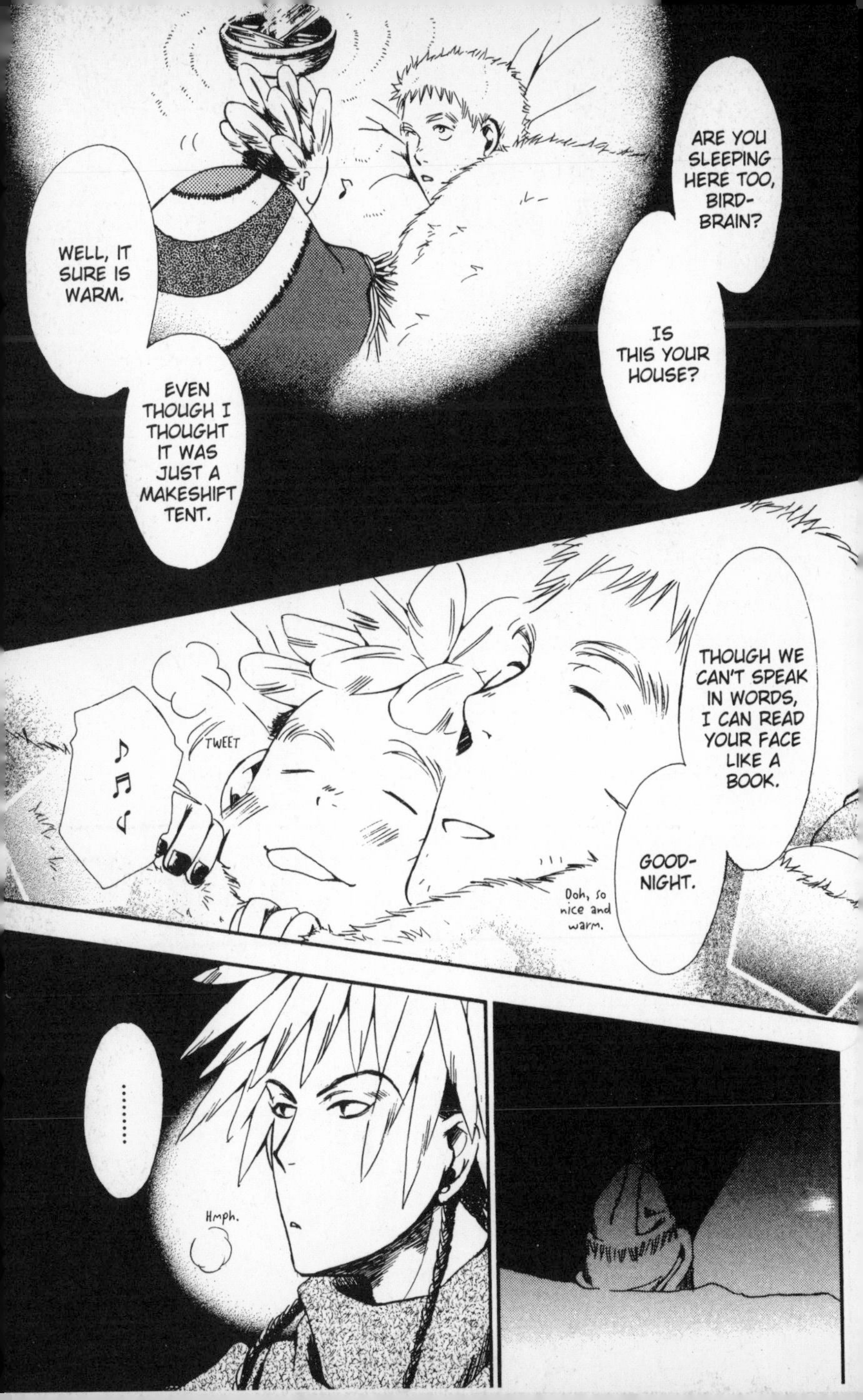

ARE YOU SLEEPING HERE TOO, BIRD-BRAIN?
IS THIS YOUR HOUSE?
WELL, IT SURE IS WARM.
EVEN THOUGH I THOUGHT IT WAS JUST A MAKESHIFT TENT.
THOUGH WE CAN'T SPEAK IN WORDS, I CAN READ YOUR FACE LIKE A BOOK.
GOOD-NIGHT.
Ooh, so nice and warm.
TWEET
......
Hmph.

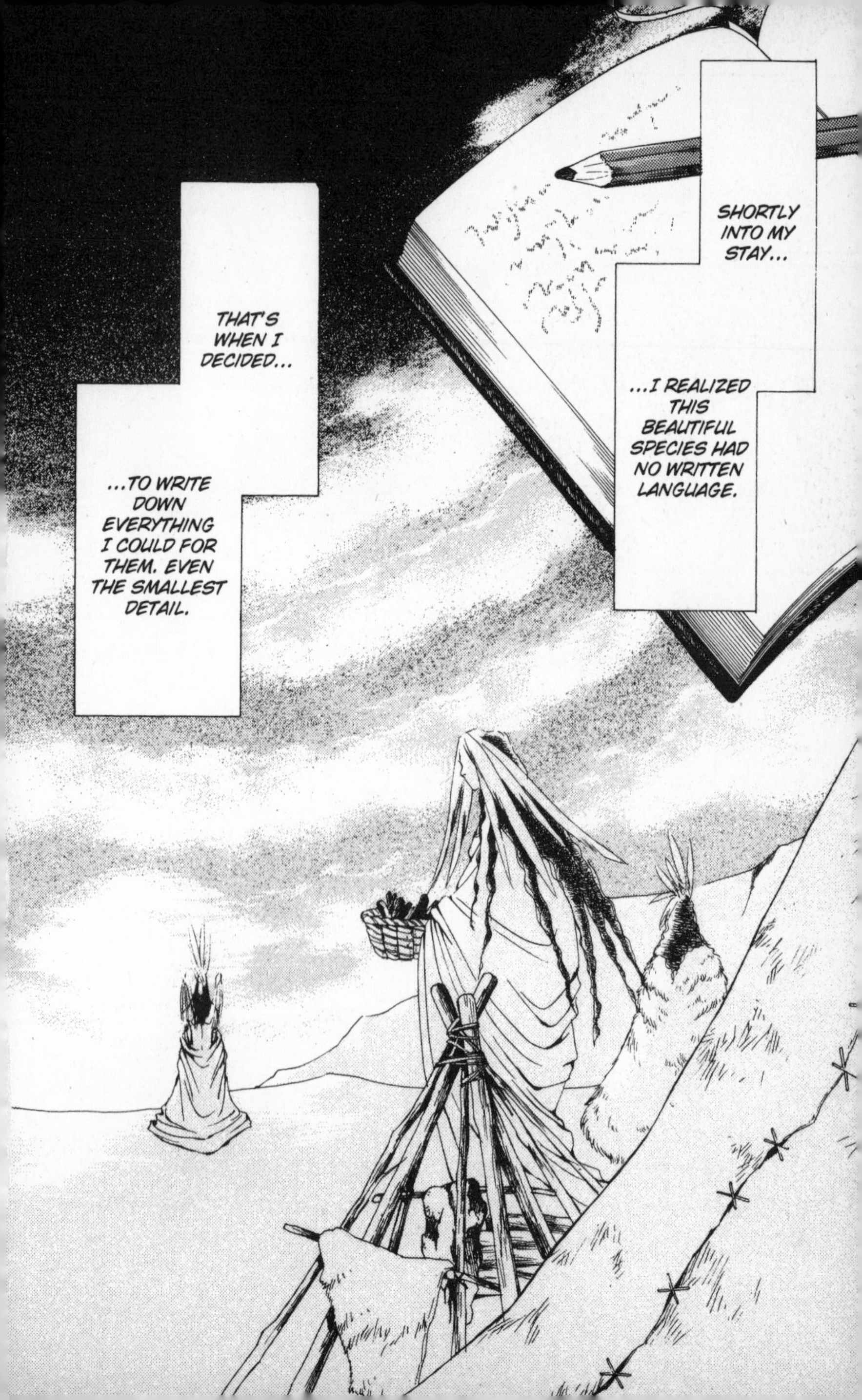
SHORTLY INTO MY STAY...
...I REALIZED THIS BEAUTIFUL SPECIES HAD NO WRITTEN LANGUAGE.
THAT'S WHEN I DECIDED...
...TO WRITE DOWN EVERYTHING I COULD FOR THEM. EVEN THE SMALLEST DETAIL.

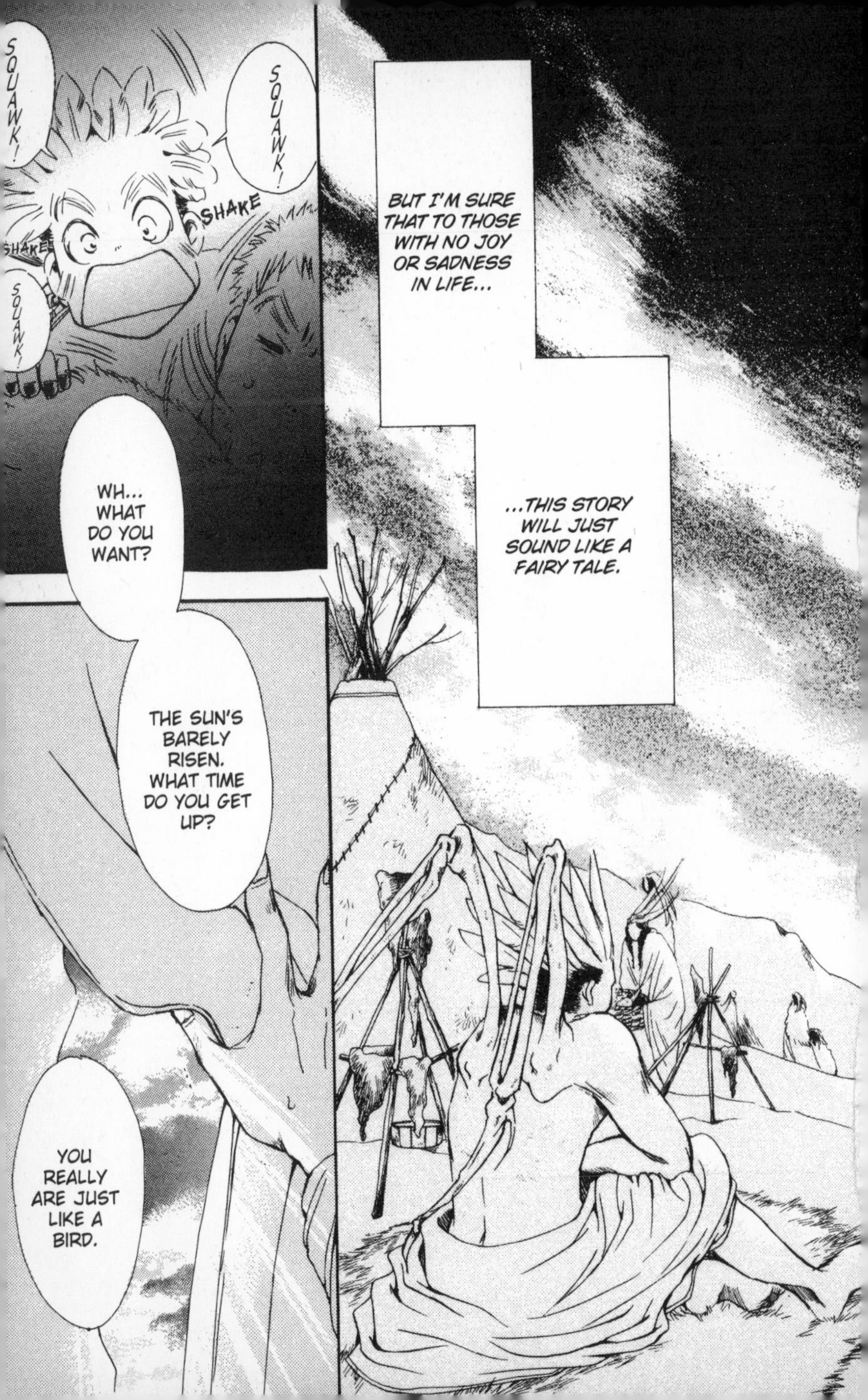
BUT I'M SURE THAT TO THOSE WITH NO JOY OR SADNESS IN LIFE...
...THIS STORY WILL JUST SOUND LIKE A FAIRY TALE.
SQUAWK!
SHAKE
SQUAWK!
SHAKE
SQUAWK!
WH... WHAT DO YOU WANT?
THE SUN'S BARELY RISEN. WHAT TIME DO YOU GET UP?
YOU REALLY ARE JUST LIKE A BIRD.

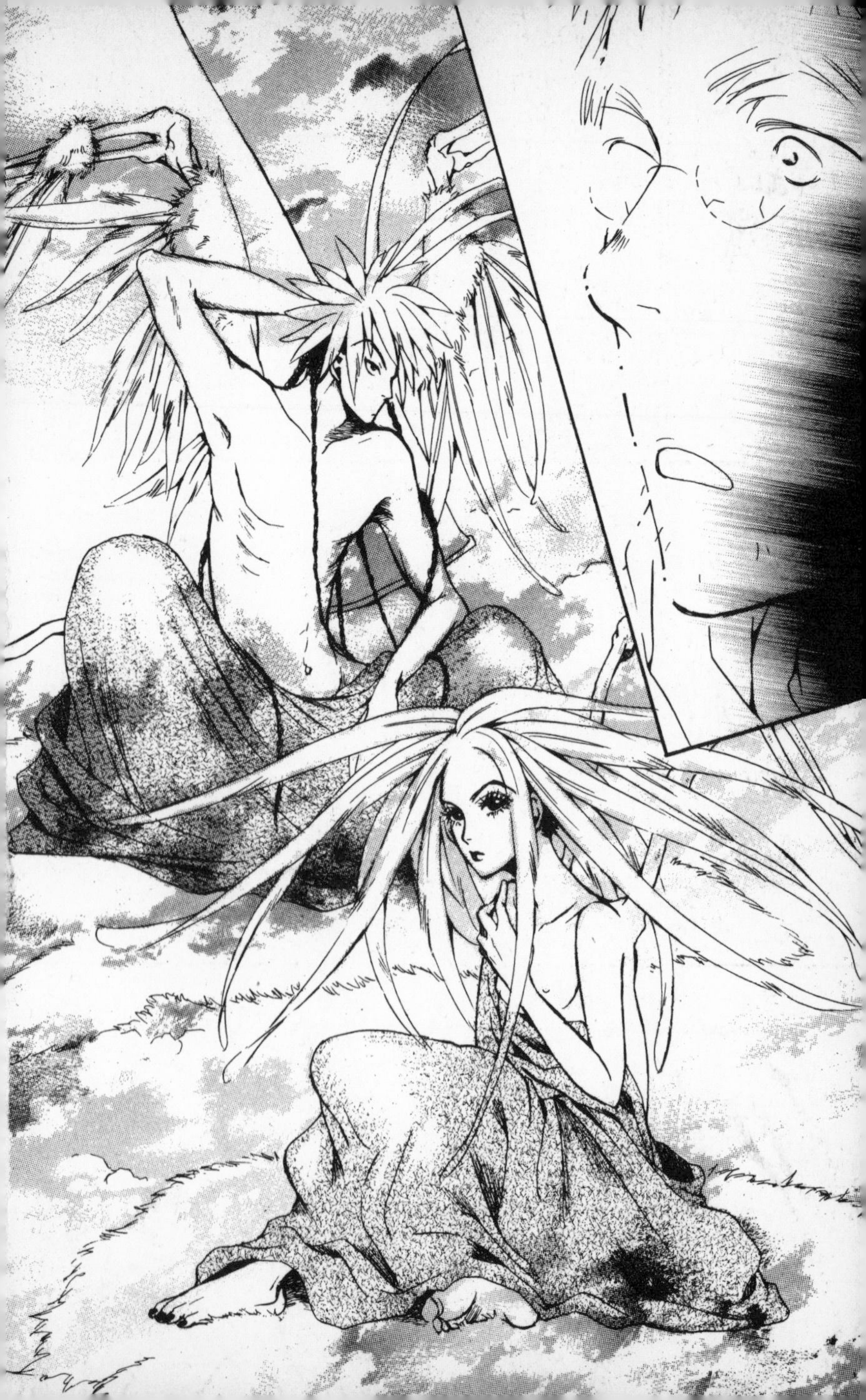

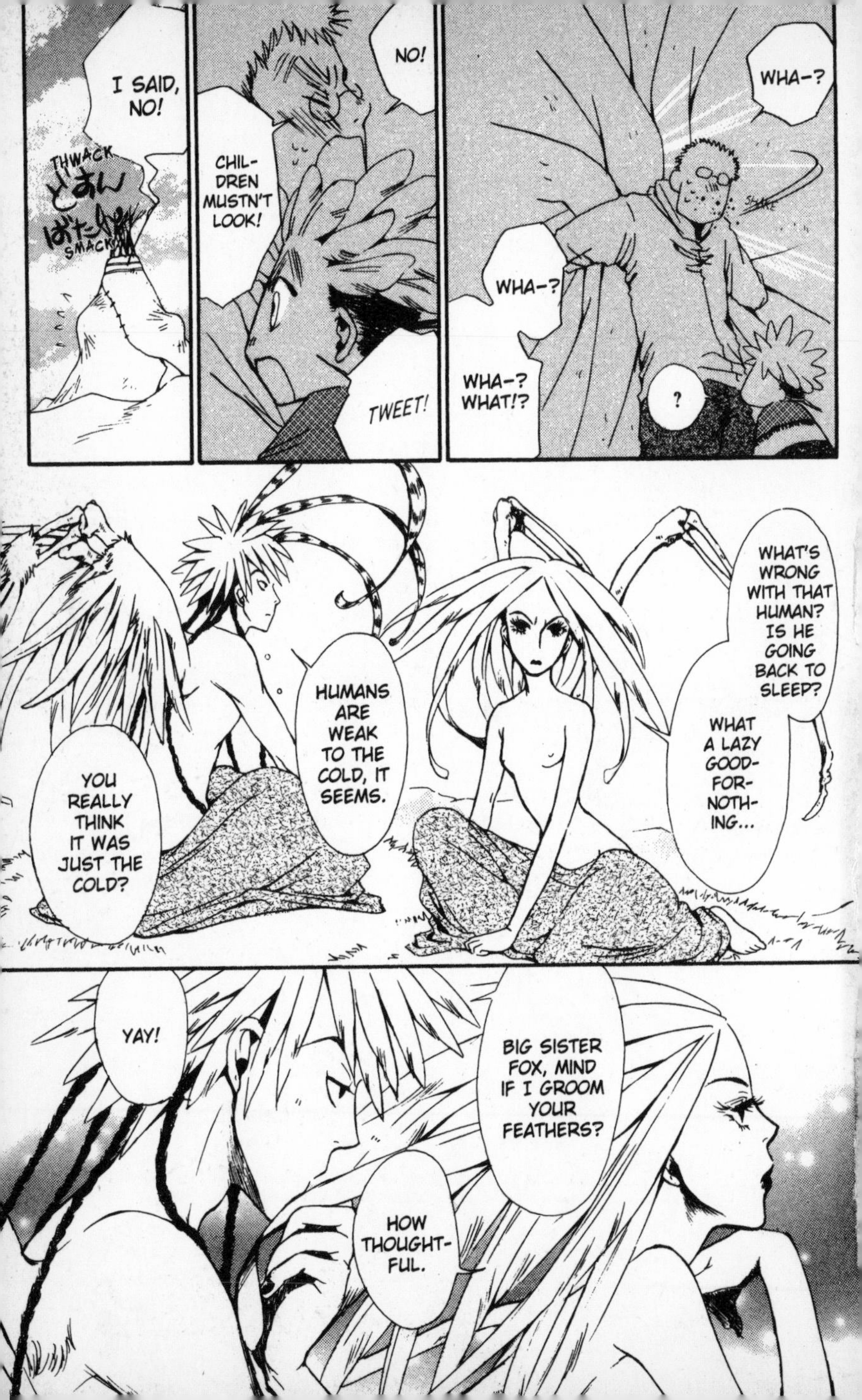
WHA-?
SHAKE
WHA-?
?
WHA-? WHAT!?
NO!
CHIL-DREN MUSTN'T LOOK!
TWEET!
I SAID, NO!
THWACK
SMACK
WHAT'S WRONG WITH THAT HUMAN? IS HE GOING BACK TO SLEEP?
WHAT A LAZY GOOD-FOR-NOTHING...
HUMANS ARE WEAK TO THE COLD, IT SEEMS.
YOU REALLY THINK IT WAS JUST THE COLD?
BIG SISTER FOX, MIND IF I GROOM YOUR FEATHERS?
YAY!
HOW THOUGHT-FUL.

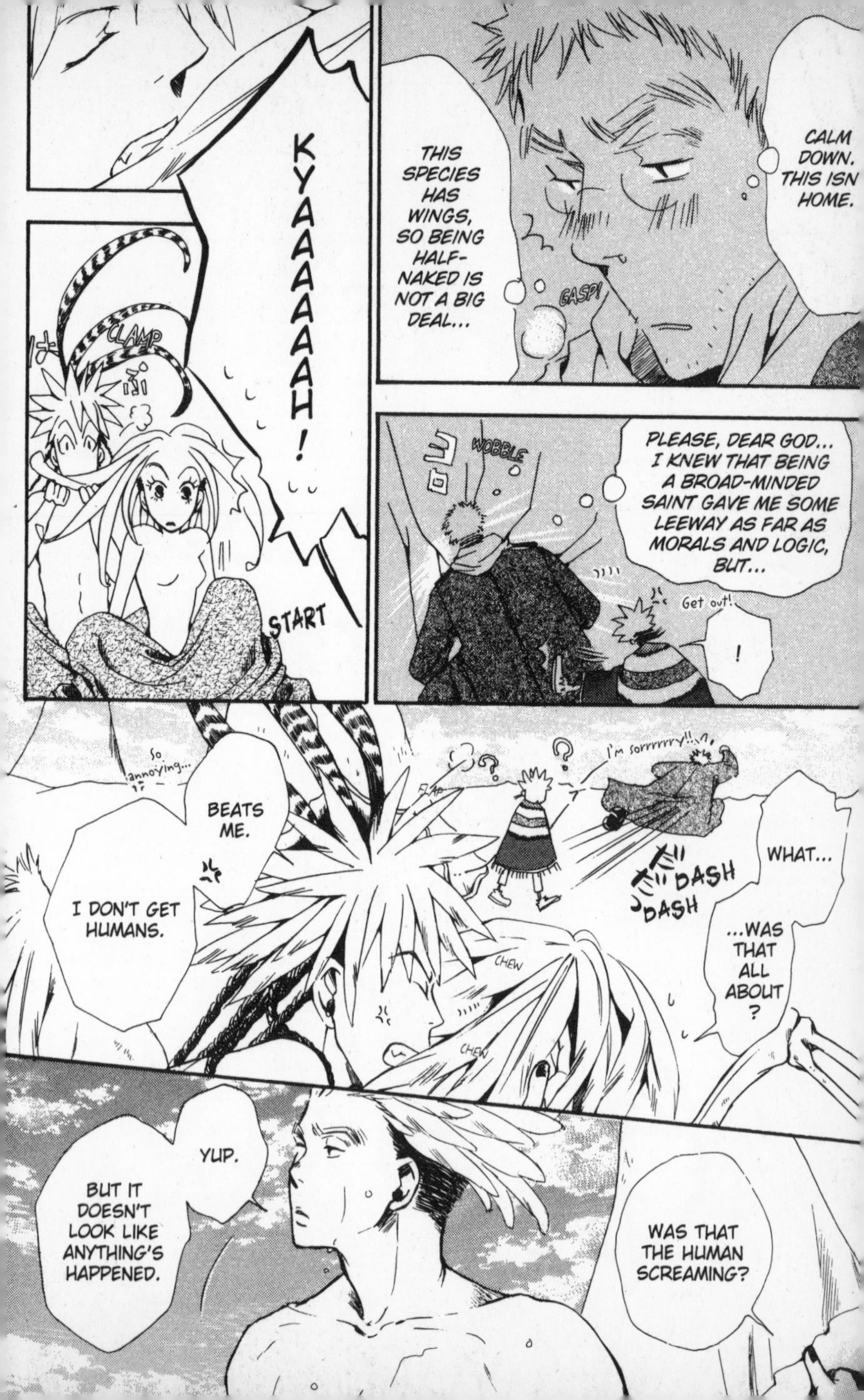

CALM DOWN. THIS ISN HOME.
THIS SPECIES HAS WINGS, SO BEING HALF-NAKED IS NOT A BIG DEAL...
GASP!
PLEASE, DEAR GOD... I KNEW THAT BEING A BROAD-MINDED SAINT GAVE ME SOME LEEWAY AS FAR AS MORALS AND LOGIC, BUT...
WOBBLE
Get out!
!
KYAAAAAAAAH!
CLAMP
START
WHAT...
...WAS THAT ALL ABOUT?
I'm sorrrrrry!!
DASH
DASH
FLAP
CHEW
CHEW
BEATS ME.
I DON'T GET HUMANS.
So annoying...
WAS THAT THE HUMAN SCREAMING?
YUP.
BUT IT DOESN'T LOOK LIKE ANYTHING'S HAPPENED.

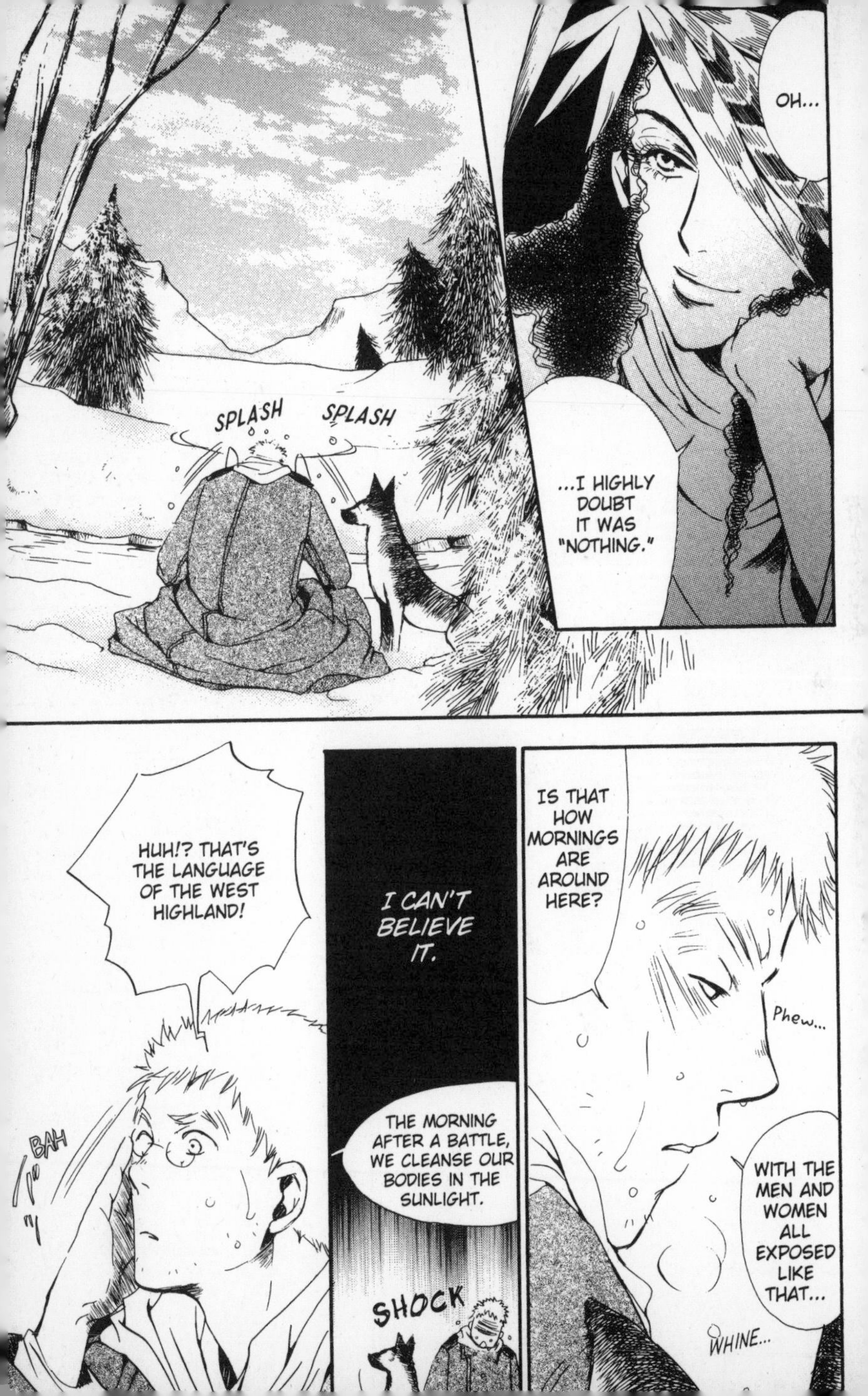
OH...
...I HIGHLY DOUBT IT WAS "NOTHING."
SPLASH
SPLASH
IS THAT HOW MORNINGS ARE AROUND HERE?
Phew...
WITH THE MEN AND WOMEN ALL EXPOSED LIKE THAT...
WHINE...
I CAN'T BELIEVE IT.
THE MORNING AFTER A BATTLE, WE CLEANSE OUR BODIES IN THE SUNLIGHT.
SHOCK
HUH!? THAT'S THE LANGUAGE OF THE WEST HIGHLAND!
BAH

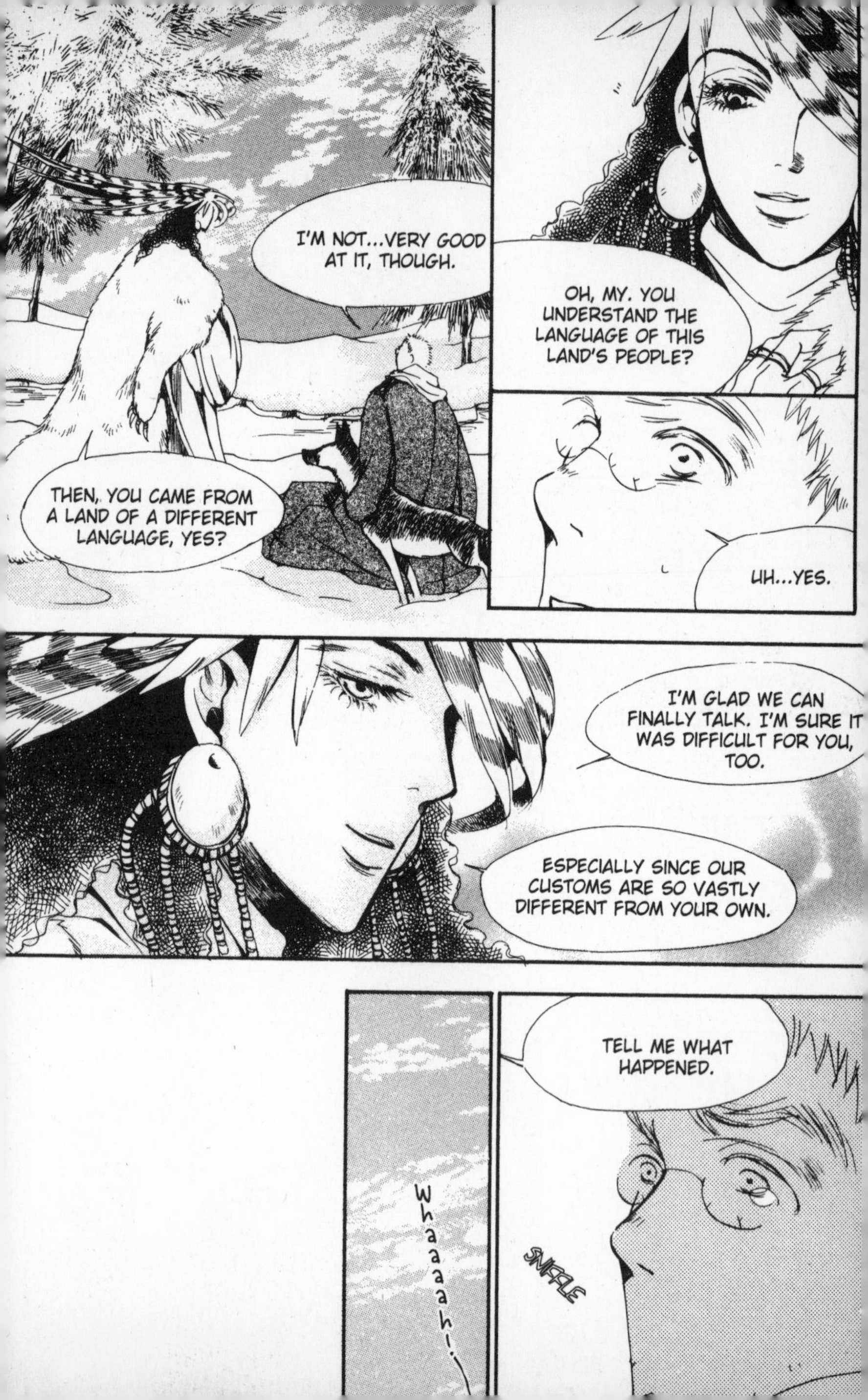
OH, MY. YOU UNDERSTAND THE LANGUAGE OF THIS LAND'S PEOPLE?
UH...YES.
I'M NOT...VERY GOOD AT IT, THOUGH.
THEN, YOU CAME FROM A LAND OF A DIFFERENT LANGUAGE, YES?
I'M GLAD WE CAN FINALLY TALK. I'M SURE IT WAS DIFFICULT FOR YOU, TOO.
ESPECIALLY SINCE OUR CUSTOMS ARE SO VASTLY DIFFERENT FROM YOUR OWN.
TELL ME WHAT HAPPENED.
SNIFFLE
Whaaaah!..

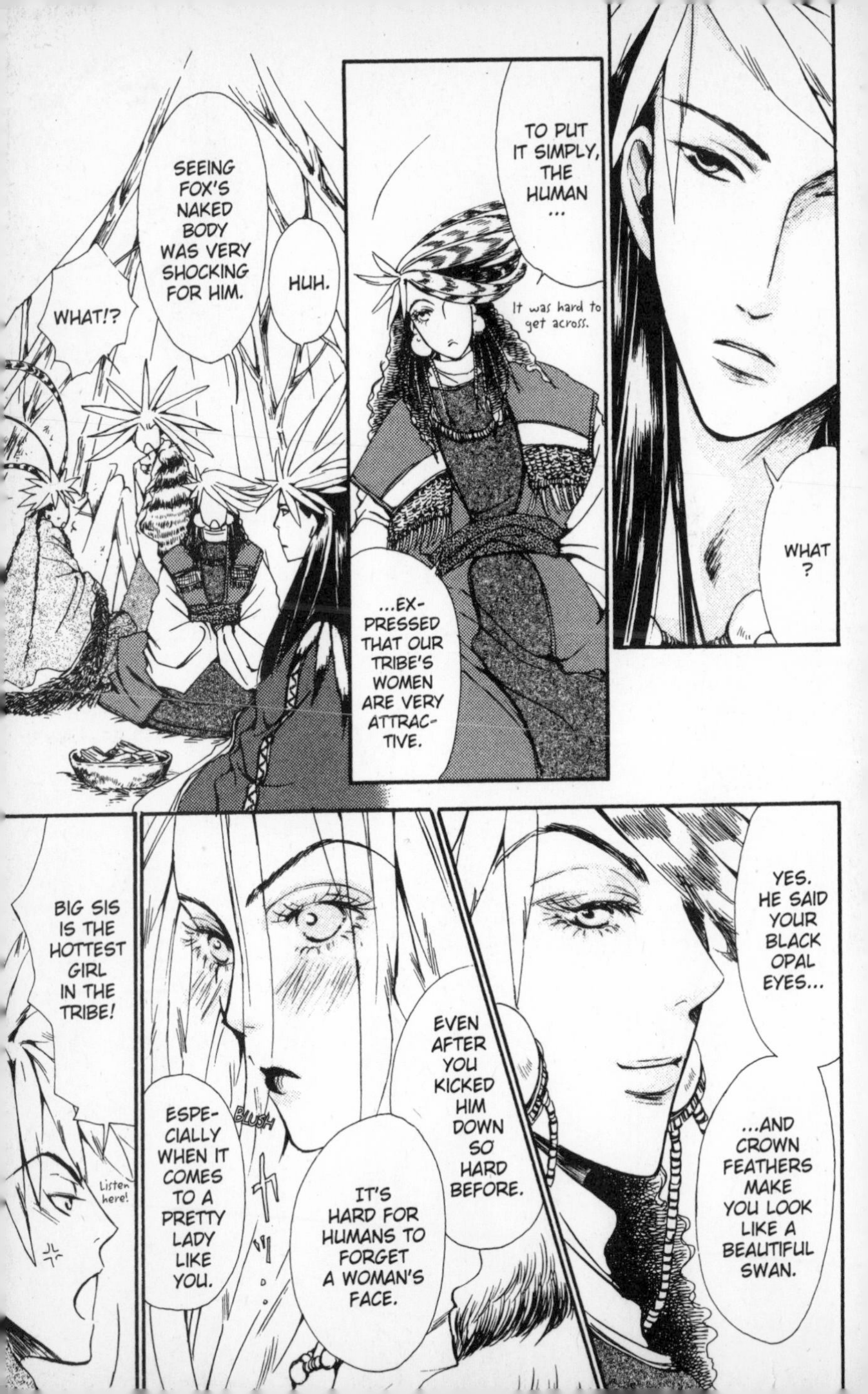
WHAT?
TO PUT IT SIMPLY, THE HUMAN ...
It was hard to get across.
...EXPRESSED THAT OUR TRIBE'S WOMEN ARE VERY ATTRACTIVE.
HUH.
SEEING FOX'S NAKED BODY WAS VERY SHOCKING FOR HIM.
WHAT!?
YES. HE SAID YOUR BLACK OPAL EYES...
...AND CROWN FEATHERS MAKE YOU LOOK LIKE A BEAUTIFUL SWAN.
EVEN AFTER YOU KICKED HIM DOWN SO HARD BEFORE.
IT'S HARD FOR HUMANS TO FORGET A WOMAN'S FACE.
BLUSH
ESPECIALLY WHEN IT COMES TO A PRETTY LADY LIKE YOU.
BIG SIS IS THE HOTTEST GIRL IN THE TRIBE!
Listen here!

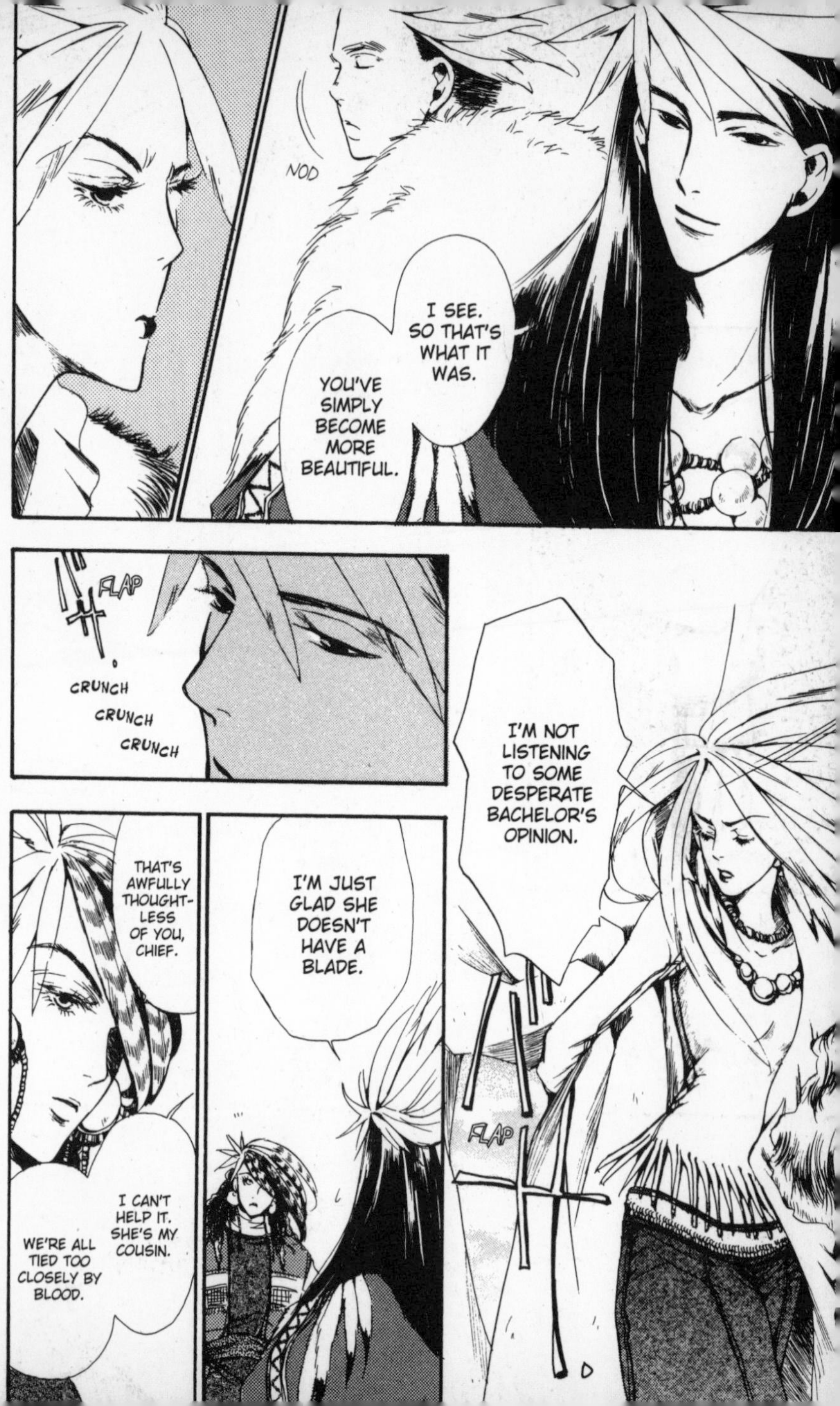
NOD
I SEE. SO THAT'S WHAT IT WAS.
YOU'VE SIMPLY BECOME MORE BEAUTIFUL.
I'M NOT LISTENING TO SOME DESPERATE BACHELOR'S OPINION.
FLAP
FLAP
CRUNCH
CRUNCH
CRUNCH
I'M JUST GLAD SHE DOESN'T HAVE A BLADE.
THAT'S AWFULLY THOUGHTLESS OF YOU, CHIEF.
I CAN'T HELP IT. SHE'S MY COUSIN.
WE'RE ALL TIED TOO CLOSELY BY BLOOD.

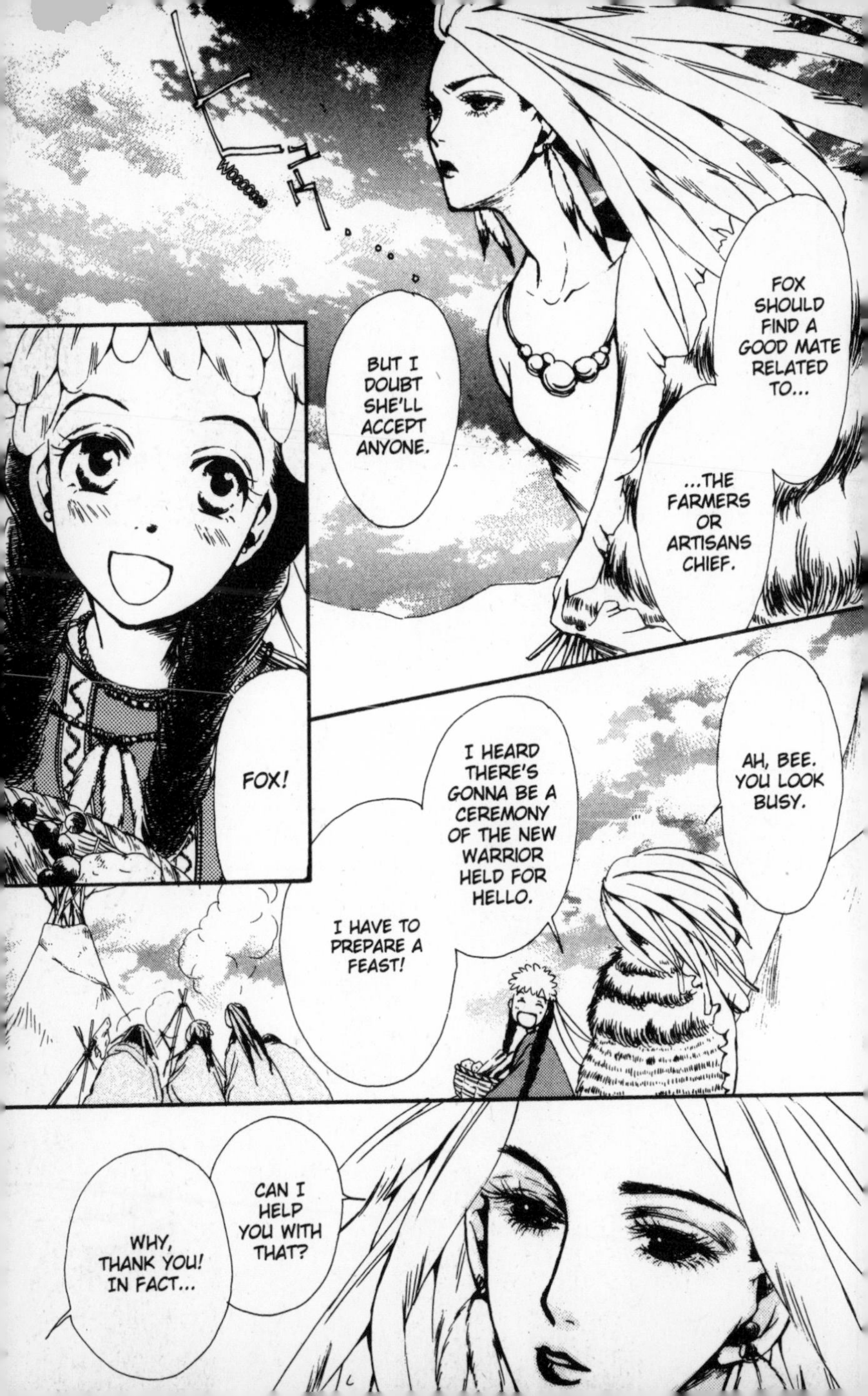
WOOOOOO
FOX SHOULD FIND A GOOD MATE RELATED TO...
...THE FARMERS OR ARTISANS CHIEF.
BUT I DOUBT SHE'LL ACCEPT ANYONE.
FOX!
AH, BEE. YOU LOOK BUSY.
I HEARD THERE'S GONNA BE A CEREMONY OF THE NEW WARRIOR HELD FOR HELLO.
I HAVE TO PREPARE A FEAST!
CAN I HELP YOU WITH THAT?
WHY, THANK YOU! IN FACT...

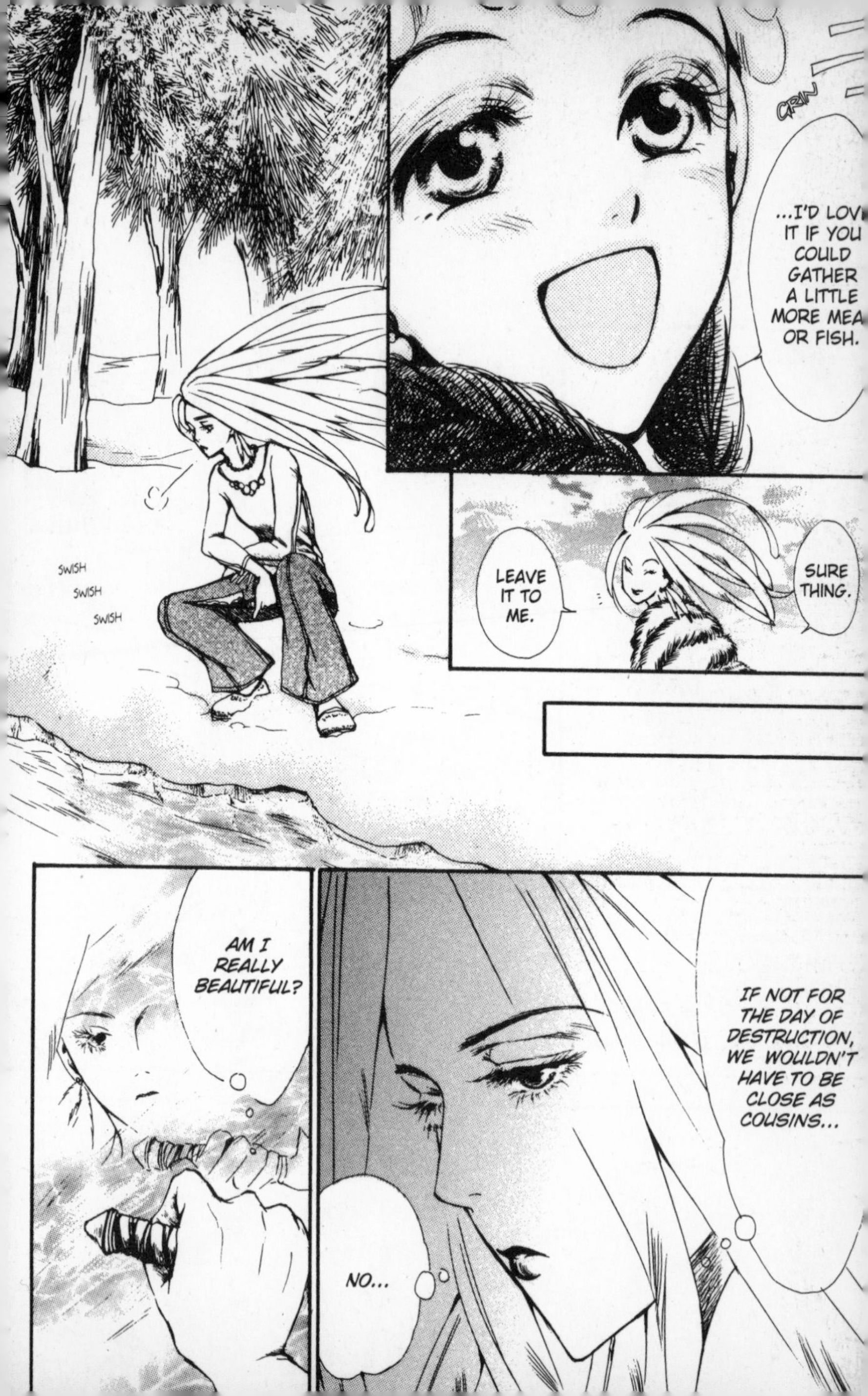
GRIN
...I'D LOV IT IF YOU COULD GATHER A LITTLE MORE MEA OR FISH.
SURE THING.
LEAVE IT TO ME.
SWISH SWISH SWISH
IF NOT FOR THE DAY OF DESTRUCTION, WE WOULDN'T HAVE TO BE CLOSE AS COUSINS...
NO...
AM I REALLY BEAUTIFUL?

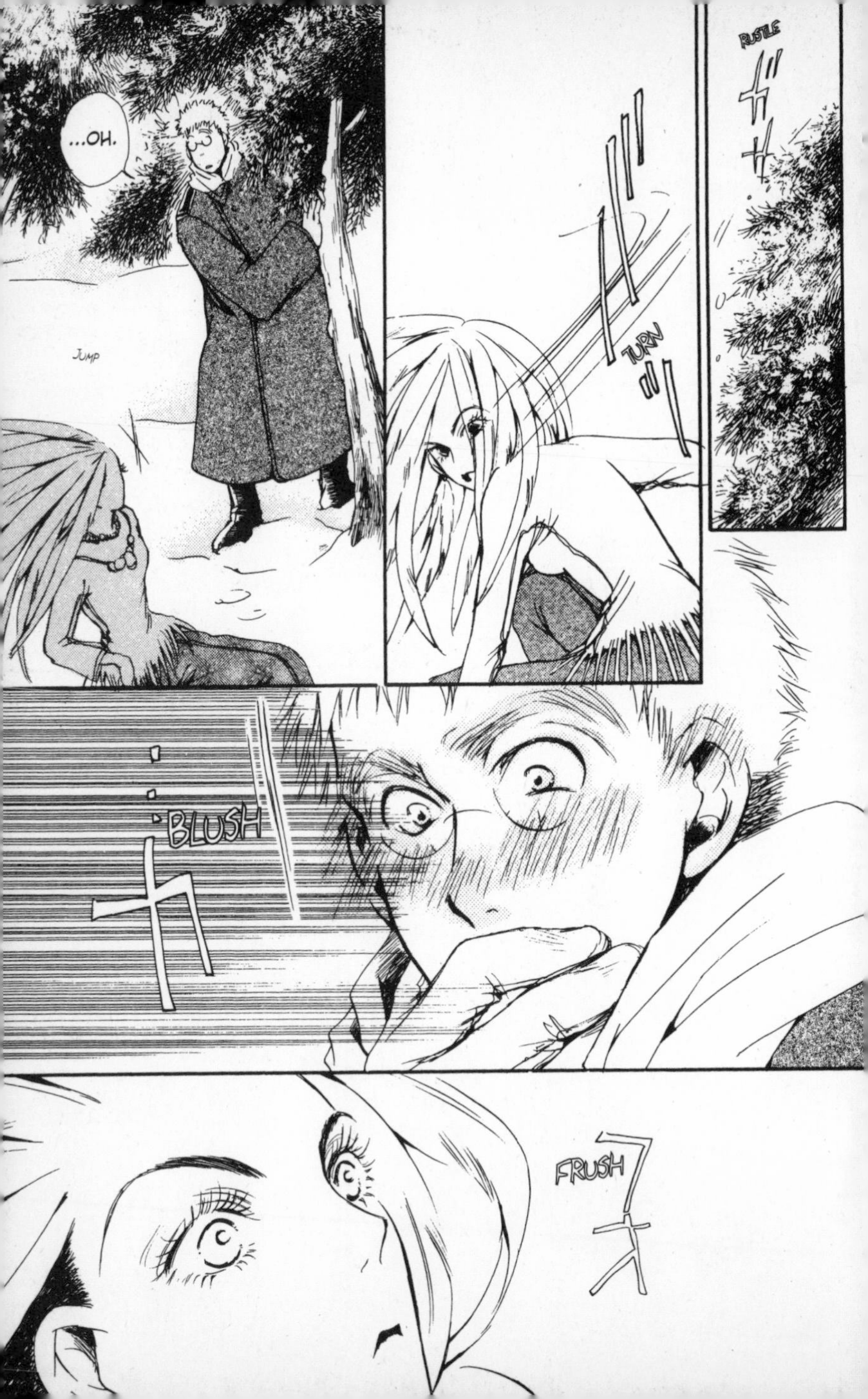
RUSTLE
TURN
...OH.
JUMP
BLUSH
FRUSH

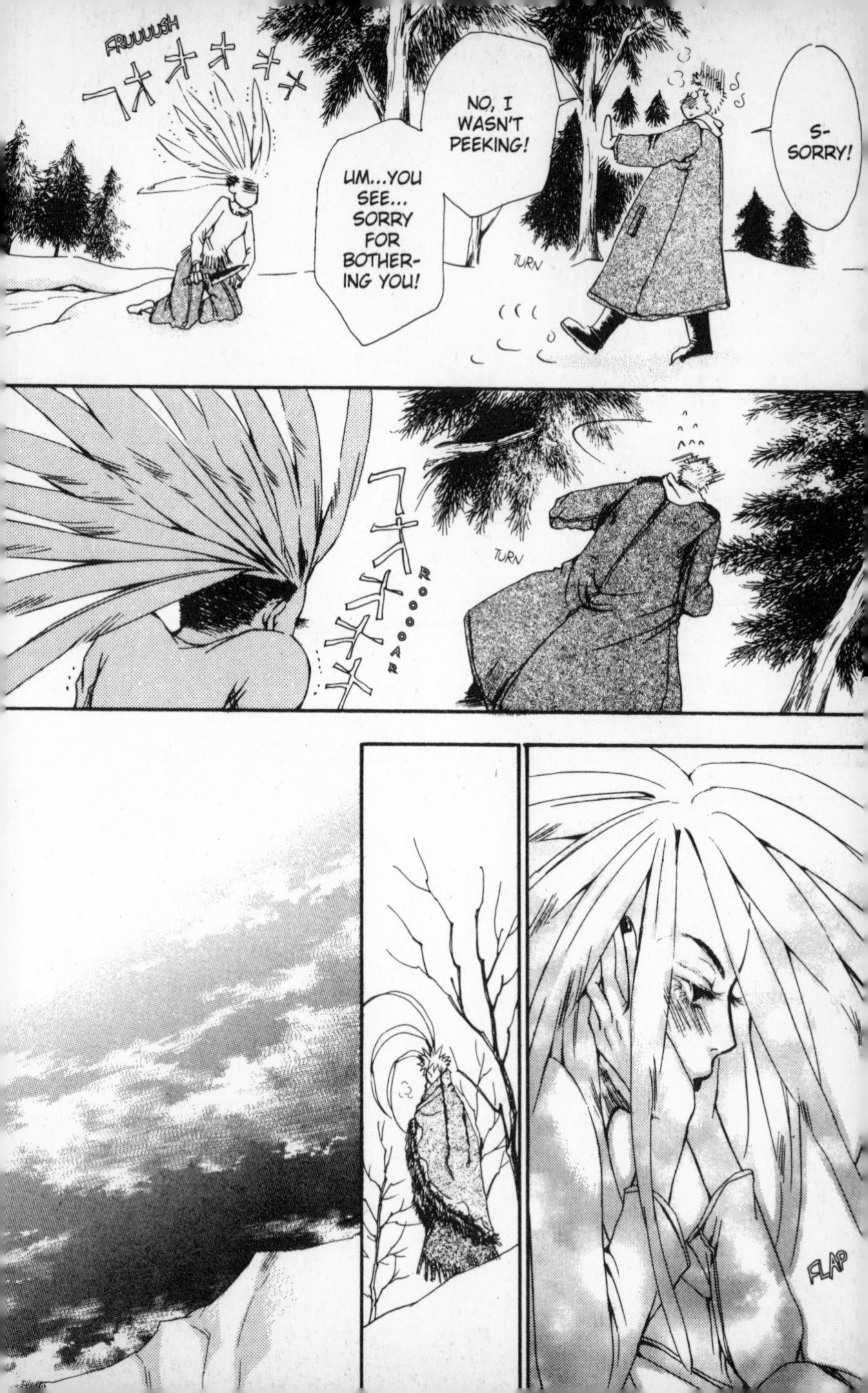
S-SORRY!
NO, I WASN'T PEEKING!
UM...YOU SEE... SORRY FOR BOTHERING YOU!
TURN
FRUUUUSH
TURN
ROOOOAR
FLAP

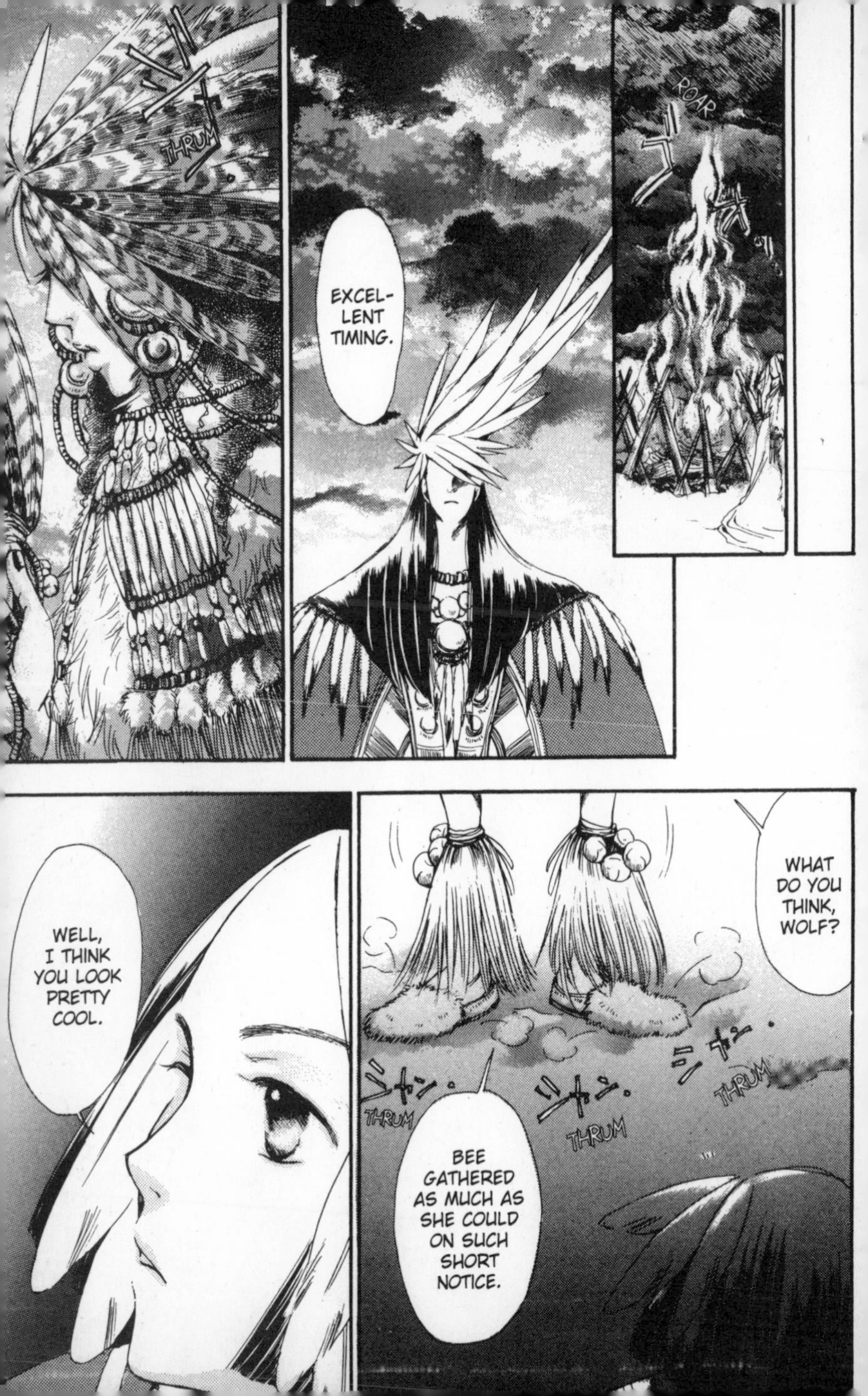
ROAR
EXCEL-LENT TIMING.
THRUM
WHAT DO YOU THINK, WOLF?
THRUM
THRUM
THRUM
BEE GATHERED AS MUCH AS SHE COULD ON SUCH SHORT NOTICE.
WELL, I THINK YOU LOOK PRETTY COOL.

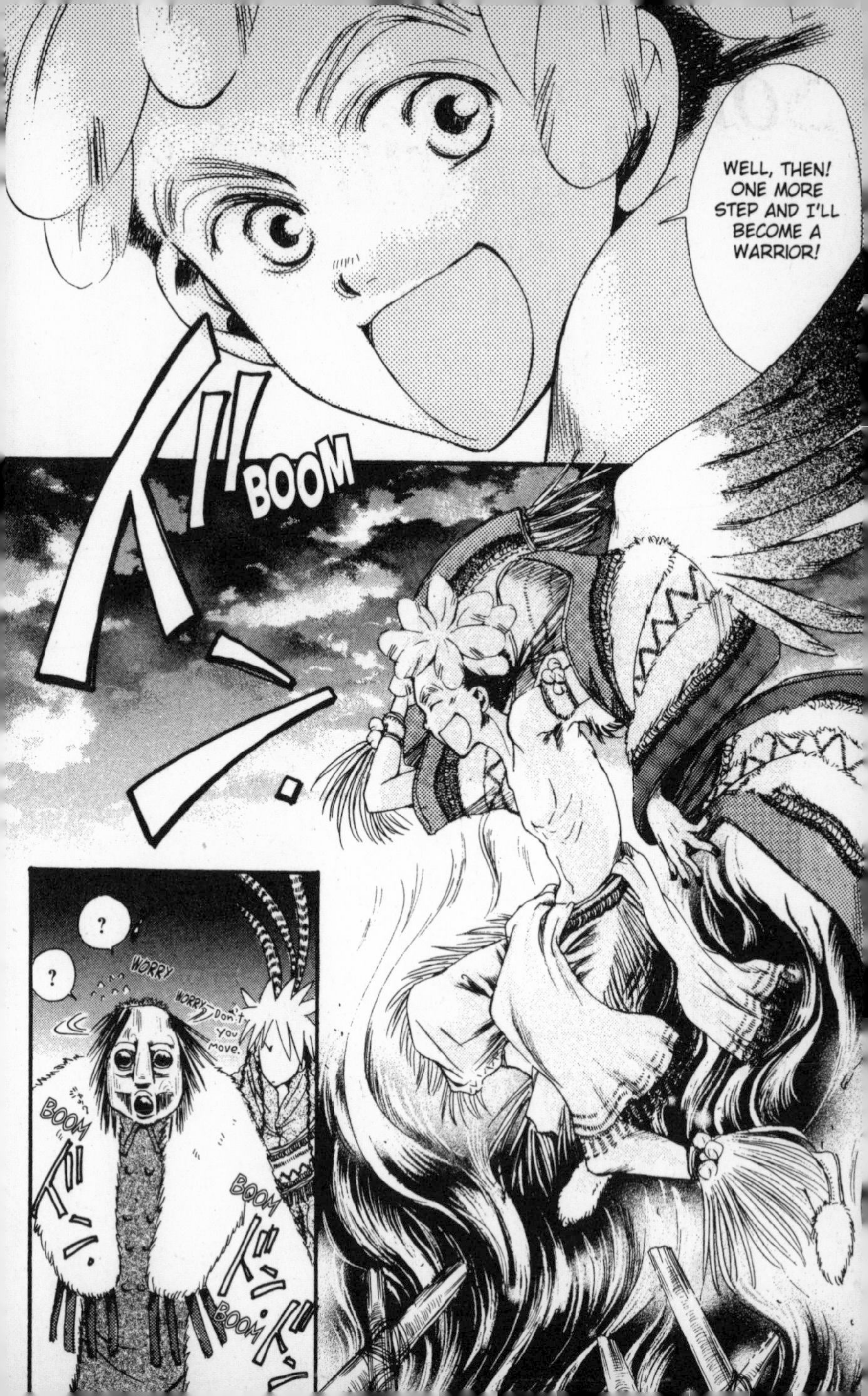
WELL, THEN! ONE MORE STEP AND I'LL BECOME A WARRIOR!
BOOM
WORRY
WORRY
Don't you move.
?
?
BOOM
BOOM
BOOM

Song of the Hanging Sky

CHAPTER 7

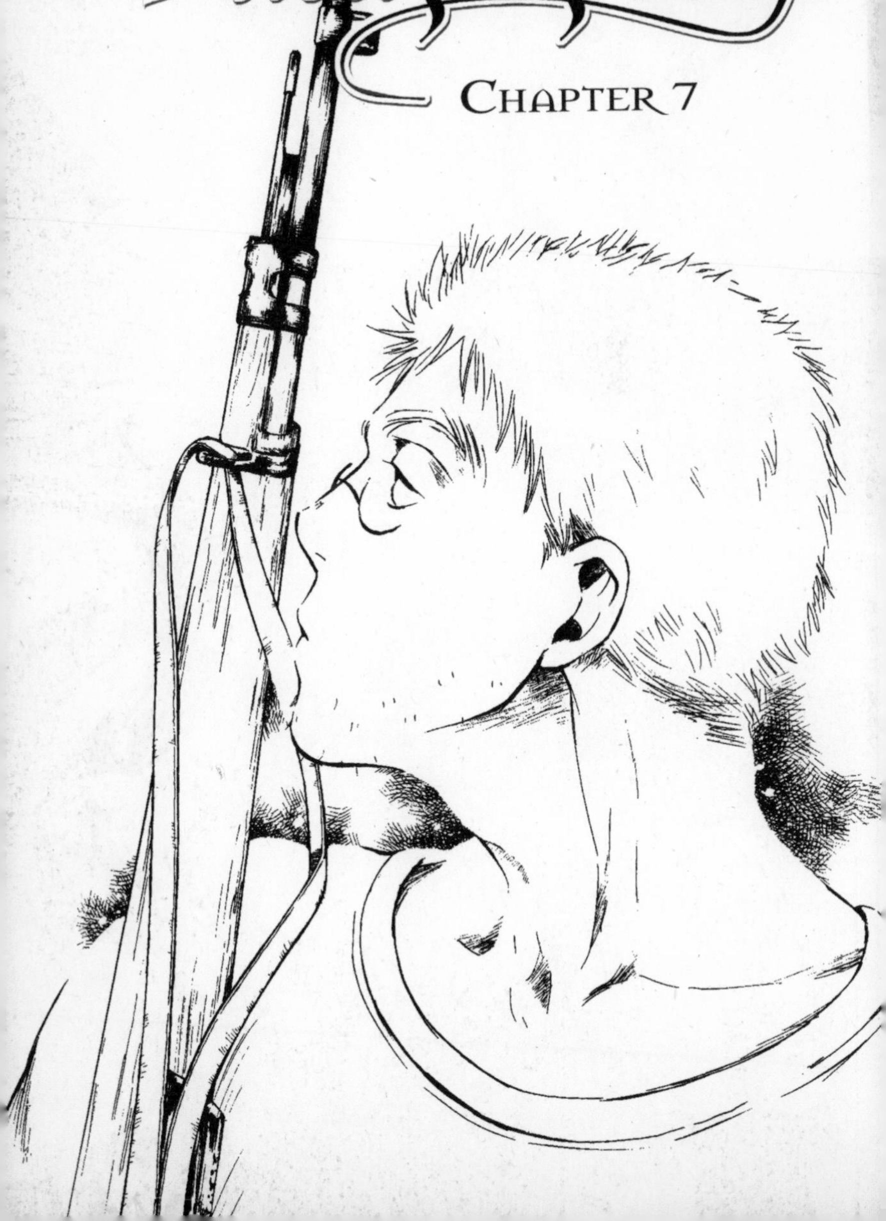

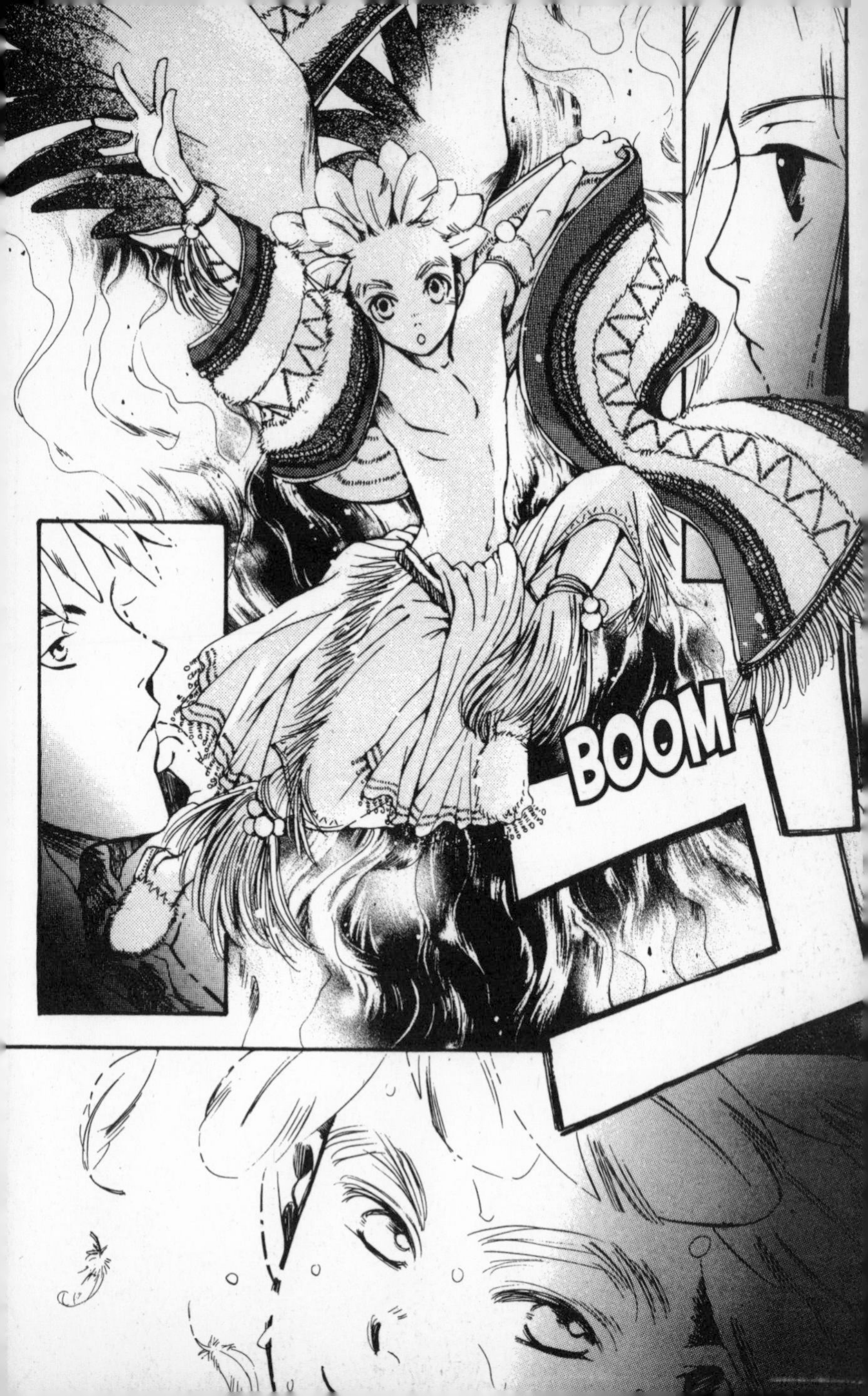
BOOM

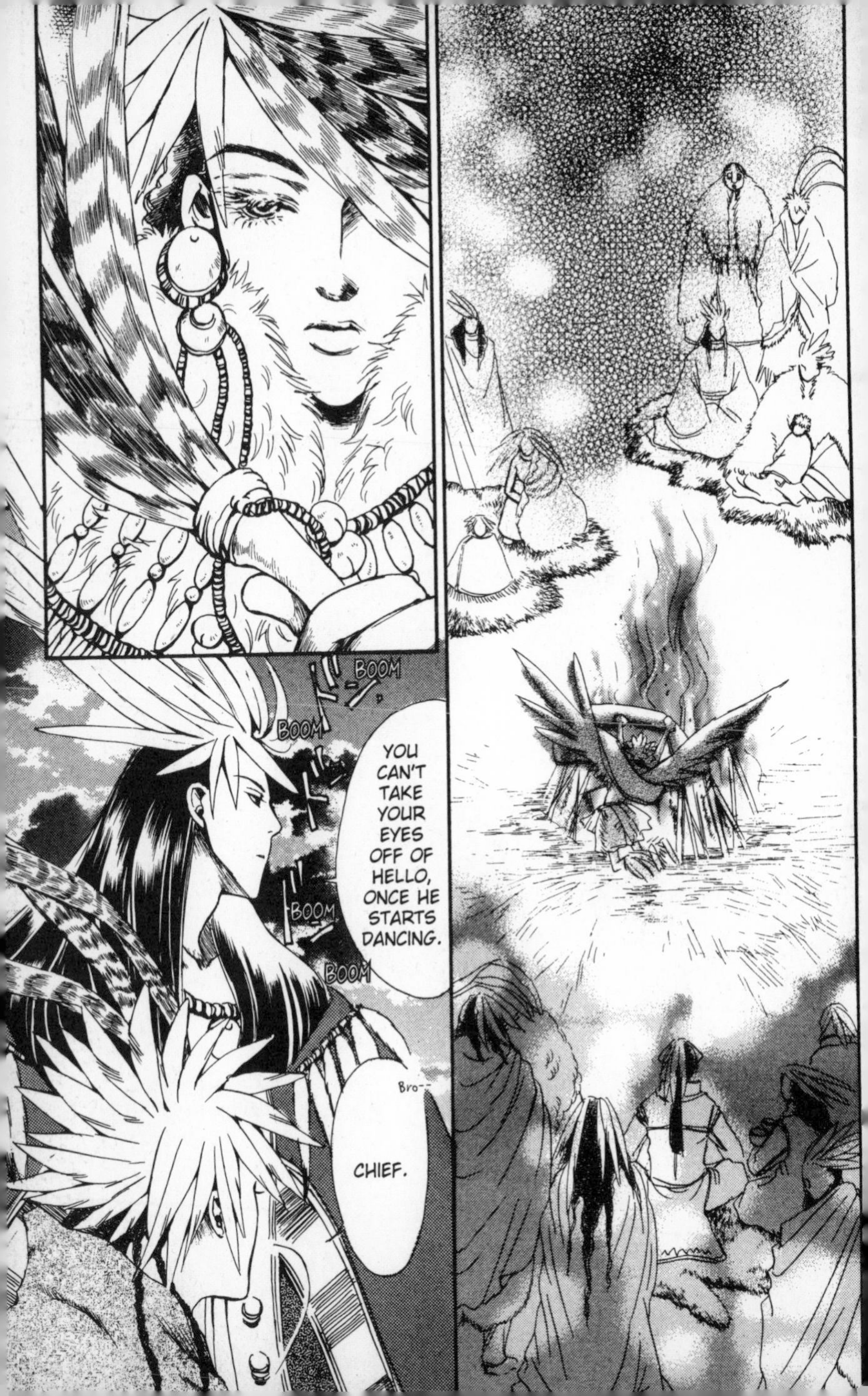
BOOM
BOOM
YOU CAN'T TAKE YOUR EYES OFF OF HELLO, ONCE HE STARTS DANCING.
BOOM
BOOM
Bro--
CHIEF.

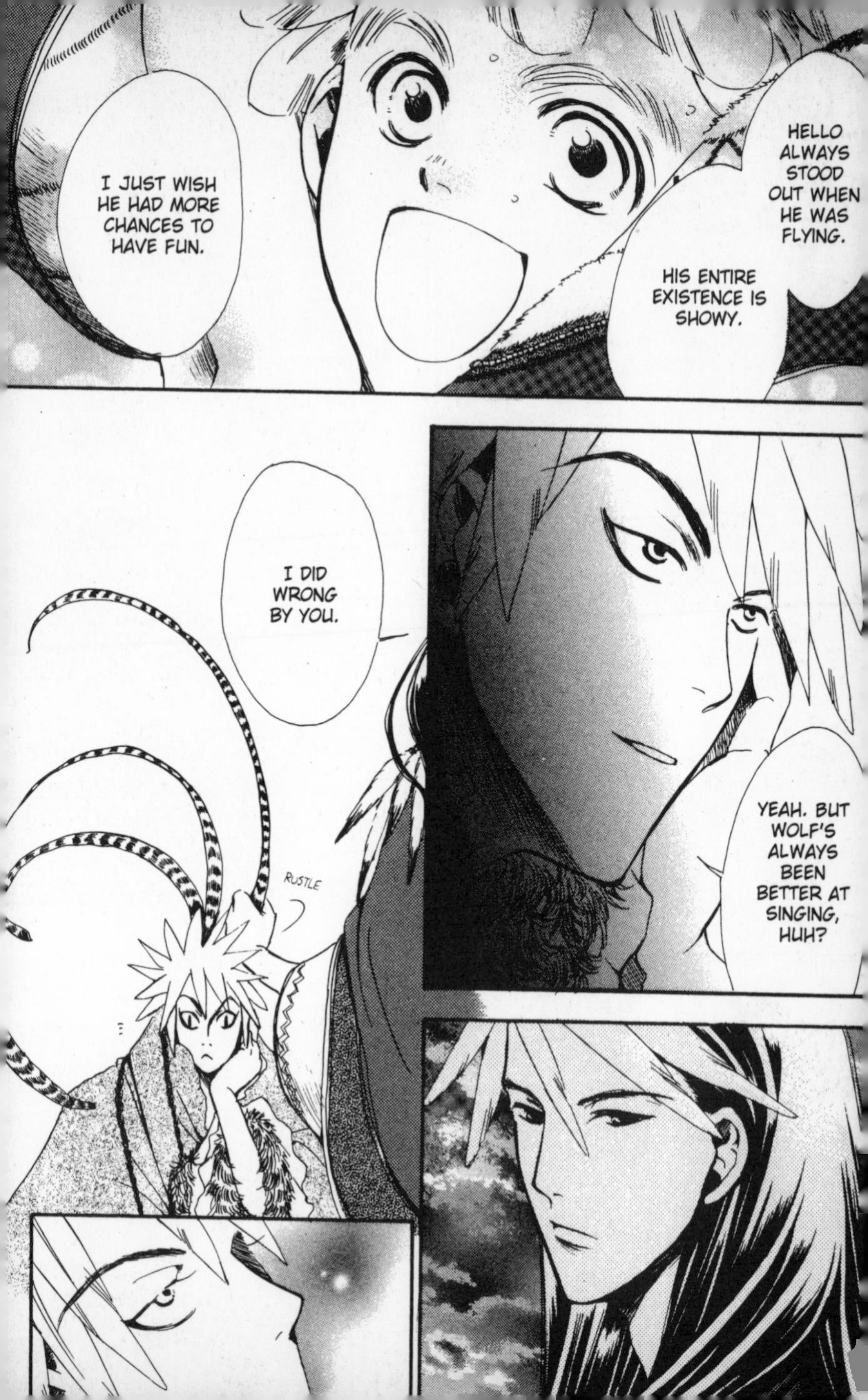
HELLO ALWAYS STOOD OUT WHEN HE WAS FLYING.
HIS ENTIRE EXISTENCE IS SHOWY.
I JUST WISH HE HAD MORE CHANCES TO HAVE FUN.
YEAH. BUT WOLF'S ALWAYS BEEN BETTER AT SINGING, HUH?
I DID WRONG BY YOU.
RUSTLE

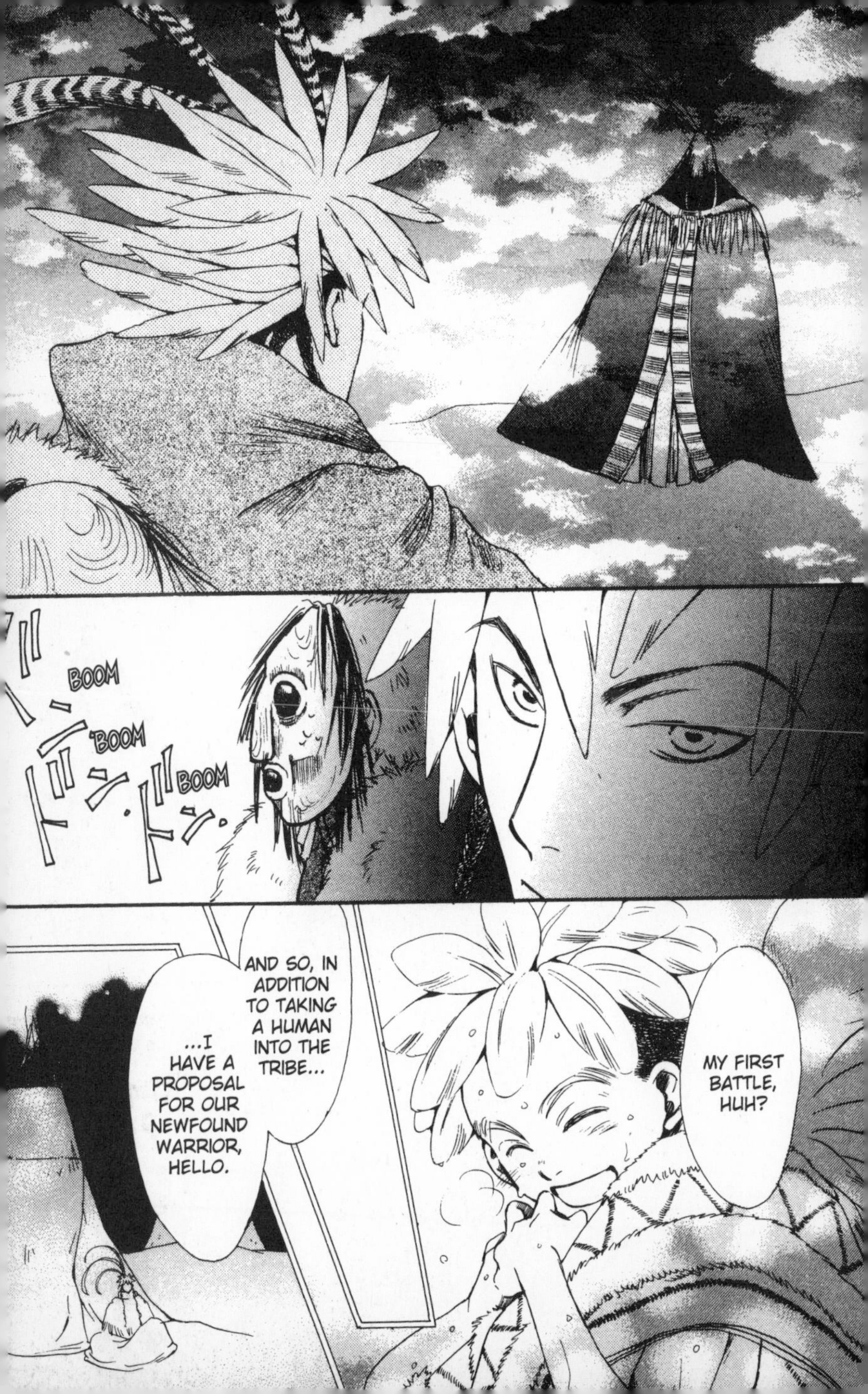
BOOM
BOOM
BOOM
MY FIRST BATTLE, HUH?
AND SO, IN ADDITION TO TAKING A HUMAN INTO THE TRIBE...
...I HAVE A PROPOSAL FOR OUR NEWFOUND WARRIOR, HELLO.

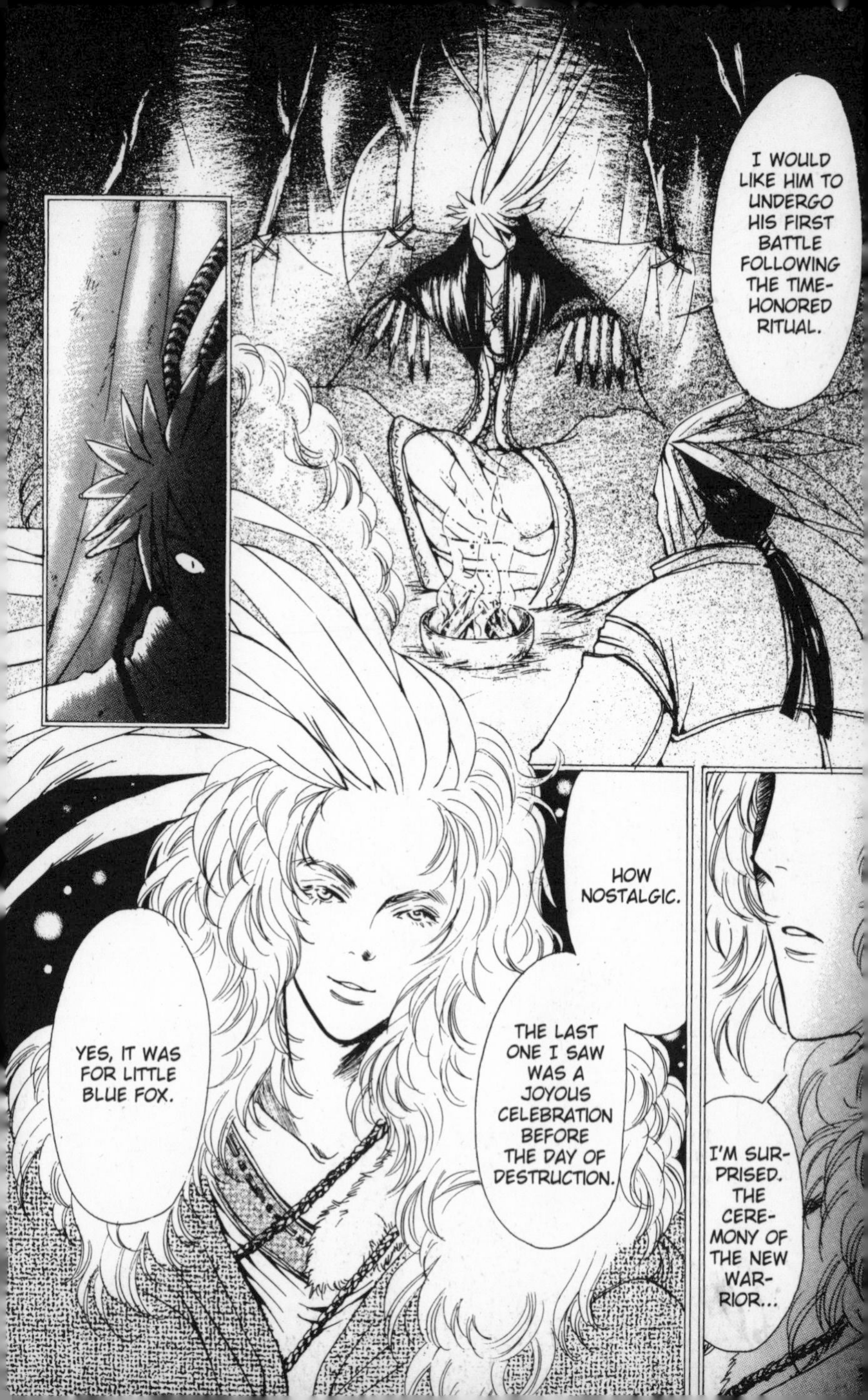
I WOULD LIKE HIM TO UNDERGO HIS FIRST BATTLE FOLLOWING THE TIME-HONORED RITUAL.
I'M SURPRISED. THE CEREMONY OF THE NEW WARRIOR...
HOW NOSTALGIC.
THE LAST ONE I SAW WAS A JOYOUS CELEBRATION BEFORE THE DAY OF DESTRUCTION.
YES, IT WAS FOR LITTLE BLUE FOX.

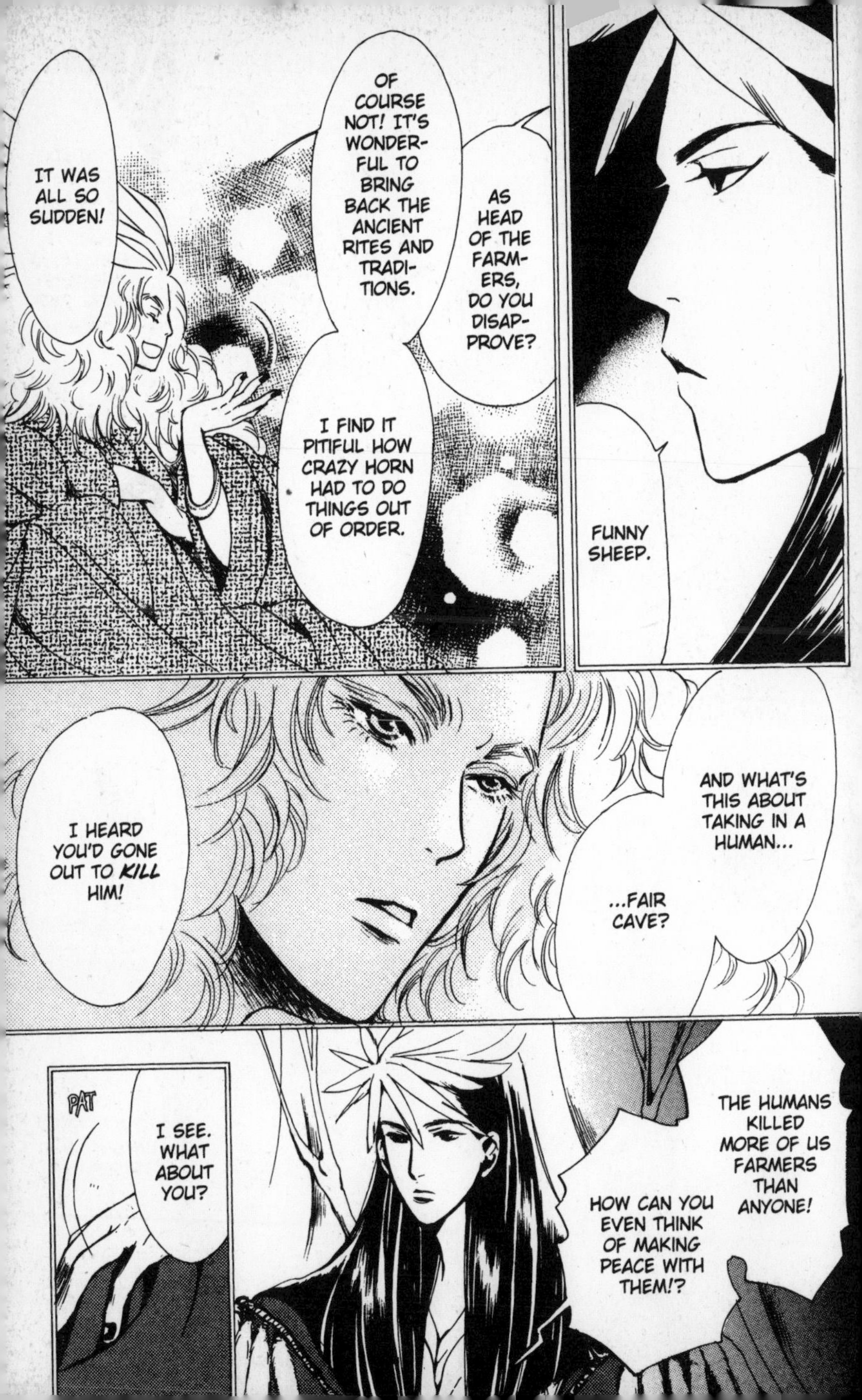

FUNNY SHEEP.
AS HEAD OF THE FARMERS, DO YOU DISAPPROVE?
OF COURSE NOT! IT'S WONDERFUL TO BRING BACK THE ANCIENT RITES AND TRADITIONS.
I FIND IT PITIFUL HOW CRAZY HORN HAD TO DO THINGS OUT OF ORDER.
IT WAS ALL SO SUDDEN!
AND WHAT'S THIS ABOUT TAKING IN A HUMAN...
...FAIR CAVE?
I HEARD YOU'D GONE OUT TO *KILL* HIM!
THE HUMANS KILLED MORE OF US FARMERS THAN ANYONE!
HOW CAN YOU EVEN THINK OF MAKING PEACE WITH THEM!?
I SEE. WHAT ABOUT YOU?
PAT
...

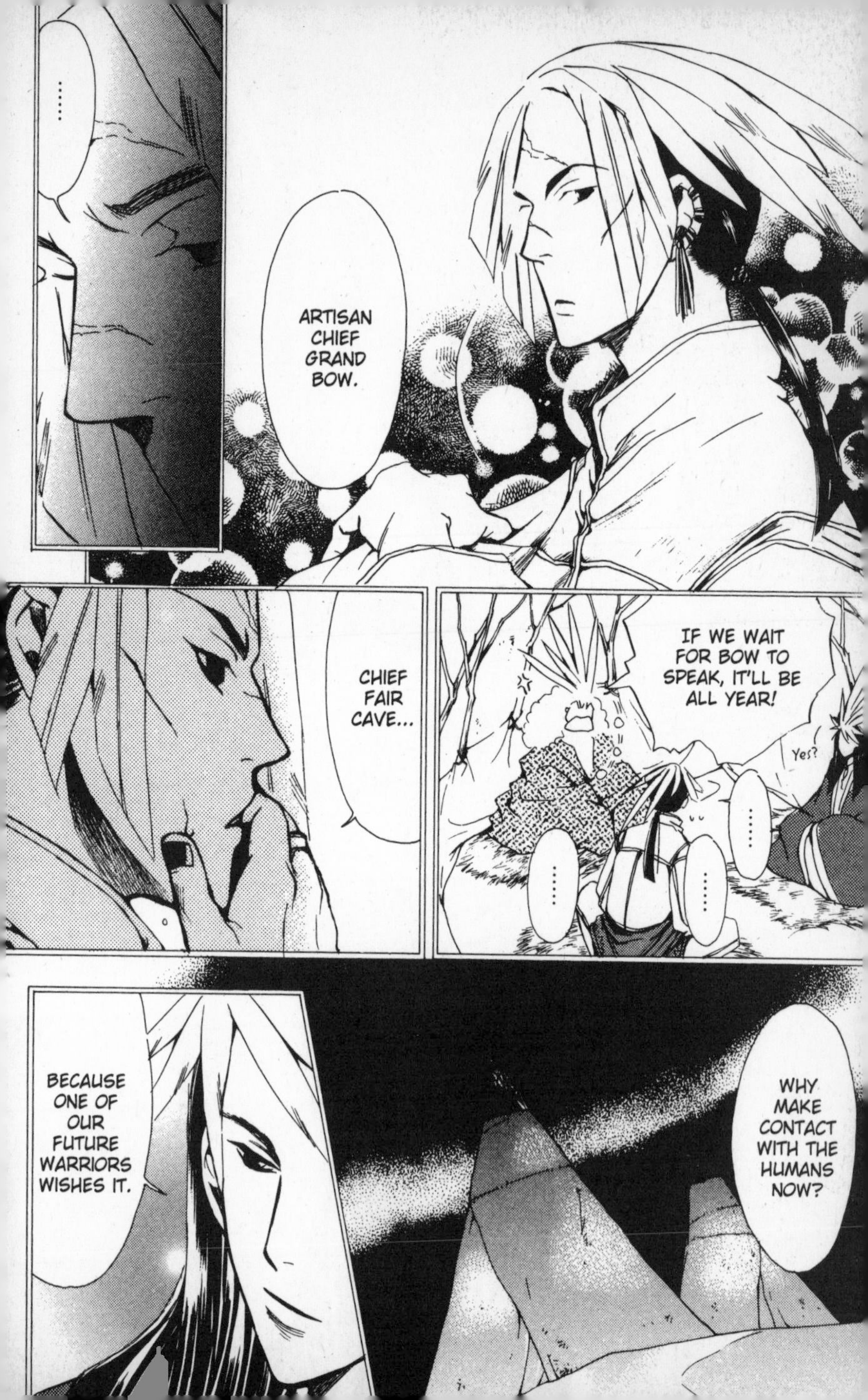
ARTISAN CHIEF GRAND BOW.
……
IF WE WAIT FOR BOW TO SPEAK, IT'LL BE ALL YEAR!
Yes?
……
……
……
CHIEF FAIR CAVE...
WHY MAKE CONTACT WITH THE HUMANS NOW?
BECAUSE ONE OF OUR FUTURE WARRIORS WISHES IT.

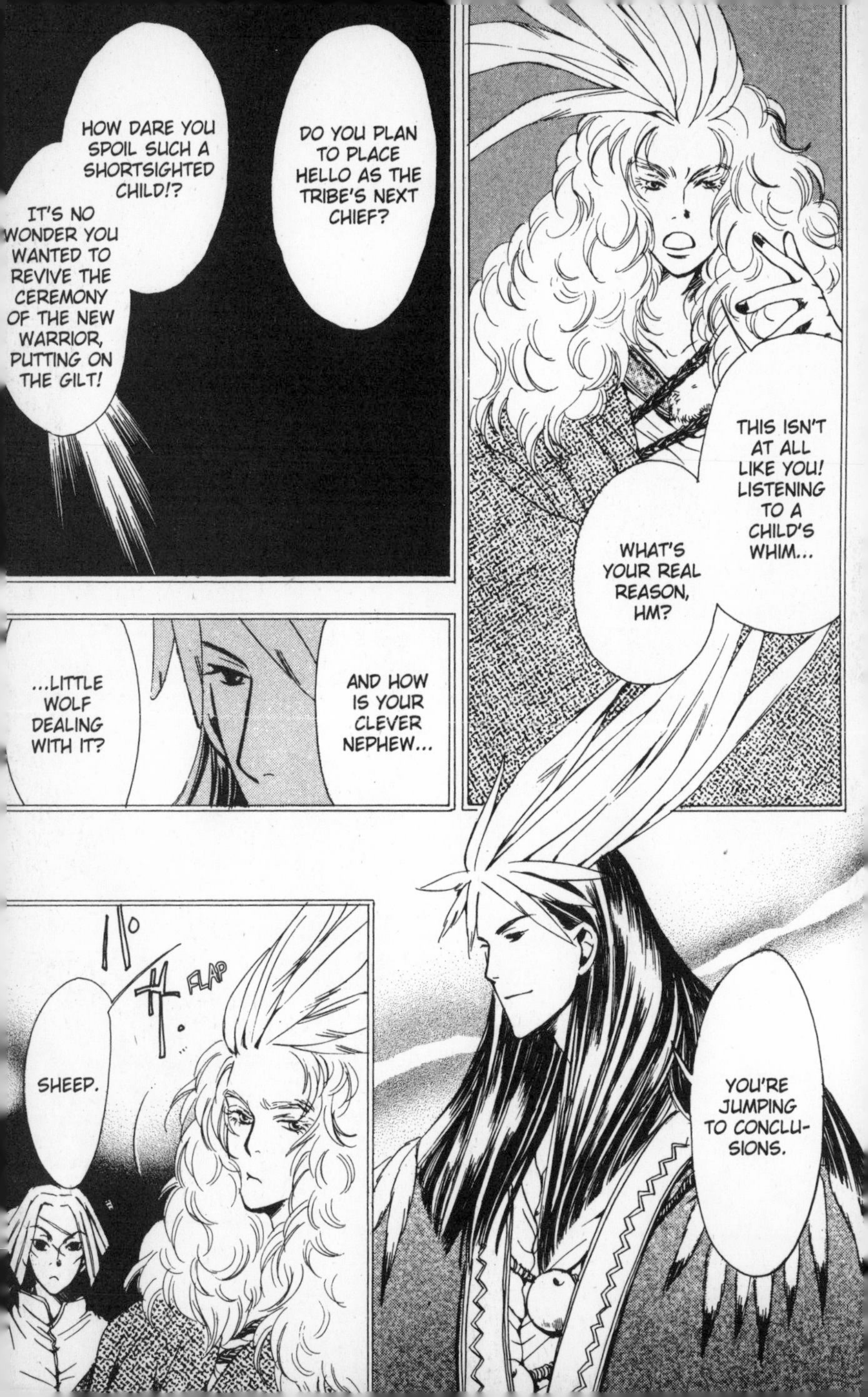
THIS ISN'T AT ALL LIKE YOU! LISTENING TO A CHILD'S WHIM...
WHAT'S YOUR REAL REASON, HM?
DO YOU PLAN TO PLACE HELLO AS THE TRIBE'S NEXT CHIEF?
HOW DARE YOU SPOIL SUCH A SHORTSIGHTED CHILD!?
IT'S NO WONDER YOU WANTED TO REVIVE THE CEREMONY OF THE NEW WARRIOR, PUTTING ON THE GILT!
AND HOW IS YOUR CLEVER NEPHEW...
...LITTLE WOLF DEALING WITH IT?
YOU'RE JUMPING TO CONCLUSIONS.
FLAP
SHEEP.

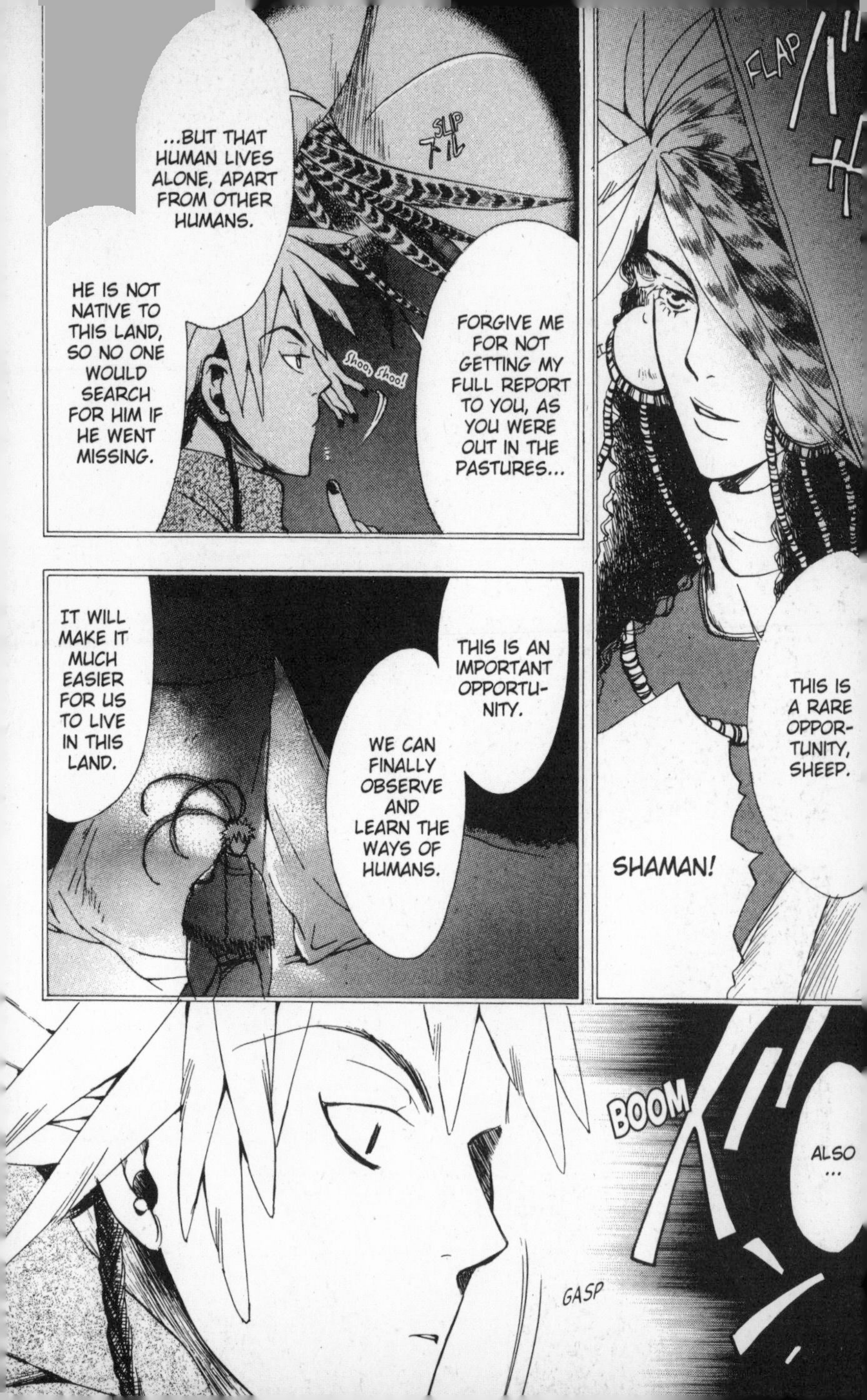

FLAP
THIS IS A RARE OPPORTUNITY, SHEEP.
SHAMAN!
FORGIVE ME FOR NOT GETTING MY FULL REPORT TO YOU, AS YOU WERE OUT IN THE PASTURES...
SLIP
...BUT THAT HUMAN LIVES ALONE, APART FROM OTHER HUMANS.
Shoo, shoo!
HE IS NOT NATIVE TO THIS LAND, SO NO ONE WOULD SEARCH FOR HIM IF HE WENT MISSING.
THIS IS AN IMPORTANT OPPORTUNITY.
WE CAN FINALLY OBSERVE AND LEARN THE WAYS OF HUMANS.
IT WILL MAKE IT MUCH EASIER FOR US TO LIVE IN THIS LAND.
ALSO ...
BOOM
GASP

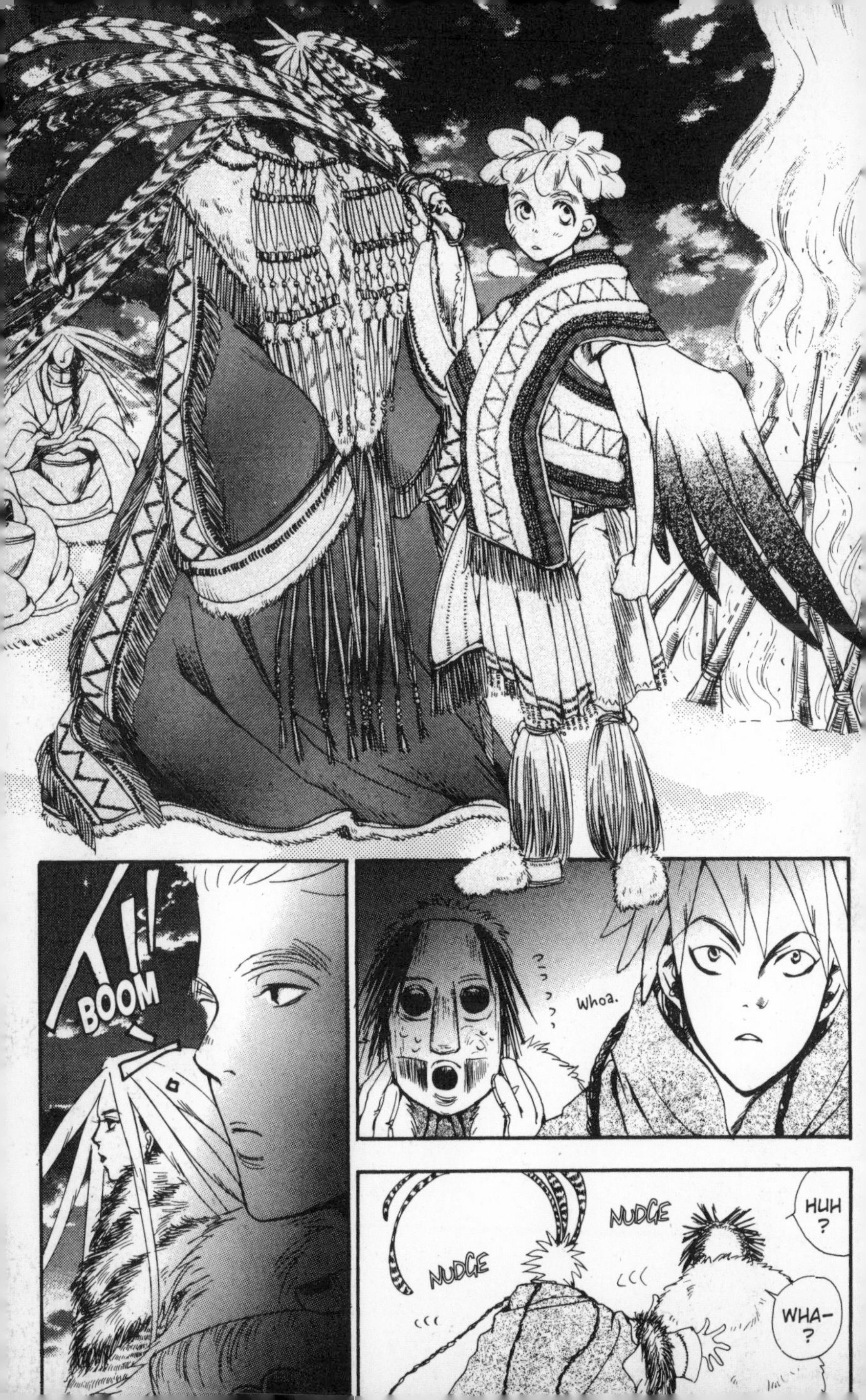
Whoa.
HUH?
NUDGE
NUDGE
WHA-?
BOOM

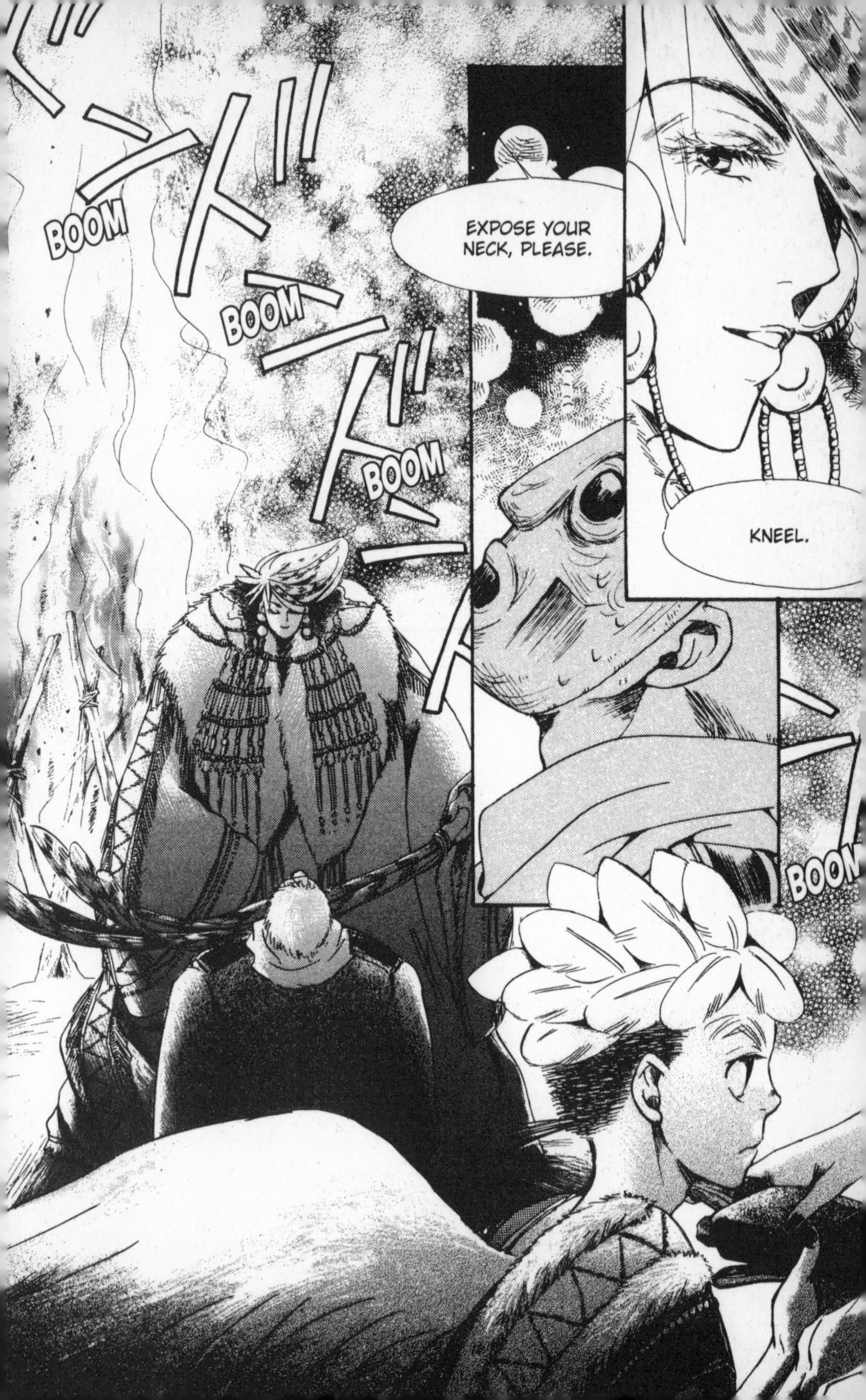
KNEEL.
EXPOSE YOUR NECK, PLEASE.
BOOM
BOOM
BOOM
BOOM

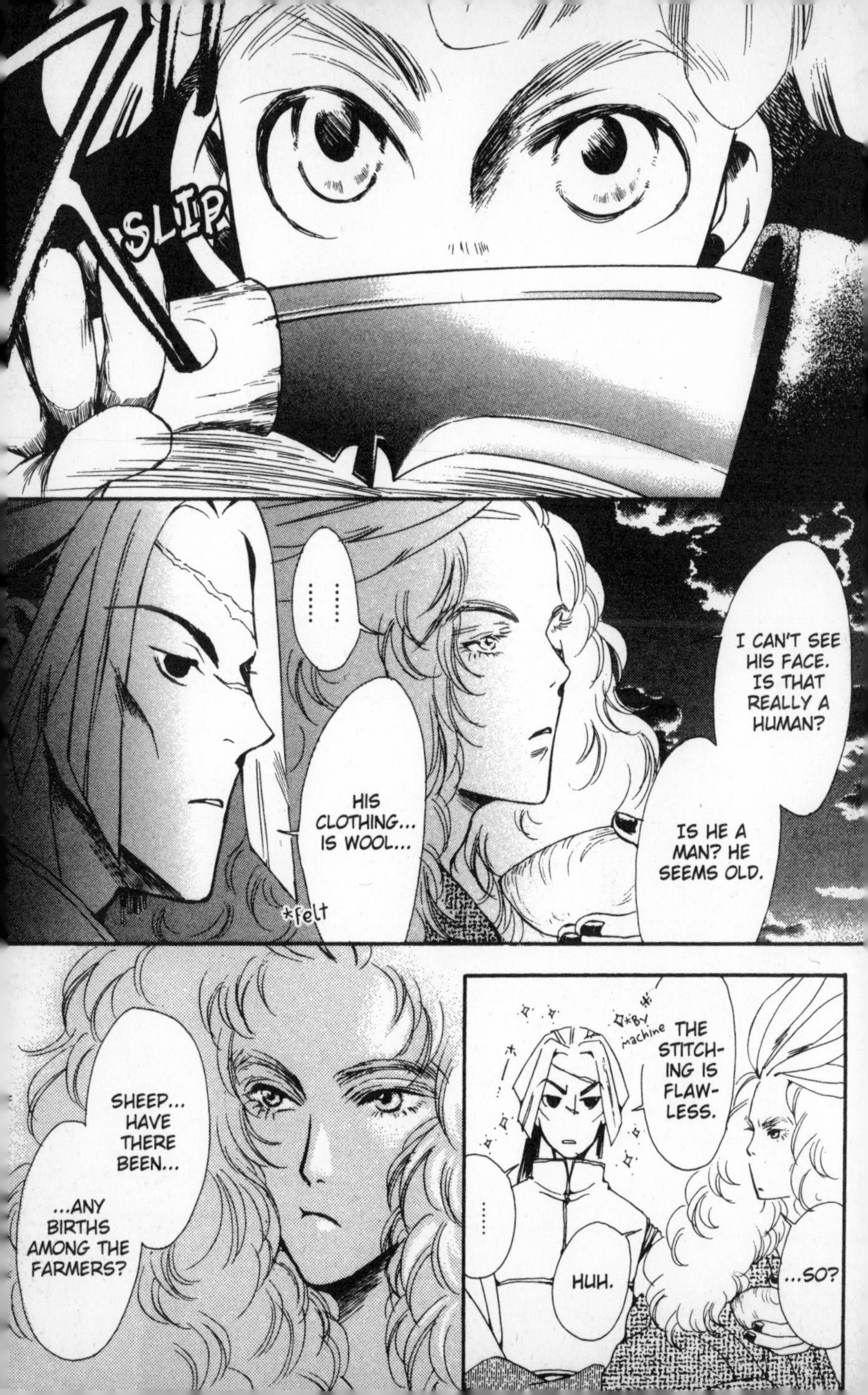
SLIP
I CAN'T SEE HIS FACE. IS THAT REALLY A HUMAN?
IS HE A MAN? HE SEEMS OLD.
......
HIS CLOTHING... IS WOOL...
*felt
THE STITCH-ING IS FLAW-LESS.
*By machine
...SO?
......
HUH.
SHEEP... HAVE THERE BEEN...
...ANY BIRTHS AMONG THE FARMERS?

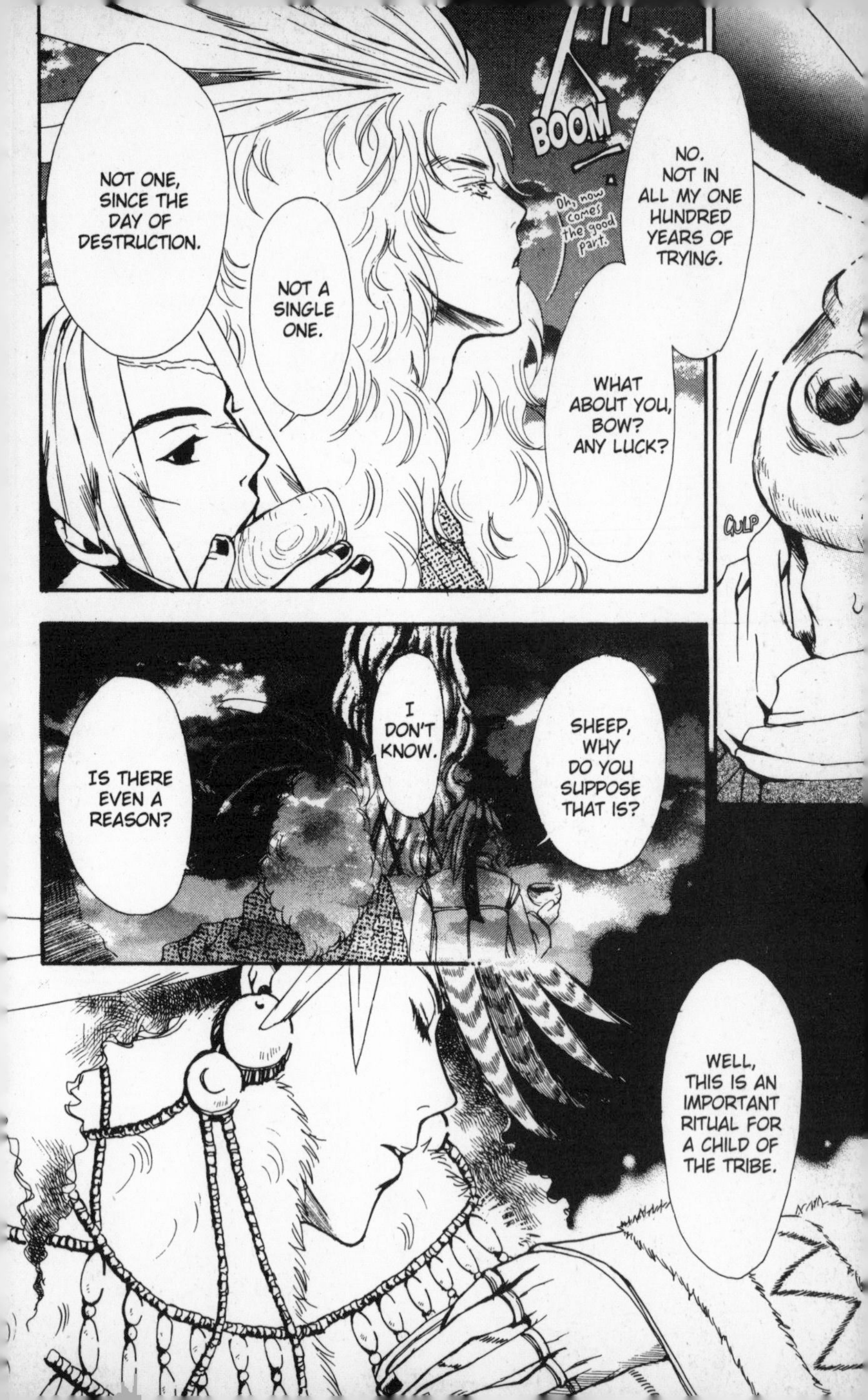
GULP
BOOM
NO. NOT IN ALL MY ONE HUNDRED YEARS OF TRYING.
Oh, now comes the good part.
WHAT ABOUT YOU, BOW? ANY LUCK?
NOT ONE, SINCE THE DAY OF DESTRUCTION.
NOT A SINGLE ONE.
SHEEP, WHY DO YOU SUPPOSE THAT IS?
I DON'T KNOW.
IS THERE EVEN A REASON?
WELL, THIS IS AN IMPORTANT RITUAL FOR A CHILD OF THE TRIBE.

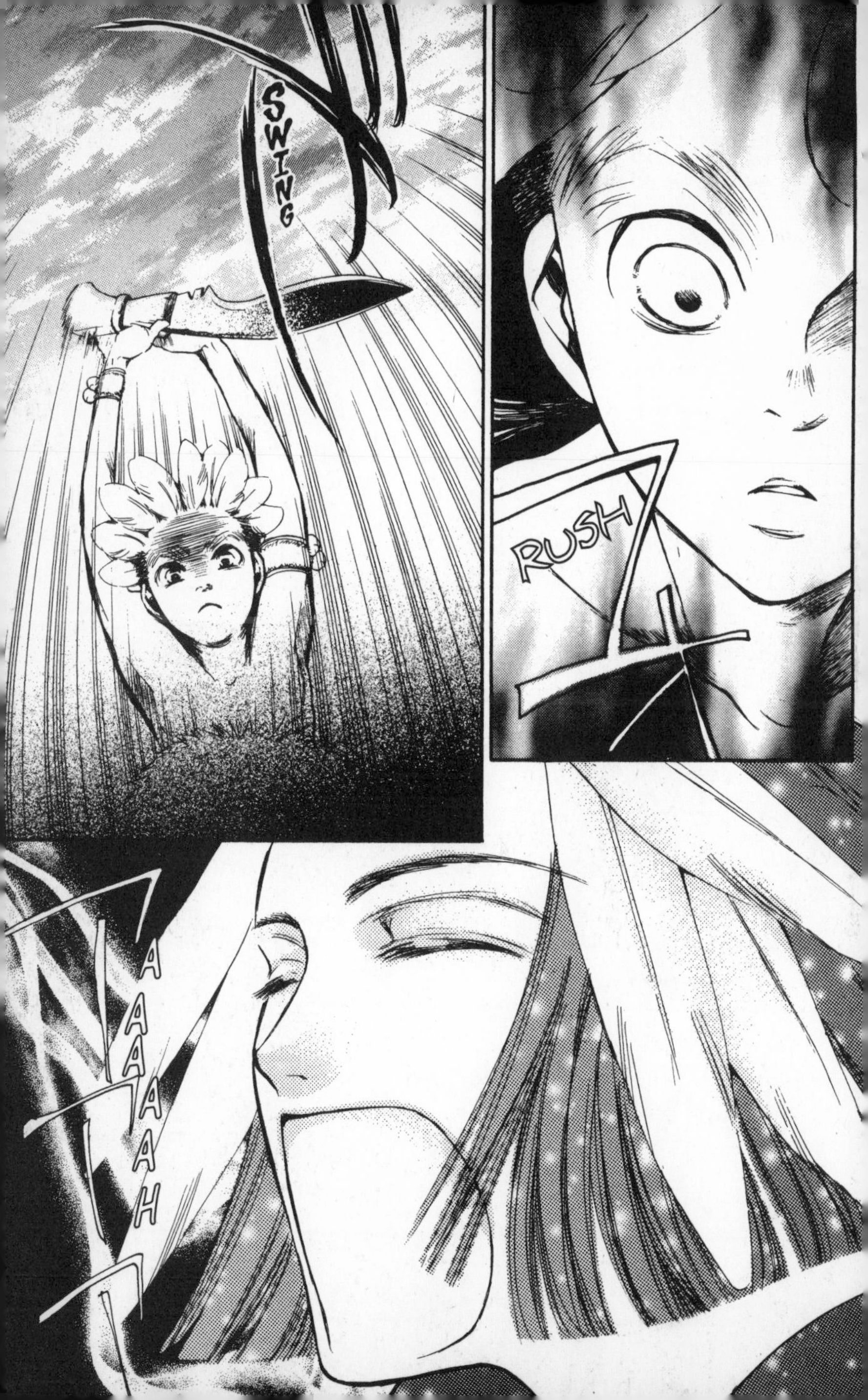
RUSH
SWING
AAAAAH

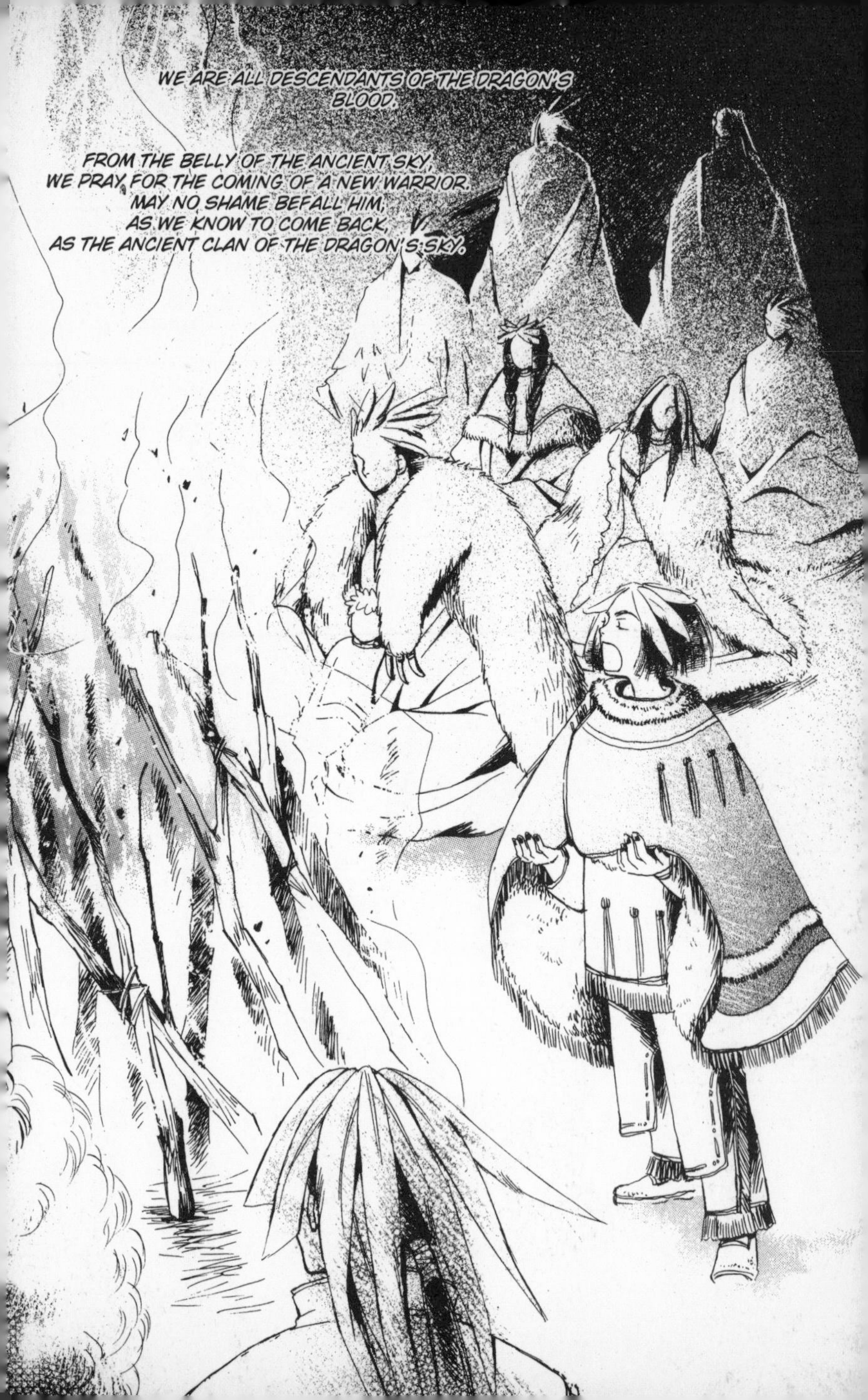
WE ARE ALL DESCENDANTS OF THE DRAGON'S BLOOD.
FROM THE BELLY OF THE ANCIENT SKY, WE PRAY FOR THE COMING OF A NEW WARRIOR. MAY NO SHAME BEFALL HIM, AS WE KNOW TO COME BACK, AS THE ANCIENT CLAN OF THE DRAGON'S SKY.

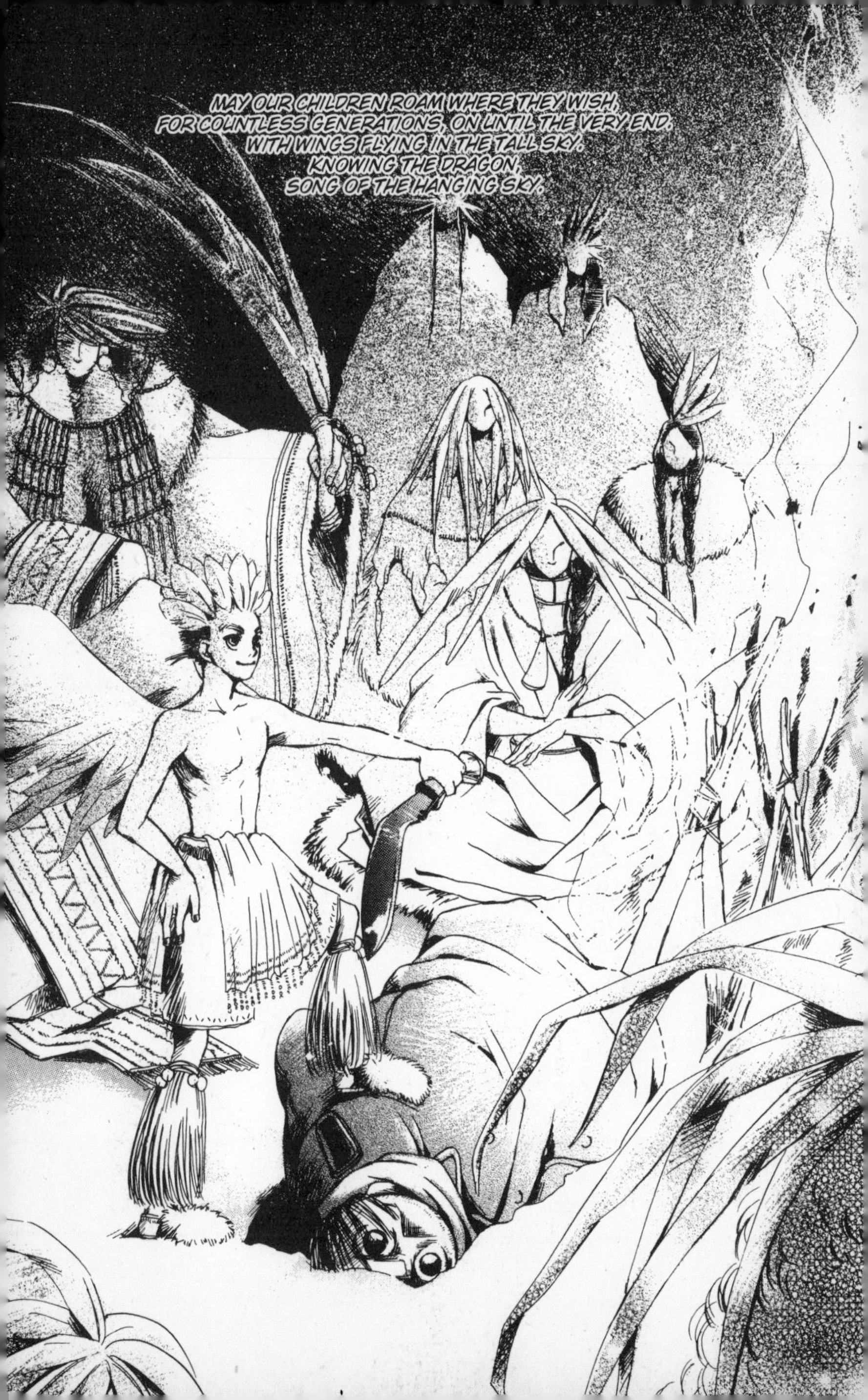
MAY OUR CHILDREN ROAM WHERE THEY WISH,
FOR COUNTLESS GENERATIONS, ON UNTIL THE VERY END.
WITH WINGS FLYING IN THE TALL SKY.
KNOWING THE DRAGON,
SONG OF THE HANGING SKY.

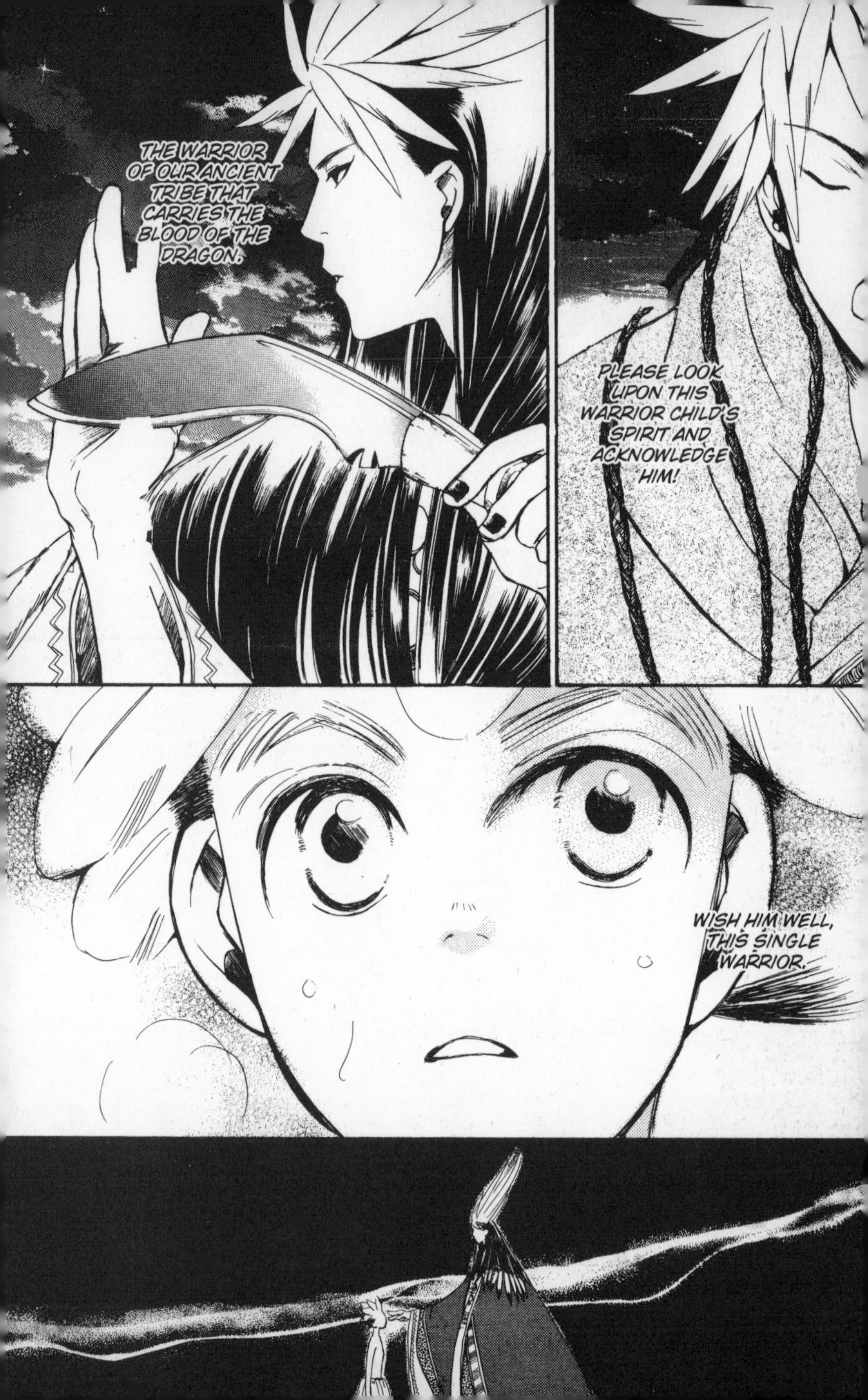
PLEASE LOOK UPON THIS WARRIOR CHILD'S SPIRIT AND ACKNOWLEDGE HIM!
THE WARRIOR OF OUR ANCIENT TRIBE THAT CARRIES THE BLOOD OF THE DRAGON.
WISH HIM WELL, THIS SINGLE WARRIOR.

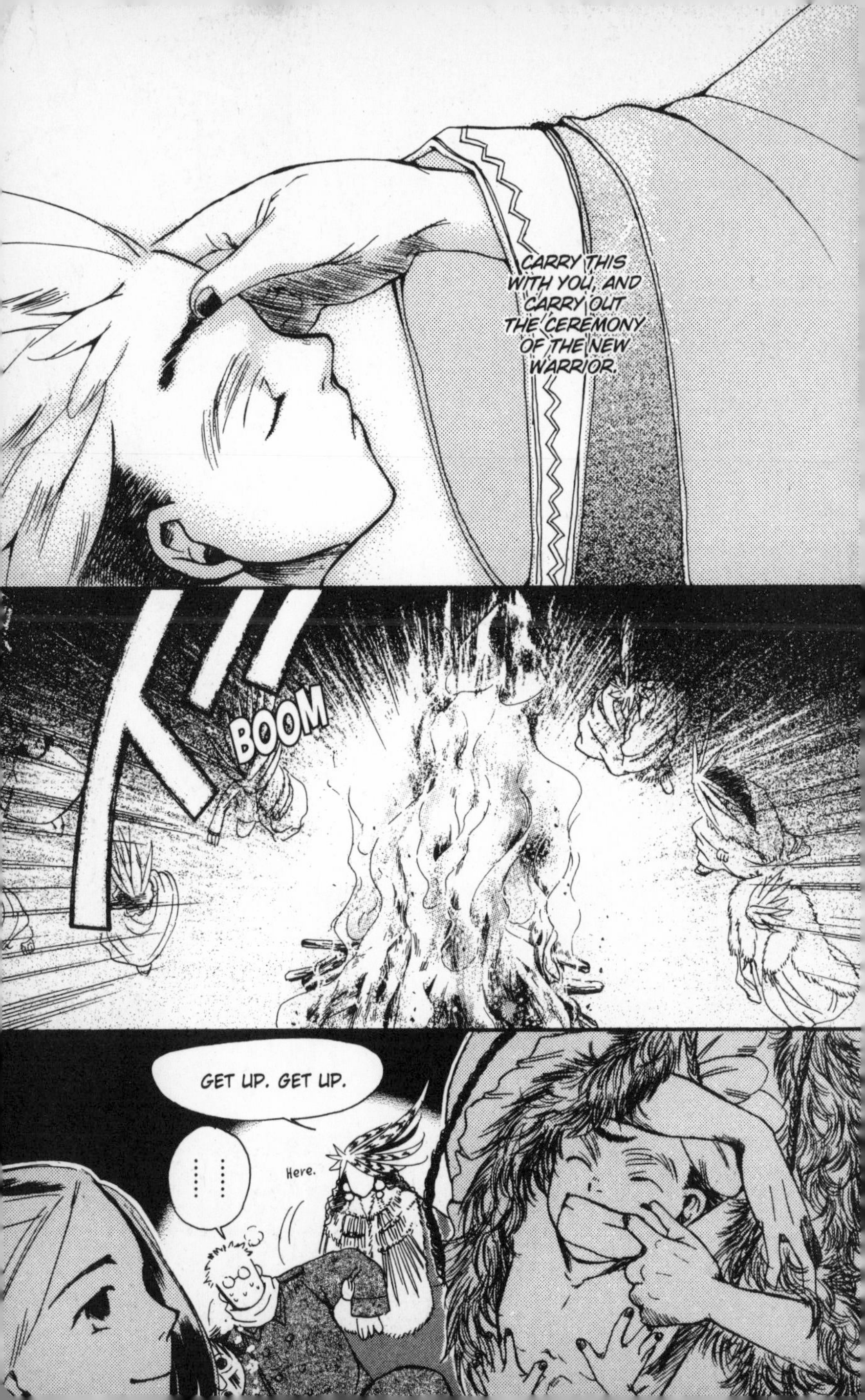
CARRY THIS WITH YOU, AND CARRY OUT THE CEREMONY OF THE NEW WARRIOR.
ド
BOOM
GET UP. GET UP.
Here.
……

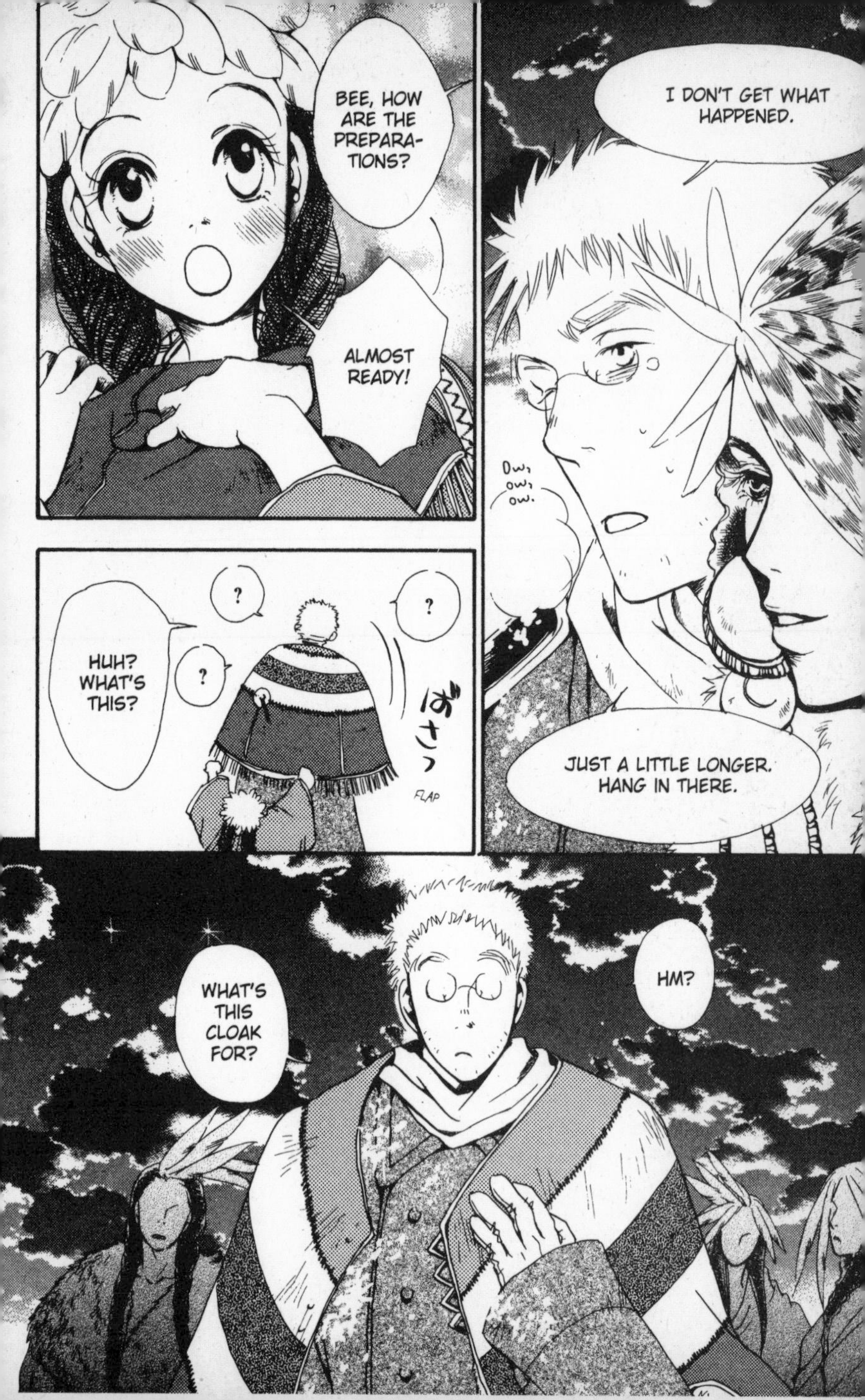
I DON'T GET WHAT HAPPENED.
Ow, ow, ow.
JUST A LITTLE LONGER. HANG IN THERE.
BEE, HOW ARE THE PREPARATIONS?
ALMOST READY!
?
?
HUH? WHAT'S THIS?
?
ばさっ
FLAP
HM?
WHAT'S THIS CLOAK FOR?

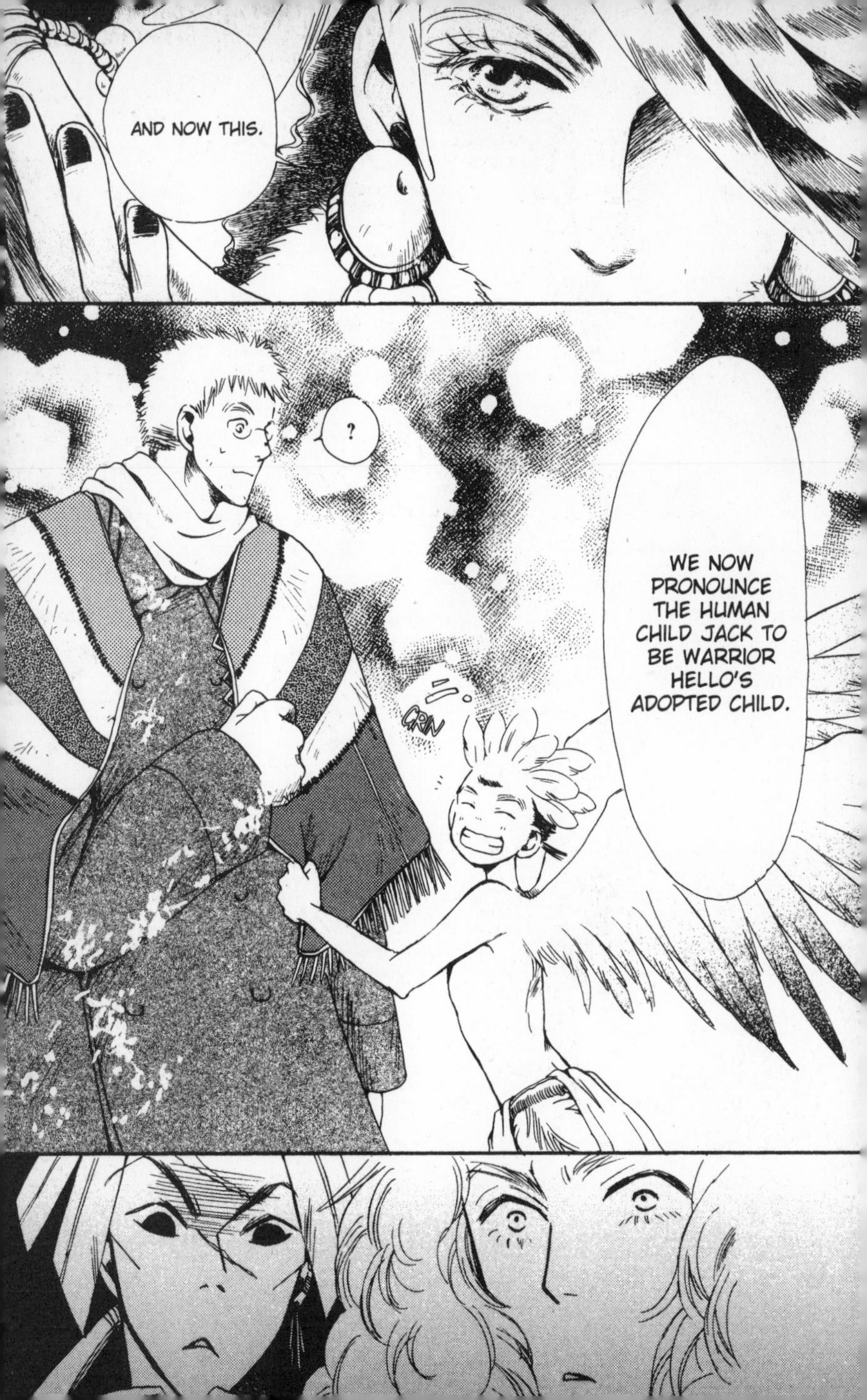
AND NOW THIS.
WE NOW PRONOUNCE THE HUMAN CHILD JACK TO BE WARRIOR HELLO'S ADOPTED CHILD.
?
GRIN

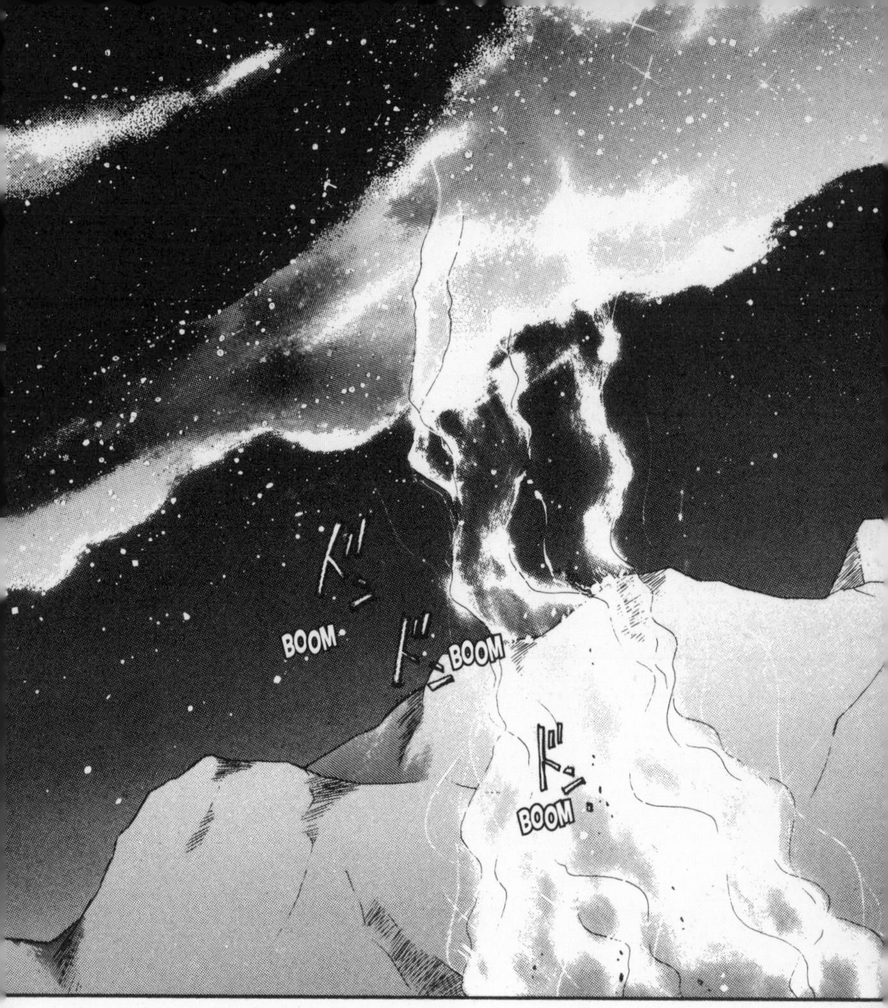
ドン
BOOM
ドン
BOOM
ドン
BOOM

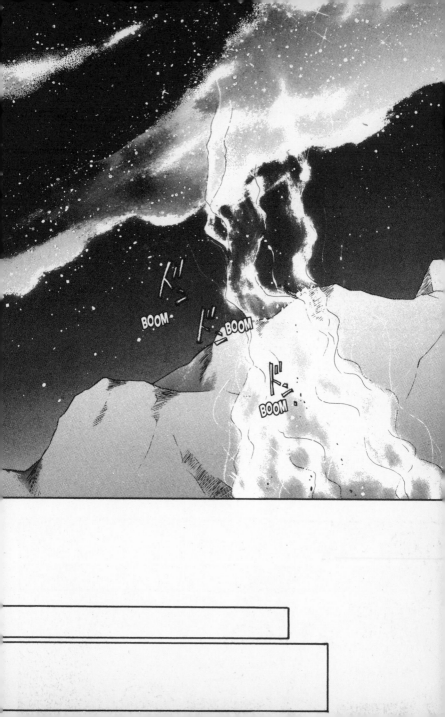

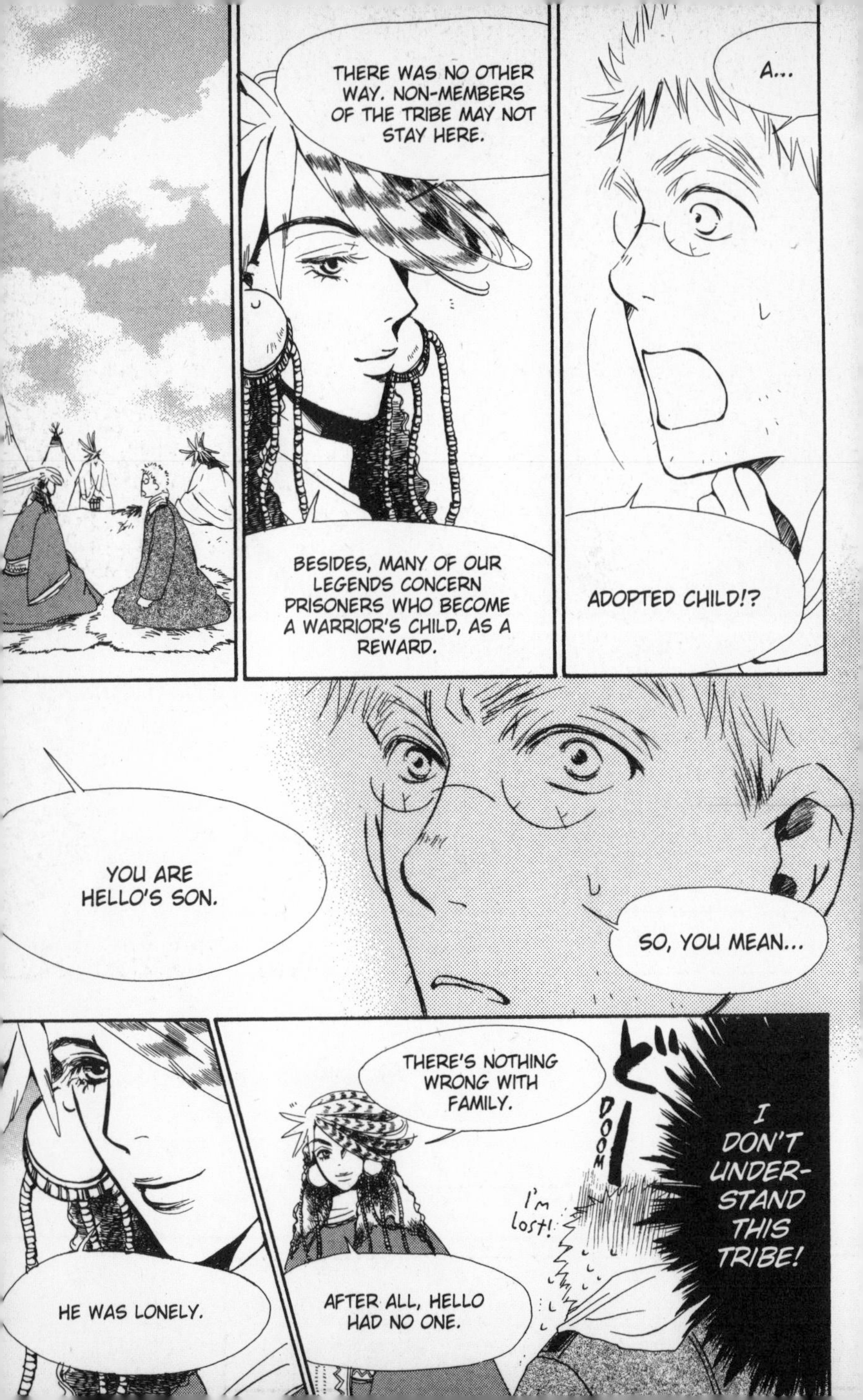
A...
ADOPTED CHILD!?
THERE WAS NO OTHER WAY. NON-MEMBERS OF THE TRIBE MAY NOT STAY HERE.
BESIDES, MANY OF OUR LEGENDS CONCERN PRISONERS WHO BECOME A WARRIOR'S CHILD, AS A REWARD.
SO, YOU MEAN...
YOU ARE HELLO'S SON.
I DON'T UNDERSTAND THIS TRIBE!
DOOM
THERE'S NOTHING WRONG WITH FAMILY.
I'm lost!
AFTER ALL, HELLO HAD NO ONE.
HE WAS LONELY.

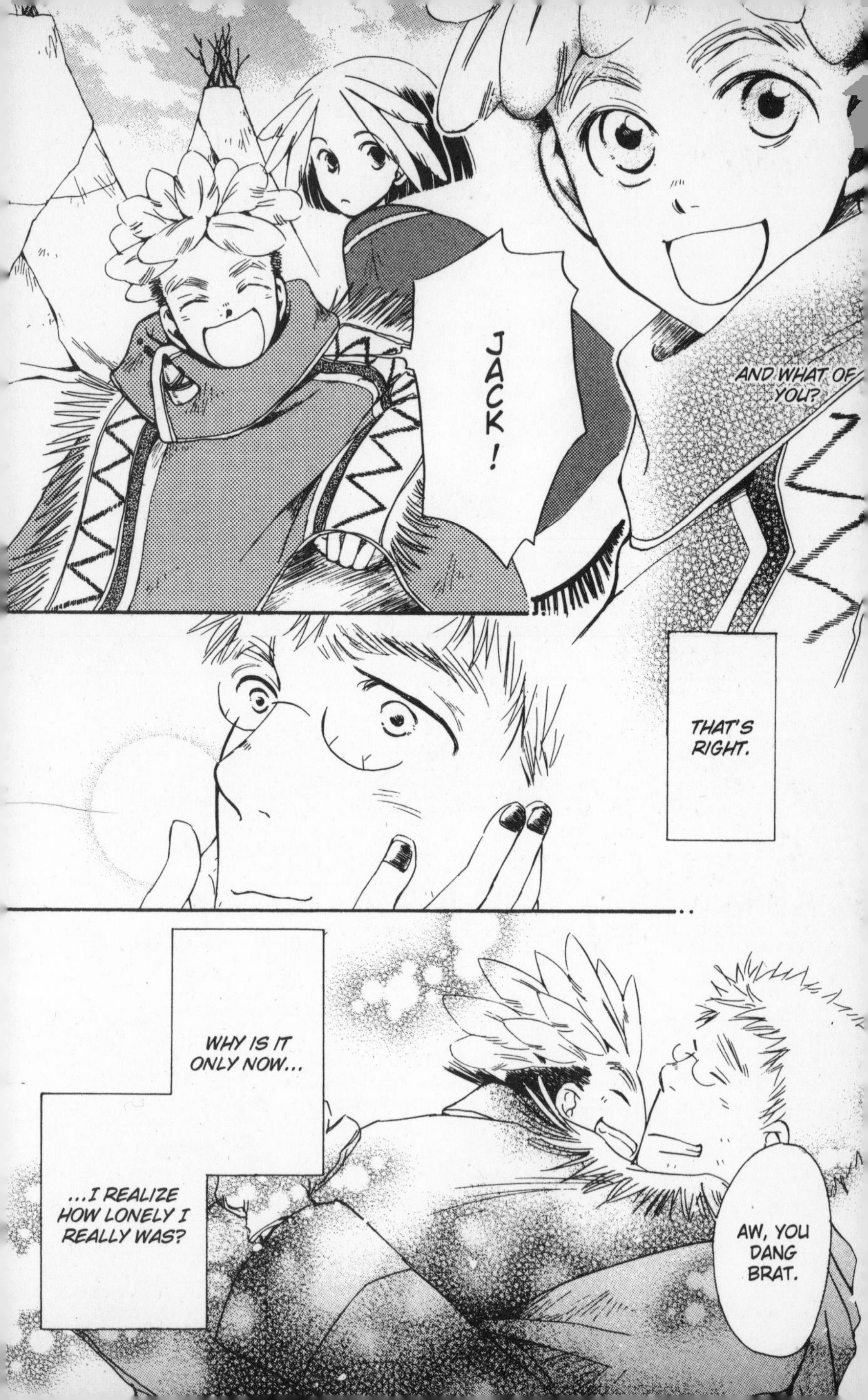
AND WHAT OF YOU?
JACK!
THAT'S RIGHT.
WHY IS IT ONLY NOW...
...I REALIZE HOW LONELY I REALLY WAS?
AW, YOU DANG BRAT.

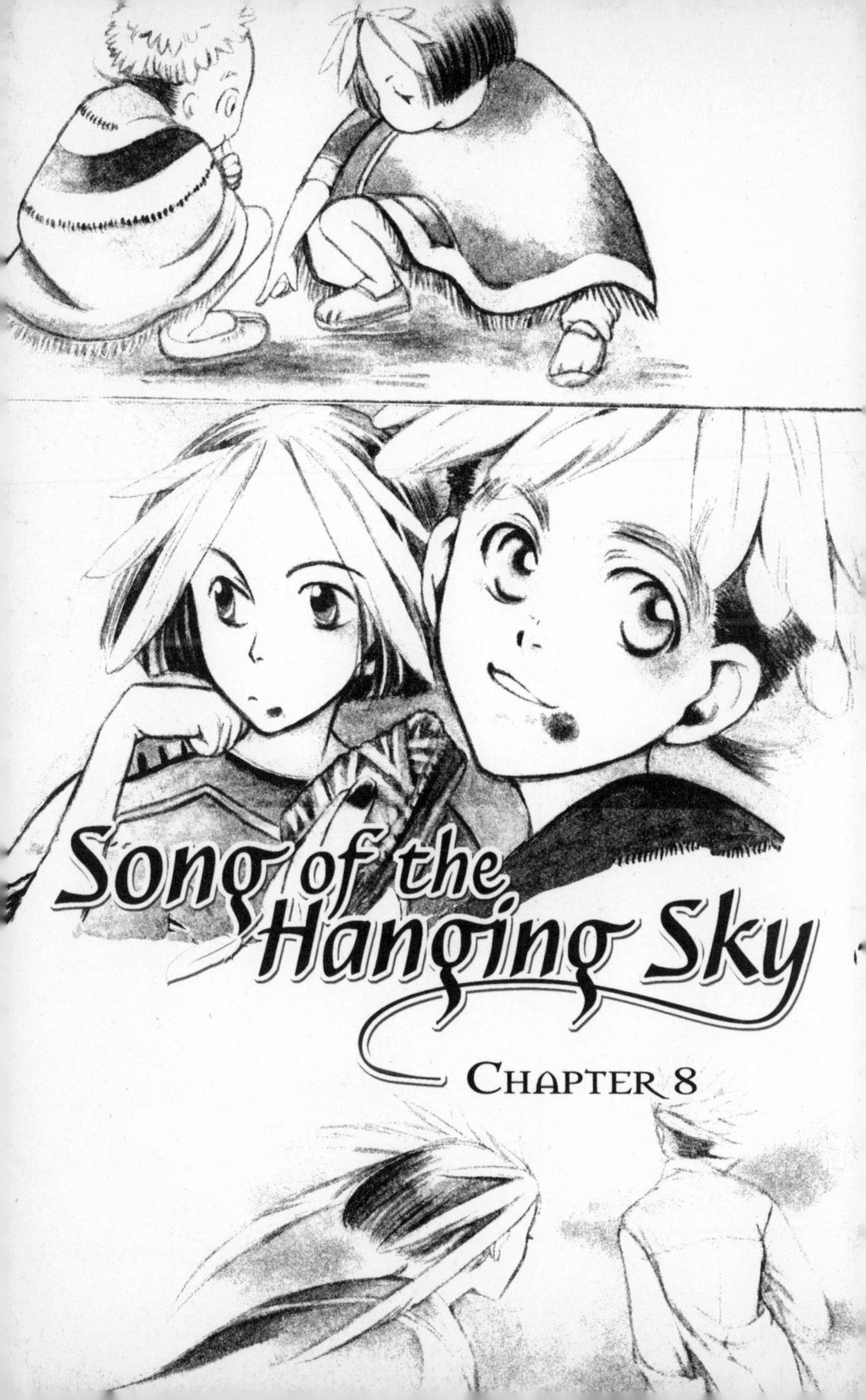
Song of the Hanging Sky
Chapter 8

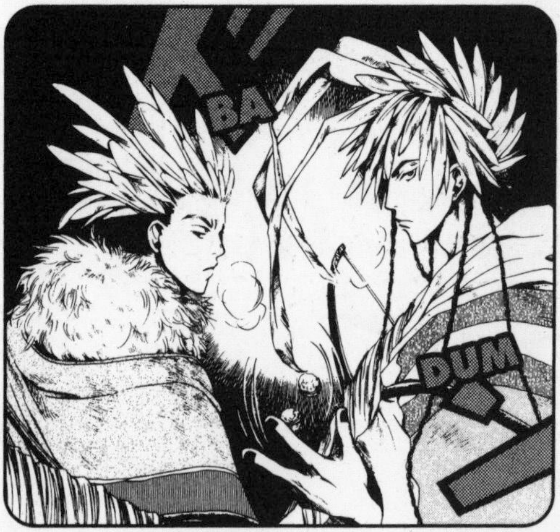
BA
DUM

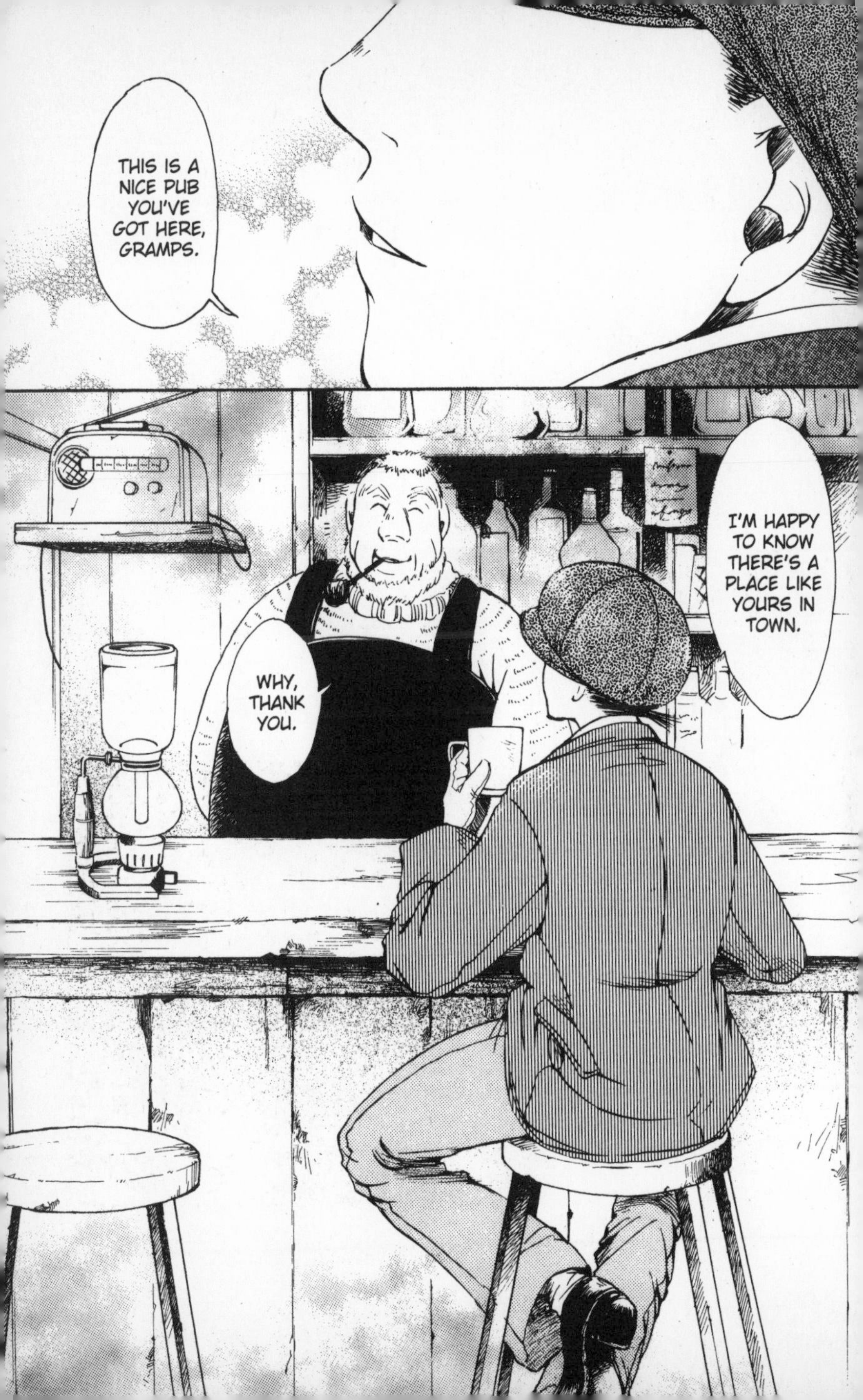
THIS IS A NICE PUB YOU'VE GOT HERE, GRAMPS.
I'M HAPPY TO KNOW THERE'S A PLACE LIKE YOURS IN TOWN.
WHY, THANK YOU.

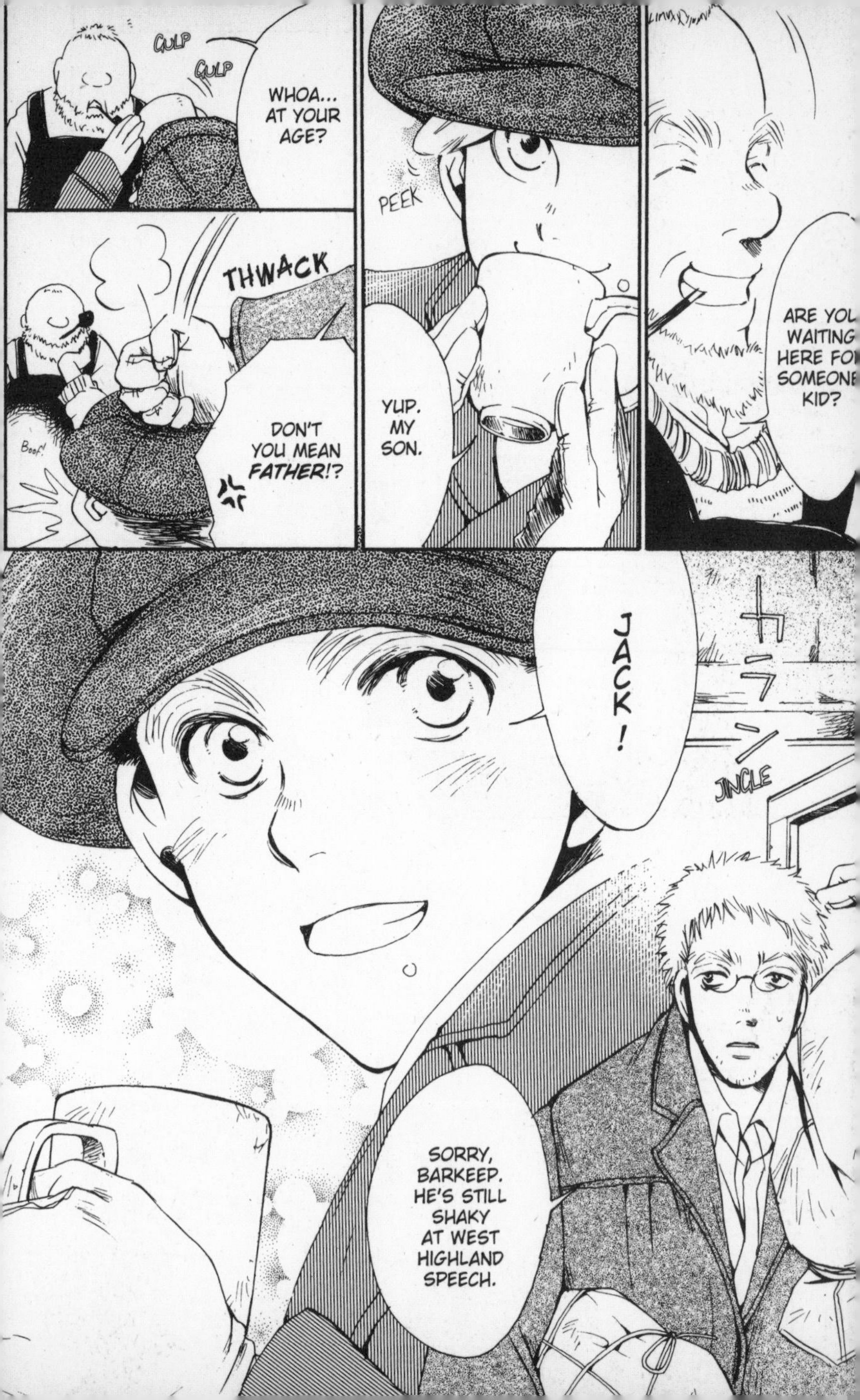

ARE YOU WAITING HERE FOR SOMEONE KID?
PEEK
YUP. MY SON.
GULP
GULP
WHOA... AT YOUR AGE?
THWACK
DON'T YOU MEAN *FATHER!?*
Boof!
JACK!
JINGLE
SORRY, BARKEEP. HE'S STILL SHAKY AT WEST HIGHLAND SPEECH.

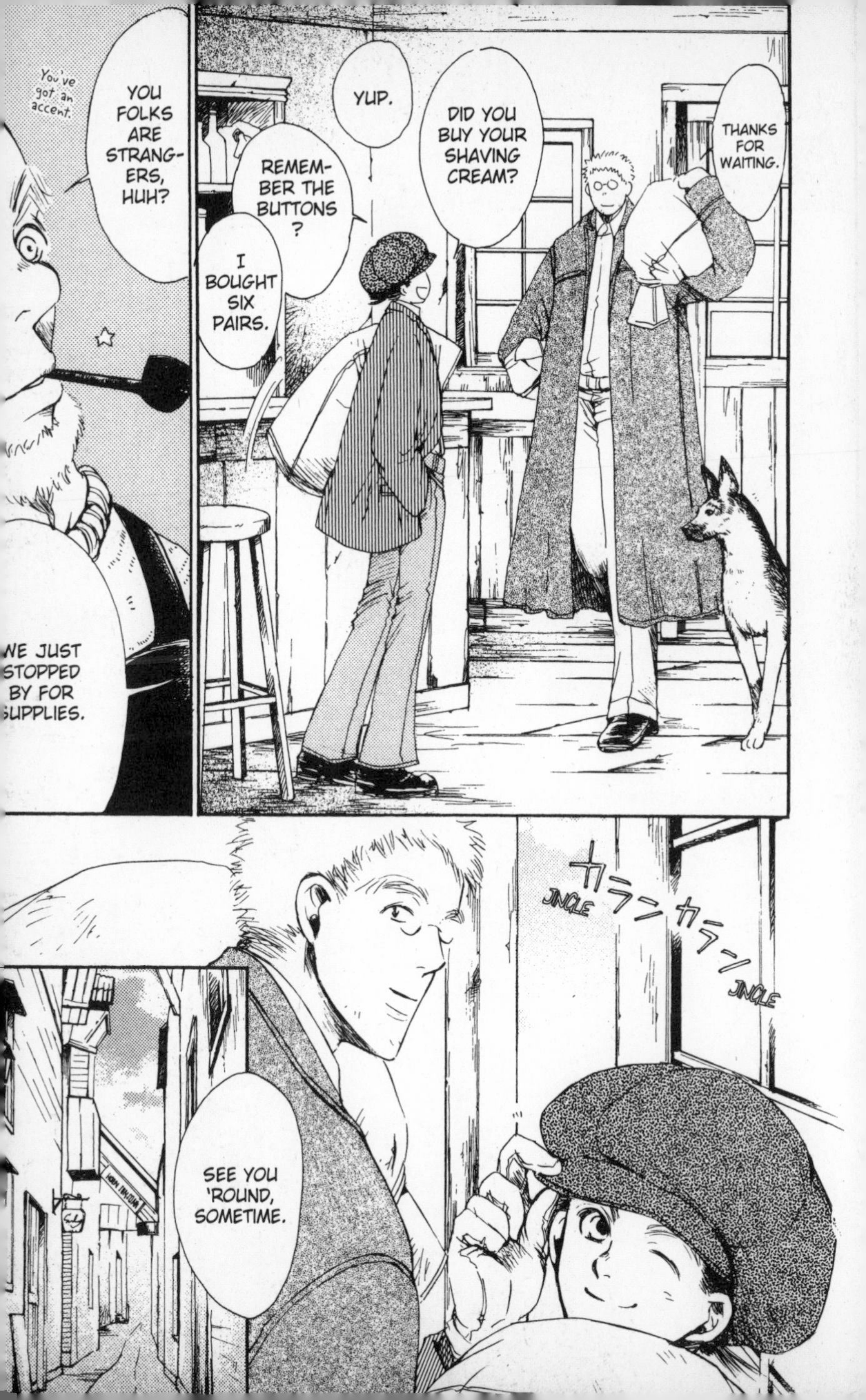
THANKS FOR WAITING.
DID YOU BUY YOUR SHAVING CREAM?
YUP.
REMEMBER THE BUTTONS?
I BOUGHT SIX PAIRS.
YOU FOLKS ARE STRANGERS, HUH?
You've got an accent.
WE JUST STOPPED BY FOR SUPPLIES.
カランカラン
JINGLE
JINGLE
SEE YOU 'ROUND, SOMETIME.

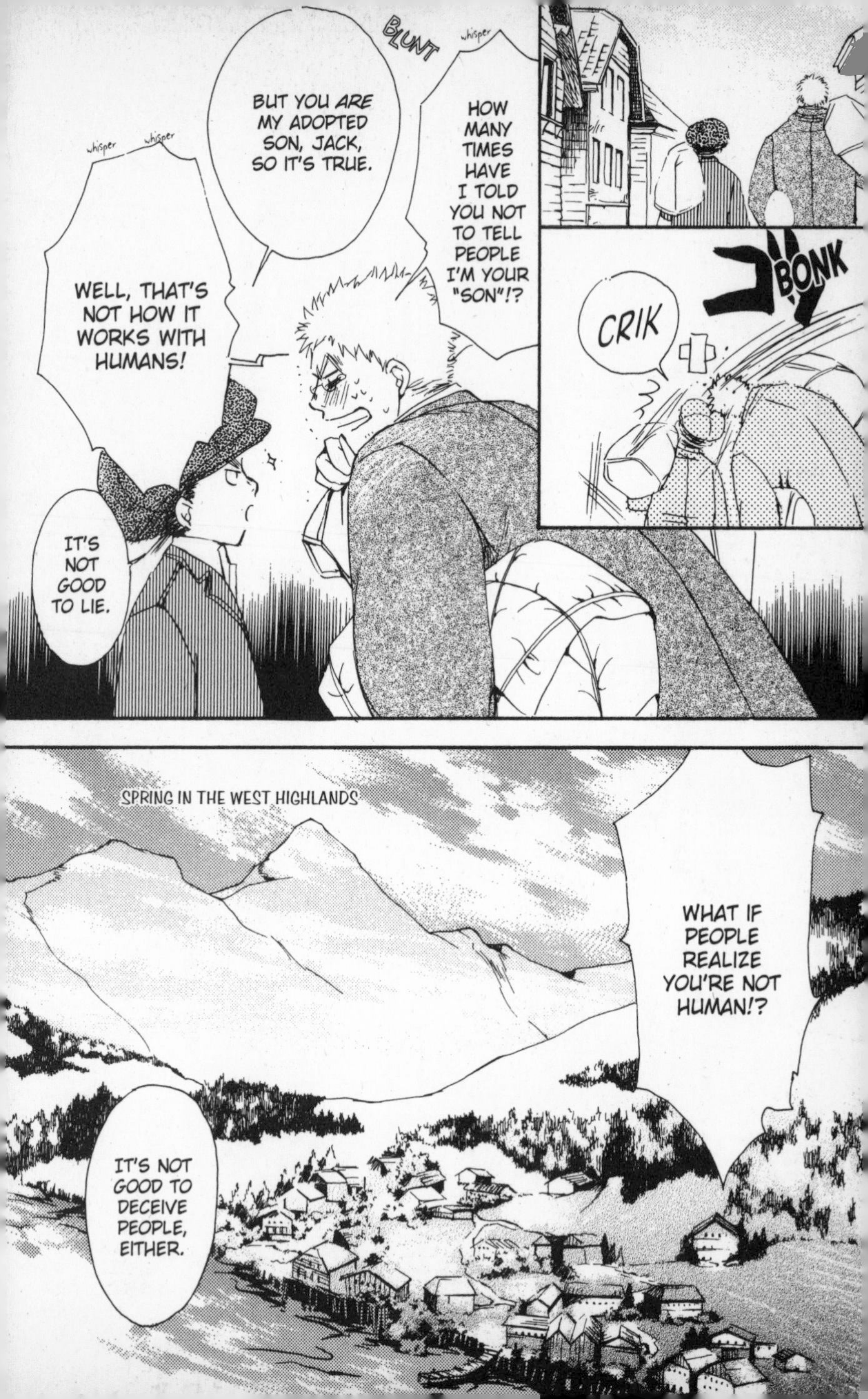
CRIK
BONK
whisper
HOW MANY TIMES HAVE I TOLD YOU NOT TO TELL PEOPLE I'M YOUR "SON"!?
BLUNT
BUT YOU *ARE* MY ADOPTED SON, JACK, SO IT'S TRUE.
whisper whisper
WELL, THAT'S NOT HOW IT WORKS WITH HUMANS!
IT'S NOT GOOD TO LIE.
SPRING IN THE WEST HIGHLANDS
WHAT IF PEOPLE REALIZE YOU'RE NOT HUMAN!?
IT'S NOT GOOD TO DECEIVE PEOPLE, EITHER.

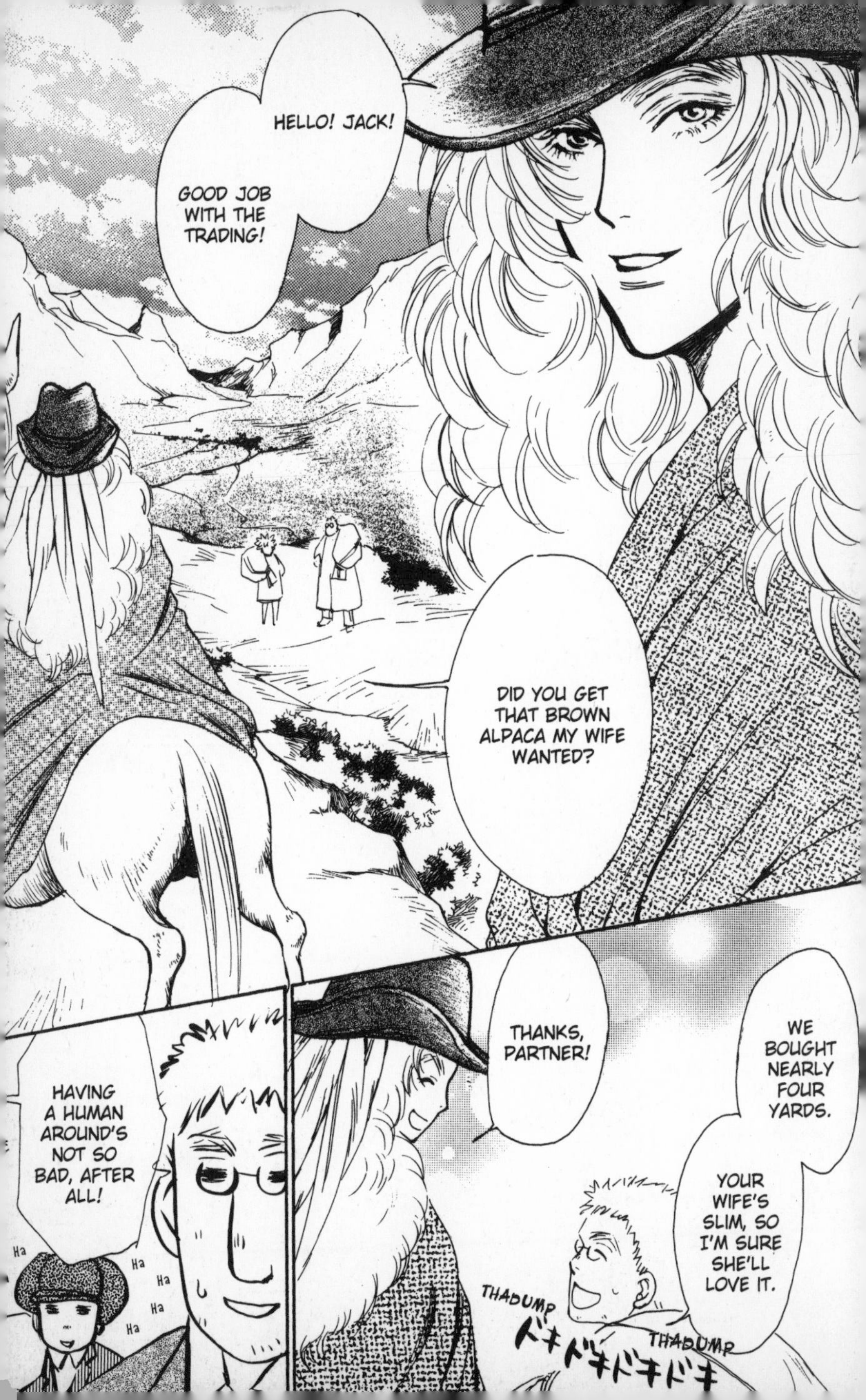
HELLO! JACK!
GOOD JOB WITH THE TRADING!
DID YOU GET THAT BROWN ALPACA MY WIFE WANTED?
WE BOUGHT NEARLY FOUR YARDS.
THANKS, PARTNER!
YOUR WIFE'S SLIM, SO I'M SURE SHE'LL LOVE IT.
THADUMP
ドキドキドキドキ
THADUMP
HAVING A HUMAN AROUND'S NOT SO BAD, AFTER ALL!
Ha
Ha
Ha
Ha
Ha

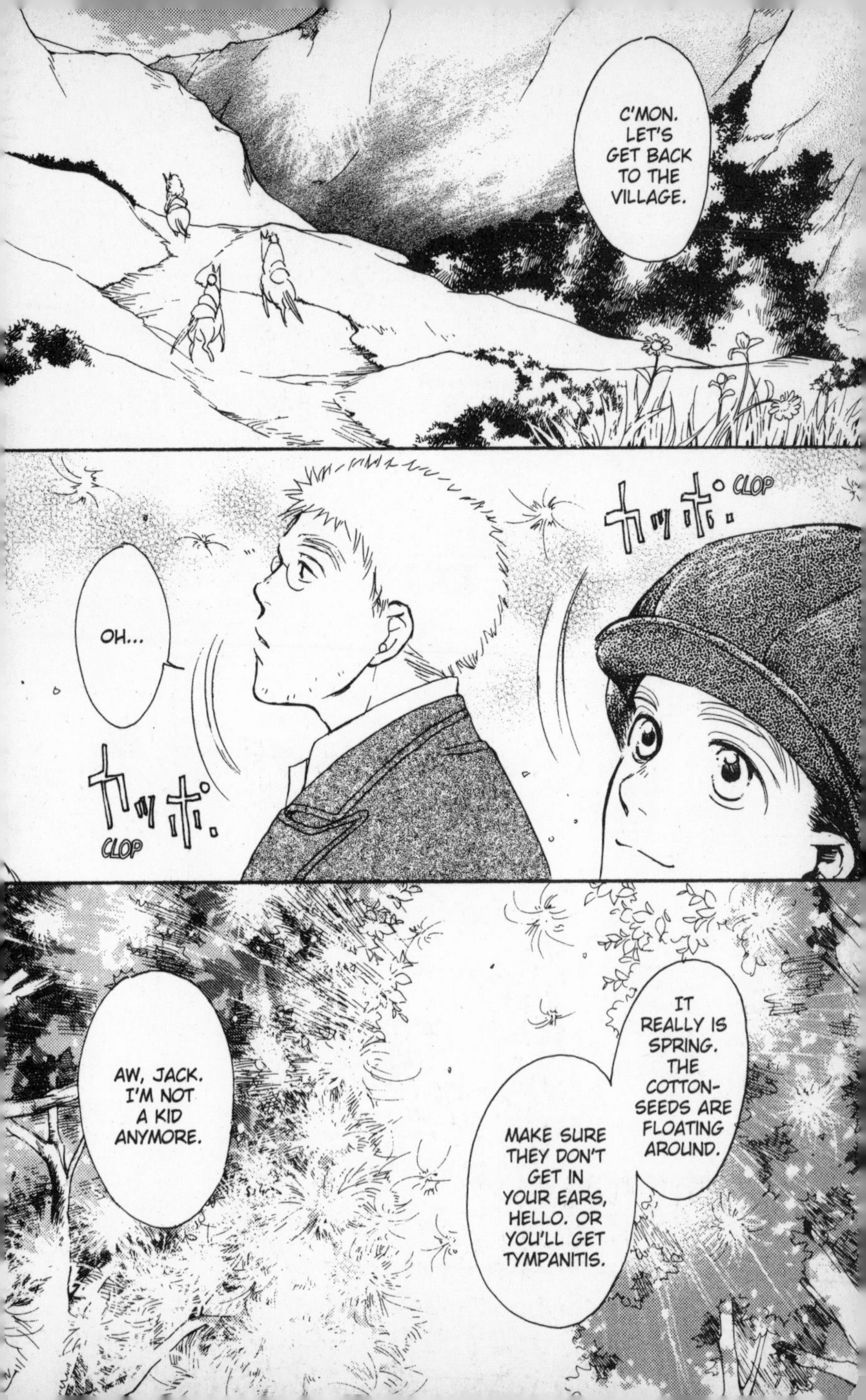
C'MON. LET'S GET BACK TO THE VILLAGE.
カッポ。 CLOP
OH...
カッポ。 CLOP
IT REALLY IS SPRING. THE COTTON-SEEDS ARE FLOATING AROUND.
MAKE SURE THEY DON'T GET IN YOUR EARS, HELLO. OR YOU'LL GET TYMPANITIS.
AW, JACK. I'M NOT A KID ANYMORE.

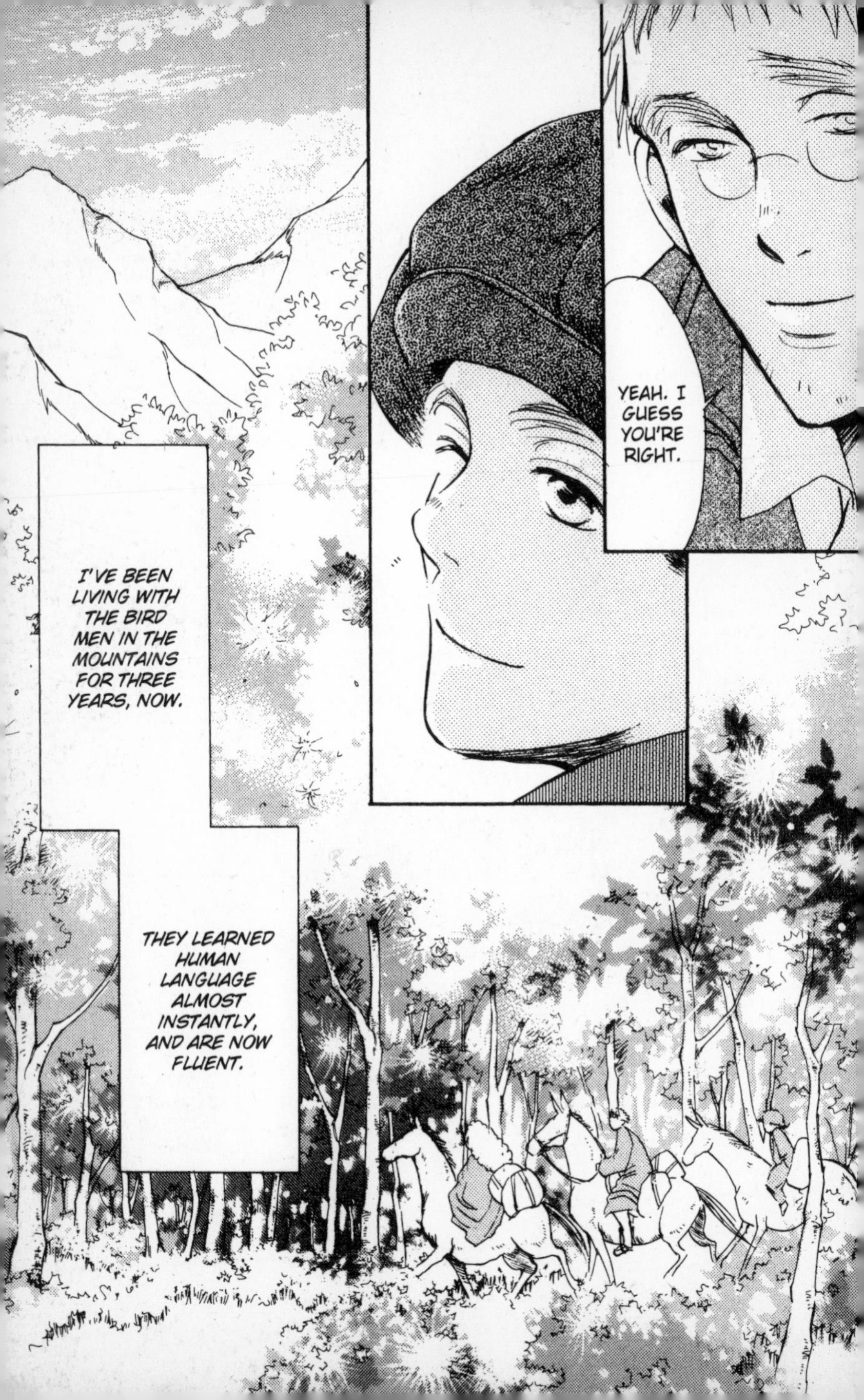
YEAH. I GUESS YOU'RE RIGHT.
I'VE BEEN LIVING WITH THE BIRD MEN IN THE MOUNTAINS FOR THREE YEARS, NOW.
THEY LEARNED HUMAN LANGUAGE ALMOST INSTANTLY, AND ARE NOW FLUENT.

THEY'VE ALSO...

...GONE THROUGH PUBERTY, SHEDDING THEIR DOWNY CHILD-FEATHERS...

...AND ARE GROWING INTO YOUNG MEN.

BUT IRONICALLY, FOR THEM...

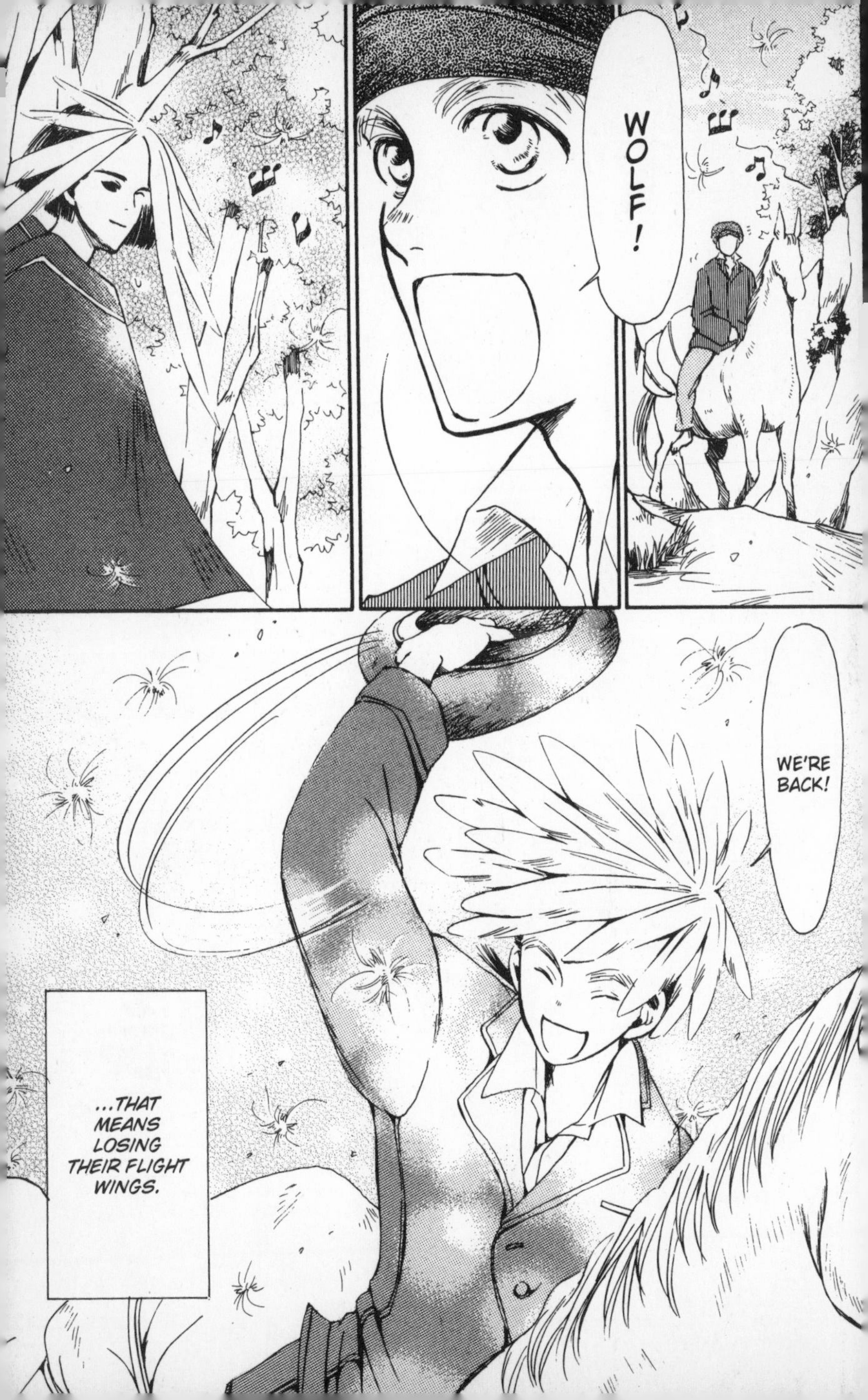
WOLF!
WE'RE BACK!
...THAT MEANS LOSING THEIR FLIGHT WINGS.

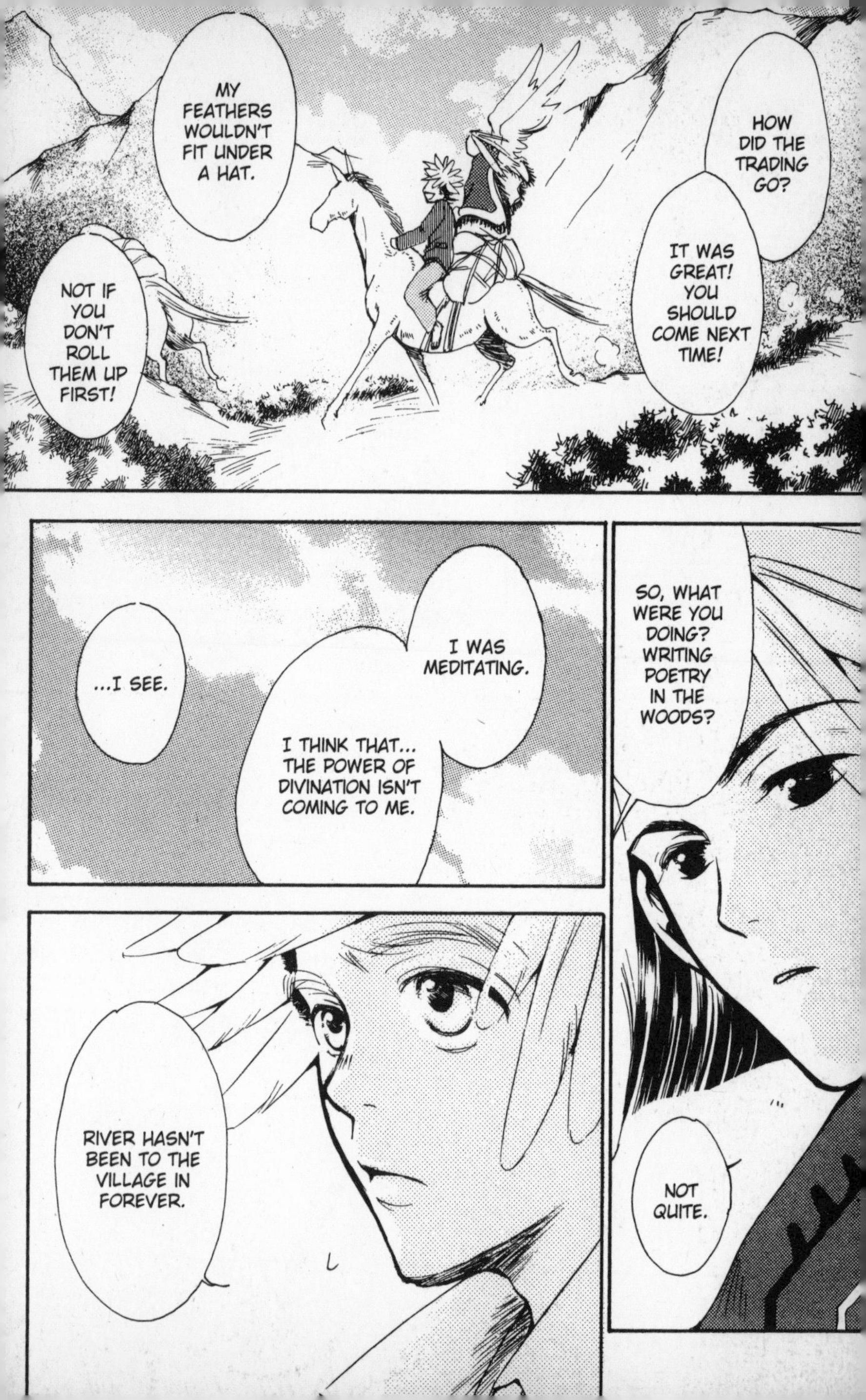
HOW DID THE TRADING GO?
IT WAS GREAT! YOU SHOULD COME NEXT TIME!
MY FEATHERS WOULDN'T FIT UNDER A HAT.
NOT IF YOU DON'T ROLL THEM UP FIRST!
SO, WHAT WERE YOU DOING? WRITING POETRY IN THE WOODS?
NOT QUITE.
I WAS MEDITATING.
I THINK THAT... THE POWER OF DIVINATION ISN'T COMING TO ME.
...I SEE.
RIVER HASN'T BEEN TO THE VILLAGE IN FOREVER.

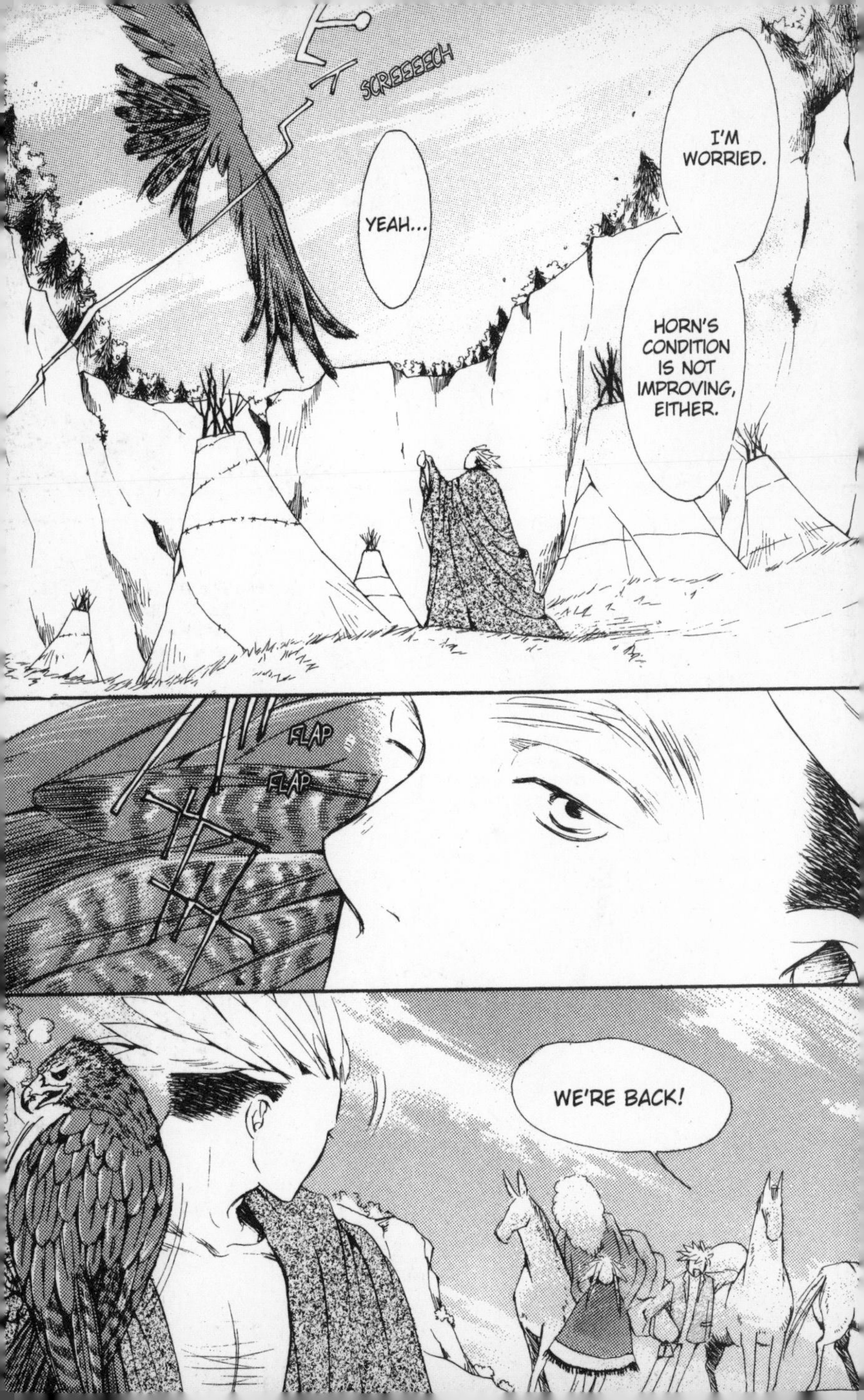
I'M WORRIED.
HORN'S CONDITION IS NOT IMPROVING, EITHER.
YEAH...
SCREEEEECH
FLAP
FLAP
WE'RE BACK!

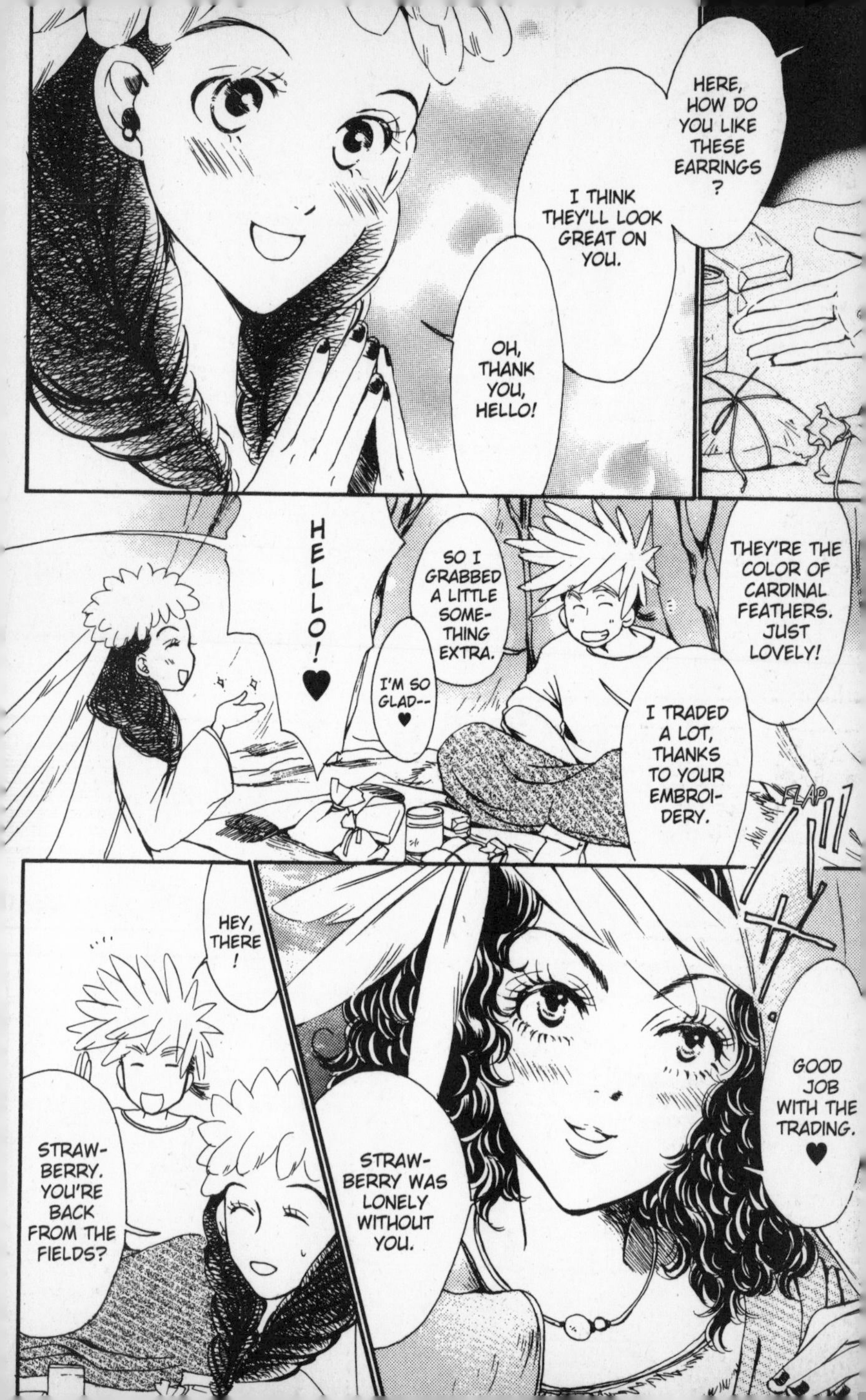
HERE, HOW DO YOU LIKE THESE EARRINGS?
I THINK THEY'LL LOOK GREAT ON YOU.
OH, THANK YOU, HELLO!
THEY'RE THE COLOR OF CARDINAL FEATHERS. JUST LOVELY!
I TRADED A LOT, THANKS TO YOUR EMBROIDERY.
FLAP
SO I GRABBED A LITTLE SOMETHING EXTRA.
I'M SO GLAD--♥
HELLO!♥
GOOD JOB WITH THE TRADING. ♥
STRAWBERRY WAS LONELY WITHOUT YOU.
HEY, THERE!
...
STRAWBERRY. YOU'RE BACK FROM THE FIELDS?

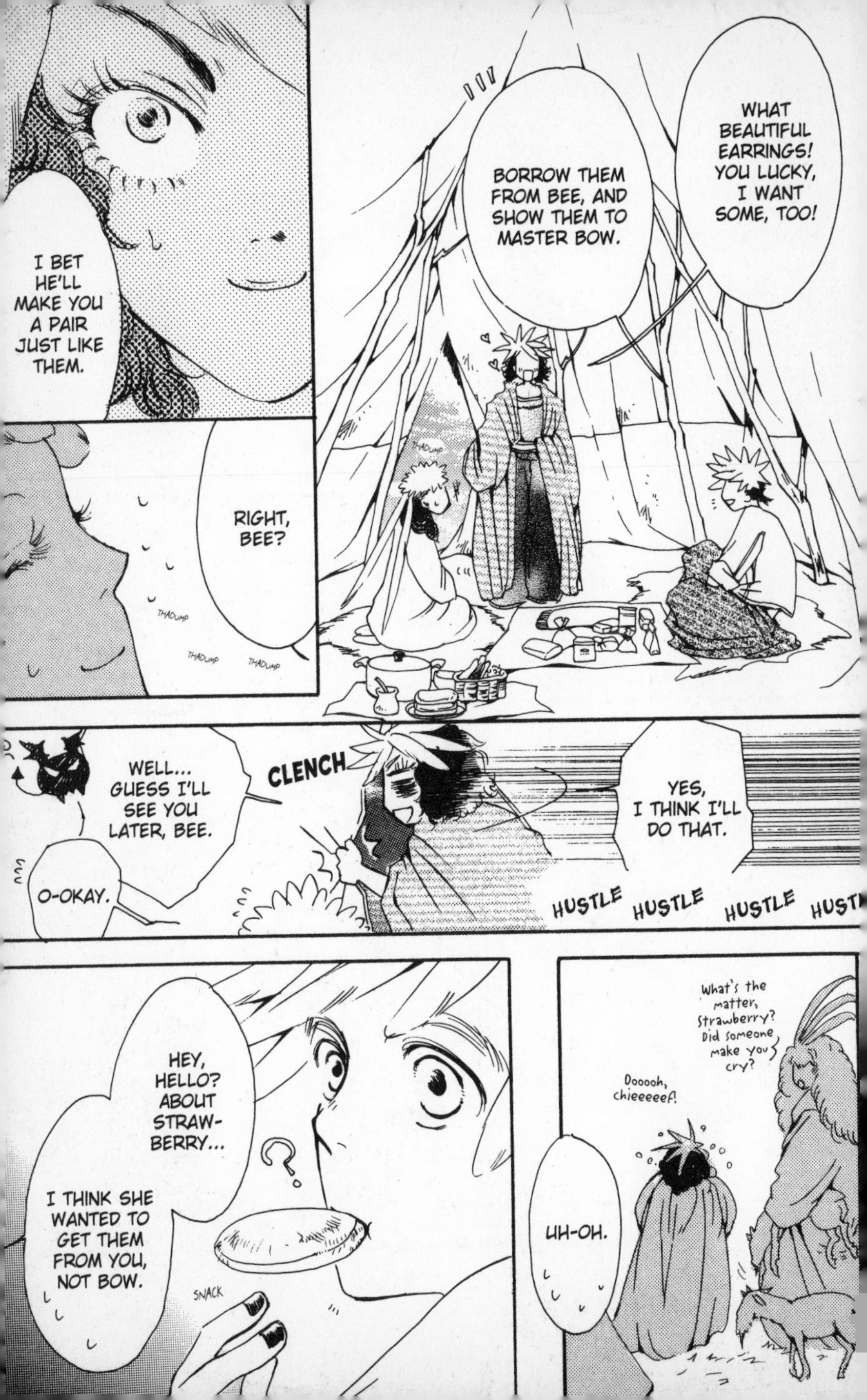
WHAT BEAUTIFUL EARRINGS! YOU LUCKY, I WANT SOME, TOO!
BORROW THEM FROM BEE, AND SHOW THEM TO MASTER BOW.
THADUMP
I BET HE'LL MAKE YOU A PAIR JUST LIKE THEM.
RIGHT, BEE?
THADUMP
THADUMP
THADUMP
YES, I THINK I'LL DO THAT.
HUSTLE HUSTLE HUSTLE HUST
CLENCH
WELL... GUESS I'LL SEE YOU LATER, BEE.
O-OKAY.
What's the matter, Strawberry? Did someone make you cry?
Doooooh, chieeeeef!
UH-OH.
HEY, HELLO? ABOUT STRAW-BERRY...
I THINK SHE WANTED TO GET THEM FROM YOU, NOT BOW.
SNACK

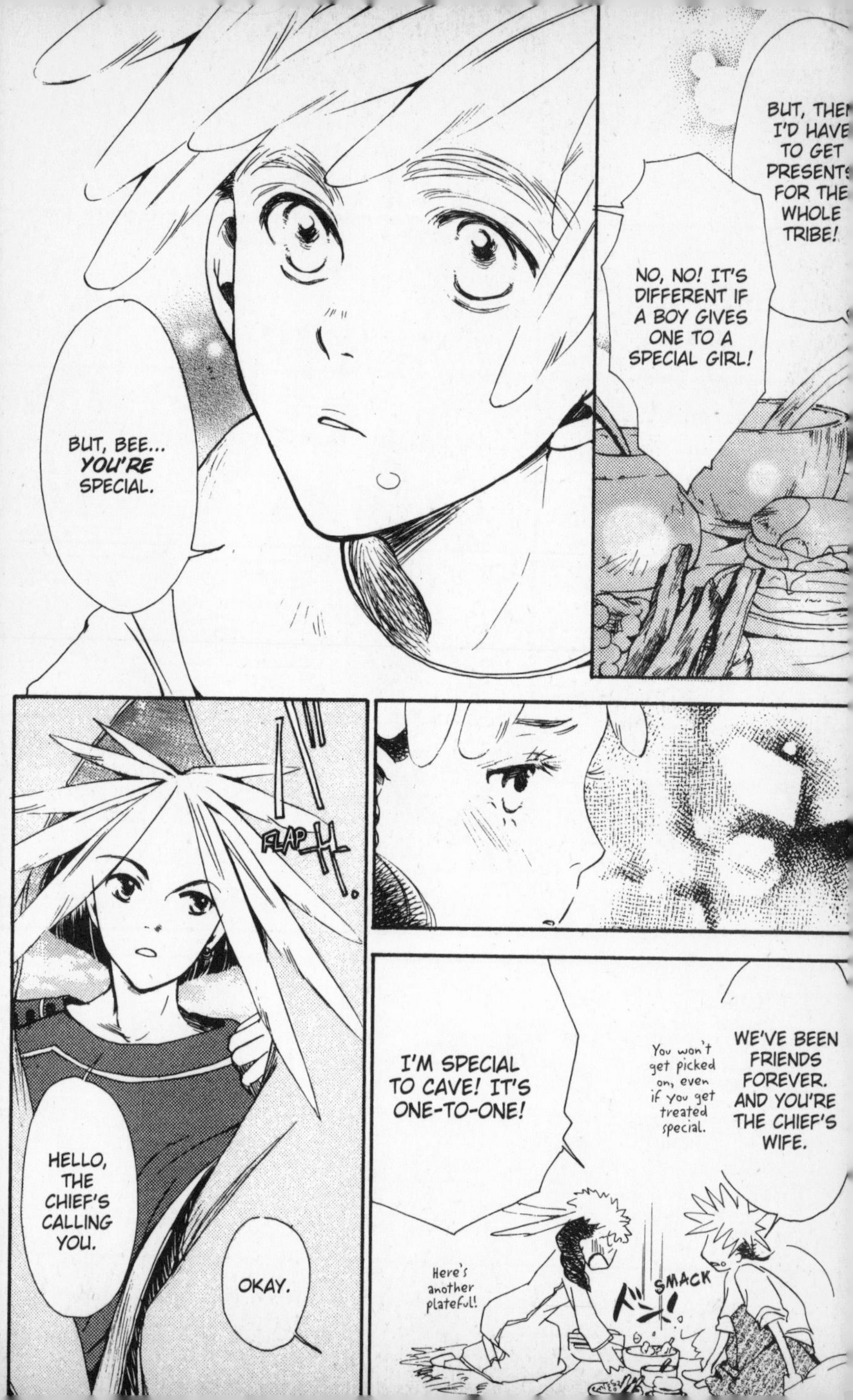
BUT, THEN I'D HAVE TO GET PRESENTS FOR THE WHOLE TRIBE!
NO, NO! IT'S DIFFERENT IF A BOY GIVES ONE TO A SPECIAL GIRL!
BUT, BEE... *YOU'RE* SPECIAL.
WE'VE BEEN FRIENDS FOREVER. AND YOU'RE THE CHIEF'S WIFE.
You won't get picked on, even if you get treated special.
I'M SPECIAL TO CAVE! IT'S ONE-TO-ONE!
SMACK
Here's another plateful!
FLAP
HELLO, THE CHIEF'S CALLING YOU.
OKAY.

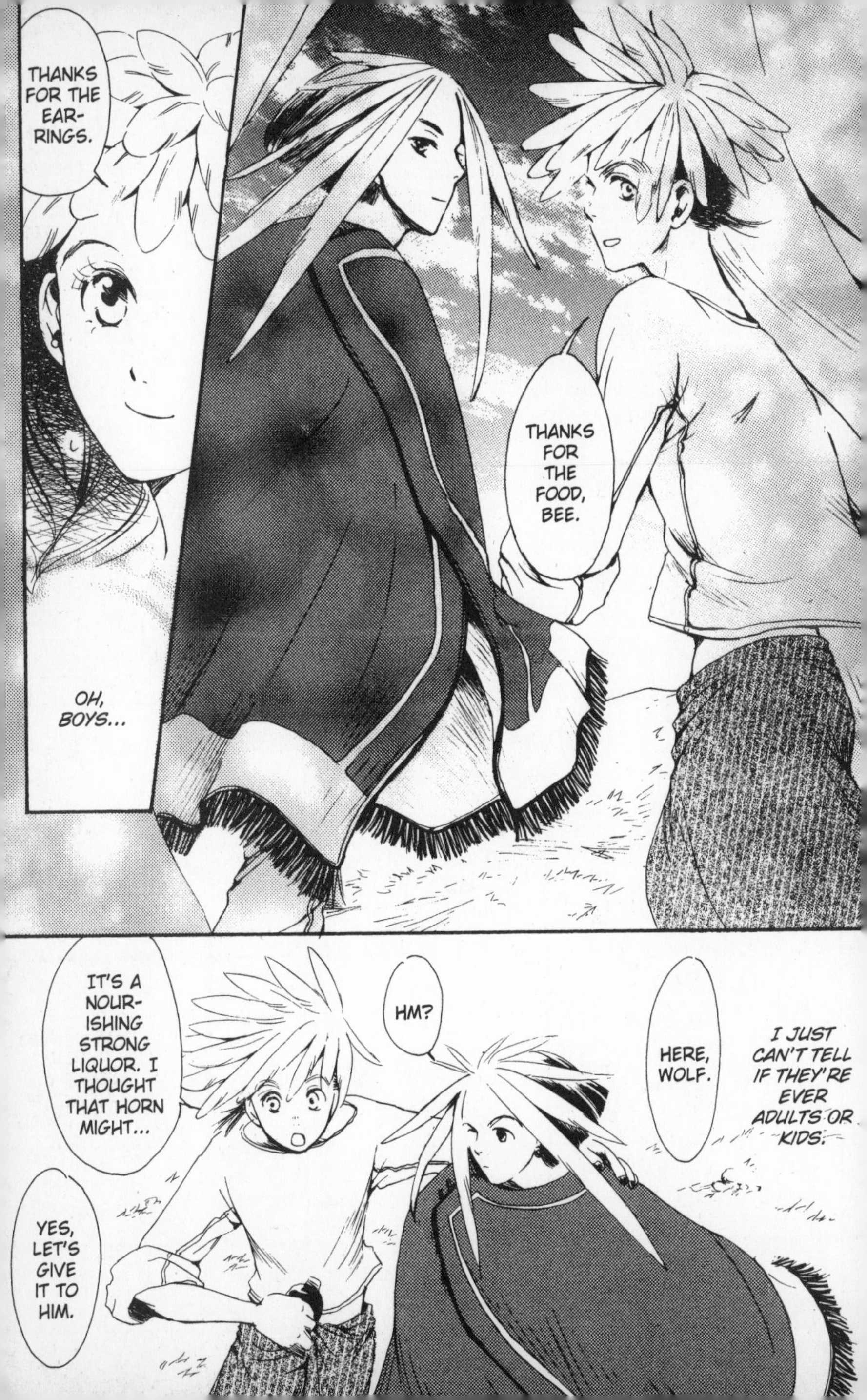
THANKS FOR THE FOOD, BEE.
THANKS FOR THE EAR-RINGS.
OH, BOYS...
I JUST CAN'T TELL IF THEY'RE EVER ADULTS OR KIDS.
HERE, WOLF.
HM?
IT'S A NOUR-ISHING STRONG LIQUOR. I THOUGHT THAT HORN MIGHT...
YES, LET'S GIVE IT TO HIM.

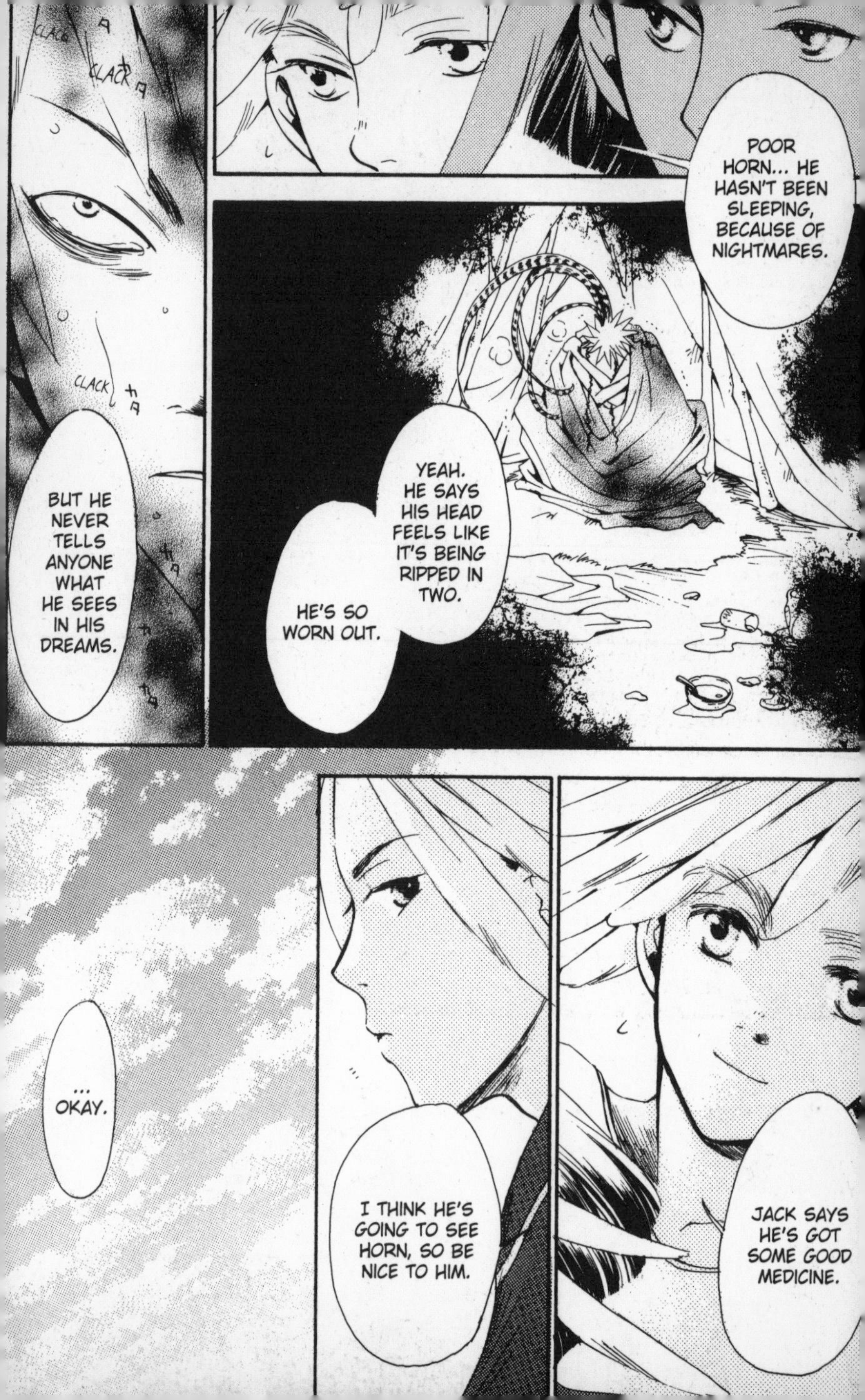
POOR HORN... HE HASN'T BEEN SLEEPING, BECAUSE OF NIGHTMARES.
YEAH. HE SAYS HIS HEAD FEELS LIKE IT'S BEING RIPPED IN TWO.
HE'S SO WORN OUT.
CLACK
CLACK
CLACK
BUT HE NEVER TELLS ANYONE WHAT HE SEES IN HIS DREAMS.
JACK SAYS HE'S GOT SOME GOOD MEDICINE.
I THINK HE'S GOING TO SEE HORN, SO BE NICE TO HIM.
... OKAY.

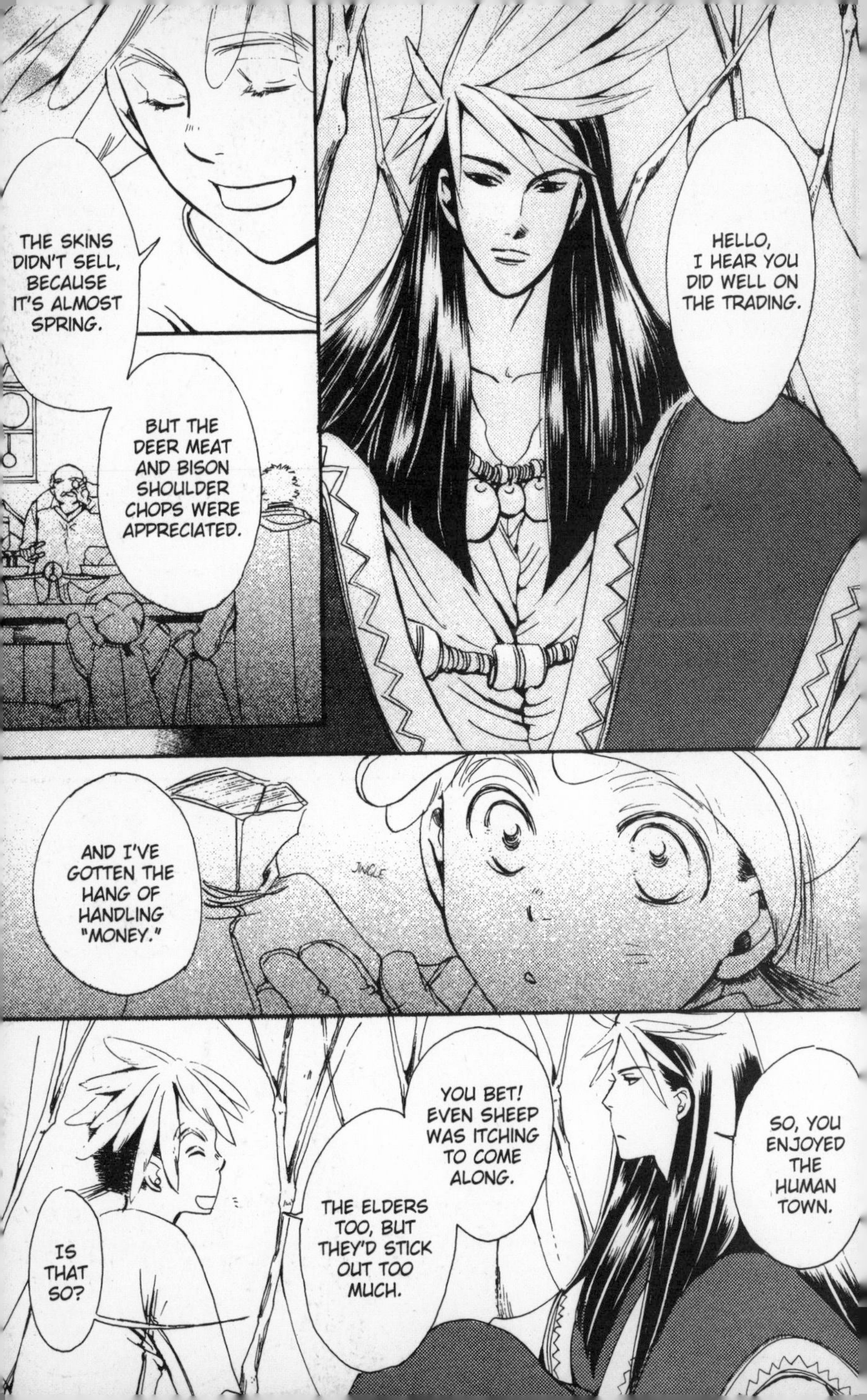
HELLO, I HEAR YOU DID WELL ON THE TRADING.
THE SKINS DIDN'T SELL, BECAUSE IT'S ALMOST SPRING.
BUT THE DEER MEAT AND BISON SHOULDER CHOPS WERE APPRECIATED.
AND I'VE GOTTEN THE HANG OF HANDLING "MONEY."
JINGLE
SO, YOU ENJOYED THE HUMAN TOWN.
YOU BET! EVEN SHEEP WAS ITCHING TO COME ALONG.
THE ELDERS TOO, BUT THEY'D STICK OUT TOO MUCH.
IS THAT SO?

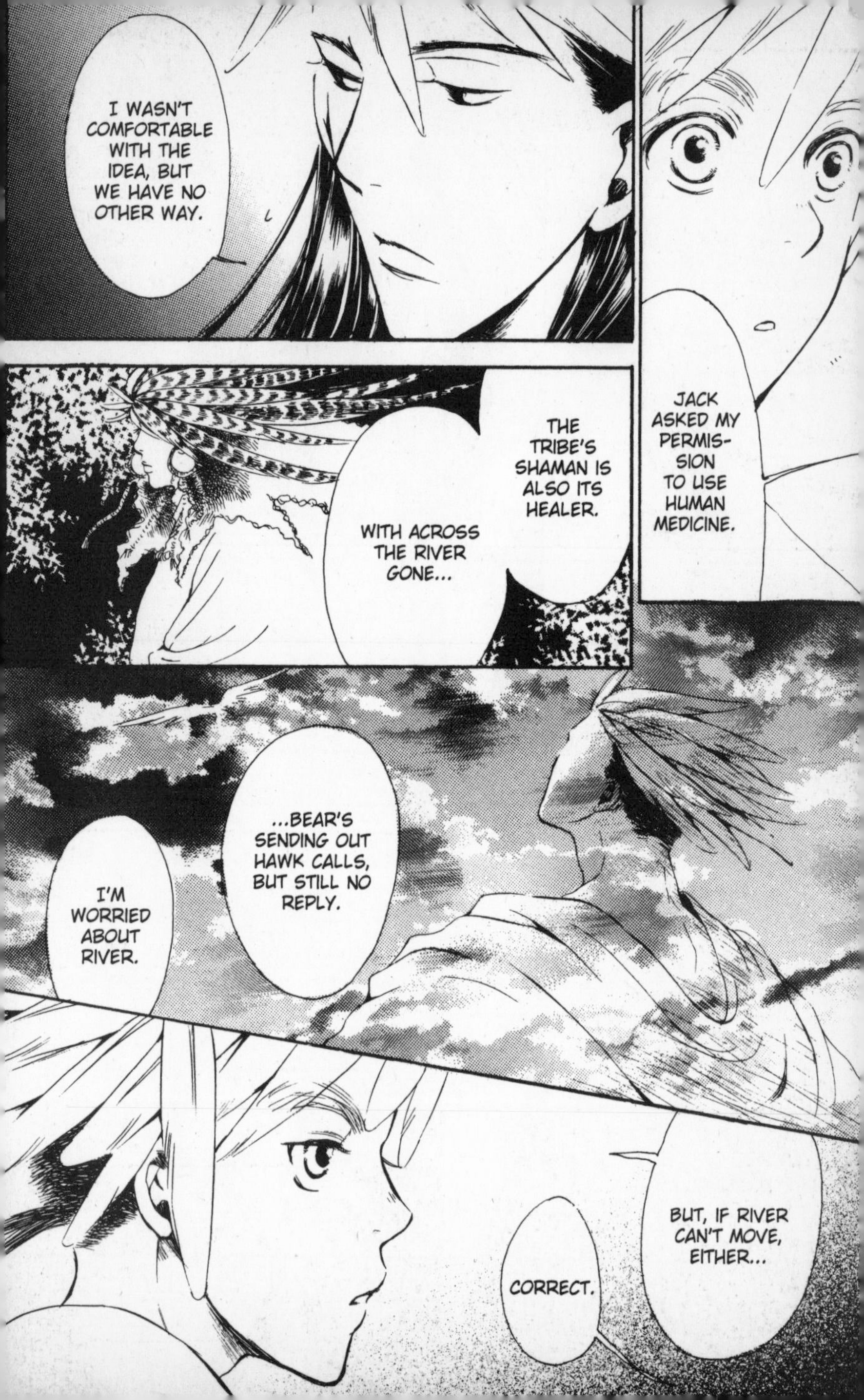
JACK ASKED MY PERMISSION TO USE HUMAN MEDICINE.
I WASN'T COMFORTABLE WITH THE IDEA, BUT WE HAVE NO OTHER WAY.
THE TRIBE'S SHAMAN IS ALSO ITS HEALER.
WITH ACROSS THE RIVER GONE...
...BEAR'S SENDING OUT HAWK CALLS, BUT STILL NO REPLY.
I'M WORRIED ABOUT RIVER.
BUT, IF RIVER CAN'T MOVE, EITHER...
CORRECT.

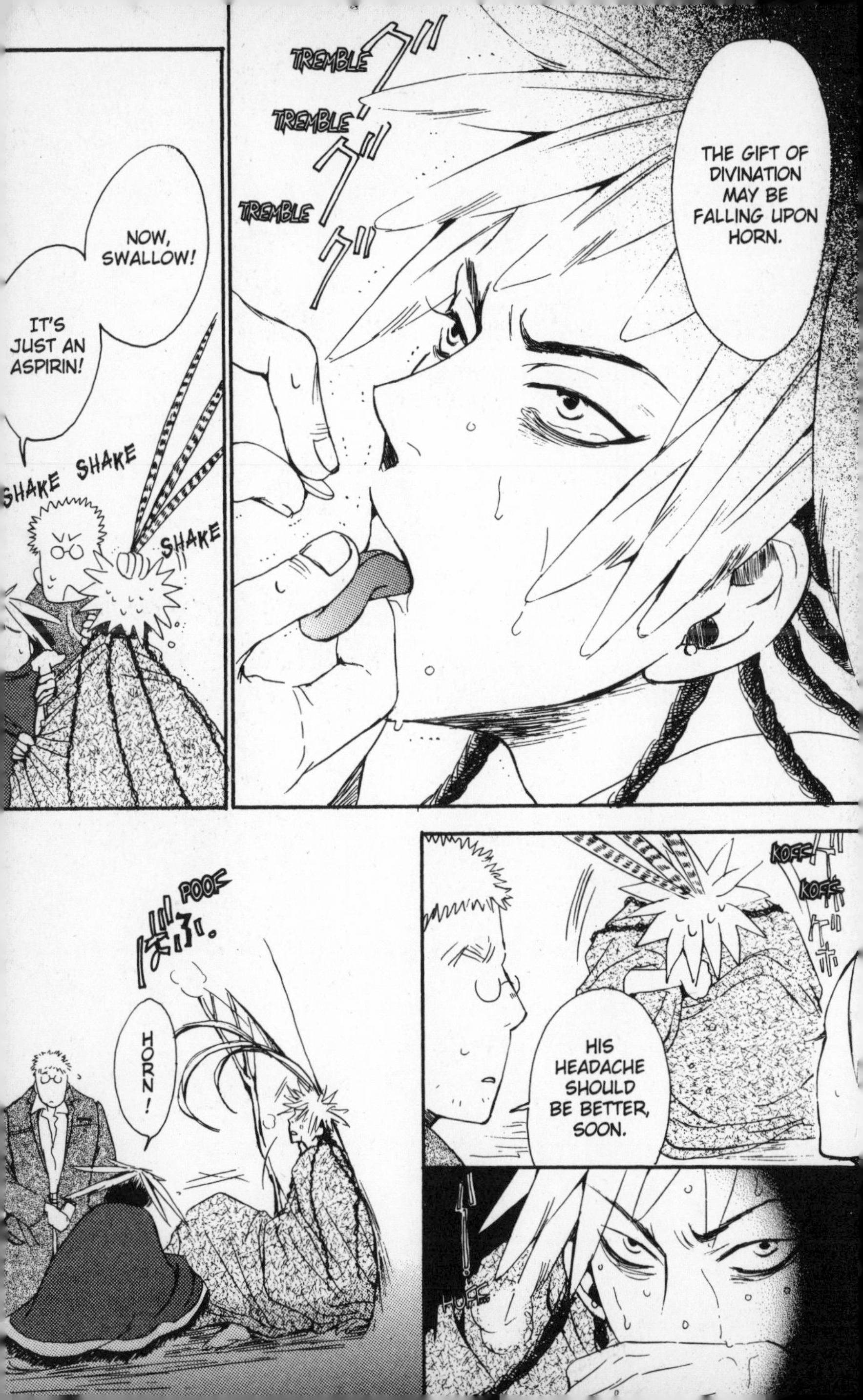
TREMBLE
TREMBLE
TREMBLE
THE GIFT OF DIVINATION MAY BE FALLING UPON HORN.
NOW, SWALLOW!
IT'S JUST AN ASPIRIN!
SHAKE SHAKE
SHAKE
KOFF
KOFF
HIS HEADACHE SHOULD BE BETTER, SOON.
HUFF...
POOF
HORN!

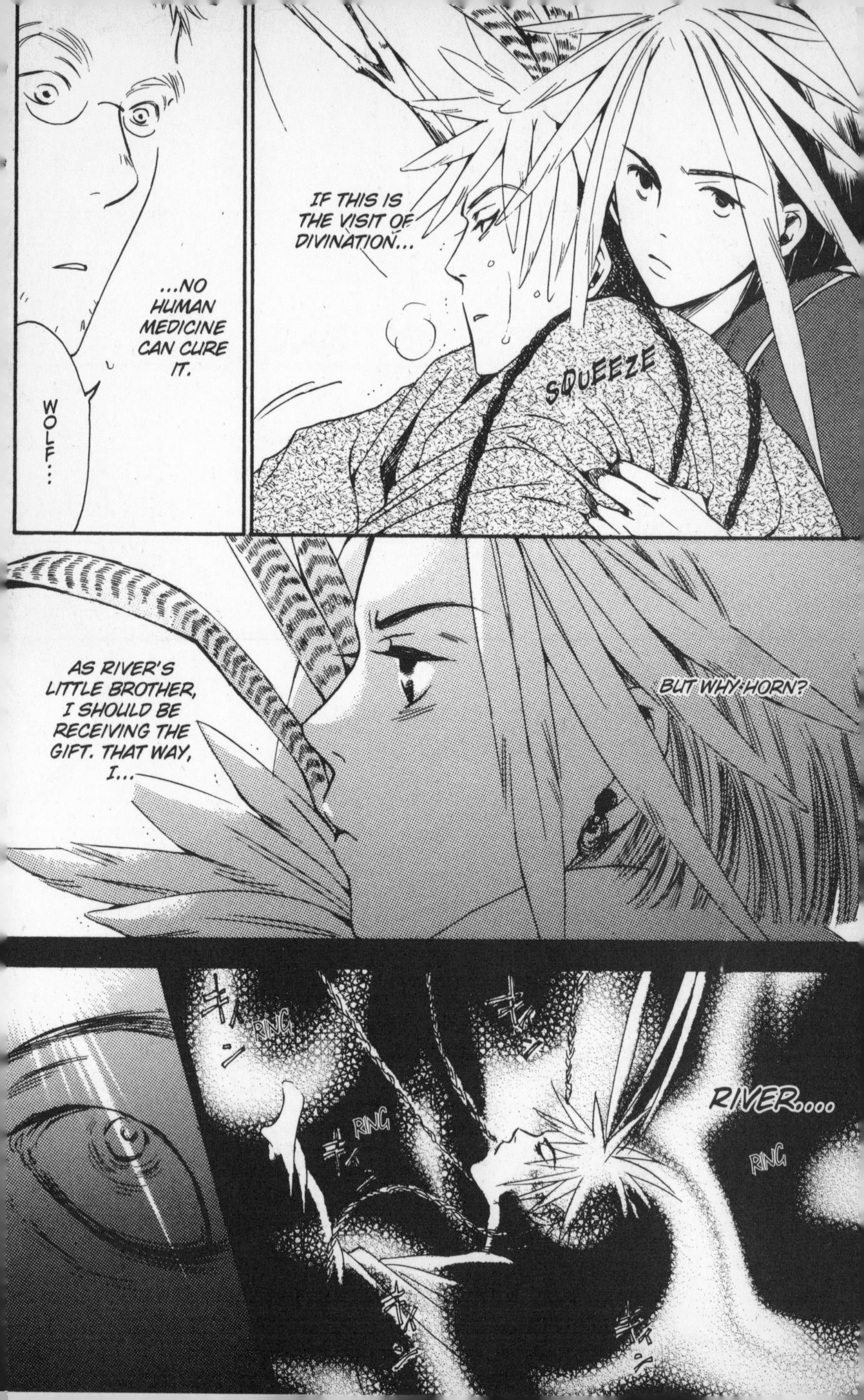
IF THIS IS THE VISIT OF DIVINATION...
SQUEEZE
...NO HUMAN MEDICINE CAN CURE IT.
WOLF...
BUT WHY HORN?
AS RIVER'S LITTLE BROTHER, I SHOULD BE RECEIVING THE GIFT. THAT WAY, I...
RIVER....
RING
RING
RING

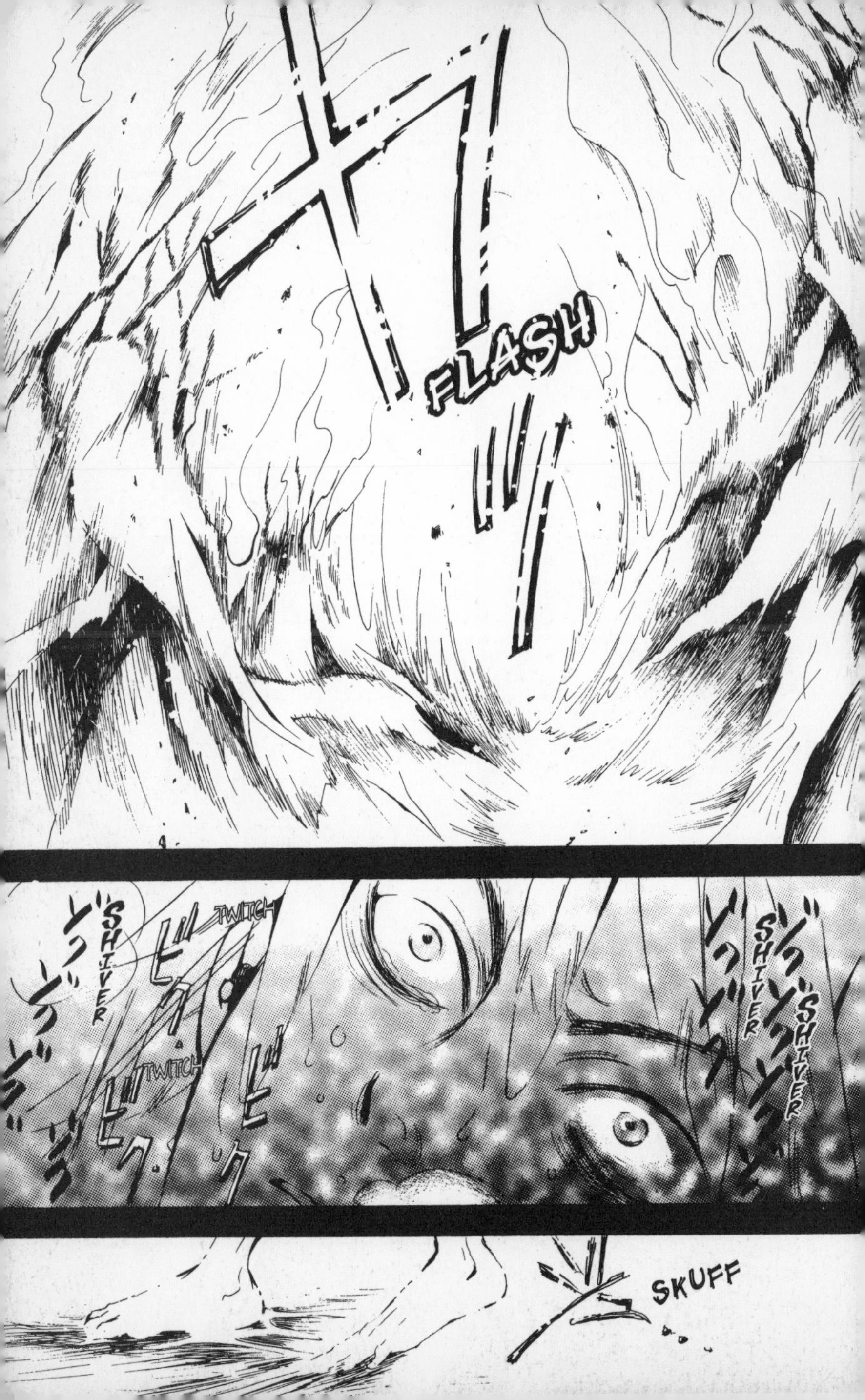
FLASH
SHIVER
SHIVER
TWITCH
SHIVER
TWITCH
SKUFF

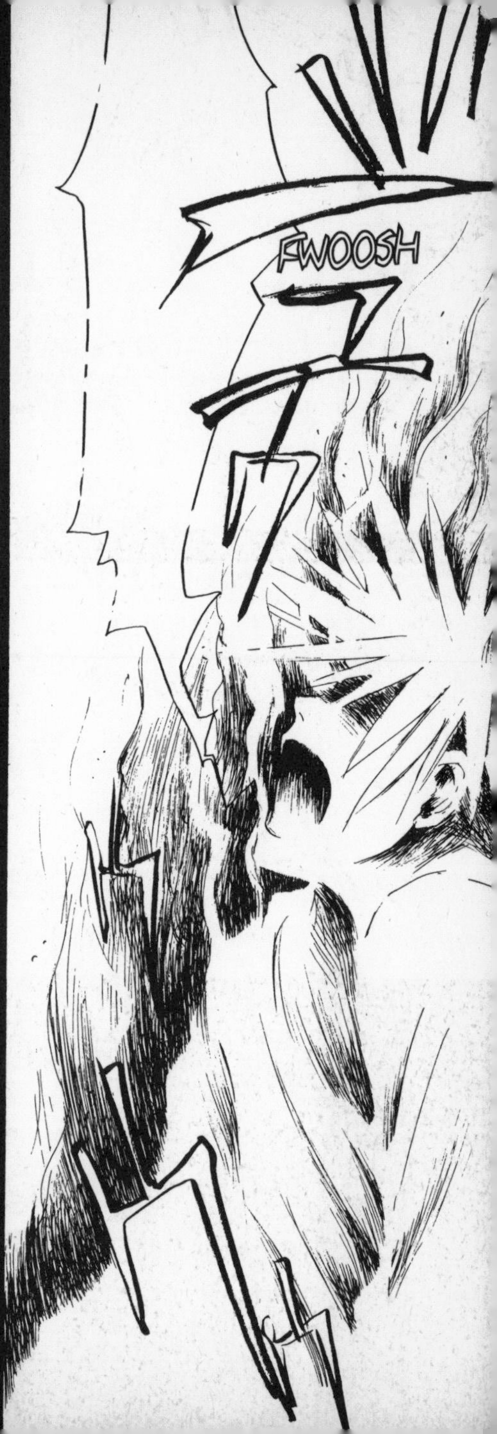
FWOOSH

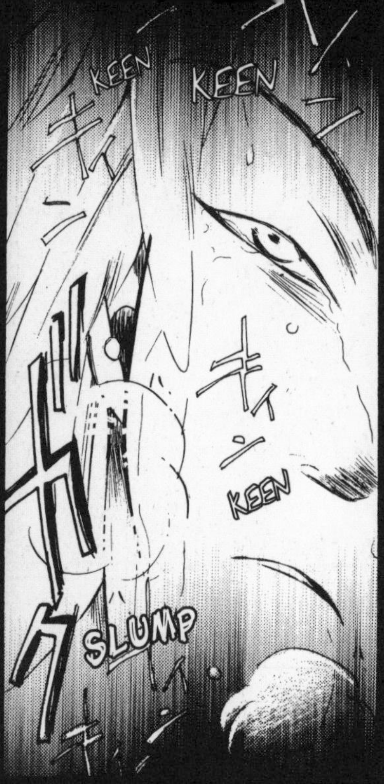
KEEN
KEEN
KEEN
SLUMP

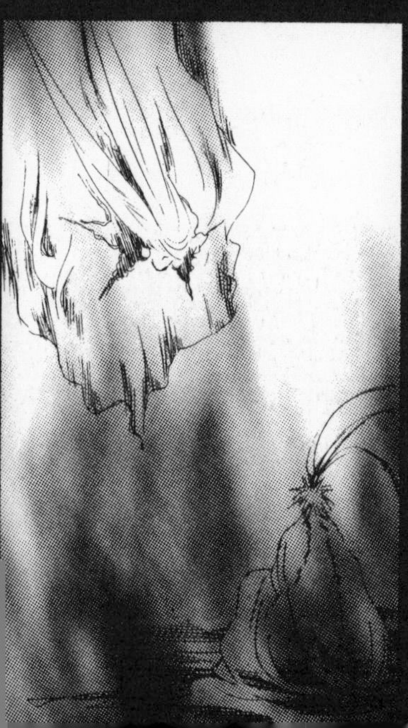

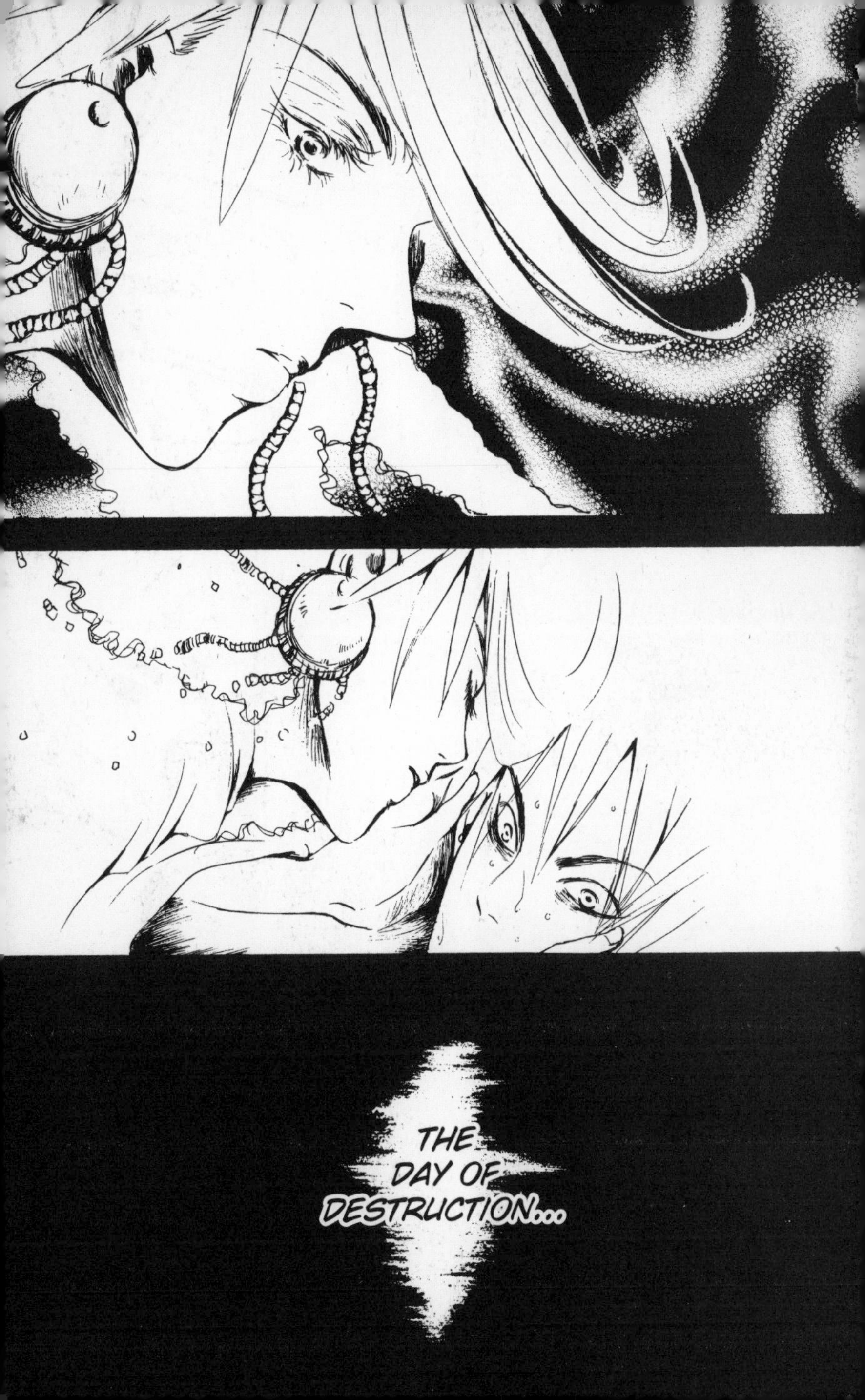
THE DAY OF DESTRUCTION...

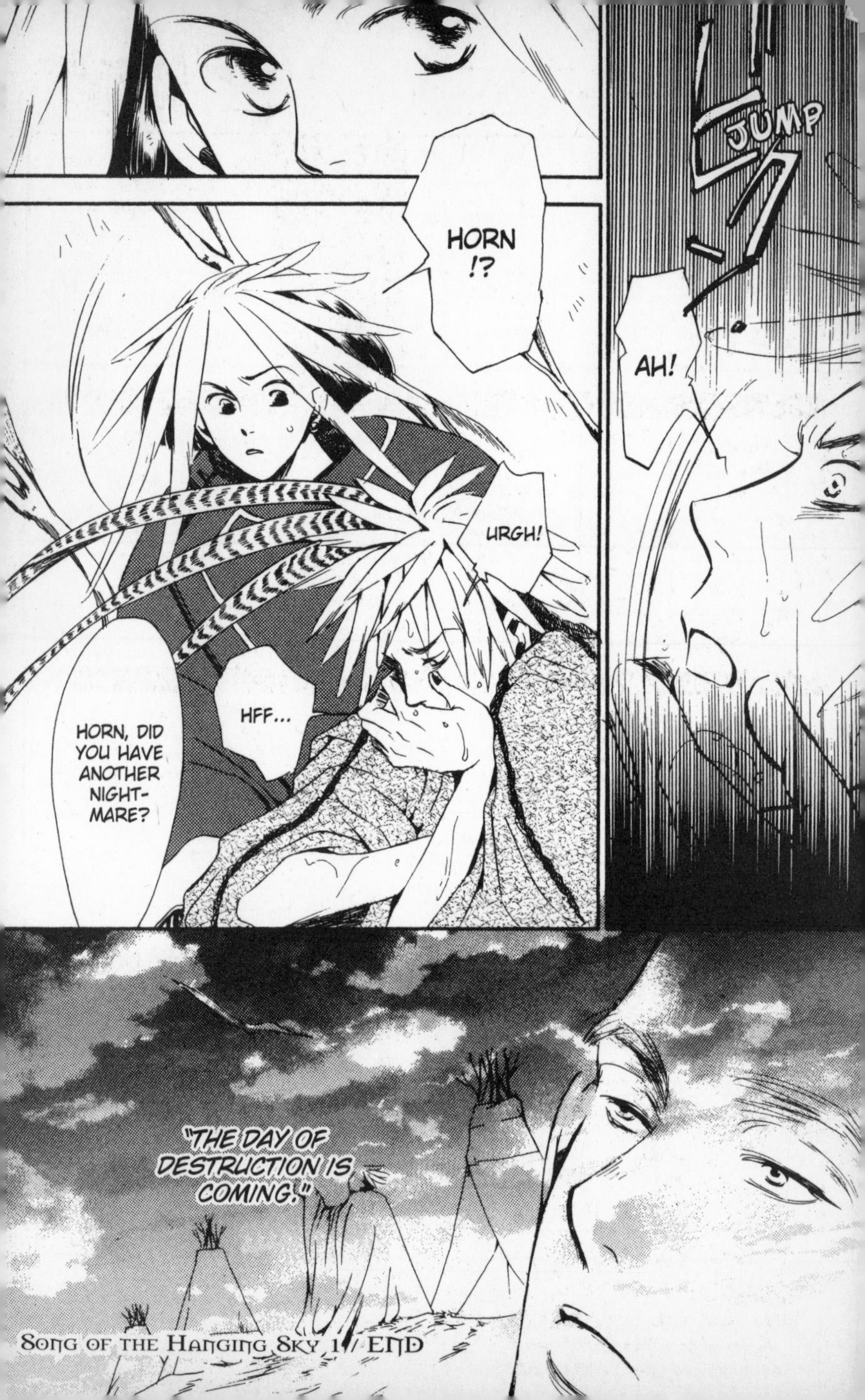
JUMP
AH!
HORN !?
URGH!
HFF...
HORN, DID YOU HAVE ANOTHER NIGHT-MARE?
"THE DAY OF DESTRUCTION IS COMING."
SONG OF THE HANGING SKY 1 / END

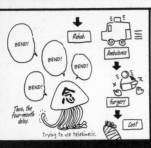

Go ← POSTSCRIPT START

■ BIG SURPRISE--! ■

Thank you for the comment on my obi, Imaichi-sensei!

Hello, This is Toriko Gin. This is the compilation of my first monthly serialization.
Thank you for purchasing it.
I was reading Bradbury this morning, so I'm a Martian for some reason.
I'm so sorry it's four months behind!
On the morning of one of my deadlines, I cut the tendon of one of my fingers on my right hand. (By accident.)
CRIK
Right about here.
BEND!
BEND!
BEND!
BEND!
Rehab.
Ambulance
Surgery
Cast
Thus, the four-month delay.
Trying to use telekinesis.
People who can bend spoons are amazing.
I'm now able to draw, again.
Extravagant
(But video games are still tough...)
I'd like to thank everyone deeply for continuing to support me online during those four months.
Via email and the message board.
That includes Tsuburaya-san of Comic B's Log, who continued to support me back to health.
Tsuburaya-san, so cool and headstrong.
She emailed me every week.
Thank you also to my friends, my family, my relatives... everyone!
I loved the picture book I got while I was sick.
Thank you, thank you, thank you!
Thank you, electro-magnetic waves!
Anyway, it's a strange manga, isn't it?
And that's how I was able to draw this fetish-ridden manga with pride.
YOU SHOULD DRAW A MANGA YOU TRULY LOVE, WITH ALL THE FETISHES YOU LIKE.
The ever-elegant Kimura-san.
Whaaaat? Are you serious?
And after continuously worrying how I'd be able to enjoy myself with a schedule of 24 pages a month...
Jellyfish Version
It was a battle with words.
Going out with a bang, in other words.
...it became a mad-dash-to-the-finish-line manga!
No time to be upset!
FWOOOOOSH
But I couldn't help it, as I was smitten with masterpiece collections of shonen and shojo stories.
This book encompassed all the tears and joy of humanity.
It got me thinking how happy I'd be, if I could be in these all-encompassing books that littered my bedside.
I wish I were in 1001 Nights.
And lastly...
...the 15-year-old dog at my parents' house finally went to Doggy Heaven. I used him as the model for Gustave who appears in this manga, so I hope he's happy where he is.
He was a silver husky.
Thank you, thank you! And I'm sorry for dillydallying so much. I devote this manga to all the love on this green earth.
Kitty Joe
Kitty Fu

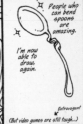

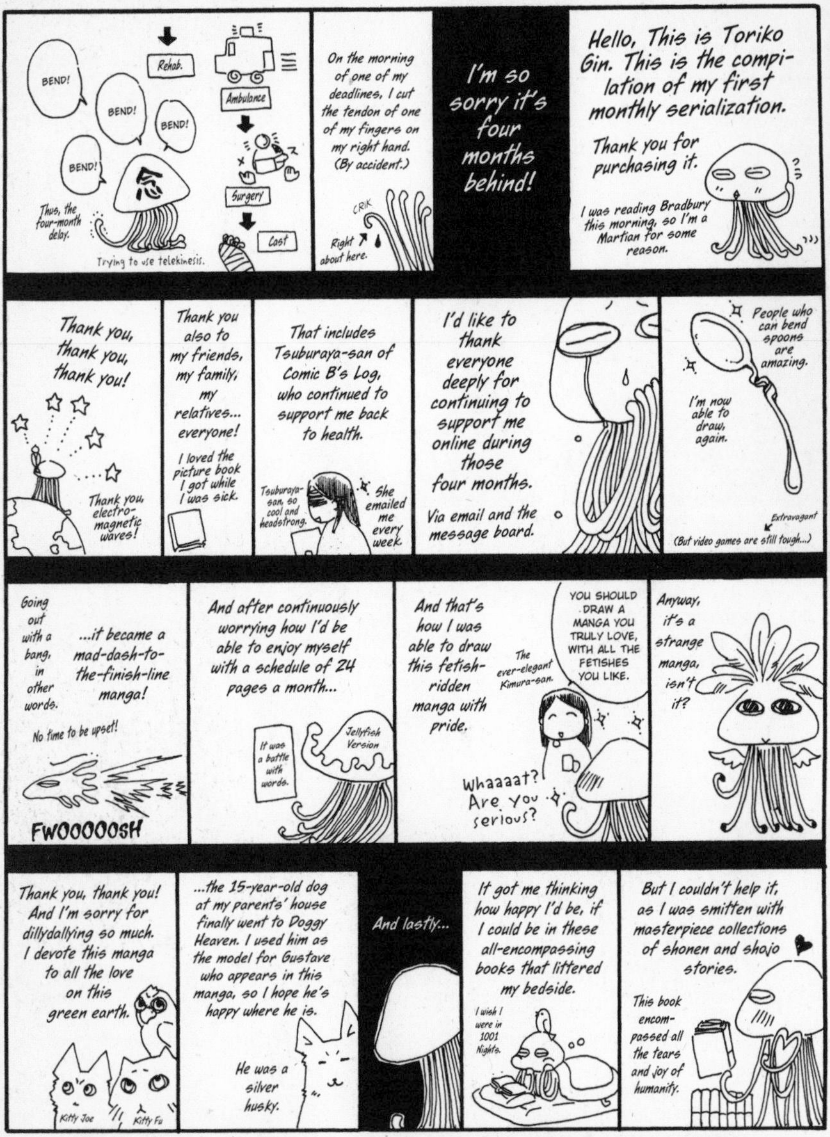

Well, hope to see you in volume 2!

http:// www6.plala.or.jp/USA/birds/

It's sort of like a "Hanging Sky" website.

This information is current as of March 2007

■ SPECIAL THANKS I LOVE YOU ■

Beserker O-san, Angel J-san, Miss Hotaru, Miss Asako.

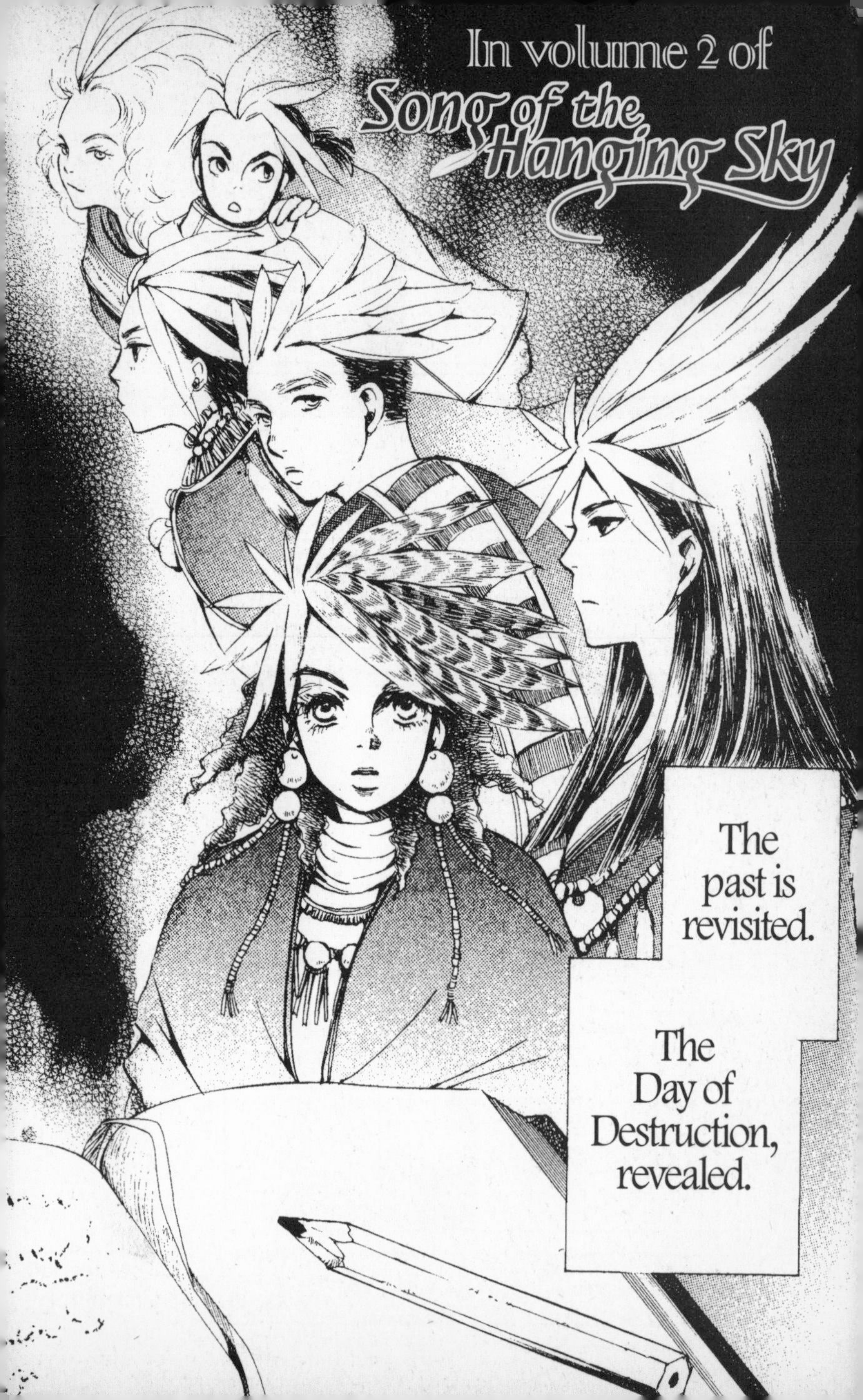
In volume 2 of
Song of the Hanging Sky
The past is revisited.
The Day of Destruction, revealed.

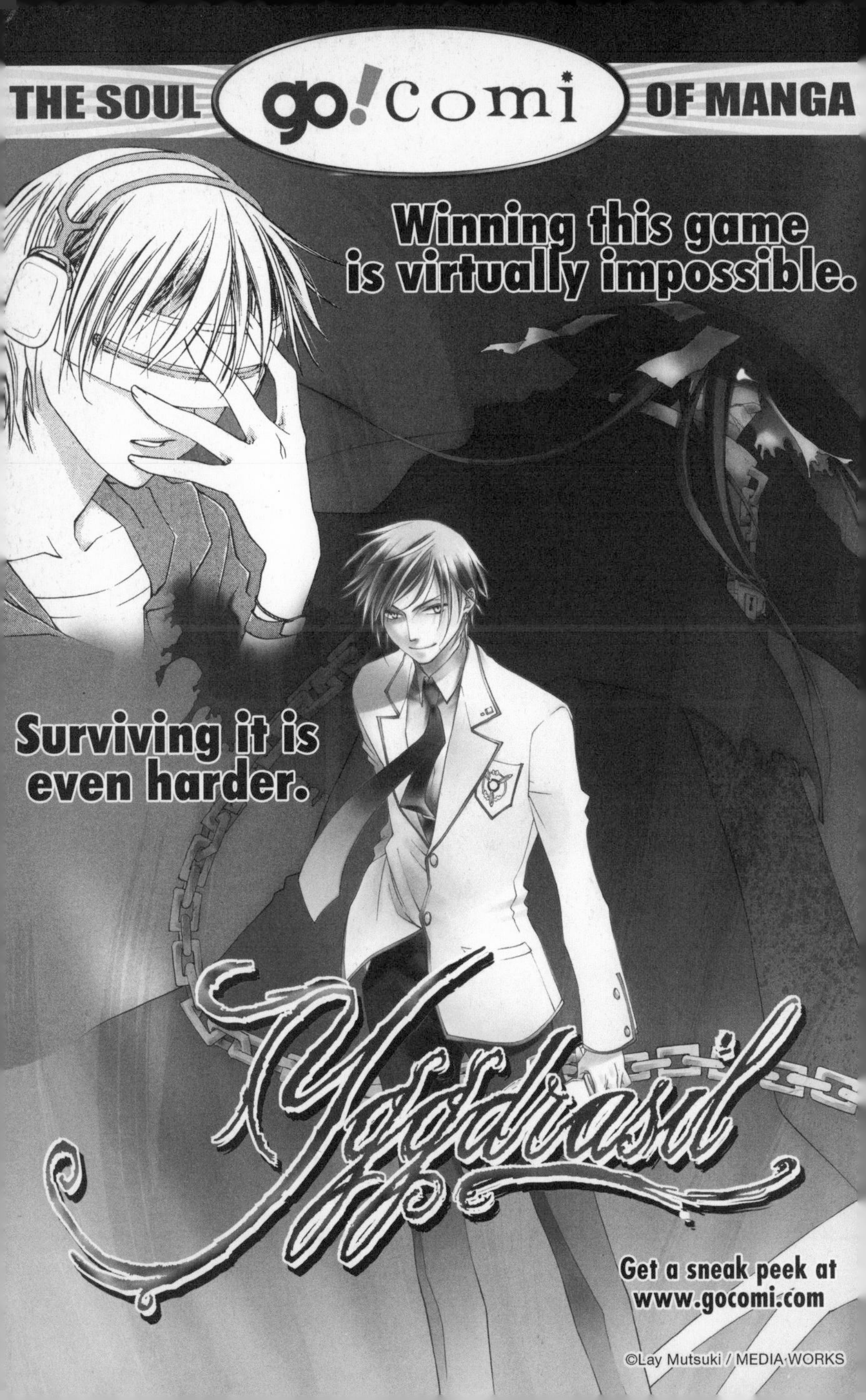